BRAIN OF
THE FIRM

The Managerial Cybernetics
of Organization

BRAIN OF
THE FIRM

SECOND EDITION

Stafford Beer

Companion Volume to
THE HEART OF ENTERPRISE

JOHN WILEY & SONS
Chichester · New York · Brisbane · Toronto · Singapore

First edition published Allen Lane, The Penguin Press 1972
Second edition published in hardback John Wiley & Sons Ltd, 1981,
reprinted 1986, 1990, 1993.
Paperback edition 1994.

Reprinted March, May 1995

Other Wiley Editorial Offices

John Wiley & Sons, Inc., 605 Third Avenue,
New York, NY 10158-0012, USA

Jacaranda Wiley Ltd, 33 Park Road, Milton,
Queensland 4064, Australia

John Wiley & Sons (Canada) Ltd, 22 Worcester Road,
Rexdale, Ontario M9W 1L1, Canada

John Wiley & Sons (SEA) Pte Ltd, 37 Jalan Pemimpin #05-04,
Block B, Union Industrial Building, Singapore 2057

British Library Cataloguing in Publication Data

Beer, Stafford
    Brain of the firm. – 2nd ed
    1. Management
    2. Cybernetics
    I. Title
    658.4′03   HD38   80-49979

ISBN 0 471 27687 1 (cloth)
ISBN 0-471-94839-X (pbk)

Photoset by Photo-Graphics of Yarcombe, Honiton, Devon.

DEDICATION

To my colleagues past and present managerial
and scientific with a motto

**ABSOLUTUM
OBSOLETUM**

— if it works it's out of date

Contents

Preface to first edition

This book is about large and complicated systems, such as animals, computers, and economies. It is in particular about the control of the enterprise, the brain of the firm. That is a difficult subject — difficult to think about or to read about, difficult to write about.

When the White Rabbit asked the King where he should begin, the King replied: 'Begin at the beginning and go on till you come to the end: then stop.' But explanation is not like that. His advice is a good example of the failure to recognize when one is up against a large, complex system. This particular system begins with two sub-systems, themselves almost unthinkably complicated, called the author and the reader. It goes on with the topic — the subject matter (also complicated) by which alone they will be connected. It then seeks to weld the three sub-systems into a meaningful whole. That is what communication is all about, and it is not easily done.

After a lot of re-arranging and re-writing, this book turns out to begin three times — which is why it comes in three parts. The first establishes some talk. The second says what I really wanted to say, using the talk. The third (hopefully) says what the reader really wanted to hear, given that he has already heard what I really wanted to say. It sounds complicated, because it is. But I hope the approach makes things easier rather than more difficult.

In communication everything depends on what you end up with, not on what was actually said or written down. Here you are supposed to end up with an insight, not with an agglomeration of facts. When everything is understood the details cease to matter very much, or can be changed, or can even be abandoned for another set. As Wittgenstein said at the end of the *Tractatus*, when you have climbed up the ladder, you can throw it away.

But the ladder must be there, and secure, and the rungs in place; the climb itself may be stiff. My only hope is that the view from the top is worthwhile. After the communication is all over, of course, we can agree to differ about all the steps on the way.

In particular, we can choose a whole new vocabulary if we like. For the moment, I have had to choose one, because I am starting this communication. Many will find it strange. But words are only names: please do not be put off by my names. Please have an agreement with me about them. I say all this because I find that cybernetics especially (these are cybernetic writings) leads people to argue with fervour about names — forgetting the ideas they name. Though all communication runs the same sort of risk.

This point is well covered by such writers as Wittgenstein. But it was brought home to me most vividly by one of my children, Matthew, when he was three years old. He had found two copper coins in a drawer. 'Daddy,' he carefully explained, 'these sixpences are half-pennies.' My sixpences may be your half-pennies, too. It does not matter as long as we both know what they will buy, because what they will buy is all they are about.

S.B.

Preface to second edition

The original edition of this book was published in 1972. Translations have appeared in Danish, French, German, Italian, and Portuguese, and preparations continue for versions in another three languages. Meanwhile, however, the original English text has been inconveniently out of print since early in 1975. The reason was that sharp changes in editorial policies and people had occurred in the original publishing house, where dozens of titles were consequently and suddenly abandoned. Publication rights in *Brain* were courteously returned to me.

By this time, however, two things had happened. A massive application of this whole approach to management cybernetics had been undertaken (1971 - 73) in Chile. The eventual overthrow of President Allende's administration was as traumatic an experience for me as for many others who, though not born Chileans, had reason to identify themselves with the nation's suffering. Years were to pass before I felt able to review all my Chilean papers, and to write a full personal account of the applications — an account which now appears in a new Part (Chapters Sixteen to Twenty) of this second edition. Secondly, if secondarily, I had been engaged in the writing of two other books: *Platform for Change,* which John Wiley published in 1975, and *The Heart of Enterprise,* which that same house issued late in 1979. The latter work, however, is the companion volume to this. Thanks to my publisher and friend James Cameron of Wiley's, *Heart* and *Brain* are now available in complementary editions that have been prepared in parallel. I hope very much that their mutual support will release synergistic energy for the readers of both.

Use of this work is certainly becoming quite widespread. It is helpful to know about applications on which I have not personally been consulted nor held a 'watching brief'. This is partly for research purposes, but also because people often write to see whether they can be put in touch with those using the approach in their own fields of management or type of organization.

The first preface, which you may just now have read, explained why the original book began three times, and therefore came in three parts (plus an Appendix). The above story is perhaps already sufficient to explain why the book now begins four times, and comes in four parts (the original Appendix becoming Part Five). There was of course a temptation to rewrite everything, but this seemed unfair to those already familiar with the first edition. In reviewing that text, I have made additions, rather than alterations. The structure and chapter headings remain as before. The final problem about the presentation of this fresh edition concerns its title. Even in 1972, the apparent limitation of the cybernetics of the viable system to 'the firm' was too restrictive — because applications to other kinds of enterprise, and especially government, were already in train. With the inclusion of all the new material in Part Four, the title is strictly a misnomer. However, it simply does not seem either legitimate or helpful to use a new title for a book the substance of which is already established.

On the question of titles, *Brain* and *Heart* shall suffice in their references to anatomy; there is no truth in a colleague's expectation that *Big Toe* would eventually be reached. Having made this resolution, I allow myself one final reference to a bodily organ — relating as it does to the business of managerial and ministerial innovation, on which this book has much to say. The figure of Prometheus is pictured on a medal that was presented to me in Sweden in 1958, and the late Edy Verlander, who was in charge of the event, asked me what this figure portended. Of course I replied that Prometheus stood as a symbol of science, since he brought down fire from heaven. 'No, no', said Edy. 'The medal is indeed for innovators, but the point about Prometheus is that he was chained to a rock and had his liver pecked out.' I did not think at the time that he was exactly joking; but now I am sure that he was perfectly serious. The reward-and-penalty structure in management heavily disfavours innovation: it is a fact which demands fresh thinking if our institutions are to survive.

Meanwhile, I commend you to *Brain,* an organ to be treated with especial respect — even with a certain reverence, since these are the brains of a planetary future with which we deal. There is a book, written by Jocasta Innes (References D), which — to judge by the frequency with which I consult it — must be of some importance. She memorably writes:
    'brains need gentle handling
    or they are apt to disintegrate'.

Amen.

S.B.

Acknowledgements

To the many friends who know that I know that they helped, and equally to those who suspect that I do not know, my very warm thanks.

I salute the memory of those three grandfathers of cybernetics, Norbert Wiener, Warren McCulloch, and Ross Ashby, with much affection.

My thanks to those managers in business and industry, government and universities, and in communities too, who have allowed and even encouraged me to develop this theory of organization on their territories over thirty years.

May I also publicly thank my wife Sallie for keeping both me and the typescript going through many years of writing and through two editions — this being the only page that I typed myself.

S.B.

PART ONE

CONCEPTUAL COMPONENTS

Summary of Part One

We begin (Chapter One) by trying to understand what is special about today's managerial problems. There does indeed seem to be something unique and it has to do with the rate of change. It could be that the lags in our systems of implementation are longer than the average interval of new technological impacts — if so there is bound to be trouble. The tool we have which might have coped with this problem, because it is fast and flexible, is the electronic computer. But we have not understood how to use it. This book is about what to do next.

We need a new insight, which the science of cybernetics can provide. I like to see straightforward English whenever possible, but I have not been able to write this book without introducing some new terms. They are there to name new concepts, or concepts which come from other sciences. If Chapter Two is read carefully, and the reader doggedly refuses to be put off, he will be armed with the first set of the tools he needs. There is a special glossary of cybernetic terms at the back of the book, so that people can refresh their understanding if necessary. You may well find that these strange terms soon become old friends — they deserve to be, or I should not have bothered to introduce them.

Next (Chapter Three), we start to use the tools. Here the really fundamental problem of management is discussed and analysed. It is the problem of complexity: how to measure it, how to manipulate it. We think of our problems as concerned with such things as men, materials, machinery and money — and their interaction. It is just that interaction that causes the difficulties, and we must get at its nature. We must also get at the nature of the way huge numbers of states in a system soak each other up — which is the subject of Ashby's Law. It turns out that organization *exists precisely to implement that cybernetic law. (There is more about this much later, in Chapter Fifteen.)*

By the end of Chapter Three the fundamental reasons should be clear why things cannot be organized down to the last iota (and why in human terms we should not even want to try). Of course, we all know that they cannot be so organized, that indeed an awful lot of things just organize themselves. But when we know exactly why, *we can approach the problem of* how. *This is the subject of Chapter Four — the nature of self-organization in very large*

3

systems. By understanding these principles properly, we may well be able to facilitate regulation without imposing it. And that is something all good managers try to do. There are some more new words here, which experience again shows to be useful to managers, with an account of a deceptively simple little machine which I call an 'algedonode'. I have explained why in the text.

But why another new word? The answer is that no one has actually isolated this mechanism before, and therefore it has no name. We all know about it, but the intention of cybernetics is to try to make such vaguely understood tricks perfectly explicit and clear, so that we really know how to use them. In Chapter Five the simple algedonode is used as a building block to construct a larger system. And the object of understanding that system is to discover the meaning of hierarchy in organizations. Hierarchies are needed for fundamental reasons given in logic when big systems are becoming organized. When they are translated into human terms, they seem to be all about power and prestige — with the result that people lose sight of their real nature and meaning in the system.

By the end of Part One we should have glimpsed a totally new perception of the nature of management, and of how to approach its task of organization and control. Please do not despair if the practical relevance of all this is by no means clear yet. As the Preface says, Part One 'establishes some talk'. We shall start talking this talk in Part Two.

CHAPTER ONE

Let's think again

At very long last something seems to be happening in management. Younger, more vigorous, more intent, and more scientifically orientated managers are to be found in senior jobs, and even in boardrooms. New modes of organization are being tried out — an experimental approach which is fundamentally scientific. The days of 'this is how we do it here' seem to be passing, and seventy years' effort in trying to make management more scientific is beginning to pay off.

I speak of these signs that something is happening in a strained voice, and with the air of a shipwrecked mariner sighting a sail. The reason is that we have really left it rather late to attempt an adaptation to new circumstances, as did the dinosaurs before us. Change — technological change — is happening all around us. It could yet leave us managerially unadapted, and, in the end, extinct.

Those two paragraphs, first drafted nearly ten years ago, opened the first edition of this book. In revision, it would seem that all that is required is to change the word 'seventy' to 'eighty'. But that would not be honest. The managerial change that I remarked has foundered, I fear. 'This is how we do it here' has become the basic slogan all over again. Witness 1978: a British prime minister, labelled 'socialist', survived on conservative policies; and an American president, labelled 'democratic', survived as a spurious republican. Adventurous ideas soon become constrained by the observed fact that their proponents cannot think them through to a proper conclusion, it would seem, and the old ideas prevail. It is not because they are successful: they are not, and the world is in a worse mess to prove it. Therefore was I at fault in drawing attention only to technological change, important as that is: I should have mentioned social and political change as well. But I see no reason not to continue as I did before — indeed the argument (until I shall interrupt it again) is the more poignant. Here it is.

There is a difficulty about saying such things from within a cultivated society. Other nations, more desperate or more brash, less conscious than ourselves of the historical process in which mankind is embedded, have forged ahead. They have not had the time to become world-weary or worldly-wise. For our part, we seem for so long to have been saying that a fantastic change in the rate of technical progress is 'only' a matter of degree; our culture does not admit of surprise, and claims to see the pattern of things. It does not allow itself to become excited. So someone invents a computer: 'it is only a faster way of doing arithmetic'. It is nothing of the kind.

The complaint which I am laying specifically at the door of our own culture is just this. We suspect that when someone invented the crossbow, warriors talked in their messes about 'this meaning the end of civilized war as we know it'. The same thing happened with the tank, with poison gas, with the magnetic mine. But with hindsight we perceive that these inventions fitted a pattern of development, and that each advance in the technology of attack rapidly drew forth (however unlikely the chance first seemed) an equivalent technology of defence. And so in industry. We still speak of the Industrial Revolution; but this again — with hindsight — no one any longer believes to have been a real revolution. It was part of evolution. Thus today people are still culturally disinclined to acknowledge anything special about the technological marvels they witness in these decades. They play it cool, and it is not my own argument that we should point to exceptional incidents and declare 'the world has radically changed'. The first lunar landing was indeed the crossbow of its time. The philosophers of science, too, would endorse the cultural verdict; they declare that the universe proceeds by continuities, and there are no 'special events'. Or, as their predecessors used to say in the Middle Ages: *natura non facit saltus* — nature does not make jumps.

Against all the cultural, historical, and philosophical evidence that there is no real problem in adaptation, because progress itself is evolutionary, there are still the dinosaurs. They were overtaken, not by hydrogen bombs or any other special events, but by *the rate of change*. So we ourselves, although we need not be bamboozled by the mere existence of a space rocket or a computer, have to look at the rate of change which such technological achievement represents. It is to the rate, rather than to the changes themselves, that we have to adapt.

Consider, then, if we are to talk of space rockets, man's capacity to travel at speed. For most of the last two thousand years the best that he could do was to climb on the back of a horse and gallop. The first alteration in this picture occurred quite recently with the invention of the steam engine. In rapid succession came the internal combustion engine, the turbine, and then the rocket itself. The curves plotting the consequent change in the speed of travel are shown in Figure 1, on which is also marked the so-called 'envelope curve' which contrives to encompass them all, and makes sense of the total rate of change.

Strangely, or perhaps not so strangely (for science is a unity and so is nature), very similar curves are obtained when we try to measure progress in any other human capability. For example, in communications the speed of message transmission was until very recently tied firmly to the speed of travel. One gave a message to someone else riding a horse, or (later) sent the letter by air-mail. The discovery which raised the speed of message transmission to something almost infinitely fast was radio — which produces an almost vertical line on the chart. Despite this there were difficulties about terrestrial transmissions, and very recently indeed it has been found better to bounce radio waves off artificial satellites rather than off the Heaviside layer. So the capacity to transmit information quickly, which not long ago seemed to have broken loose from the capacity to travel quickly, is now geared to it again.

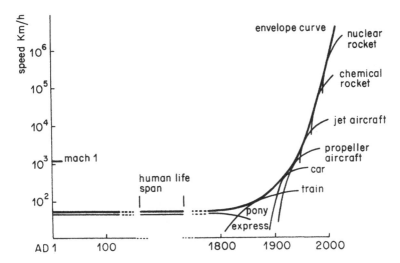

Figure 1. Man's capacity to travel at speed (After *Science Journal*)

In computing, the position is the same. For most of the two thousand years under review, people were mostly limited in computational facility by their ability to count on their fingers or with pebbles. Even *savants* were restricted by the elementary forms of calculus (such as plain arithmetic using the Arabic notation, and much later logarithms) which they were able to invent. Pretty well the first technological breakthrough was Pascal's wheel, which could add and subtract an infinitely long series of digits mechanically. This was in the mid-seventeenth century. But it was not until the 1820s that Babbage had invented a much more complicated, though still mechanical, computer, and the typical mechanical office machine was not in use until the last decade of the nineteenth century. Such machines were later electrified, but we waited until 1946 for the invention of the electronic computer. The present-day computer (1970) is already 1,000,000 times faster than the original machines of the late 1940s, and by the year 2000 they will predictably be a thousand million times faster.

Here is the second intervention of the new edition. The prediction above is on course. Computers are now somewhere between ten and a hundred million times faster than they were in the late 1940s, and the prediction for the year 2000 may be an underestimate. But their sheer speed is as nothing compared with their cheapness. The development of microprocessors will constitute a much bigger revolution than the invention of computers themselves, because they can be afforded by anyone with the credit to pledge on the scale of a television set. That takes computers out of the hands of big business: a devastating development. But let us return to the first edition once more.

Whatever human accomplishment we study, we seem to obtain a curve similar to that drawn in Figure 1, a curve which is itself compounded of smaller curves each representing an epoch of the relevant technology. There is another human accomplishment which notoriously follows the same pattern; procreation. Fairly well authenticated estimates of the population of the entire world over the two millennia since BC became AD are available, and now the rate of expansion is almost vertical on the chart. Eventually it actually becomes vertical, according to one mathematical model that is consistent with the known data. If this rate of change continues, then it is computed that the population of the world will be infinitely large by the year 2026. That would mean that Malthus was at least half right in thinking that the earth could not in the end sustain an exploding population — except that we shall not be starved, but squeezed to death! There are two lessons to be drawn from the arguments so far.

If we take a typical human life span, and impose it on the curve of Figure 1, we find that for most of history the 'lines of force' of technological change run through it horizontally. That is to say that a man found the world much the same when he left it as when he arrived in it. Incidents like the invention of the crossbow may have surprised him at the time, but it is true that they fitted the pattern and offered (hindsight again) relatively little challenge. But if we impose this life span on the chart over our own decades, we find the technological lines of force tearing upwards through our own viscera. All our capabilities are expanding by factors of perhaps a million times or so within our own lifetime, and simply cannot be regarded as normal to earlier human existence in general. No wonder we have a problem of adaptation to change. I repeat: it is not a question of *incidents*. The whole rate of progress is explosive, and there is hardly a human capability which remains static long enough for us to adapt to it. We therefore feel unease. Consider the problem posed by our own children. There is a cultural as well as a psychological gap between the generations, which seems to have existed throughout history. But today people wonder whether the gap in our own generation is not profoundly more significant. All I can say is that I hope it may be so. For the whole structure of society has this same problem of adaptation, and unless our children can invent what amounts to a new way of living in a single generation our species may be doomed. We ourselves are trapped in our own social and cultural patterns, so the more incomprehensible to us our children seem, the better it probably is.

When we come to management, whether of the firm, or of the country, or of international affairs, the same problem of adaptation exists. This seems to me to identify the managerial challenge. And if it is the rate of change in technology which poses these problems for us, there seems to be no alternative but to turn to science itself for their solution. Modern management must be about this. It is not a question, as it is so often represented to be, of using 'better methods' or 'advanced techniques'. This view of the matter was all very well when the exponential curve of development was only just beginning to take off. What is needed now is a total reappraisal of our way of managing, which entails in turn a reconsideration of our traditional organization for the purpose.

The second line of thought which emerges from the original consideration is of a different kind. It is provoked by the suggestion that the population of the world 'looks like' becoming imminently infinite. No one, I suspect, will believe that this is really going to happen. Why not? It may of course be sheer terror. But a cooler judgement suggests that, just as nature does not make jumps, it does not lightly run to infinities. Inifinities are the boundaries of mathematical processes rather than physical ones. Infinities are abstractions; realities are finite. In the case of the curves we have been considering, we should note that they are envelope curves composed of smaller curves dealing with technological epochs — which themselves *tail off*. Now this tailing off is typical of growth processes in nature. Their curves tend to be S-shaped, or sigmoid; mathematicians call them 'logistics'. And if the component curves tail off, then it seems probable that the *total* curve we are considering will also tail off — or at least be itself a component curve of some larger, and so far unimaginable, technological era.

In Figure 2, then, appears the typical growth curve which is found in nature. We may study it in the biological context — in our own growth for example; in the economic context, such as the growth of markets, or even in the inanimate world wherein things are made to grow. For instance, when men build a plant, or a large machine, they begin by incurring a basic cost — laying down the foundations or a base plate. This investment usually remains almost static for some little time, while materials and labour are assembled to begin serious work on construction. The rate of growth, in this case the cost of the investment, then rises steadily and quite rapidly as work proceeds in an organized fashion. Towards the end of the job, however, it is common to observe a flattening out of effort and therefore of extra investment committed. This is the phase during which one waits for a final set of parts which were under-ordered — and no one can find the funnel to put on top.

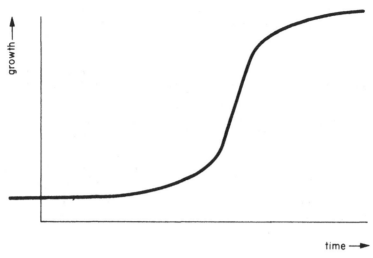

Figure 2

In tracing the advance of progress through a technological epoch, we find much the same phenomena. There is a slow start, because the technology is not fully established; there are teething troubles. During the middle phase of the epoch everyone is learning rapidly, discovery follows discovery, and a successful industry is created. In the third phase, things begin to stultify. Although they may continue to be highly profitable for some time, operations do not continue to improve. This is characteristic of all learning processes as they approach their theoretical limit. We find that for every equivalent slice of time that passes, and more particularly for each extra unit of investment, a decreasing improvement occurs. It is then usual, in both human performance and business development, to truncate the effort and to settle for something slightly less than could ideally be achieved. This is in acknowledgement of the law of diminishing returns. The technologies used in businesses, and indeed the businesses themselves, will normally follow this pattern.

What happens next is fairly alarming. The level of performance, however it may be measured, will continue perhaps for some time. After that, if it does not simply stultify, it may actually *decline*. Just as senescent people may forget what they once knew, just as the biological organism which was fully grown may begin to shrivel, so markets may decline following saturation, so businesses may fail and become bankrupt. Even successful technologies, considered in relation to competitive technologies, may cease to be economic any longer. When these symptoms appear, there is only one remedy. It is fruitless to imagine that extra effort, extra capital, can resurrect the moribund organism. A decision must be taken to superimpose a new growth curve upon the old. In the case of technology, this means embarking on fresh research; or it means acquiring new staff and facilities in a proven but novel field, which is quite foreign to both the managers who run things and to the work force who operate things. So that experience is likely to be traumatic. In the case of the firm itself, the decision may be to acquire (or perhaps to merge with) another firm, with a view to establishing a business synthesis which is greater than the sum of its parts.

In either case, we should note, two serious conditions apply. Firstly, we have to overcome a host of practical difficulties associated with mammoth change — while keeping everything running at full blast. The second difficulty, strangely enough, is even more serious because it is conceptual. If the people concerned regard the change as 'a new venture', as some 'diversification', or as a means of giving their quiescent patient a shot in the arm, they will fail. They have to stand back and take a much larger view. They have to see and to understand that the new growth curve is superimposed on the old growth curve in order to create part of an envelope curve which will drive upwards to higher and possibly quite other things. They are not enhancing an old technology but embracing novelty. They are not improving the business they have known and loved, they are devising a new business of unknown characteristics.

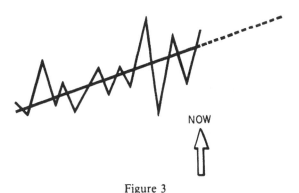

NOW

Figure 3

In considering the prospect of new investment, whether in mergers and acquisitions or in the development of a new technology, the firm is faced with an intractable problem of statistical analysis. Consider a senior manager or a board which is seeking to establish what are euphemistically known as 'the facts'. We want a run of figures to show how we are progressing — whether as to profitability, as to return on capital employed, as to turnover or production or any other measure. A little graph is produced, looking like Figure 3, showing an upward trend over the last few years. If we are prudent, our immediate reaction is to ask someone to give the information for twenty years prior to the start of this run. If he in turn is prudent, he is likely to refuse. He will remind us that it is only four years since the takeover, or the fire, or the new tax, or the war in the Far East. For any of these reasons or many others, he will argue, we ought not seriously to consider information earlier than that which he has already given. The conditions were not comparable. And so we look at our little run of data, and we fit a line. Perhaps we do this by eye, or we employ a mathematical statistician to undertake a regression analysis. In either case, this line is about all we confidently know; and in either case we are likely to extrapolate it. This is the meaning of the thick line in the figure, and its dotted extension.

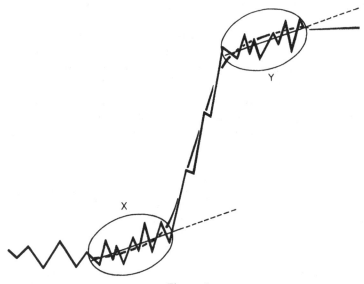

Figure 4

Now if growth in nature were normally linear, this would be fine. But as we have seen, growth curves tend to be sigmoid in shape. Where, then, on the sigmoid curve does this small piece of pattern belong? Perhaps it fits at the first inflection of that curve (marked X), where the growth rate is beginning to rise rapidly. In that case, as Figure 4 shows, the straight-line extrapolation will wildly underestimate the growth potential: we shall be outstripped by competitors who are making a larger investment. But if our curve belongs to the second point of inflection (marked Y), as is also shown in the new diagram, we shall be entertaining expectations which are due to be sadly disappointed. There will be over-investment. In either case the business has lost out. It may seem at first sight quite easy to identify where 'now' lies on the overall growth curve. But this would be true only if we knew in advance *what* was growing. Unfortunately, we do not. We know what we think the business is, what we think is our technological basis. What the business will turn out to be, and what technology we shall by then be using, are quite unknown. As was argued earlier, our biggest difficulty is the conceptual one of keeping an open mind on these very matters.

The nature of this problem may be identified, if once again we are prepared to use hindsight. In Figure 5 is the envelope curve of the business (marked E). Technology A is the one with which we are familiar: technology B is the one which (unknown to us now, because the time is not yet ripe) is going to dominate our industry in the next epoch. Here we are at time t_1. It would be clear to us, if we could see ahead, that by time t_2 a new technology will have overtaken our affairs. At this moment, however, it is very far from clear. The business will succeed or fail depending on our wisdom in first identifying technology B, and then investing in it at the right moment. Of course, this is not an all-or-nothing decision taken at a special instant. What would be preferable would be a mixture of investment at all times between t_1 and t_2 in *both* technologies. We should have to go on investing in technology A — in order to ensure the continuation of our profits and the ultimate pay-off of our much earlier investments in it. We should also be investing in technology B, so that a smooth takeover could be accomplished when technology A became stultified.

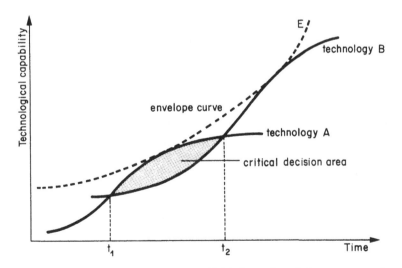

Figure 5. (With acknowledgement to Erich Jantsch and *Science Journal*)

But remember the time *now* is no more than t_1, and the rest of the graph is quite hypothetical. Therefore the psychological problem implicit in this course, quite apart from the technological problems it poses, is immense. Someone within the firm's upper councils may perceive the emergence of technology B, and its relevance to the business. Other people, in the nature of things, are going to declare that the man is mad. After all, anyone who really knows the firm would know that technology B has nothing to do with it. Suppose the battle is won, and people are eventually convinced of the relevance of technology B. Investment decisions still have to be taken, and many problems remain. Some people will, quite rightly, point out that an investment in technology B may exhaust the company's resources. By mistiming, they could fail to support technology A to its real pay-off period, and at the same time fail to reach profitability in technology B before the funds have run out. These objectors are making points of great validity. But, on the contrary, if their counsels prevail for too long, the firm will quite clearly lose its market share to competitors who have got their timing right.

This argument identifies the problem of corporate planning. Management has heard little of this topic in the past, but the phrase is suddenly fashionable. Perhaps this is another passing fad of the business schools and consulting companies. I would contend that this is not so, for the reasons set out at the beginning of this chapter. Companies have always had corporate planning problems, but they solved them fairly casually because the lines of technological force were almost horizontal (remember Figure 1). Today, as we have noted, these lines are shooting upwards at an ever steeper angle. Therefore the problem of company adaptation, which is the problem of corporate planning, cannot be dealt with casually any longer. It is a matter of the most serious import. In short: it took five hundred years before Sikorsky developed Leonardo's helicopter into a commercial proposition, but in twenty years from the building of the first computer at the University of Pennsylvania it was not merely a commercial proposition but bidding fair to run the world. Science in fact is only just beginning, and almost all scientists who have ever lived are still alive. This is the explosive growth curve of science itself, and this it is which impinges on the world today. How to run companies, how to organize them, how to service them, how to do anything at all in government or business or industry is just not known any longer. Both knowledge and experience seem to have run out. We are in an experimental situation.

It is against this background that management confronts the electronic computer. This instrument offers management its own 'technology B' — something which makes the managerial world utterly different. But management has addressed itself to the possibilities in a way which virtually precludes the emergence of a new managerial order. It has tried instead to assimilate the computer into managerial technology A — improving, or let us say simply souping-up, the ways of regulating matters with which managers are already familiar. I think I have detected four phases in this process.

The first phase was amazement. Publicists called computers 'electronic brains', while people in the know were saying that they were not much like brains at all. What could they really be expected to do? This question was answered according to temperament, but many managers suspected two things. Computers might turn out to be incomprehensible to the manager himself, and therefore a substantial personal threat; in any case the cost might be ruinous. But the good manager is made of sterner stuff than this. In the second stage he very properly came to grips with the nature of the machine, and made a serious effort to understand its basic method of operation. He soon found out that the machine is a moron. Not only did this discovery remove unjustifiable fears, but it took away all sense of wonder, and that was a pity.

Although present-day computers fall very far short of the human brain in so many capabilities, they are in just as many ways very much superior to the computers in our skulls. But in this second phase people lost sight of the fact, and they fell to discussing rather trivial problems about the relation between office machines and scientific machines in terms, for example, of the input/output requirement. Thus the managerial issues rapidly became political, because people used these trivial arguments to justify different computers in the office and the research laboratory, and a different computer again in the production context. Anything which inflames the appetite for empire building not only becomes a vice, but detracts from the issues which ought to be discussed.

For the manager, this was to be the age of electronic dataprocessing — referred to by the slick acronym EDP. Regardless of the purposes to which the processed data would be put, all effort was now focused on the argument whether more and better data could be provided faster and more cheaply by installing a computer or by streamlining orthodox clerical procedures. This done (and of course this is a process that still goes on) some managers decided to go ahead and install computers. And that brought us to the third phase, in which most businesses remain. There is a rather widespread use of computers in the role of new lamps for old. Routine office work is done by machines; sometimes staff have been saved, sometimes not. More and better output has been obtained; sometimes people have known how to make use of it, and sometimes not. A variety of benefits has been sought; sometimes money has been saved, but all too often the pay-off has been negligible. Many who introduced computers during phase two became disappointed in phase three, while many who did not came to feel that they were well out of it.

Meanwhile, however, the leaders in the field have entered a fourth phase of development. It begins by facing the following dilemma. Enough has happened in the computer world to demonstrate that these machines are now permanently with us. History has painfully demonstrated that once mankind knows how to perform a function by machine, the machine is in and man is out. And yet there is disappointment, and the economics of the whole business look somewhat rocky. The answer to the dilemma is becoming clear. Too many managers have been dazzled in EDP terms by the 'more and quicker' argument, with the result that little fresh thought has been given to the purposes which the information duly handled is supposed to serve. This, it is being declared in phase four, is management information. And so the magic letters EDP are being replaced by the equally magic letters MIS — management information systems.

This certainly appears to be another advance. It looks as if it takes seriously the question about the purposes of EDP. But in reality we become more and more embedded in managerial philosophies of the past. We continue to replace one thing by another which is indeed more effective, and now we have a great vision whereby all these bits and pieces will be *integrated* in a vast informational network. The whole firm will run on a basis of 'instant fact', because managers will draw any item of knowledge they require from a huge data base into which all the facts about the business will be poured. In a later chapter I shall show explicitly why this vision of the future is actually incapable of fulfilment. The argument for the present rests on the fact that, even if these prognoses were reasonable, we should still have missed the point.

Items of fact about a business are profuse. They proliferate with every second that passes. Most of them are worthless — in the sense that they have no bearing on managerial decision. By recording them, sorting them in different ways and printing out huge quantities of tables, nothing useful is accomplished. On the contrary, managers become engulfed in a sea of useless facts. Doubtless some valuable facts may be included, but if so they will be lost without trace. The manager wants information, not facts, and facts become information only when something is changed. The manager is the instrument of change (otherwise what is he doing?) which is to say his job is that of *control*. This means that the job is not to design a data-processing system at all, but to design a control system. And if we use the computer simply to undertake a souped-up version of the old kind of control system, which was inadequate simply because we did not have computers, we are no better off than before. It is the same with our planning techniques, which are part of the manager's control armoury, and which so desperately need to be improved in the context of technological change. For again we are concentrating on slicker ways of doing things rather than on *what* we do. What is the use of the ever-faster, ever-slicker, more nearly perfect implementation of rotten plans?

The question which asks how to use the computer in the enterprise, is, in short, the wrong question. A better formulation is to ask how the enterprise should be run given that computers exist. The best version of all is the question asking *what, given computers, the enterprise now is.* Underlying the problems of good practice in the modern firm are the problems of control, and underlying these in turn is the problem of control to what end.

Central to these issues, the control problem sits like a fulcrum. If the manager is to run the business at all, or for that matter the government the country, a new order of control sophistication is required — and can be made available through the computer. If we wish to answer the questions about the nature and purposes of the enterprise, the control system itself should make manifest the evidence on which judgements can be based. This is possible in the sense that the controls needed do not simply relate to the internal economy, but to the relationship of the enterprise itself with the world outside.

Now the study of control is a science in its own right, known as cybernetics. If we wish to design new managerial control systems, they ought to have a cybernetic validity, and to be more than a pooling of computer applications evolved on the new-lamps-for-old approach. I am speaking now of structure, which is to say organization, rather than of facts and the flow of information. Perhaps what managerial technology B has to offer over managerial technology A is precisely a cybernetic shape.

The main discovery of cybernetics after a history of twenty-five years, and indeed what gives it the right to be called a coherent science, is that there are fundamental principles of control which apply to all large systems. The principles which have been discovered have been investigated in living systems (such as the brain), in electronic systems (such as computers) and in social and economic systems too. This book is entirely concerned with the contribution which cybernetics, the science of control, can make to management, the profession of control.

At the outset of this project I have a suggestion to make about the way we should look at the topic of management itself. The thought comes by analogy with a consideration of arithmetic. Ordinary arithmetic has to do with calculations using the natural numbers, 1, 2, 3, 4, 5, etc., but there is another subject, belonging to advanced mathematics, called 'the higher arithmetic'. This is concerned with the exploration of the laws which govern the way these natural numbers behave in general. Clearly this is a study of a more elevated order; we expect children to be able to add two digits together, but it takes a mathematician to understand the nature of the process which is happening when, for instance, this manoeuvre is carried out for arbitrary pairs of numbers arranged in arbitrary ways. The analogy is this: In most of the training courses arranged for managers, the topic of concern is known as 'management studies'. This, as customarily presented, is essentially concerned with the manipulation of data about a business. How to calculate a discounted cash flow, for example, seems (at a suitably more difficult level) the same sort of activity as adding two digits in arithmetic. We might then define a new subject, to be called 'the higher management', concerned with the laws which govern the behaviour of these data. How do the measures used in business behave in general, and in particular how are they related to each other? In short, I seek to promote the study of management at an elevated level, where we should be more concerned with the nature of things and their structural relationships than with operational matters which are strictly consequential. The higher management is about a policy calculus.

The issue before us which above all needs to be considered from this standpoint is the relationship between man and machine. We have seen the computer used in the role of a fast adding machine, regarded as a quicker and possibly more accurate way of 'doing the sums'. We shall need to regard it as something more than this, and to use it far more intelligently. For, moron though the computer may be, its huge capacity to store information, its fantastically rapid retrieval capability, and its vastly suprahuman capability to juggle with thousands of quantified variables simultaneously, offer man an asset which as it were entitles the machine to an equal partnership.

An end is rapidly approaching to the medieval dichotomy between the animate and the inanimate machine. We have seen vast machines which swallow the men who work them, for the men are no more than clogs in the whole assembly. We have seen machines embedded in men, such as electrical pace-makers for the heart. We have seen machines which limit men, and machines which are extensions of men. The computer is a machine which rises above the amplification of muscular effort, and the effort of control which is needed to be precise. It is something which can be used as an extra lobe of the brain. There can now be, indeed at some point there certainly will be, some kind of merger between man and machine — a symbiosis.

Earlier in this chapter we saw that science nowadays tends not to recognize the special event, but only the continuous process. I personally think that part of the message of cybernetics is to say that, by the same token, there is no unique control mechanism recognizable by its fabric. The brain may be made of protein, and the computer of semi-conductors. Brain-like behaviour, perhaps of a more sophisticated kind than either can achieve alone, is not a function of these special fabrics. It is a function of the laws of control through which they can be organized to operate in unison.

Let's Think Again — Again

This is now the second edition speaking in its own right. You will have noticed that it was necessary to interrupt the first edition only twice, as a matter of updating the facts. Recent pages could have been amended to say that cybernetics is by now *thirty*-five years old; and that there is some evidence that the exploding growth curves referred to may turn out to be not merely exponential, but *hyperbolic*. However, I am not accustomed to apologizing for understatement, and the curves must take care of their own hyperbole.

The arguments deployed in this chapter as originally written still hold. I have often been denounced as a 'prophet of doom'; but it turns out that only my optimism was unfounded. It should be worth discussing why this was so, and obviously the keys must lie in those two early interventions that it was necessary to make. The first of them included these words:

> 'Adventurous ideas soon become constrained by the observed fact that their proponents cannot think them through to a proper conclusion, it would seem, and the old ideas prevail. It is not because they are successful: they are not, and the world is in a worse mess to prove it.'

There are two main reasons, I suggest, why this customarily happens. They appear to be very different at first sight.

People embrace adventurous ideas because they appear *liberating*. Things have always gone wrong: here are new notions that will put everything right. Adventurous ideas are in this sense the intellectual and pacific means of engaging in guerilla warfare against the embattled strength of outdated and oppressive Establishments. The problem is this: we are not confronted merely with the attractiveness of one idea as juxtaposed against another. That may happen for the individual in search of God, or for a family or other small group in search of a more satisfactory way of living. But even in these cases, the embodiment of the idea — its realization in a societary context — encounters systemic reaction. That is to say, the system to which the individual or the small group belongs is catering for something which (within fairly narrow limits) it designates to be 'normal behaviour'. Deviation from that norm is not only puzzling and unsettling to others in the system: with the best will in the world, the system is not so organized as to accommodate it. Any married woman in our society, for example, who seeks to behave as a free individual, soon finds out that (despite all Acts of Parliament to the contrary) she is hemmed in by old ideas. She will be asked for her husband's signature in relation to contracts that she is legally entitled to engage in herself, and so forth. All this happens because reforming zeal is not enough on the part of reformers: they fail to work through the *systemic consequences* of their adventurous ideas.

This is yet more evident in the arena of entrepreneurial management, because the systemic ramifications of any truly novel proposal are inevitably legion. The naivety with which an adventurous idea is launched often sounds its own death knell in the very enthusiasm of its half-bakedness. I am frequently struck by the fact that whenever an example is needed to illustrate what I am writing, there is always one available in the news of the day concerned. Today — this very day — a trade union leader in Britain has demanded that all laboratories handling pathenogenic bacteria should be removed to remote areas, to be guarded by wire and dogs. That is a new idea, prompted by a very understandable and proper concern over the failure of biological security in an existing laboratory, which recently led to the death of a member of this leader's union. But the only reason why these lethal bacteria are cultivated at all is for teaching purposes. Even if medical students can be transported to 'remote areas' to be taught, it is a safe bet that the few specialists capable of the teaching will not manage to arrive. And that is not because they are wicked people, but because the *system* in which this whole problem is embedded urgently requires their presence in the very metropolitan teaching hospitals which are at some possible risk.

Let no manager 'on the other side' chortle because the example-of-the-day concerns a trade unionist: managers on *all* sides simply fail to perceive the system into which their short-term palliatives are introduced, and therefore also fail to work out the systemic consequences. Having said all this, I am once again everyone's enemy. But it might just be that the human brain is too small, and the human spirit too irresolute, to handle the ramifications of the system with which it perforce must deal. It was human ambition and human avarice, however, that created that 'system' in the first place. It is to the brain that this book turns for answers.

This first reason as to why adventurous ideas often fail, and old ideas prevail, is benign. It reflects merely on human weakness and inadequacy. It is not a 'theory of conspiracy', which declares that sinister forces are mustered against any kind of innovation. And yet there is a malign explanation as well — although it is not a 'theory of conspiracy' either. The word *malign* means simply *inimical to viability*. We do not have to be paranoid to recognize that we are actually ill.

This second explanation says that the new idea is not only beyond the comprehension of the existing system, but that the existing system finds it threatening to its own status quo. Of course it does. That is not necessarily because of its determination to hang on to power, although that is often a factor. It is mainly because the existing system does not know what will happen if the new idea is embraced. The first explanation said that the innovator fails to work through the systemic consequences of the new idea. The second explanation says that the Establishment cannot either, and with better reason — and, what is more, that it has no incentive whatsoever to do so. It was not its own idea for heaven's sake. The onus is on the innovator. That seems perfectly reasonable. It is perfectly reasonable until we remember the power equation: it turns out that the Establishment **controls the resources** that the adventurous idea needs ...

Consider the cybernetics of the prestigious bodies that are created to administer research monies on behalf of the government. In regulatory terms, the mechanism is geared towards (a) spending money as voted, and (b) making sure that such expenditure can be defended. Now if the money goes towards the expansion of existing knowledge, under the aegis of academics of solid reputation who already dominate the field concerned, the system cannot fail to demonstrate that the money was 'well spent' — especially because the arbiters of that judgement are the committeemen who *receive* the grants (or were the year before, or will be next year). If however 'adventurous ideas' are pursued, they may fail — by definition; then all members of the body, and those who appointed them, would be vulnerable to criticism.

This analysis is not idle barracking of the status quo machines that these bodies constitute, nor have I personally sufferred at their hands. Having never applied for, nor been awarded, a research grant in my life, nor yet accepted membership of a grant-awarding body, I lay claim to a reasonable degree of objectivity. And unless my recollection has failed, I know of no case in which I have been in favour of an adventurous idea that has received its grant, nor of any case in which I have disfavoured an idea because it was unadventurous where the grant application has not succeeded.

It is worth noting that any conscientiously adventurous person who comes to this realization has no choice but to opt out of the grant-awarding system. If support guarantees failure, while objection guarantees success, the only strategy that would be effective is to recommend the contrary of one's considered judgement; and that strategy is indefensible. But in opting out, one strongly reinforces the status quo machine — which is that much more free to be unadventurous. The dilemma could be resolved, but not by any rebellious individual: as usual, the cybernetic answer is *structural*. It is not until some proportion of research money is demonstrably wasted that there is a chance that the rest has been truly well spent; and that proportion cannot be fixed as a matter of accountancy, because no-one can show what the percentage should be. That has to emerge as a *physiological limit* of the *homeostat* that regulates research expenditure .... But the terminology gets ahead of the explanations offered in this book, and the hope for genuine regulation of public research expenditure gets ahead of its (even attempted) realization.

Meanwhile, of course, 'the old ideas prevail'. In this instance, it is predictable that the foregoing analysis will be labelled an over-simplification. That is an initial tactic in trying to ensure that nothing will be done. As to the evidence adduced, it is predictable that this will be called 'typical exaggeration': that is the classic *ad hominem* technique. Serious critics are referred to the Social Science Research Council for the facts — if they can still be found.

As promised, the two explanations for the collapse of adventurous ideas prove to be basically different: the first is benign and the second is malign. But, as was also mentioned, the difference is one observed only at first sight. The two explanations share a common root: it is the failure to treat problems as symptoms of systemic malorganization, and to imagine instead that they are either evils penetrating the system that can be exorcised, or technical gremlins that can be thumped on the head. The scientific and managerial pursuit of systemic consequences is a general solution. In the benign case, it means noting how the system will necessarily react to a novelty that it perceives as a mere perturbation of input; in the malign case it means evaluating how the system is likely to respond to *threat* — threat, that is, to its own integrity. In most cases, an adventurous idea will result in both benign and malign reactions. Failure by the would-be innovator to distinguish between the two may render him impotent as a strategist. In the limit, it may render him psychotic as a person.

But however the details work out, *the old ideas prevail*: so 'let's think again', again.

The second intervention in the first edition of this chapter concerned the microprocessor. This is a recent innovation — an adventurous idea indeed, but also a concrete fact. That distinction needs to be made. There is no philosophical difference, I think, between a valid new idea and a piece of hardware that works; if there is, it is certainly clouded by the facts that a valid idea is quite concrete to those who understand it, while no amount of ironmongery has any potency unless it has its appropriate software support. The distinction needs to be made on other grounds, and those grounds are *units of money*. It is not legally possible to patent an idea, nor even to retrieve royalties on the photocopies that people illegally make of the books in which that idea was expressed. But it is legally possible to make vast sums of money out of gadgetry, because it can be patented: which is just what the computer manufacturers have done. That is fine, in our kind of society. What is far from fine is that the power of money to control the first quarter-century of computing has totally blocked off its truly adventurous ideas — for both benign and malign reasons in systemic terms. There is, however, good reason to think that the reign of money is over, even in our kind of society, where computation is concerned.

As the second intervention remarked, the point about microprocessing is its *cheapness*. 'That takes computers out of the hands of big business: a devastating development.' And so it is. In the past, brilliant young people who wanted to work with computers had to toe the line — a line drawn with vigour and often ferocity by those who were making the money. The generally disastrous results are plain to see; more will be said about that in subsequent chapters. The challenge to management renews itself after twenty-five years....

The unchanged part of this chapter detected four phases in managerial response to the arrival on the management scene of the electronic computer:

'The first phase was amazement.'

'In the second stage ... he soon found out that the machine is a moron.'

'... the third phase, in which most businesses remain. There is a rather widespread use of computers in the role of new lamps for old'

'... phase four, is management information. And so the magic letters EDP are being replaced by the equally magic letters MIS — management information systems.'

After explaining why this approach would not work (nor has it), the analysis asked the question as to *what, given computers, the enterprise now is.*

Microprocessors, the second intervention declared, 'will constitute a much bigger revolution than the invention of computers themselves'. As this is being written, the managerial response to these developments is *amazement*. We are back, all of a quarter-century later, to phase one. The other phases cannot reduplicate themselves in the same way, because the power of money will not exert the same influence. Managers will surface, in this second electronic revolution, who will support the brilliant young men — because the money involved will be trivial. Appropriations will not have to go to board level, to be consistently misunderstood, and to be shot down by the vested interests of monied manufacturers. Moreover (publish this not in Gath), some of these managers will themselves be brilliant young people, and some of the brilliant young people will themselves be managers; and others there will be to command and to afford this technology who are not brilliantly young, nor managers, but who have different concerns about the future of the world — some benign, and some malign ....

I shall not interfere with the flow of this book again by making interventions and special additions, as in this chapter, but merely revise the text in the light of experience.

The message holds: *let's think again.*

CHAPTER TWO

Concepts and terms

If we are to approach the cybernetic realities of large control systems, we must inevitably break with the general style of thinking used in the first chapter. If there are principles of control, we shall have to start specifying them. And this is to be done on the established understanding that the concepts and terms that are familiar in management studies will be of little help. In this chapter, therefore, we shall discuss the nature of systems and their control in a new language, and without much reference to the firm at all. The idea is that we should really sit down and *think*. What is control all about?

The first principle of control is that the controller is part of the system under control. The controller is not something stuck on to a system by a higher authority which then accords it managerial prerogatives. In any natural system, whether we speak of animal populations or the inner workings of some living organism, the control function is spread through the architecture of the system. It is not an identifiable thing at all, but its existence in some form is inferred from the system's behaviour. The controller moreover grows with the system, and, if we look back through time, we see that the controller evolved with the system too.

For these reasons it is best to ask how a system under control is aware of itself and its own states, rather than to ask how a controller can become aware of the state of the system. 'Aware of itself', by the way, means something different from self-consciousness. I do not think we need run the risk of endowing the system with a *persona,* or with any identity other than that demarcated for it by an observer. Let us define awareness behaviourally, that is, by specifying the behaviour which is to count as typical of an aware system. Take the system as given. We define an assemblage of entities as a system because those entities are observed as acting cohesively. Take some kind of routine activity as exemplifying the system's natural dynamics. That is, we often observe the assemblage of entities acting in this way. Then what happens if we interfere with something — poke a stick into the system, or shout at it, or change the temperature of its environment? If the system responds to this stimulus, then we say that it is aware. Note that we do not have to say: aware of the stimulus, which implies an act of cognition about the world outside the system. All that we know from our experiment is that the system is aware of a change wrought in itself. The distinction is important.

This explanation provokes a new question: what is to count as a response to a stimulus? If we interfere with a running car-engine by switching off the ignition, is it right to say that the system responds by dying out? No; because we have annihilated the dynamic system that we discovered, not offered it a stimulus. If we shoot an animal, it dies — and for the same reason. Equally, if we were to drop a matchstick on to the car's cylinder block or on to the back of an elephant, nothing would happen. This time it is because our interference does not count as a stimulus.

It is not difficult to make sense of all this. Clearly what is to count as a stimulus is an interference which affects the system's operation in some way, being neither so mild as to be insignificant to the operation nor so drastic as to destroy the system itself. What is to count as a response is some change in the system which makes sense only in terms of the stimulus offered. If the system changes arbitrarily when we happen to offer what we think is a stimulus, then perhaps it would have changed anyway. A cat which happens to leave the room after inspecting a board bearing the inscription 'go away' is not responding to the message content, and is therefore (by our definition) not aware of it. But we might well train the cat to leave the room on seeing the board. If it always did so we would abandon the idea that this was a coincidence and talk about a response to a stimulus, and an aware cat. A stimulus is something which alters the operation of the system. The system's response is something it does that has to be interpreted in terms of the stimulus. In general, this means that the system avoids or otherwise counteracts a stimulus which disrupts its activity, and embraces or seeks to increase a stimulus which favours its activity. Note that we accept evidence that these things are happening when we judge that the observed action of the system is not haphazard. And that judgement depends either on the dramatic quality of the whole incident (which can be misleading) or on its highly reliable repetition (which is the scientific criterion). A system conforming to this behaviour is aware — to some degree at least. If it conforms to this behaviour in almost all circumstances, we shall call it aware without any qualms or reservations at all. Nor is this a desperately unscientific judgement to make, because the universe is governed by probabilities, not by certainties. In physics, in genetics, in social science alike, we rely on descriptions and even on laws which are based on the balance of chances. It is only the special and artificially constructed field of mechanical engineering in which effect follows cause in a determined way which is fully understood to be inexorable. Even then things may go wrong.

In general, we were saying, responses to stimuli by aware systems are either negative or positive. The former tend to avoid inimical stimuli, the latter to reinforce favourable stimuli. It follows that the aware system has, in some sense, the ability to judge which is which. Care is needed in understanding that conclusion. Awareness is still not to be equated with self-consciousness; the system does not have to make value judgements. All it needs is a mechanism which registers the stimulus as opprobrious or salubrious, and these terms are in no way ethically loaded. For if a system has a criterion of smooth operation, it can be organized to work towards that criterion. We said at the outset: 'take some kind of routine activity as exemplifying the system's natural dynamics', and this is really the clue to thinking about control. Systems *are* and systems *work*; if not, they are not systems at all. Control is what facilitates the existence and the operation of systems. We said before that being aware (intransitive) and being aware of a stimulus were two different things. We now begin to see why. It is because this criterion of smooth operation is a criterion based on *internal* stability. We may suppose that a stimulus arises from outside the system; unintelligent systems do not know this, intelligent systems infer or perceive the fact. Even so, for both systems the control action is a response to change that is internal, once the stimulus has registered itself in some way. We withdraw from pain — that is the physiological fact. The idea that we shrink from the needle or the burning cigarette-end is an intellectual construction. We actually shrink from the sensation of pain, which exists inside us, because it upsets our internal environment. If we shrink before the pain is sensed because we see the danger coming, we are simply anticipating the internal consequences of a forecast external event. This is because we are (and this is a refinement) learning systems. If we had not learned to associate the external event with its internal consequence we would not shrink in advance. Typically our thinking about control becomes muddled because we ourselves are very advanced systems, and we introspect too much. We have learned about stimuli; we have classified stimuli, therefore we suppose we react to stimuli rather than to stimulation. We are then led to a particular erroneous conclusion — namely that systems can know how to respond only to those stimuli which they know about in advance and have classified. After all, we argue, an engineer cannot make a machine or a construction proof against unknown, unforeseen disturbances, but against those alone that are listed in advance. We must define what counts as stability, the argument says, and then enumerate what interferences will count as upsetting stability. Then and only then shall we be able to design or to programme the system to produce a 'correct' response. All this is mistaken. What the system really needs, and all it needs, is a way of measuring its own internal tendency to depart from stability, and a set of rules for experimenting with responses which will tend back to an internal equilibrium. Then there is no need to know in advance what might cause a disturbance; there is no need to know what has caused a disturbance. To be aware of something happening and label it disturbance, and to be able to alter internal states until the effects of the disturbance are offset, is enough.

28

A system that can do this, that can survive arbitrary and unforecast interference, is know to cyberneticians as an *ultrastable* system (following Ashby's nomenclature).* For example, there could be a stable computer which, when its building caught fire, would go on churning out figures while its fabric melted. People might think that to guard against this possibility the designer should foresee the risk, and install thermometers. Not so. An ulstrastable computer would detect not the fire (no thermometers) but 'something wrong', because internal check calculations would not come right. It would then start up its driving wheels and simply leave the burning building. People might then think that the computer could 'smell fire', and again they would be wrong. Intelligent behaviour often relies on simple mechanisms such as this, which trick us into imagining that they are based on profound insight. The simplest version of a controller, the control function of a system, that we can depict would therefore appear to be Figure 6.

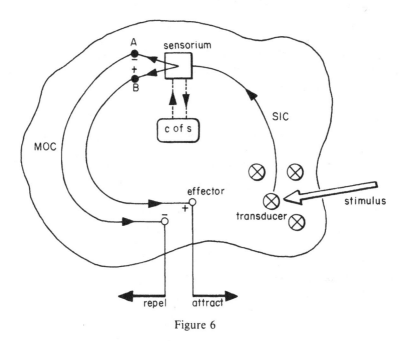

Figure 6

The sensorium, which is the square box in Figure 6, is defined as anything within a system that can register and classify the existence of a stimulus. The controller should now either avoid (−) or reinforce (+) this stimulus, depending on its deleterious or beneficial effect on the system as a whole. To do so it must switch on, or fire, the A or B round dot, which will then take action bearing on the stimulus. To decide between A and B the controller must compare the outcomes of making either choice against its criterion of stability

*Design for a Brain. See Bibliography.

(c of s). To do this, its simplest strategy is to do a *little* avoiding and a *little* reinforcing, testing out the results on its criterion, and then firmly setting its switch. If it goes on experimenting too long, the system will go into oscillation. This is what the engineer calls hunting and the physiologist ataxia. All systems are prone to the disease — for such it is. If this is the simplest kind of controller, we should now see that we fully understand how it works and master the basic terminology needed to discuss it.

The stimulus, as shown, derives from outside the system. It may arise from within, but this point remains: there must be a device which registers that something has happened, and translates whatever it is into terms that have meaning to the controller. This device is part of the system; it is not the stimulus itself, it is what detects the stimulus. It is called a *transducer,* meaning that it 'brings across' the stimulus to the system, and is marked with a cross on the diagram. The system probably has only one sensorium, with its power to classify stimuli, but many transducers. Indeed, the major classification initially made by the sensorium is to say which transducer has been stimulated.

When the transducer has operated, a message about the stimulus is passed into the system. The channel along which the message flows, which is the thick black line (SIC) on the diagram, is called the *sensory input channel.* Sensations are indeed sensory input data. The other half of the control loop, which closes the circuit, is the *motor output channel* (MOC). The adjective 'motor' is attached to output, because output has meaning only in so far as it leads to effects. In physiology, for instance, the nerves constituting output channels are said to convey 'effective' impulses (which may be either stimulatory or inhibitory, our + and −), while the sensory input is 'affective'. So the motor output leads to effectors (the empty circles on the diagram) which are capable of action in relation to the stimulus. In the simple case of Figure 6, one of these steers the system towards, and the other away from, the stimulus. Throughout, please note, the system is unconcerned about what it is that may be interfering with it.

In a real-life control system, the circuitry will be much richer than this; volleys of impulses will flow through a large number of input and output channels. This is true in the body, and in managerial situations too. This fact does not alter the entirely basic structure of sensory and motor halves in the control loop; we must however take it into account when considering the switching operation that constitutes decision, for in large, complex systems this process is never the simple switch that the diagram depicts.

In the case of a piece of control engineering this switching procedure is fully understood. The rule which governs how it works is known as the *transfer function*, because it specifies mathematically what kind of transition goes on between the sensory and motor halves of the control loop. The mathematical form of a transfer function is a differential equation, and this can be very complicated. The complication arises because the kind of response the system gives is often dependent on the portion of the range of stimulation which a given stimulus invokes, or on the frequency with which the stimulus occurs. In living control systems the most straightforward example of a transfer function would be the neuron, or individual nerve cell. McCulloch has assessed the complication of the transfer function involved here, and he considers it would take an eighth-order non-linear differential equation to specify it. The human brain contains perhaps 10,000,000,000 neurons and for all we know no two of them have the same transfer function. We find the same sort of problem in discussing the transfer function of a manager. A business decision may involve a dozen managers, which is a simplification by comparison with several thousand neurons. But the transfer function governing each of them is clearly impossible to specify — if only because it is the sum of the interacting neurons of his own brain. And we know about those.

There is worse to follow. When considering the control of a whole system, which was our appointed task, we may well find that we cannot even identify the individual input and output channels, but only whole bundles of them. Still less can we identify the individual switches whose transfer functions cannot, therefore, be investigated — still less measured. There is a vital structural reason for this, which is detected in physiological structures such as nervous systems and in social structures such as company organizations. What happens is that the sensory input arrives at the sensorium in disseminated form, while the triggers of motor action are also spread widely and thickly on a whole plane corresponding to the two points A and B so far recognized. The switching problem therefore involves connecting a whole batch of inputs and a whole batch of outputs. Instead of a single switch in between, we necessarily have a tangled network of connection. Such a network is called by its Latin name — *reticulum* — and the variety of reticulum we expect to meet in cybernetics is called *anastomotic*. This refers to the fact that the many branches of the network intermingle to such purpose that it is no longer possible to sort out quite how the messages traverse the reticulum. The word simply means that the input channels have outlets such as are found in a river delta. There are many streams flowing to the sea or to the flood plain, and the streams branch repeatedly, flowing into each other. There is no way of tracing the route by which a particular pailful of water taken from the sea arrived there; there is no way of saying from which source or sources it originally came.

It is important to grasp this notion of an anastomotic reticulum, because decision processes inside bodies and inside managerial societies work like this. We observe information being received, we observe action being triggered; we detect the affective and effective channels by which each respectively is made to work. It is then all too easy to leap to the model of an electrical circuit, and to try and discover the switching system underlying the decision-taking circuits in between. Moreover, when we considered Figure 6, it seemed a sensible procedure to show the connection as a switch (A or B) in the diagram. But this was because we considered the simplest case. No doubt there are some simple situations in management too — when a manager answers the telephone, is told that course A or course B must be taken at once, gives his decision, and puts down the telephone. In such a case a transfer function might be expressed in terms of cost minimization. But these are trivial cases. Normally it is as difficult to say how the managerial group of decision-takers has been internally influenced as it is to follow the course of water down the delta. So now we must modify the major loop in the first diagram to be more realistic, like this:

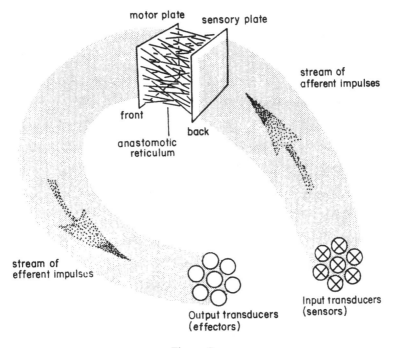

Figure 7

The important points about this new version are as follows:
The stimulus alerts a whole colony of input transducers, or sensors, and the system's response is implemented through a whole colony of output transducers, or effectors. Both sets of transducers are serviced by a stream of impulses using many channels. The sensorium and its associated switch are replaced by a sort of box, having a sensory plate at the back and a motor plate at the front. These plates are connected by the particular sort of switching network which we called an anastomotic reticulum.

The dicussion so far in this chapter has been of control in large complex systems from first principles, although the terms that have been introduced have had an increasingly biological flavour. The control engineer has had some mention, however, but mainly to say that it is difficult for him to help us! But now he comes forward again to supply further terms and the most important concept of all: *feedback*. It would not on the face of it be correct to describe a stimulus-response arrangement as a feedback system. The term is used so loosely in some quarters that almost anything which procures a reaction to itself is described as a feedback. What the term means strictly is so fundamental to cybernetic thinking that its connotations should be unravelled with some care. There is a little mathematics in the following explanation, which is simplified from general usage in the hope that the argument can be properly understood by the non-mathematical reader.

A system has input and it has output. What goes on inside the system that turns the first into the second has already been called a transfer function. In control engineering, as we said, this function is a differential equation: it measures the rate of change of the input-output relation with respect to time. The operator in this transaction is usually given the letter p. There is no need here to go into the typical details of the equation; it is enough to say that they are in general functions of this operator p. When we said earlier that the transfer function of a neuron might well be an eighth-order non-linear differential equation, it could still be written $f(p)$. The trouble is, of course, that although we can write down this transfer function we do not actually know what it is. The difficulty is exactly the same as in saying: 'let x be the number of people in the city'. We go on using x in our calculations quite happily, and maybe we can express the number of families in the city as a function of x, but sooner or later we shall want to know what actual value corresponds to x.

In control engineering, there is a way of finding out what is the actual differential equation for which $f(p)$ stands. After all, it converts the input to the output. This means that we can define $F(p) = \dfrac{o}{i}$ where i is the input variable and o is the output variable. When dealing with electrical circuits, as control engineers do, the input and the output are directly measurable. Moreover, if the output is plotted against the input over its whole range, we may be sure that a pattern emerges. The transfer function is the equation which fits that pattern. It may be highly complicated, but it can be discovered, especially as there is usually a lot of information available about the switches and circuits that constitute the system. Knowledge of the system's structure enables the mathematician to predict the kind of equation that will be found. To find the value of $f(p)$ in a typical cybernetic situation may, however, prove to be impossible. We have seen that it is difficult and not always meaningful to say what counts as input and as output in a physiological, social, or managerial situation. The variables concerned may prove impossible to isolate, let alone measure. So we may never obtain a verifiable curve relating input to output. And if the circuit structure is, as was argued, an anastomotic reticulum, then it is difficult to form any mathematical expectation as to the form of transfer function involved.

But we must return to the control engineer and his *servo-mechanism,* as his control device is termed. He knows the input, output and transfer function of his system. His problem now is this: The output of the system may not be exactly what is needed. Suppose, for example, that when the input is steady the transfer function produces a steady output which is exactly right. Now the input begins to change in a regular way — what happens to the output? It may follow the input, whereas it is supposed to be steady. Worse still, it may amplify the input fluctuations, and produce huge oscillations that are a danger to the next system which this system's output is feeding. Whatever happens, at any rate, it is possible to measure the continuous change in the output variable, and to compare it with what it is supposed to be. Thus a measurement is obtained which detects the system's deviation from some norm. It is this measurement, which may itself have to undergo some modification, which is *fed back* to adjust the input so that the existing transfer function determines a corrected output.

To concoct a simple arithmetical example, a transfer function may be doubling the size of the input. At a given moment the input value is 3, so the output value is 6 — and 6 is just what is wanted. Suppose that suddenly, for no reason that we knew in advance, the output reading changes to 8. Then the deviation of 2 will be sensed at the output, which means that the input value must for some reason or another be *effectively* registering 4. The feedback circuit, which accepts as its own input the output deviation 2, must now operate on this figure. For if it simply feeds back the deviation 2 as a correction to the system's input, then that input (now reading 4, remember) will be reduced to 2. The transfer function will double that and the new output will be 4 instead of 6. Clearly the feedback circuit needs its own transfer function, which will take the output deviation of 2, reduce it to 1, and adjust the original input downward by that amount. The system's output will now return satisfactorily to 6, because its input has been corrected to 3.

This example indicates the mechanism of negative, error-correcting, feedback well enough, but it is defective; we have frozen the whole system in order to consider some actual numbers, and then allowed it to move again for the finite time interval needed for the feedback to operate. But the cause of the whole trouble is most probably an unexpected variation in the input signal, and this will have varied again by the time corrective action is taken. Hence what happens to the deviation measurement in the course of its being fed back is more complicated than merely reversing the original transfer function. If that were the sole operation, it is easy to see that a systematic variation of the input which occurred in phase with the time cycle of the feedback circuit would not be damped down but amplified. The mechanism would detect the original + 2 deviation, and be subtracting 1 from the input, at the precise moment when the input had set off an impulse which would result in a − 2 deviation. That is, the input would be effectively 2, setting out to generate 4 rather than 6. Along comes the feedback, reading from the first (positive) deviation, and reduces the input from 2 to 1. The output now goes to 2 instead of 6, which is worse than ever.

It follows that a feedback has its own transfer function, which may be written *F(p)*, and that this will need to be cleverly designed to produce a dampening rather than an amplification of input fluctuations. Given that it can be done, however, we have that impressive result we were seeking: a self-regulating mechanism which does not rely on understanding *causes* of disturbance but deals reliably with their *effects*. For the cause of variation may be a change of temperature (which the system was not designed to detect), or a faulty connection (which was not intended), or a failure in another system generating the input to this one (of which this system has never heard). What matters is that control should be exerted regardless of the cause of disturbance.

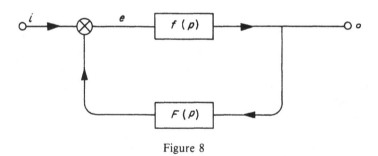

Figure 8

To distinguish between the original transfer function *f(p)* and the new one *F(p)*, we shall refer to the forward network and to the feedback network — which are controlled by these two functions respectively. 'Network' is still a good term, because real systems are more complicated than the simple notional ones considered here, where everything can be visualized in terms of single lines and loops. 'Network' is said in ordinary English, too, rather than 'reticulum' in Latin as before, because we are now designing systems with specifiable connections. A reticulum will be taken to refer to the general and possibly unspecifiable case of interconnection, which was the context in which the word was introduced. Now look at the diagram of a simple servomechanism: we shall examine the characteristics of feedback by inspecting its mathematical form. This does not mean that particular differential equations will be studied: the whole discussion is couched in algebra of an extremely elementary kind, and is worth following.

The input to the feedback is the output of the forward network, o. The output of the feedback network is a modification of this value, after the feedback transfer function has been applied, which is therefore written: $oF(p)$. The input to the forward network, which was originally i, becomes e after the feedback is applied. So we may define:

$$e = i + oF(p)$$

This being so, the form of the forward transfer function itself changes. It was originally written: $f(p) = \dfrac{o}{i}$, but that will not do now. The input to the forward network (represented by the box labelled $f(p)$) is no longer i, but is now e, representing the combined effect of the input i and the feedback $oF(p)$. Since $f(p)$ accepts e and produces the output o, we write $f(p) = \dfrac{o}{e}$. To obtain the transfer function of the total system we must return to the basic definition that this compares output with input, and write down a new function $\phi(p)$ which subsumes both $f(p)$ and $F(p)$ in their proper relationships. Well $\phi(p) = \dfrac{o}{i}$ quite simply. To work this out we need only to manipulate the forward transfer equation $f(p) = \dfrac{o}{e}$ and the equation for e itself. We obtain:

$$\phi(p) = \frac{o}{i} = \frac{f(p)}{1 - f(p)\,F(p)}$$

Several conclusions follow from the inspection of this equation. First, it is evident how feedback becomes either positive or negative. Consider the term which multiplies the forward and feedback transfer functions by each other, namely: $f(p)F(p)$. Suppose that the system called for no correction at all, so that the feedback transfer function had no effect at all. Then this multiplicative value would be zero, and the total transfer function $\phi(p)$ would work out correctly as $f(p)$ itself. If the multiplicative value is larger than zero, the denominator will be less than unity, and the value of the total function will be greater than the forward function alone — positive feedback. If the mulitiplicative value is less than zero, the denominator will be greater than unity, and the value of the total function will be less than the forward function alone — negative feedback. Evidently the same system may generate either positive or negative feedback, depending on the form of variation afflicting the input, and the phase shift involved in relating the two internal networks.

Second, there is a very interesting result that has to do with negative feedback. Error-correcting feedbacks are necessarily negative if any deviation from a given norm is counted as an absolute value; it is a positive discrepancy. Then the equation for *e* must be re-written: $e = i - oF(p)$ since we know that the absolute value of the error transfer function must be substracted from the original input. This has the effect of changing the equation for the overall transfer function to:

$$\phi(p) = \frac{f(p)}{1 + f(p)\,F(p)}$$

Inspecting this equation, we may observe what happens if the forward transfer function is made very large. So long as the value of $f(p)$ is very much greater than unity, the effect of the 1 disappears, and the $f(p)$ terms then cancel out. This leaves the reciprocal of the transfer function of the feedback network as determining, all by itself, the overall transfer function of the system. Formally,

$$\text{if} \quad |f(p)| \gg 1$$

$$\text{then} \quad \phi(p) \simeq \frac{1}{F(p)}$$

The outcome is startling. We may have a weak input signal, as is likely in both biological and managerial contexts. We may amplify this signal greatly in the forward network, and that certainly happens too. One would suppose, then, that any 'noise' in the input, which means any sort of mis-information included in the original feeble message, would be hugely amplified as well. But in fact the total system is dominated, not by the forward network, but by the feedback network. The output signals will be of greater 'purity' than we had any right to expect.

We are now well on to the track of that normally desirable systemic property, ultrastability. Negative feedback corrects output in relation to fluctuating inputs from any cause. It does not matter what noise gets into the system, how great it is compared to the input signal, how unsystematic it is, nor why it arose. It tends to disappear.

NOTE

The results of this enquiry are interesting, and important to the understanding of ultrastability. The mathematics involved are not at all difficult: despite the use of functions, the argument is couched in schoolboy-algebra. Some readers have not understood how the original equation for $\phi(p)$ was derived, nor how the term *e* vanished. Since this term was chosen to stand for 'error', its disappearance is especially interesting. So here, in relation to Figure 8, is the algebra, with the intermediary steps filled in:

definitions:

$$f(p) = \frac{o}{e} \qquad (1)$$

$$e = i + oF(p) \qquad (2)$$

cross-multiplying (1):

$$o = ef(p) \qquad (3)$$

and transposing (2):

$$i = e - oF(p) \qquad (4)$$

using results (3) and (4) to find the overall transfer function $\phi(p)$:

$$\phi(p) = \frac{o}{i} = \frac{ef(p)}{e - oF(p)} \qquad (5)$$

substituting for o in the denominator according to (3):

$$\phi(p) = \frac{o}{i} = \frac{ef(p)}{e - ef(p)\,F(p)} \qquad (6)$$

and now the term e disappears, to leave:

$$\phi(p) = \frac{o}{i} = \frac{f(p)}{1 - f(p)\,F(p)} \qquad (7)$$

CHAPTER THREE

The dimensions of the problem

There are three fundamental components of any control system, as we have seen: an input setup, an output setup, and the network that connects the two — which in the most general case is an anastomotic reticulum. Our next consideration will be the numbers which quantify such a control system. Quite a lot can be said about the dimensions of the problem from first principles.

First of all, then, there must be an input arrangement, starting with a set of receptors which transduce information about some external situation into the affective channels, and concluding with a sensory register (or sensorium) on which this information is collected. This basic sensory arrangement is to be found everywhere, in living and artificial systems alike. A telephone uses the different modes of vibration of a diaphragm in the mouthpiece as its set of receptors, by which a voice is transduced into the input channel — the telephone wire. At the other end, the diaphragm in the listener's earpiece collects the sensations which have been transmitted along the channel and acts as a sensorium. In television, on the other hand, the transmitting channels are not wires but radio emissions. Even so, the scanning system used by the camera constitutes a set of receptors transducing a picture which is collected together again on the face of the television set, which makes another good example of a sensorium.

It is at once obvious that the capacity to distinguish detail at each end of the input arrangement (receptor and sensorium) should be equivalent in an efficient system. For if the sensorium has more power to distinguish details than the receptors, its power will be wasted — because insufficient messages will be generated to activate some part of it. If, on the contrary, the receptors have more power to distinguish detail, and that detail is transmitted to a sensorium of an inferior distinguishing capacity, then some of the detail will be crowded out. The other obvious conclusion is that the capacity of whatever channels are used to transmit the information between receptors and sensorium must be sufficient to take the traffic. This is especially clear when the transmitting channel is mechanical.

Consider, for example, a typewriter as the input setup of a system. (It could be considered as a total system in its own right, for there is no doubt that what counts as a system is determined by the observer who demarcates its boundaries for his own purposes.) The keys on this typewriter constitute receptors having the power to distinguish between (say) ninety-two different symbols. There will be forty-six keys, and an arrangement (the shift) distinguishing between the two symbols on each key. These keys are used by the typist to transduce a message into the system which is collected on the sensorium — the paper. If there are forty-six keys, then there must be forty-six type-bars capable of transmitting the metal symbols to the paper, and the shift arrangement acts as a kind of amplifier, because it doubles he number of symbols (however many there may be) represented by the number of keys. It is also important that the transmitting channel should have sufficient capacity, not only in terms of an ability to distinguish all the different signals, but in terms of its speed of response. An expert typist trying to use an old, worn-out machine will find that the arms carrying the symbols cannot get out of each other's way quickly enough, with the result that two of them may jam together.

What is true of the input arrangement is also true of the output arrangement — the second component of any control system. There is a motor plate which transmits instructions to a set of effectors, and here again there is no value in having more capacity to distinguish at one end than at the other. A complicated set of intentions to act which either cannot be transmitted down the available motor channels or cannot be translated into distinguishable actions later on is no use to anyone. Someone shouting elaborate and valuable advice from the quayside to a yachtsman in difficulties down in the harbour is in a frustrating situation if his words are carried away by the gale; he lacks the effector channels. A knowledgeable musician, reading the score of a Chopin *étude* may know precisely which notes on the keyboard ought to be hit, and since he is equipped with the standard human body he has the channel capacity to transmit this requirement to his muscles. But if he has never learnt to play the piano, he also is frustrated in being unable to obtain effective action. He lacks the effectors (the output transducers) themselves.

The third part of the control system is the anastomotic reticulum which connects the sensory to the motor plate, and there will be much discussion later of this component. For the moment we shall try to assess the scale of the problem that faces the control system for any complex organism, such as a human being or a firm, in terms of input and output. And now that these two terms are again mentioned in the same breath, let us note one more interesting fact. We spoke of the capacity of the parts of the control system to distinguish detail. On the input side this capacity needs to be equivalent for the set of receptors and the sensory plate; on the output side, it should be the same for the motor plate and the effectors of action. Putting the whole control system together then, we can see that this capacity needs to be the same for both input and output considered as a whole. The reasoning is exactly the same as before, and we are still assuming that the criterion is an *efficient* system. The common case in which (for example) the transmission channels by their nature degrade the information they pass will be different. Here we shall need a greater amount of input data than can ultimately be used, and the surplus can be employed to offset degradation in the channel. For example, if every messenger we send with a message stands a fifty per cent chance of being killed on the way, we ought to send two messengers with the same message — even though only one message is needed at the other end.

In cybernetics, the number of distinguishable items (or distinguishable states of some item) is called the 'variety'. So we may sum up by saying that the output variety must (at least) match the input variety for the system as a whole, and for the input arrangement and the output arrangement considered separately. This is a vitally important application of Ashby's Law of Requisite Variety, which says that control can be obtained only if the variety of the controller (and in this case of all the parts of the controller) is at least as great as the variety of the situation to be controlled. This, like all profound statements of natural law, is perfectly obvious — once it has been pointed out. There is no great difficulty, however, in finding examples of attempted control systems which disobey this law quite flagrantly, and therefore do not succeed. From traffic control to the control of the national economy, this fallacy is apparent — indeed, this is one of the key problems of control in a firm. For management always hopes to devise systems that are simple and cheap, but often ends up by spending vast sums of money to inject requisite variety — which should have been designed into the system in the first place.

The scale of the variety problem within a firm is of crucial importance. In order to understand it, we shall need gradually to acquire an insight into the way variety proliferates, and the way proliferating variety may be absorbed, for that is the act of control. Consider first the problem of reading, and take this problem in terms of its basic component, the recognition of letters. We want to be able to distinguish between 26 letters of the alphabet — ignoring the complications of upper and lower case, type-face, and so forth. So we imagine a series of twenty-six separate cards, on each of which a letter of the alphabet is printed, and we arrange for a receptor to look at each one.

Now a single visual receptor is simply a device for distinguishing between light and dark. A photo-electric cell, for instance, can do this, and the threshold between light and dark at which the cell changes its state can be preset. The cell has two states — on and off — which we will call 0 and 1. If a single receptor looks at a card bearing the letter A it will register a degree of grey derived from the mixture of black and white on the card. It is not seeing the pattern that to us is A; but it is seeing something which may be unique to the letter A in our series. That is, the letter B may produce a different mixture of black and white, a different gradation of grey. Since we may set the threshold at which the cell registers either 0 or 1 at will, it becomes possible (at least in theory) to set the cell to operate so that it can tell A from B. When the letter C comes along, unfortunately, the variety of the receptor has been used up: there is nothing we can do about C, D, or any letter through to Z. Clearly, one receptor is not enough. Moreover, it looks as though we shall need twenty-six receptors, each carefully tuned to recognize the distinctive grey of its own special letter. If so, that would accord with the law of requisite variety: a value of 26 attaching both to the input transducers, and to the sensorium, which matches the 26 states of the world under consideration.

Now if we had only this one original receptor, we could do another sort of trick with it. We could divide the whole alphabet into two piles of cards so that every member of the first pile registered a lighter grey than any member of the second pile. (This still assumes that it is possible to design the letters so that every one of them has a unique ratio of black to white.) This arrangement will still not distinguish more than two states, because that is given in the receptor's capacity to handle variety. But it will deal with all of the cards, sorting them into two piles — the lighter (for which the receptor reads 0), and the darker (for which it reads 1). If we arrange this cleverly enough there will be thirteen letter cards in each pile. The receptor will be able to transmit twenty-six messages, one after the other, as a series of 0's and 1's, thereby throwing each card on to its appropriate pile.

The advantage of all this is that a single receptor, of variety two (namely 0 or 1), is capable of *halving* the problem of deciding which of twenty-six letters is which. We are talking about a 13-variety for the price of a 2-variety. This may not sound as if it were much help, but in fact the point is of prime importance. In general, a binary classifier (the 0, 1 receptor) halves the *uncertainty* with which it is dealing — if it is efficiently used. All problems, whether they are regarded as problems of recognition, or classification, or indeed decision, are problems about uncertainty. If there is no uncertainty about an industrial situation a manager has no decision to take. If there is no uncertainty about which letter is which we are able to read letters. High-variety situations are hard to handle just because the measure of their variety is the measure of their uncertainty. This is why the trick we have just discovered is so important. However big the problem, its variety can in principle be halved by *one* decision element. Take another example. You are looking for one person in a dance hall where five hundred couples are present. This represents a problem of variety one thousand; that is an uncertainty factor of 1:1000, or a probability of ·001 of making a correct selection at random. That is the scale of the problem. But if you can find out whether the person you are seeking is a man or a woman the problem is halved forthwith.

Returning then to the problem of the whole alphabet, we have seen that thirteen lighter letters can be distinguished from thirteen darker letters by one sufficiently discriminatory receptor, capable of finding the mid-point in a range of greys. Taking one bundle of thirteen letters, and a second receptor, we can see that this will be able to separate six of the letters from the other seven using the same device, a photo-electric cell the threshold of which discriminates half-way between the darkest and the lightest grey. Of course, this same second receptor could be applied to the second bundle of thirteen too, when the time comes to sort that. A third receptor would take a bundle of six (or seven) and cut the problem down to half its new size, producing a bundle of three or four. With a fourth receptor we can halve *that* bundle, so that we know that every given letter being examined is one of two letters of the alphabet. Thus a fifth receptor will discriminate between those two. The uncertainty of one in twenty-six with which we started has now vanished — we *know* which letter is which, and we have done it with five photo-electric cells.

In principle, then, we need only five receptors to read letters with, because they are sufficient to distinguish $2^5 = 32$ letters, given that each letter produces a black-to-white ratio, or greyness measure, which is unique. In general, n is the minimum number of receptors capable of distinguishing between 2^n possibilities. Note that there is an impressive economy in receptors as the number of possibilities increases. Ten receptors will distinguish between $2^{10} = 1024$ letters or whatever. Forty receptors will distinguish between 2^{40} — which is more than a million million. At any rate that is the theoretical number, but we must note that in practice so many possible letters (or states, or pictures of the world) will not be uniquely distinguishable. This is partly because the thresholds of greyness involved become too close to each other to permit a practical measuring instrument to tell them apart, and partly because the letters are not printed with so great an accuracy anyway. In other words, smudged outlines will produce a measure of greyness for one letter which is exactly that required to determine another letter printed properly. So now we encounter the problem of variety in channel capacity, as distinct from input variety.

We may start on this same problem of variety reduction from the other end. There are hundreds of lines in a television scanning system, and hundreds of quanta of black-or-white dots transmitted to each line. There are thus, in effect, tens of thousands of binary receptors in use to generate a picture on a TV screen. Similarly, there are roughly a million binary receptors in the retina of each eye. No wonder, then, that either the camera or the eye can distinguish between twenty-six letters of the alphabet — for we have seen that the job could be done with only five receptors. So here is another key point; by using far more receptors than are theoretically necessary we can in fact accommodate an enormous amount of confusion in the input. This point is analogous to the one about having two messengers carrying one message, although this time we are dealing with receptors rather than channels. Thus people go on watching television pictures fairly happily, and certainly with understanding, when the picture is broken up quite seriously by electrical disturbance. Similarly, the eye will successfully read excruciatingly bad handwriting. This is because it has sufficient receptors to distinguish between millions of letters, rather than just twenty-six, and if we take all possible alphabets, including hand-written ones, into account we may well need most of them.

The distinction between yes and no, between 0 and 1, is the *element of decision*. Managers may evade responsibility by giving equivocal or bogus decisions, if they wish, or by making qualified utterances; but when the crunch comes the answer is binary. And in fact managers do use the process of dichotomous classification (which has just been described) though rather informally. A managerial problem may have hundreds of possible solutions, and the manager may refuse to do more than say that he thinks the answer will be towards one end of a scale rather than the other. This sounds extremely vague, but in fact he is dividing the possibilities into two groups, which may not be of equal size, and leaving the threshold between the two groups muzzy. His people will go along with this for some time, performing actions which tend to push the situation in that one direction rather than the other, and trying to avoid the doubtful zone. But sooner or later they reach a point where they cannot decide what to do, and the manager is presented with a narrowed-down uncertainty. And so the process goes on, effectively splitting the universe of possibilities into two parts, until one day the manager is faced with saying yes or no to some final proposition. It can be shown mathematically that the most effective way of going through a sequential set of decisions of this kind is to divide the possibilities exactly in half each time, but it does not matter much if the division is not in fact equal. One may have to use an extra receptor (which entails taking an extra decision) beyond the number which is strictly necessary — but the general procedure holds.

In computers it is extremely well-known that all the messages are composed of 0's and 1's; in the body too a nerve cell is either activated to transmit an impulse or it is not. In natural systems, such as the social system of management just mentioned, or inside the living body, there is usually a muzzy area between the 0 and the 1 instead of a clear-cut threshold. This is why it is necessary to distinguish between analogue computation and digital computation. Computers working from punched cards or magnetic tape are digital in form, just as the abacus is digital. A bead on the abacus is either pushed up or pushed down, there is no equivocation. But a slide rule is an analogue computer, in which it is not always certain which number is indicated; there is a muzzy area. The nerve cell in the human control system has analogue characteristics in itself, because no one is quite sure what its threshold of firing actually is. But it receives digital inputs, because the electric impulses travelling down nerves arrive in volleys, the intensities of which vary in terms of the *rate* with which they arrive and not in terms of their amplitude. Thus, for example, a pain becomes more intense because there are more impulses travelling per unit time than before, and not (as many people intuitively think) because the electrical potential is increasing. Equally, the nerve cell either fires an impulse or it does not — there is no question of firing either a tiny impulse or a very large one. But the translation by the nerve cell of input into output (that is to say, its transfer function) is a much more difficult problem.

Most of the control systems in which cyberneticians are interested mix analogue and digital computation. But the point of the present argument is to say that in either event we can still measure variety in terms of binary decisions. Muzziness, after all, is only another kind of uncertainty, and it has to be resolved sooner or later. It turns out, then, that the elemental decision between yes and no, 0 and 1, is the raw material of control theory. It is called a binary digit, and is contracted to 'bit'. We shall have to make extensive use of this word, so do not be misled into thinking that bits are things which computer experts use, and which are of no interest to the rest of us. In measuring the scale of a problem it is a very good idea to discuss its complexity using bits as our measurement, for this is the operational unit. If a situation has a variety of 1024, the only advantage in knowing this number is to be able to say that it will take ten decisions to eleminate the uncertainty implicit in that variety — because $1024 = 2^{10}$. This simply means that we must halve the number ten times over to get a unique answer of one. In other words, the bit as a measure is the exponent in our formula 2^n: it is exactly n.

This then is the nature of the fundamental mechanism which enables us, whether as people living in the world or as managers dealing with an enterprise, to handle the immense variety with which we are faced. We can recognize, or select, or decide between a million million alternatives with only forty well-planned receptors, or classifiers, or decisions. Even if we are very inefficient in designing our system or planning our procedures, the result is very impressive. We have also discovered what kind of measurement to use in thinking about these problems of control and in designing controllers. Then what happened to the Law of Requisite Variety? The answer is that we may devise variety-generators in control mechanisms, just as nature disposes variety-proliferators in proposing problems of control.

So far, so good; but now nature takes its revenge. If we, the controllers, can generate very large numbers from a small number of components, so can nature. That is what variety proliferation means. Consider this: We said that we needed five receptors to read the twenty-six letters of the alphabet. Imagine, then, five lightbulbs which can be lit up in any number of ways. (The first bulb is lit and the rest are off, two are lit and three are off, and so on.) The fact that five receptors will distinguish between thirty-two letters means that these five bulbs can generate thirty-two different patterns, and of course if we want to know what our environment is all about we have to recognize the patterns it displays. So if the outside world consisted solely of *forty* lightbulbs, we know from our previous argument that we could be presented with a million million different patterns. True, it will take us only forty bits of informational effort to distinguish between them — the situation is quite symmetrical. But the world does not consist of forty lightbulbs, but of milliards of things and events.

If we are concerned in fact with n things or events, each of which is or is not 'lit up' at any one moment, then this world may propose itself to us in any one of the 2^n possible shapes of n things. Having understood how rapidly this function 2^n increases, the prospect is fairly alarming. But provided we are efficient in our design of controllers, it is not too alarming, because it means to say that we need as many receptors as there are things and events. These n receptors will generate 2^n variety at the sensorium. The motor system will unscramble 2^n patterns to n possibilities of distinct action. We are preserving requisite variety. But recall an earlier argument: if there were more things and events to concern us than receptors to recognize them and transduce them into the control system, we could not know it. Here is the Law of Requisite Variety again. At any given moment, we can be concerned about what we know about and no more — and the variety is n. 2^n patterns will be generated from this n, but our selection procedures enable us to cope with this by drawing n distinctions, or making n selections, which is just the number we have available by definition. No, the trouble really arises when it comes to taking some action.

We said that the input and the output arrangements are symmetrical and obey the Law of Requisite Variety. So the argument just applied to input applies to output too. The real problem of control, the problems which a brain is needed to solve, is the problem of connecting an input pattern to an output pattern by means of an anastomotic reticulum. If the variety of the situation presented to us is n, then the variety at the sensorium is 2^n. And if, by requisite variety, the action needed has variety $n,$ then the variety of the motor plate is 2^n as well. What is the variety *inside* the network connecting the sensory and motor plates? It is the number of ways of combining 2^n with 2^n, and that number is $2^{n.2^n}$. The diagram at Figure 9 makes the point clear.

If we refused to be frightened just now, this is the time to give way to genuine alarm. For this kind of number is unthinkably large. We must understand how it comes about. The reason why an n-variety situation generates 2^n input states, or patterns of input, at the sensorium has already been explained. The explanation was given in reverse, in so far as we saw how variety is halved by each selection that is determined. Each selection that is made available *doubles* the variety. Starting with a single possibility, we allow it to generate an alternative, 0 or 1. If we do this again, then we get 0 generating either 0 or 1, and 1 generating either 0 or 1, and so on. So consider a box with just two inputs and two outputs. On either side, sensory and motor, this $n = 2$ generates $2^n = 2^2 = 4$ possibilities. They are: 00, 01, 10, 11. How many patterns of connections are there? That is, how many possible states has the system? The answer is: the motor variety (4) raised to the power of the sensory variety (4), namely $4^4 = 256$.

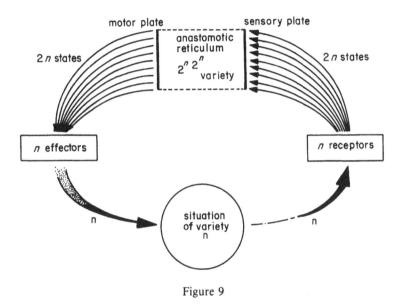

Figure 9

This may seem hard to credit, since we began with no more than two binary inputs and two binary outputs. But consider one of the four possible output patterns, say 00. It may or may not be registering a connection with any one of the four input patterns. Indicate a failure to be connected by a 0 and a live connection with a 1; the following table shows the possible states of the system:

	0000	0000	1111	1111	←	00
00	0000	1111	0000	1111	←	01	input states
output	0011	0011	0011	0011	←	10
	0101	0101	0101	0101	←	11
	↑↑↑↑	↑↑↑↑	↑↑↑↑	↑↑↑↑		

16 distinguishable states

The system has sixteen states, recognizably different states, when just one of the output states is considered. But there are *four* output states, equally capable of generating sixteen patterns inside the system. The total interaction of the input patterns and the output patterns produces the system's total variety __ $16 \times 16 = 256$. As we said, the formula to use is 4^4; and since each of those 4's is really 2^n where $n = 2$, it is clear why the original formulation of the conclusion was written as $2^{n.2^n}$.

Why should we probe so much into this matter and why is there talk of alarm? The reply is that any real control system generates so much variety by this mechanism that there is literally no possibility of analysing it, and therefore no way (it would seem) of finding out how best to connect up an anastomotic reticulum. 'Literally' here means just what it says: the task appears to be scientifically impossible, not merely hopelessly large. If this is true we must not attempt it, nor hopefully suppose that one day there will be large enough and fast enough computers, nor pretend that we can do what we cannot do. The facts have to be faced, and they look like this.

Consider the smallest 'brain' that would be worth having to cope with a complex real-life situation in a firm. The environment is characterized by how much variety, shall we say? Whether we think of ourselves or our firms, an environmental variety of $n = 300$ would surely be very low. The figure is highly conservative. Many companies have more than 300 employees, for a start, with more than 300 machines, more than 300 products, more than 300 customers. For an environmental variety of only 300 all told there is both a sensory and motor variety of 2^{300} patterns. The anastomotic reticulum needed to connect this together has variety $2^{n.2^n} = 2^{300.2^{300}}$. Now measuring variety in bits (because, as explained, this is the natural measure to use in a decision-taking milieu) we have 300×2^{300} bits, which is approximately 3×10^{92} bits. That is the uncertainty implicit in the situation we have chosen — a firm with no more than 300 inputs and outputs, each of which has no more than two states.

The next part of the argument comes from physics, and is due to H.J. Bremermann (see Bibliography). According to quantum mechanics, there is a lower limit for the accuracy with which energy can be measured. That is, there is a permanent and fundamental degree of uncertainty in matter. Any attempt to improve the accuracy of one relevant measurement will, according to Heisenberg's Uncertainty Principle, perforce drive accuracy out of an associated measurement. The quantities involved are very small, but they turn out to matter very much. What Bremermann did was to apply the quantum law to one gram of matter for one second, and to show that the lower limit for accurate measurement places an upper limit on the information-processing capacity of the material. Beyond that limit, noughts will become confused with ones, and computation must become ambiguous. In one second, he concludes, this gram of typical matter cannot cope with more than 2×10^{47} bits of data. Of course, no one has a gram of anything which can actually be used to compute so great an amount of data; microminiaturization has not advanced that far. But, and this is his point, even at the end of the technological road it would be impossible to cram more than 2×10^{47} bits into a gram of matter in one second — because the bits would be confused by Heisenbergian uncertainty. Bremermann has conjectured, with this argument, the requisite variety of matter itself.

The number sounds large; indeed we have just been studying the explosive power of 2^n — and here n is 10 followed by forty-seven noughts. Moreover, we can build larger computers than a gram weight, and use them for longer than a second. But even people who are accustomed to thinking in terms of exponentials may be taken aback by the next stage of the argument. Suppose we turn the whole of this earth, the terrestrial globe, into a computer, and run it for its whole history. What variety has this fantastic machine? Well, says Bremermann, there are about $\pi \times 10^7$ seconds in a year, and the age of the earth is about a thousand million years. Its mass is about 6×10^{27} grams. So the earth-computer, in its whole history, could have handled (2×10^{47}) $(\pi \times 10^7)$ (10^9) (6×10^{27}) bits. And that works out at something like 10^{92} bits.

It is now apparent why I chose the variety $n = 300$ for my example about the brain of the firm. A few paragraphs ago we saw that the reticular variety capable of being generated by that brain, with its conservative estimate of environmental variety, was 3×10^{92} bits. It now turns out that a computer the size of the earth, running as long as the age of the earth and in the ultimate condition of technological perfection is needed to do the sums for this tiny firm.

The firm's environment, just as man's environment, has variety much greater than 300. In the living brain, the raw variety measure (on the basis that the motor variety must be raised to the power of the sensory variety) is probably something like $2^{10^6 . 2^{10^7}}$ which has well been described as perhaps the largest number that has ever been taken seriously. If we really want to cope with the firm's environment properly, there is surely no reason to think that the brain of the firm needs to handle any less variety than this. The brain of the firm, just as man's brain, has more potential states than can ever be analysed or examined by an enormous factor — an unthinkably large factor. Information, then, has to be thrown away by the billion bits all the time, and without making nonsense of control. It must be noted at once, most especially, that there can be no question of finding absolute optima of behaviour — either for men or companies — because all the alternatives cannot be examined. It is, by the laws of nature, fundamentally impossible.

Thus the anastomotic reticulum is no good by itself. Something must be done to make things work, to get the whole system under control. Proliferating variety must be stopped; the potential must be cut down, and down, and down — even though we cannot prove the best way to do it. There is no sensible way even to record and retrieve information on this scale — let alone compute with it. Heinz von Foerster has given a graphic example of this 'memory' problem. He computes the size of a multiplication table which does no more than record the results of multiplying all numbers up to (only) ten digits by all other numbers up to (only) ten digits. He proposes to print these results in a reference book, the pages of which are 21 × 28 centimetres and of normal thickness. The whole book is then 10^{15} centimetres thick. Again, for the non-mathematician, there is the difficulty of becoming accustomed to these exponents. The bookshelf to accommodate this book will have to extend roughly a hundred times the distance between the sun and the earth. A librarian moving with the velocity of light, declares von Foerster, will require half a day to find a single entry in this book.

The full-scale handling of proliferating variety is completely impossible for the brain of the man or for the brain of the firm. Yet both men and firms actually work. They do so, they *must* do so, by chopping down variety on a mammoth scale. It takes more than an act of faith in electronic computers to achieve this. The question is: how does a system conveniently and effectively undertake this fearful task? The answer is: by *organization*.

CHAPTER FOUR

The organization of unthinkable systems

The systems under discussion are unthinkable, in the sense that they really are too complex to fathom. We have just seen that the earth itself is not a big enough computer to explore thoroughly a fairly small system of proliferating variety. Yet nature is stuffed with systems of equal complexity and equal activity, and nature works.

Just as the best map of a country is the country itself, so the best computer of natural systems is the natural system itself. Think of the sea: it is calm. The tide turns and a great wind arises. The water is grossly disturbed. Can we imagine having to programme a computer with the relevant inputs of this situation in order to discover the precise output — in terms of ruffled water? The task is hopeless. Yet the sea works; continuously, inexorably, it produces the answer. That answer *is* the waves and the current, the vortices, the flying spray.

Consider the biosphere, the film of life that covers the earth (or geosphere). From the microbe to the elephant life-forms interact. In particular, they feed on each other, and in complicated ways. We humans could not eat enough vegetation to supply our physiological needs; we have insufficient chemical processing plants to fabricate the elaborate protein molecules we must have. And so we use animals as our protein factories, eating them and their products. But what of proliferating variety here? How are the sizes of animal populations computed, so that there is enough food for the entire system? Part of the answer is the very proliferation. It has been calculated that a single plant louse, a cabbage aphis weighing one milligram, given enough plant food and no interference with its breeding processes, would turn into 822,000,000 tons of aphids in a single season. That is five times the weight of the whole human population. Why then are we not inundated with lice, or caterpillars, or anything else?

The fact is that this ecological system is self-organizing. It is *itself* the vast computer that gets the answers right (or roughly so, give or take a few plagues, famines and so forth). But it has no programme, no planning department, no licences to breed, no bureaucracy. It just works. We, the intelligent humans, interfere with this system, unbalancing it for our own ends. Thus we increase crop and livestock yields. But we treat the 'lower orders' of life as if we were gods outside the ecological system, forgetting that we ourselves are very much part and parcel of the whole. The result is that we can fairly effectively control the proliferation of *Pasteurella pestis,* the bacillus which gives rise to bubonic plague, but not the proliferation of our own species, *Homo sapiens.* We can see that our cows are fed, but not our own brothers over half the world.

There is, it would seem, a capability inherent in natural systems to self-organize the anastomotic reticulum in ways which we do not properly understand. They are not, we can be sure, optimal ways in a mathematical sense. There is not the computing capacity, it can hardly be too often repeated, to evaluate all possible outcomes and to choose 'the best' on some criterion of efficiency. There is instead a mechanism which selects particular modes of organization that are survival-worthy.

Here we must introduce and discriminate between two terms which will permit the discussion of the distinction just drawn. The first of these terms is *algorithm.* An algorithm is a technique, or a mechanism, which prescribes how to reach a fully specified goal. A typical air pilot's flight-plan is an algorithm. The instruction: 'turn left at the crossroads, take the second turning on the right, turn left at the Red Lion and our house is 120 yards up on the right' is an algorithm. A method for finding the square root is an algorithm, and so is a computer programme. This last is important, because we shall soon have to clear up some confusion about the capabilities of computers. A computer can do only what it is precisely told to do. The programmer has to write an algorithm, then, which will exactly determine the computer's next move in any set of circumstances whatever.

The second of the terms we shall need is *heuristic.* This is an English adjective, not often used perhaps, meaning 'serving to find out', which has been turned into a noun by contracting 'an heuristic method' into 'an heuristic'. An heuristic specifies a method of behaving which will tend towards a goal which cannot be precisely specified because we know *what* it is but not *where* it is. Suppose you are trying to reach the peak of a conical mountain enveloped in cloud. It must have a highest point, but you do not know the compass bearing. The instruction: 'keep going up', will get you there, wherever 'there' is. That is an heuristic. 'Take care of the pence and the pounds will look after themselves' is an attempted heuristic for 'being wealthy'. Heuristics prescribe general rules for reaching general goals, then, and do not typically prescribe an exact route to a located goal as does an algorithm. There are after all an infinite number of paths up the mountain, and it does not matter much which path is taken (although some routes may be quicker than others).

These two notions are very important in cybernetics, for in dealing with unthinkable systems it is normally impossible to give a full specification of a goal, and therefore impossible to prescribe an algorithm. But it is not usually too difficult to prescribe a class of goals, so that moving in some general direction will leave you better off (by some definite criterion) than you were before. To think in terms of heuristics rather than algorithms is at once a way of coping with proliferating variety. Instead of trying to organize it in full detail, you organize it only somewhat; you then ride on the dynamics of the system in the direction you want to go.

These two techniques for organizing control in a system of proliferating variety are really rather dissimilar. The strange thing is that we tend to live our lives by heuristics, and to try and control them by algorithms. Our general endeavour is to survive, yet we specify in detail ('catch the 8.45 train', 'ask for a rise') how to get to this unspecified and unspecifiable goal. We certainly need these algorithms, in order to live coherently; but we also need heuristics — and we are rarely conscious of them. This is because our education is planned around detailed analysis: we do not (we learn) really understand things unless we can specify their infrastructure. The point came up before in the discussion of transfer functions, and now it comes up again in connection with goals. 'Know where you are going, and organize to get there' could be the motto foisted on to us — and on to our firms. And yet we cannot know the future, we have only rough ideas as to what we or our firms want, and we do not understand our environment well enough to manipulate events with certitude. Birds evolved from reptiles, it seems. Did a representative body of lizards pass a resolution to fly? If so, by what means could the lizards have organized their genetic variety to grow wings? One has only to say such things to recognize them as ridiculous — but the birds are flying this evening outside my window. This is because heuristics work while we are still sucking the pencil which would like to prescribe an algorithm.

The failure to understand the role of heuristics in complex systems at large slops over into much computer thinking. The computer itself can be analysed, can be understood in detail; after all, we designed it. We have already declared roundly that a computer programme is an algorithm. Some thought is therefore needed to understand where heuristics come into the computer picture. Firstly, the need for them arises once the computer becomes alive with fast-flowing information. If we know what we are trying to do with the input data, such as striking the average of a list of figures which then constitutes the output, there is no difficulty. The total system is understood; and the algorithm $\Sigma x/n$ (which means: add up the figures and divide by the number of the figures) solves the problem. The whole thing is simple because we have specified the goal, the system and the algorithm, and have largely forbidden the entire arrangement to proliferate variety. Once the concern is to link a high-variety input with a high-variety output, however, we have the basis for an anastomotic reticulum.

Now the computer needs to be programmed (that is, needs supplying with an algorithm) that will organize the reticulum, and this can be done only if there is a known goal.

The subtle point is this: if the goal is not recognized in detail, an heuristic is required, so the computer must be supplied with an algorithm determining an heuristic. That is the basic trick. Suppose we say: 'The computer must learn from its own experience, as do we ourselves.' Learn what? We do not know; what we meant was that the computer must find out over a period, by trial and error, the courses of action which lead to better results of control. *We* shall say what is a better and what a worse result, but the computer has to determine a better strategy, a better control system, than we ourselves know. And of course it can do it. Because its algorithm, what it is programmed to do, specifies an heuristic. Alter the solution you are now using a little bit, says the algorithm, and compare the outcome with the erstwhile outcome. If this is more profitable, or cheaper, or whatever else we say, adopt it. Go on like this until any variation you make leads to a worse result than you already have. Then hang on to this solution, until the situation changes; whereupon you may do better once again by producing a new variation.

Here in this simple, innocuous statement, which a child could follow, we have the secret of the essentially biological process. We have burst through the barrier which two thousand years of conventional thinking have erected between mechanical and living systems of control. This is really a barrier between the algorithmic and the heuristic modes of control. When we have eschewed the mystical-sentimental approach to biology ('isn't nature *clever!*') we observe that nature is simply using its algorithms to specify heuristics. Genetic material is algorithmic: the DNA molecule consists of a complicated specific code. Thus progeny is built according to a blue-print. But variations and mutations occur in the codes, so that progeny has a proliferating range of possible patterns. Then — in another language, the language of ecology — judgements are made about the 'profitability' of the progeny. The survival-worthy variations survive, and hence the variations and mutations that led to them are reinforced; the failure-generating mutations are extinguished. The genetic heuristic works towards the unknown goal; a form of life that is competent to survive in circumstances, and by techniques, which are too complicated to analyse, and for which there exists no optimizing computer.

There are several important points to be made about heuristic control, which ought to be carefully considered and appreciated. Hence, at the risk of spoiling the narrative, I shall set thirteen of them down in numbered paragraphs which can be studied carefully. Here they are.

1. An heuristic will take us to a goal we can specify but do not know, and perhaps cannot even recognize when we reach it. The algorithm (such as: 'to

get to the highest point, try one step in each direction, and move to the next higher position') specifying this heuristic stipulates the eventual discovery of a strategy. The strategy says: 'The best thing to do is to go up here for so far, round this, along that, then up the other.' This strategy cannot be worked out in advance.

2. If we give a computer the algorithm which operates the heuristic, and wait for it to evolve a strategy, we may find that the computer has invented a strategy beyond our own ability to understand. This is quite possible in so far as it can make trials more quickly, more systematically, and more accurately than we can, without pausing for play or rest, and without forgetting the results. It is just like a man who plays chess all the time, and memorizes all the lessons of all the games. We expect him to beat casual players like ourselves.

3. This being the case, it is time to start recognizing the sense in which man has invented a machine 'more intelligent' than he is himself. The thought is annoying, even alarming, and stands to be rejected by self-satisfied humans — on the grounds that 'we told the machine what to do'. But think it out. If the machine ends up with a better strategy than we have got, and if we cannot understand why it is better but only that it is, it is small consolation to know that we taught it the heuristic trick by an algorithm. Einstein's primary school teacher was in the same position. (Those last two sentences repay much thought.)

4. The argument that 'computers can do only what they are told' is correct, but highly misleading. It suggests that they must remain the moronic slaves of their inventors. In fact we are telling them to learn, and giving them a training algorithm; but they learn more efficiently than we do and must pass us in the ability to achieve heuristic control.

5. The argument that the output of a computer is only as good as its input, summed up in the phrase 'garbage in, garbage out' (sometimes called GIGO), is true for algorithms specifying algorithms, but not for algorithms specifying heuristics. For it is easy to tell (algorithmically) the computer to *suspect* (heuristically) its own input — to test it for consistency. See how this happens. If one input line pumps in data which do not correlate with anything else in the system, the likelihood is that this input is probably a random disturbance — noise rather than information. The heuristic can then begin to diminish the weight its control strategy gives to this input. If it then mixes only 0.9 of the suspect input with every whole unit of every other input, and the result is better control, it will try 0.8 — and so on, until the 'garbage' input is ignored altogether. Please note: we shall not understand why this has happened, because we are very bad at intuiting statistical correlations, and may well have a strong *belief* that the garbage input is terribly important. But the system will have eliminated its misleading source of information just the same.

6. The mechanism we are using is precisely the old servomechanism discussed much earlier, in which error-correcting feedback is derived by a comparator from actual outcomes contrasted with ideal outcomes. But the outcome is measured, not in terms of the input data transformed by a transfer function, but in terms of the whole system's capacity to improve on its results as measured in another language. This is the language in which we say it is better to increase or decrease the value of the output, which the closed system itself could not know. For instance: if the output of the system measures profitability, and the system has an heuristic which produces fluctuations in profit which it learns how to extinguish or to reinforce, it must be *told* that higher profits are better and lower profits are worse. All it can learn for itself is that some patterns of events push profits up, and others down.

7. Secondly, the servomechanism's feedback does not operate on the forward transfer function as such. It operates on the *organization* of the black box which houses the transfer function. That is, it experiments with the connectivity of the anastomotic reticulum. As effective structure emerges, this is what cuts down the capacity to proliferate variety.

8. Although paragraphs 6 and 7 above give better ways of thinking about the servomechanism, they do not appear to change the mathematics which govern its stability. Hence the conclusion (Chapter 2) that feedback dominates the outcome still holds. Hence everything depends on the other-language criteria (see point 6 above) which the system is given to decide what to learn and what to unlearn.

9. Then suppose the control system has become so effective, and has learnt so well, that it is now 'more intelligent' than we are. Perhaps we shall no longer be clever enough to specify these other-language criteria that it should use. We may no longer understand what they are. In that case there must be *another* control system, using the output of the first system as input, and operating in another plane. This higher-order, other-language system would experiment with the fluctuating outputs of the first system, and produce new outputs in the other plane. Feedback from there (compared with some other-plan criteria) would establish the meaning of 'better' and 'worse' for the first system. For example the first system might be controlling production to produce more or less of each product, utilizing all the plant. The second system would then evaluate this in terms of market demand, taking the output — profitability — and telling the first system whether to learn higher or lower production strategies for each product.

10. But this criterion of profitability in turn might not be specifiable. Human thinking tends to give up the ghost when trying to compare short-term and long-term profitabilities. A short-run, maximum-profit strategy may break the firm in terms of goodwill and lead to bankruptcy. Then clearly the second system needs a *third* system to evaluate its outputs in a higher-order language,

and to say what counts as more or less profitable. This third system would experiment heuristically with the time-base of the second system's economic evaluations.

11. This argument continues until the hierarchy of systems, and the levels of language that go with them, reach some sort of ultimate criterion. What is this? It can only be *survival*. The firm (like the man) makes things in order to be rewarded, in order to show a profit, in order to continue to make things, and so, round and round, in order perhaps to generate all sorts of side effects, in order to ... go on being.

12. And what is true of the firm in this generation of management, and true of *this* man, son of his father, becomes true of the firm as a continuing entity in perpetuity, and of all men, fathers of their sons. That is, the training process for here and now is the evolutionary process for the epochs ahead.

13. So when we said that an heuristic organizes a system *to learn* by trying out a new variation in its operational control strategy, we might equally have said that an heuristic organizes a family of systems *to evolve*, by trying out a new mutation in its genetic control strategy.[1] The aim of *adaptation* is identical.

All this may sound very elaborate, but it is not really. We have to accustom ourselves to a new kind of thinking, perhaps, but it is not difficult thinking once its rudiments are understood. Indeed, it has to be easy thinking or computers could not handle it; it has to be easy thinking, or the population of plant lice could not handle it. Nature's mechanisms are simple, in short, but we need a suitable way of talking about them. Above all, in the case of natural control systems, we need to feel at ease with the concept of a metalanguage. The Greek prefix *meta* means 'over and above', so a metalanguage is a language of higher order in which propositions written in a lower order language may be discussed.

In logic, the bases of metalanguages really are abstruse. It can be shown that (virtually) any logical language must contain propositions whose truth or falsity cannot be settled within the framework of that language — logical paradoxes are the familiar example.[2] These propositions will then have to be discussed in a metalanguage, at which level we may understand what is paradoxical about them. But for present purposes we need not look at the logical foundations. It is enough to realize that if we build a machine, or write a computer programme, then this system has a language — a language in which not everything can be expressed.

---

[1] I have dealt at length with the possible equivalence of the problems of learning in the individual and of evolution in the species in *Decision and Control*, pp. 363-7. See Bibliography.

[2] I have explained the reason for this situation in *Cybernetics and Management*, Ch. 8. See Bibliography.

This is like having a small child, who has a limited language. There are things which we cannot explain to him in his own language — not only because his vocabulary is too small, for it would be possible to define new words to him — but because he is short of *structure*, that is syntax, too. We try to convince him that something should or should not be done. Why? he asks; and why? again when we have answered him once. We struggle in his language with these questions. The process may prove impossible, just because the language is inadequate. When we conclude: 'Because I say so', we have made a metalinguistic statement. (Incidentally, was it true to say that we could define new words through the existing language? And if not, if for instance we need to demonstrate things as part of the definition, shall we not have swallowed the original language in a metalanguage by so doing? Thinking about such questions is helpful in mastering the new concepts.)

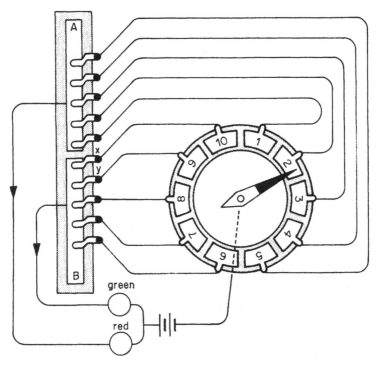

Figure 10

With this preamble, let us now invent a simple machine for doing heuristics. The sensorium consists of a strip of wood, on which are mounted two brass strips A and B. Figure 10 shows that they are insulated from each other. The afferent part of this machine consists of ten fixed terminals (the dots) bearing spring clips which make electrical connections with the brass strips — five on each. Input arrives down one of the ten wires leading from the roulette wheel, which represents the outside world. The wheel is spun, and the afferent system recognizes that the world outside has taken on one of the values 1 to 10. The efferent part of the machine now goes into action. It has two effectors: the wires leading from A and B to two lights, red and green. One of these bulbs must light up, but there is no way of knowing which. If we go on spinning the wheel it is obvious that, on average, each will light up on half the occasions.

The description just given is written in machine language. All the statements are verifiable in terms of the machine itself. We may use this language, for instance, to declare that red has a 50 per cent chance and green has a 50 per cent chance. The machine itself could 'understand' such a statement, because it is derived from its own structure. But there is no way of stating in this language that red is in any sense preferable to green or vice versa. As far as the machine is concerned, such a statement is neither true nor false. It is not verifiable or testable. It is strictly meaningless. In machine language it cannot be said.

Along comes a speaker of metalanguage one — call it Meta 1. This is a language designed to talk about colours and the emotions which colours evoke. He says: 'I like red, but I don't like green.' He cannot interfere with nature, which is spinning the wheel. He reckons he wants to train the machine to go red, and this is just like training a dog to respond to a command. He cannot explain in machine language, and the machine does not understand his language. So he communicates with the machine through an *algedonic loop*. Here is another new term which must be explained.

A trainer and his dog are in the same situation as the Meta 1 speaker and this machine. The dog trainer does not understand 'how the dog works', and the dog does not understand human speech. The trainer therefore stimulates the dog somehow, and observes its response. The dog's response may be altered by punishment or reward. This entails altering the connectivity of the dog's anastomotic reticulum. Of course that does not mean that neural switches must be thrown in the dog's brain. It means only that somehow a new output pattern has to be associated with a given input pattern. The dog at first responds to a repeated stimulus arbitrarily. So the trainer tries to extinguish the response he dislikes by a sharp rebuke (ἄλγος — *algos* — means 'pain') or to reinforce the response he approves by administering a reward (ἥδος — *hedos* — means 'pleasure'). These activities create an algedonic mode of communication between two systems which do not speak each other's language. The trainer is using an algedonic loop which translates Meta 1 into machine language. It involves a new receptor in the machine, an algedonic receptor, which will change the internal environment of the machine.

In our invention, it follows, we must provide the machine with an algedonic receptor, through which the speaker of Meta 1 can communicate. This consists of two switches, either of which will move the wooden strip vertically up or down the diagram. The strip in Figure 10 carries and now moves the brass plates A and B; but the contacts from the roulette wheel do not move. The red light, which our observer likes, is activated by the brass strip A. To reward the machine for shining red, we shall tell him, one presses the switch marked *Reward*. This will move the strip down a notch, and bring the contact marked X on to strip A, whereas it used to rest on B. (Remember that the contacts are fixed). This alters the 50-50 probability of the outcome to 60-40 in favour of Red. If the green light comes on nevertheless, as it may, the machine has to be punished. The observer is told to press the switch marked *Punish*. (Both switches in fact pull the wooden strip one notch down, but no one but ourselves know this.) The contact Y will now rest on strip A as well, and the probability of a red outcome is now 70 per cent. It is readily seen that the algedonic loop will cause the machine to adapt its behaviour to a red outcome, since that is the decision in Meta 1. The machine does not understand why its behaviour is being conditioned, and the operator does not know how the trick is done. We do, because we are omniscient with respect to this situation. If we were not, we might be puzzled too; most people are, as a matter of fact, when they see this machine working.

Pause for a moment, however. Why does this first man, speaking Meta 1, prefer red to green? It is just a psychological quirk. Now suppose a second man comes along who happens to be the first man's boss. He is observing the effect of these two lights in another context. He finds that when the green light goes on, someone gives him ten pounds; but when the red light goes on, he is told to pay a ten pound fine. At first he tries to tell the Meta 1 man about this. 'Change your preference to green,' he says. 'I know how to make money that way, and I will share the proceeds with you.' But the first man cannot understand him. He speaks Meta 1, a language of aesthetics; he has not heard about money at all, and does not want to know. The second man is a speaker of metalanguage two. How is he to convey his point, expressible in Meta 2 alone, to the Meta 1 speaker? He will also need an algedonic loop, connecting him to the first man, if we assume that he cannot spend his time operating the switch himself.

Accordingly, Man 2 says to Man 1: 'I hold you responsible for this machine. I am going abroad, but I am recording the greens and reds. If when I return I find that red has predominated, you will be replaced by another operator, and lose your bed and board in my house. But if green predominates, your room will be floodlit with the red light you enjoy.' Note that it is no use trying to talk about money in Meta 1, which is an aesthetic language, and profitability is a notion which only Meta 2 speakers understand. The second algedonic loop translates Meta 2 into Meta 1, and Meta 1 can be translated into machine language by the first algedonic loop.

If all this happens, and Man 1 succumbs, the operating procedure is reversed. He still does not know why the machine responds to his switches, and still less how. He no longer knows why he is due to produce an outcome (green) which 'goes against the grain' for him. All he knows is expressed in the one language he understands, Meta 1, — namely that it will be better in the long run for his colour sense to start training the machine to shine green. To do this he must press the *Reward* switch whenever the green light shines, and the algedonic receptor is so arranged that this (and the *Punish* switch for the red outcome) pushes the wooden strip *up*.

The fable we are recounting, however, really begins like this. Once upon a time there were two philosophers discussing cupidity. They considered it possible that a man might be persuaded to undertake an entirely pointless task for a suitable reward. So by way of a trial, they sent for a member of their staff. They told him that in another room was a box with an operator, and that the whole purpose of this box was to light either a red or green bulb. We will give you ten pounds, they said, every time the green light comes on — but you will have to give us ten pounds if the red bulb lights. They spoke to him, of course, in Meta 2 because that was his language, but they were really using an algedonic loop. He knew nothing about the test of his own greed, and had never spoken the philosophical language in which cupidity is discussed — which is called Meta 3.

This example could be continued indefinitely. The point is that heuristic techniques are determined within a framework specifying the mode, the limits, and the criteria of search. And if that framework is itself an heuristic, then it too requires a framework; and so on indefinitely. At some point the nth framework must be reached which, from this system's internal standpoint at least, will have to be declared an absolute framework. In good logic, this cannot be done; but in all practice it has to be done. Hence all finite systems are limited and incomplete. We ourselves, our firms, our economies — all suffer from this limitation. And because we do, and must, the best possibility for change directed towards ever more successful adaptation lies in a reorganization of these hierarchies of command. We shall not beat the ultimate limitation like this, but we can choose its form. There will be more of this in the next chapter.

Meanwhile, let us return to the adaptive machine. We have already seen how the probability transfer function is changed by algedonic feedback so that one bulb lights more regularly than the other. If the environment of this system, which is its next senior hierarchic level, keeps changing its mind about the utility associated with the red and the green outcomes, then the machine will follow these changes. But if we take the limiting case, when the environment settles for red, the machine eventually adapts completely to red — because all ten of its contents are sweeping the same brass strip. This is the analogue of overspecialization in a biological evolutionary situation. The system is so well, so very thoroughly, adapted to its environment that if this should suddenly and grossly change the system would have lost the flexibility required for adaptation. We can stop rewarding our machine and try to punish it, but the slide has rusted in.

This state of affairs illuminates the need for a constant flirtation with (what we usually call) *error* in any learning, adapting, evolutionary system. In the experimental version of the machine, the one I actually built, two of the ten contacts by-passed the transfer function — one always lit green, and one always lit red. Thus, in a fully adapted red outcome, the machine still made mistakes for 10 per cent of the time by exhibiting a green light. That is a high rate of error; but if we had a hundred contacts we could reduce it to one per cent. The vital point is that mutations in the outcome should always be allowed. Error, controlled to a reasonable level, is not the absolute enemy we have been taught to think it. On the contrary, it is a precondition of survival. Immediately the environment changes and begins to favour the green outcome, there is a chance-generated green result to reinforce, and the whole movement towards fresh adaptation begins too. The flirtation with error keeps the algedonic feedbacks toned up and ready to recognize the need for change.

Although this point emerges clearly from a consideration of biological fact for viable systems, and although it is well illustrated by our simple machine, it is not understood by management. In the firm, error is anathema. This is not to say it is avoided — of course not. But it is treated with hostility, not as having a value of its own. A perspicacious manager would review every mistake made within his command as mutant behaviour, and make himself receptive to the algedonic feedback the incident invariably generates. His observed tendency is, on the contrary, normally to concentrate wholly on correcting the fault. Thus the system's errors are wasted as progenitors of change, and change itself is rarely recognized as required. All the managerial emphasis is bestowed on error-correction rather than error-exploitation. In turn, errors themselves are reiterated as being essentially bad. Thus it follows that when change is really understood (for some extraneous reason) to be necessary, people resist the need, because to attempt change is automatically to increase the error rate for a time, while the mutations are under test.

CHAPTER FIVE

Hierarchies of control

The discussion in the last chapter needs to be extended. It was about heuristic methods which, alone it seems, are capable of organizing the sort of system we called unthinkable. We have already seen how the basic control device works. It is an algedonic loop, consisting of an algorithm stipulating an heuristic. But, as we have also seen, the required algorithm is itself specifiable only in a metalanguage. This means that a second-order system is required, linked to the first, and connected by its own algedonic loop. The process goes on, forming a command hierarchy, and could go on indefinitely. In logical theory, we could show that the total system strictly requires an infinite number of metalanguages; we should never finish building it. Sooner or later, then, we have to adopt — illogically — an ultimate metasystem as paramount.

This unsatisfactory conclusion, however, no more than parallels the ordinary facts of institutional life. In a business, departments are co-ordinated into divisions, divisions into groups, groups into giant corporations. The various levels are themselves largely autonomous, and the controls exerted are mainly algedonic. (We shall talk more about this in Part Two). The head of the corporation himself looks upwards to a metasystem called 'the industry', and beyond that to another called 'the government'. Both of these are linked to his corporation by algedonic loops. But although one can readily envisage the rest of the hierarchy until a total system of cosmic size is envisioned, one must in practice settle for a particular level above as the ultimate arbiter of one's own affairs. None of us can manage to influence more than one or two metasystems above our own, and normally, we accept the next-level algedonic input as speaking an 'ultimate' language.

It is interesting to begin the analysis of hierarchic control structures by asking about the basic decision elements of which ranks and orders of command are in general composed. In nature, and if we consider that most sophisticated control system the brain, this element might be identified as a single nerve cell — or neuron. In industry or government — indeed in any strongly cohesive social group — the element is some sort of manager.

Both the neuron and the manager have one really basic task to perform: to decide. In the neuron's case, a pulse must either be triggered down the output nerve (the axon) or not. For the manager, the fundamental task is also to say yes or no. It is true that managers do not spend their lives uttering these two words; they may never utter them. None the less, this is their task — and the subtleties, the nuances, the might-I-suggests and the perhaps-you-woulds are really socially intricate ways of saying yes or no.

In order to reach a binary decision the decision element has to establish a threshold of decision. We may think of it as saying 0 until it is prompted to say 1 instead. This would be a permissive kind of management, in which the decision element does nothing until activated. It must not be activated by any stray impulse or noisiness that happens to be floating around the system, and this fact establishes the need for a threshold. Oversensitive neurons would soon send either men or firms mad. When things really begin to happen, the decision element accumulates its evidence. When it is sure that there *is* real evidence demanding action, which is to say when the sum of inputs exceeds a threshold value, it fires.

The language here may seem a trifle strange. But I seek descriptions that will be useful in general, whether we apply them to managers or neurons. And if the description is reasonable so far, we shall be able to invoke quite general control systems theory by describing the threshold as a transfer function. There is a set of inputs which, submitted to some criterion, is transformed into an output — 0 or 1. Because, as we have seen in the last two chapters, organizations cannot hope to command events in detail from on high, it is best to consider the transfer function as providing a modest degree of algedonic applause when in the normal state. If there are twenty algedonic input channels, perhaps fifteen of them are at 1 while things are running normally. The five at 0 represent the extent to which the algedonic feedback system as a whole is poised to administer rebuke. If events begin to go out of control in the lower level system all twenty algedonic channels may turn to 0, but, if things go especially well, some of the original 0's may change to 1's.

Suppose, however, that the transfer function itself turns out to be wrong — wrong that is in terms of an environment within which the neuron or manager is effectual or ineffectual. This judgement would be made by the metasystem, of course. Then (we could say) the transfer function must change its sign, but that is drastic advice; we cannot afford to have transfer functions flip-flopping their outputs from 0 to 1 and back again in a trigger-happy fashion just because the environment is a little unstable. It would be better to change the threshold slowly, so that the decision element tends to change in response. The best way to understand that is to contemplate a series of judgements in which an apparently valid output is produced with more or less keenness, and the effects noted. That is to say, there is feedback which adjusts the transfer function itself. Note that some environmental conditions may demand more sensitive neurons or managers, and other conditions less sensitive ones.

This account offers a special and refined case of the control theory set out in Chapter 2. There is still a sensory input and a motor output, driven by afferent and efferent impulses respectively. There is still an anastomotic reticulum, which we do not pretend to analyse in detail or to control by ad hoc commands. Moreover, this account is faithfully reflected (so far) in the machine of wood and brass devised in the last chapter.

Consider the sensorium of that machine. There were ten contacts which collected data transduced to them from the world outside, represented by the roulette wheel. We said at the time that there might be a hundred. Indeed, there could be any arbitrary number of contacts, scattered randomly across the sensorium. The machine would still work. Suppose moreover that the transfer function, represented by the A:B proportionality of the two brass strips at any given time, were not quite so crude a device. We might imagine, for example, a chemical cell in which the threshold were represented by the pH value, or by some electrical property, which altered as the results read in language Meta 1 were reinforced or suppressed by the algedonic feedback.

In such a case the connectivity between input and output would in practice be untraceable. Part of it, the peripheral part, would be digital in character — streams of binary pulses would be arriving and departing through an extremely intricate network of lines. Tracing all that would be difficult enough, and actually impossible if the network kept changing — lines might atrophy, or mysteriously go into and out of use. But if there were enough of them, the machine would still work. Inside the cell, worse still, the connectivity would be traceable at the molecular level alone. In practice, we should be dealing with statistical effects in the mass. The most likely descriptive name that the observer would award to this inner part of the neuron would be 'analogue device', because the basically binary character of the system would have been lost. All in all, at any rate, the entire connective network and interaction would be a perfect example of an anastomotic reticulum.

It seems that a real-life neuron looks rather like this. Furthermore, the description fits a manager rather well too. In considering the sense of that remark, beware of confusing the different degrees of resolution (in the optical sense) involved. We are considering the neuron (whether natural or artificial) and the manager as simple decision elements in a network of neurons (a brain) or of people (a managerial society). The fact that there are ten thousand million neurons in the manager's brain is irrelevant to the comparison. It is none the less an interesting point when we are also considering the hierarchies of command. There is after all a wonderful homogeneity in all this, and the manager's own language is obviously an nth-order metalanguage in relation to the machine language of one of his own neurons.

Incidentally, if the sensorium of the machine we invented can be represented by a large, possibly unknown, number of inputs instead of the original ten, the algedonic loop can operate successfully on a less precise basis too. We said that the triggering of algedonic feedback would cause the wooden strip to move so that a contact, one of ten, changed from strip A to strip B. But if there is an indefinite number of contacts, carelessly positioned, this rule becomes silly. In any case, there is no reason why the algedonic move should be a discrete, predetermined little jump. Let us think of this conditioning process as a kind of pressure, which normally moves the wooden strip ever so slightly, gently correcting mistakes. Now we know by this time that the algedonic function is itself determined by a metalinguisitc decision — something that has to do with pay-off in a senior hierarchy. Whatever system it is that determines the sign of the algedonic loop knows not only that the answer being given by the lights is right or wrong, but *how seriously* right or wrong it is. Then let this knowledge be tapped, and applied as a force to the movement of the wooden strip. Normally, then, its movement is slight: the A:B probability might change from 50:50 to 51:49. If the 'wrong' answer is suddenly (metalinguistically) dangerous, the pressure goes up; 50:50 might change at once to 99:1 (not 100:0, however, as this would kill off mutation). Again, the managerial analogy in terms of the pressure with which rewards and penalties are applied is abundantly clear.

Before looking at any actual hierarchies, a note of recapitulation is in order. All our training teaches us to think about command networks as being specially designed, as having nodal points which are in effect switches, and as depending on feedbacks in the engineering sense defined in Chapter 2. But viable systems reveal in actual fact an anastomotic reticulum, rather than a properly designed network, in which the elements form and reform themselves into appropriate structures. These elements, which are the nodal points, are governed by transfer functions which change — they are best described as continuously modified conditional probabilities, rather than the immutable operators which standard control theory depicts as differential equations. Thirdly, the feedbacks are not simply error-correcting devices which adjust outputs to 'correct' values. They are algedonic loops arriving from a higher-order system which effect the first two kinds of change. Even so, these systems remain dominated by their feedback functions as they do in standard control theory.

The contention, as far as we yet have it, is that neurophysiological and managerial systems (to take two viable systems which will turn out to have much in common) are best understood in these terms, and that their basic elements — the neuron and the manager — both work on the model provided in its simplest form by the wood and brass machine. For ease of reference we need to name it, and I choose the name *algedonode*. It is, I know, tiresome to keep introducing words which are new to the reader, especialy when (as now) I am compelled to invent them myself. And yet the vocabulary available to managers is manifestly deficient. Here is the concept we have reached as precisely as I can say it. A decision element in a control system consists essentially of an input (or afferent) and an output (or efferent) sub-system connected by an anastomotic reticulum. All three parts of the control system were defined at some length earlier. This decision element consitutes a *node* in a network of decision elements making up the control system. But this node, the decision element, is conditioned (in the ways we have been studying) by a metasystem which uses the pain-pleasure heuristic method which we named an algedonic loop. The whole of this package is the algedonode. Our wood and brass machine is a crude example, but the brain's neuron and the individual manager in a management team are also examples of algedonodes.

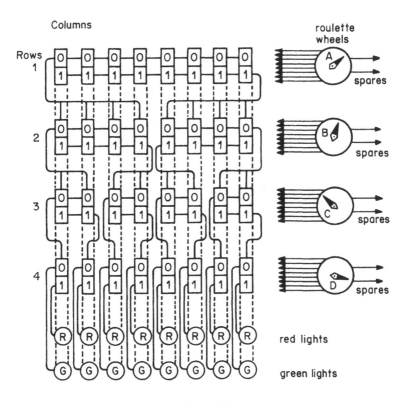

Figure 11

Our next step is to extend the original machine to a command hierarchy, and to see how it works. The next wood and brass machine, then, is composed of thirty-two elements, each of which is itself an algedonode. If our rows of eight algedonodes are arranged as in Figure 11, we have a device capable of making eight binary decisions instead of just one. (There is no magic in these numbers — they were just chosen as convenient.) The bottom row looks like eight separate algedonodes, their outputs being the familiar pair of red and green lights in each case. The light outputs have been suppressed in the first three rows, and the binary output of each algedonode is used to select the next group of elements to be used. On the right of the diagram are shown four roulette wheels, each representing an unknown input from the world outside.

Spinning the four roulette wheels selects a 'state of the world'. It is easy to see that if each wheel carries the number 0-9 the total number of input states is 10,000. (Think of the inputs as a bank of dials which registers any number between 0000 and 9999.) There are just eight contacts associated with input A on the eight columns of brass strips, and they lie alternately on 0 and 1 across the board. (The actual connections are not shown on the diagram, as it becomes too complicated, but see Figure 12 later.) The two contacts left over from the roulette wheel's ten positions, in accordance with the laws of mutation elucidated earlier, by-pass the system's logic. The first row of algedonodes then selects either the left-hand or the right-hand group of four algedonodes in the second row. One of the spare contacts goes *directly* to each of these groups. Thus in the initial state of play there is an exactly 50-50 chance that Row 1 will activate either the left- or the right-hand group of four algedonodes in Row 2.

Row 2 has eight contacts too, responding to the random input B. These are arranged on *both* the 0 *and* the 1 of each algedonode in each group of four algedonodes. This means that there are sixteen contacts in all, and any B input activates two of them — one in the left-hand group and one in the right. But Row 1's decision has already eliminated one of these groups. So Row 2 activates a *pair* of algedonodes in Row 3, either through this system or directly (as before) from its two spare inputs. There are two pairs to choose from, either the left-hand or the right-hand set of two pairs, depending on the decision of Row 2. Which of the pairs is selected depends on input C. There are four contacts on each of the algedonodes in Row 3, two on 0 and two on 1 — again arranged in parallel. Thus there are thirty-two contacts in Row 3, only eight of which (plus the two spare from input C) are concerned in the third decision — because three of the four pairs in Row 3 have already been eliminated. Row 3 now determines which *one* of the algedonodes in Row 4 is to be active.

Row 4 takes the last decision, based on input D. This time all eight contacts are arranged in parallel on each algedonode (there are therefore sixty-four connections in this row), four on 0 and four on 1. Row 3 decided which of the columns to use, and now Row 4 decides whether the answer is green or red. Once again, the two spare inputs, from D this time, will by-pass directly to one light or the other.

Since, in its starting position, this whole reticulum is based on thirty-two algedonodes proffering equal amounts of 0-valued and 1-valued brass strips, the outcome of any play is wholly indeterminate. The four roulette wheels spin. They randomly activate a contact in the row, and each row randomly halves the variety of the next row. Any one of the eight lots of output may fire, and the chances are even that the lamp then lit will be red or green. Here is a 2^n expansion of binary decisions in physical being: there are four rows of algedonodes which are therefore capable of deciding between $2^4 = 16$ outcomes — which are the sixteen bulbs. The theory behind this kind of expansion was explained in Chapter 3.

To make the machine work in its electro-mechanical form we shall need relays to 'take the decisions', and these relays will be activated by the crossing of an input appropriate to the row with an output determined from the previous row. One relay will be needed as the output of Row 1, and this will decide between the two groups of four algedonodes in Row 2. The outputs of Row 2 and 3 will obviously require two relays and four relays respectively. Row 4 needs no relay at all, because it lights the bulb directly. It will be realized that we need $2^{n-1} - 1$ actual decision elements (the relays) to deal with n ranks generating 2^n possible outcomes. In the present case there are: $n = 4$ ranks, $2^n = 16$ outcomes, $2^3 - 1 = 7$ relays. If another rank were added we should have: $n = 5$ ranks, $2^n = 32$ outcomes, $2^4 - 1 = 15$ relays — and there would be sixteen columns. But this machine would accept another input E, and could deal with 100,000 world states.

'Deal with' is all very well, in the sense that the reticulum connecting input and output is not overloaded; it can still differentiate one set of responses from another. But 'deal with' so far means 'produce a random result', and it is not worth having a machine at all to do that. The next step is to connect the algedonodes together by *columns*. One vertical column of the machine is redrawn in Figure 12 to show how this looks. Note that it is no longer conveniently possible to show the hierarchical connectivity we have just been discussing. Now we have, in each column, eight brass strips — all mounted on one strip of wood. They are insulated from each other, and alternate 0,1 down the column. In fact, of course, they remain (because of their electrical connections) four sets of algedonodes. They are marked in the way shown simply because some 'spare' 0 or 1 brass strip is needed when the wooden strip is moved up or down — as the diagram shows.

Now it is possible to bring algedonic feedback to bear. To begin with, consider its crudest form. If the wrong bulb lights, the punishment will be severe. The whole of the brass strip in Row 4 which gave rise to this result will vanish, too, in every other row belonging to this column. But there will be no change in adjacent columns, because they have not been moved. Hence the balance of probabilities of the whole machine changes in an interesting way. Consider only one pair of bulbs — that lit by this column's Row 4 algedonodes. The chance that the red bulb (say) will light is now 9:1. (All eight contacts are on *one* brass strip, one spare input is connected straight to red, the other straight to green.)

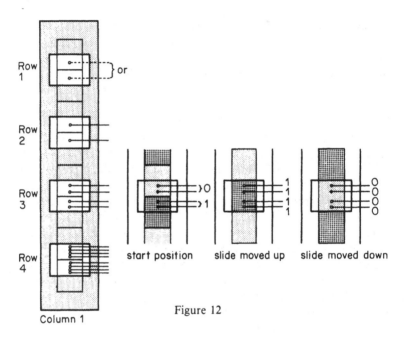

Figure 12

However, the chance that this fully adapted algedonode (Row 4 of Column 1) will be selected at all has also changed. The selection is done by the Row 3 algedonodes of Column 1 and Column 2. There used to be a 5:5 chance that this pair would select either Column 1 or Column 2, Row 4. But once the Column 1 slide is fully moved, two of the four separate areas (0 and 1, 0 and 1 in the two columns) have changed to 0. Thus three expose the 0 strip, and one exposes the 1 strip. Of the eight contacts arranged on these strips, then, six connect to 0 and only two to 1. Taking the two spare inputs into account, the chance that Row 3 will select this column's Row 4 has changed from 5:5 to 7:3.

Working backwards up the decision tree we come to Row 2, which contains quadruples of algedonodes. Here the decision was originally taken through eight contacts connecting with eight areas (four 0, four 1); but now the balance is disturbed so that what were a 0 and a 1 area in Column 1 are both reading 0. Hence there are now five 0 and three 1 areas. Given the spare leads, the probability of selection in this rank is 6:4. When we reach Row 1, and consider the probability with which it will select *this* quadruple in Row 2, we find sixteen areas of brass, only eight of which are touched by contacts. This situation is formally equivalent to that of Row 2.

Hence the probabilities affecting the whole decision tree which lights the bulbs of Column 1 can be understood. At the start, each row produces a 0.5 chance of taking the decision that ends in lighting the red bulb. The chance that it *will* light is therefore $0.5^4 = \cdot0625$, or one sixteenth. Since there are sixteen bulbs in all and the starting state of the machine is equilibrial, this is just what one would expect. But after making a crude (that is, total) algedonic adjustment to Column 1, the probability is the product of 0·6 for Row 1, 0·6 for Row 2, 0·7 for Row 3 and 0·9 for Row 4. The probability is 0·2268 — between a fifth and a quarter. The chance that the green bulb of Column 1 will light is 0·6 $\times$ 0·6 $\times$ 0·7 (for the selection pattern of the first three rows is identical) $\times$ 0·1. And the answer to that is ·0252 — only once in forty plays.

After this, understanding what is happening becomes quite difficult. A crude algedonic feedback applied to Column 2 on the second pass of the game will yield a 9:1 chance of lighting the correct bulb in Row 4. But once Row 2 has selected the left-hand pair of algedonodes in Row 3 we have a 90 per cent chance of a right answer *altogether* — for it does not matter whether Row 3 selects Column 1 or 2 in Row 4. Moreover, because the algedonic feedback makes a reinforcement (of diminishing effect) right back through the hierarchy, Row 1 is more likely to choose the left-hand quadruple of Row 2, and that is more likely to choose the left-hand pair of Row 3.

It is not worth expounding a full theory for these probability shifts, because we have already over-simplified this apparently simple device. If the algedonic feedback is *not* crude (and why should it be?), the slides will be moved on an infinitely variable scale. This complicates the theory very much. Moreover, we do not really want to be stuck with eight contacts per row: we may have a random scatter of a huge number. The mathematics become more complicated again — but that need not daunt us. What is important is that the mathematics become quite arbitrary. In detail, the probability transfer functions *for any state* of this thirty-two element array are immensely complicated and not really worth knowing. Only a little more elaboration, only a little less precise design, and our machine genuinely is an anastomotic reticulum. The strange thing is that it does the job. It adapts 10,000 combinations of input states to 16 output states so that an observer speaking Meta 1 judges the result to be profitable. The machine, then, learns to behave successfully. If the environment changes — in terms of the metasystem's criteria of success — the machine rapidly adapts to the change. That is what we want.

If all this is understood, the next question is: how can such machinery be made useful? The first point is that the artefact described is purely illustrative, and even this is difficult to make. I have made it in cardboard so that it plays with counters. It works perfectly well, but it takes a very long time to demonstrate. I have also tried to make the electrical version, as described, which should work much more quickly. But there is a huge number of mechanical and electrical traps. In particular, the electrical circuits in practice are full of cross-connections — so that the only practical version bristles with the diodes necessary to control the direction of the logic. Then the simple machine, which I still think is easy to understand conceptually, looks hideously complicated — which defeats the object of the illustrative exercise, although it brings home the variety-handling capacity of algedonodes. A full-scale demonstration model, which looks extremely handsome, was finally built by T.C. Macnamara Ltd. and N.T. Griffin of Exeter University, whom I thank.

Thus it is that we have to think in terms of a far more sophisticated technology. There are two alternatives, and the choice between them is an important choice, as we shall see later. The first involves programming a general-purpose electronic computer to behave in this way. The second involves building special-purpose systems, using solid-state physics. But much more important than anything technological at all is the recognition that algedonodes exist; because just this sort of complex switching goes on inside management groups — using people as the elements.

PART TWO

THE FORM OF THE MODEL

Summary of Part Two

Before beginning the analysis of Part Two, it would be an excellent plan to read once again the summary beginning Part One. This should help to consolidate the thinking we have experienced up to this point.

We can now start 'talking the talk'. The object is to construct a model of the organization of any viable system. The firm is something organic, which intends to survive — and that is why I call it a viable system. There are many examples of such systems in nature. Yet instead of using any of those (which are known to work) as models of the firm, we try to use organization charts that are really devices for apportioning blame when something goes wrong. They specify 'responsibility' and the 'chain of command', instead of the machinery that makes the firm tick.

The problem is discussed at the outset (Chapter Six), as is the very nature of a model. Models are more than analogies: they are meant to disclose the key structure of the system under study. So if we want to understand the principles of viability, we had better use a known-to-be-viable system as a model, and that is why Part Two embarks on an account of the way the human body is organized and controlled by its nervous system. We could have used another viable system — such as the amoeba, or a whole animal species — as the model. The results are the same, as they must be if viability as such has its own laws and enshrines its own principles (as cyberneticians contend).

But the human body is perhaps the richest and most flexible viable system of all. Besides, there is an extra advantage: all of us have bodies and inevitably we have a good deal of insight into their characteristics. Most people know little, however, about 'how it all happens'. For that reason, there has to be quite a lot of explanation about the physiology of the nervous system. You can see why I am not too embarrassed about putting this forward. After all, any human being is likely to find his own neurophysiology interesting — whether he is studying management or not. You will find, though, that this book continuously compares the unfolding story of corporate regulation in the body with its manifestations in the firm. The process begins in Chapter Seven.

By Chapter Eight the story is developing well. We are dealing with one of the most vexed questions in modern management — the topic of autonomy. If a division of the firm were really and truly autonomous it would not be part of the firm at all. In the same way, if the heart or the liver were really and truly autonomous, they might decide to renegue on the body. On the other hand if the heart and liver were not more or less autonomous, we would have to remember to tell them what to do all the time — and we would be dead in ten minutes. In the same way, if a division of the firm is not more or less autonomous, the main board has to run it directly — which is equally impossible. Besides, the divisional staff would resign.

The body has understood this dilemma for several hundred thousand years, and we can learn from it. Its solution is called the autonomous nervous system, appropriately enough. By the end of Chapter Nine we shall have seen how it works, and we shall also have worked out its relevance to the management task. Three vital systems are identified as prerequisites of all autonomous control.

In the final chapter (Ten) of this part, the need for a System Four is disclosed. Systems, One, Two, and Three are concerned, automatically, with the regulation of internal stability — but the organism needs also to maintain dynamic equilibrium with the external world. More than that: if the challenge of change and increasing complexity discussed in Part One is to be met, there must be systems for arousal and adaptation. All this is modelled by the brain, before the level of conscious *direction (attributable to the board of the firm and to the cerebral cortex in the brain) is reached. That final level, System Five, is reserved for discussion later.*

In Part Two cybernetics is put to work to create a model of the management of any viable system. There are passages of fairly tough going, as the nature and the implications of some of the neurophysiology are elucidated. But remember that once the issues are properly understood, there will be no real need to remember all the details.

CHAPTER SIX

The anatomy of management

In the foregoing chapters, in which the business of control within complex systems has been talked about, all sorts of concepts and terms have been introduced. These are some of the tools of the cybernetician's trade. They are not yet the tools of the manager's trade — although they ought to be.

The firm, which is the entity a manager controls, is a good example of a system of high complexity in which the input and the output are themselves high-variety sub-systems. What connects the input to the output is the domestic firm itself — that is the men, materials, machinery, and money which are based in particular locations with a company sign outside. The whole complex of activity going on inside is an anastomotic reticulum. What sort of description of all this would be useful in discussing such typical managerial problems as organization, efficiency, and objectives?

The orthodox answer to this question is of the following kind. We need an organization chart of some sort which will indicate how each part of the business relates to each other part, with the main intention of determining where responsibilities lie. Since 'part' might mean anything less than the whole, we may have a set of organization charts. In this the major parts are first exhibited, and the minor parts are exhibited later on in subsidiary charts — which could carry the detail down to individual people at the lowest organizational level if need be. These charts are, or more usually are not but could be, supported by detailed job descriptions intended to show how the whole thing works. So the charts themselves specify an anatomy of management, while the job descriptions specify its physiology.

So far, so good; but we are left with the question as to how all this is to be done. There are normally (I speak from fairly extensive observation) three phases in this task. The firm has not to be invented — it is there. First and foremost, then, the task is one of description. But whoever sets out to supply the description knows a lot about this kind of structure in advance. He knows about the basic divisions of firms into such parts as 'production' and 'sales'.

He knows about the functional divisions which are commonly used: for instance there are 'line' and 'staff' relationships. Thus he will, for example, expect to find an accounting function which will be 'staff', groups of middle managers 'line' responsible to senior managers, and so on. He may well expect, what is more, a good deal of disagreement about certain twilight areas — of which production control and management accounting are both typical. We shall see why in a minute.

Thus the second phase of the job involves not only description but prescription. Whoever is undertaking this task has a limited number of concepts to work with, if he remains orthodox — concepts which are generally current with the manager concerned. He has a limited collection of physical equipment, too — basically a two-dimensional piece of paper and as many ways of drawing on it, in thin, thick, dotted and coloured lines, as he thinks people can stomach. Somehow he has to stretch the firm he studies on the Procrustean bed of this paper structure. If he is knowledgeable about management theory he will also have 'principles' to guide him. These principles ('one boss for one man', 'five is the ideal number of immediate subordinates', 'you should not mix a line and a staff responsibility in one man') are distillations of managerial culture. There must be some substance in them, but I put the matter kindly.

The third phase of this job is, frankly, breakdown. The formal statement of the company's structure in the managing director's office is typically something we are working towards, something we know needs revising, or something we are up-dating through a process of evolution. As to the job descriptions, where they exist, they turn out to be descriptions of *men* and not of jobs at all. For the fact is that jobs do not do themselves, but men do them. And the result is that people describe what the man is doing, or what the boss thinks the man ought to be doing, and not any such impersonal thing as a job. If a big clinical effort is made to describe the job, the odds are that no actual man can be found to fill it. So the job has to change. Actual company structures are heavily dependent on the particular people who fill the acknowledged roles, and when those particular people leave the structure often has to change.

It is not surprising. 'Production Manager' is a line job, and 'Chief Metallurgist' is a staff job. But if the manager is, temperamentally, an administrator and the metallurgist is a personality who commands high respect in the works, command may actually vest itself in the scientist while the manager is happily computing discounted cash flows for the five-year plan. That job belongs to the accountant; but he is busy deciding on an expenditure of a million pounds for a new computer. That job in turn belongs to the managing director, but he is not going to have a chance by the time his 'adviser' has buttoned the case up. It is just as well, because the managing director used to be a personnel man who knows nothing about computers, cares even less, and is at the moment trying to resolve a strike threat — which he will do very well in the absence of the real personnel manager who is on a course about operational research. This latter service to line management comes, of course, under the Office Manager (because someone regards it as a kind of O and M activity) and he has appealed to Personnel because the OR scientists 'don't seem to fit'.

That is all invented. Even so, real life is just like that, and it is a lot of fun. It would be disastrous if some neurotically disposed chairman or consultant tried to insist that everyone behave like the organization chart. But the questions whether real life in the firm is best described by this three-phase effort, and whether if so a structure specified like this really helps best in solving the problems that arise in transforming input to output, are unanswered. I shall answer them quite flatly in the negative, and for three key reasons.

Firstly, this mode of description is wholly arbitrary. I said earlier that the rules of this game were part of a managerial culture, and this is all that can be said for them. They are frozen out of history. And it looks as if their form is due more to a rough classification of men than of jobs — as the game pretends. Think about the history of management for a moment. The origins of large modern enterprises were in small companies controlled by autocratic entrepreneurs, and these men did everything that mattered themselves. Those who worked for them followed a leader, and did as they were told. Small firms to this day still usually begin like this, recapitulating (as the biologists say) a development scheme which was common at the time of the industrial revolution. When the firm grows larger the boss is compelled to delegate or bust. It certainly seems to be true that bosses who cannot delegate do indeed destroy either their firms or themselves — frequently both. Now it is natural that a man in these circumstances should first delegate the things he least enjoys doing. Some men will delegate anything rather than the financial control of the business, while others see this as mere figure-work and let it go first. Some see the business as manufacture, and others as a collection of customers. The entrepreneurial orientation of the boss conditions these things, and the entrepreneur today is further conditioned both by the way in which his predecessors have carved up the business activity, and by the success with which their arrangements met. Nor is all this independent of the national weal. There are times, for example, when only an accountant has much chance of succeeding to the top job, because the influence of banks is dominant. Or there may be a vogue for engineers.

All this is real enough, and not something that can be set aside lightly. It is not the existence of different entrepreneurial orientations which I question, for these demonstrably exist. What is arbitrary is the description of the control of the firm in just these terms. It used to be true that the control of the firm was a function of these different types of people interacting with each other, and nothing more. Then there was reason to draw up ad hoc organization charts showing which of these actual people were actually doing what. But to allow this heavily personalized structure to become depersonalized was a mistake, because it erected a structural convention which has no particular *raison d'être*. It made generalizations about management structure in just the dimension (the group personality of a set of actual people) in which generalization is impossible. Much less negatively, it ignored the dimension that really matters — the dimension of control itself. The convention did not answer the question: how shall input be optimally converted to output? Worse, the convention tended to obscure the very existence of the question and stopped it from being asked.

Today, however, control in a business is something much more than the interaction of its senior managers. It has to do with information of an extent and complexity beyond the capacities of those senior people to absorb and interpret it. Therefore it has to do with the structure of information flows, with the method of information handling, with techniques for information reduction, and so forth. All these features of information's role *used* to be determined by the cerebral capacities of the senior staff. The brains of these men constituted the only media for information handling, and therefore the way the men interacted was equivalent to the way information interacted. This is why the orthodox description of the anatomy and physiology of management worked fairly well, even though it was arbitrary.

But if arbitrariness was the first reason given for objecting to this orthodoxy, the second is much more powerful. It is that there exists today a capacity to cope with information vastly in excess of the human capacity, with the result that the manager is no longer the arbiter of sophistication in control. He must delegate this role to the electronic computer, just as he delegated other managerial prerogatives in the past — thereby losing them, be it noted, to people who were more expert than he but junior. And just as he retained his seniority over these juniors, just as he remained in command, just as he used the efforts of his more expert underlings to build a bigger and more profitable firm, so now he must use the computer. The manager no more abdicates in favour of computers because they are more sophisticated in control than he, than in favour of maintenance men because they can keep the plant working and he cannot. But he has to know how to organize the maintenance men to keep the plant working, and he has to know how to organize computers to effect the firm's control. Moreover, he has to organize the plant so that it can be maintained; he has also to organize the firm so that it can be computed with.

There is the rub. People do not want to re-organize their firms. More particularly, they do not know how to do so. More precisely still, they have no tools or means of description which would enable them to work out a new mode of organization as distinct from a reshuffle of responsibilities. That is one reason for the sermon you have just been reading: we can hardly go on unless we agree that a new language and a new model (something different from the archtypal organization chart) are required. The other reason for the sermon is to warn managers that if they persist in drawing in computers on their existing organization charts, they cannot possibly succeed in doing more than bolster the humanly limited control system they have already got. Things may go more slickly; the firm may even save some money (though this is little more than a pious hope in most standard applications), but the human filters remain, and they remain the limitation.

The third key reason for objection to orthodox company descriptions and ways of discussing organizational structure derives from the other two. If the distinctions we currently use are wholly arbitrary and indeed archaic (first objection), and if they are constrained by human limitation in a way which modern facilities falsify (second objection), then there is no guarantee that what really matters in modern management can be expressed like this at all. It is, after all, one thing to express something ineptly, and quite another to have no way of drawing attention to it at all. But this latter tragedy is quite possible, and often happens with any grossly simplifying language.

You really cannot explain relativity theory to a savage; you really cannot draw a child's attention to the precept that obligation implies possibility. This is not because either of them is not sufficiently intelligent; certainly not. It is simply because there are no words to use. And this in turn is not due to a shortage of vocabulary (that can quickly be taught), but to an insufficiently rich conceptual framework. That child for example knows very well what 'must' and 'can' mean. He does not understand any sense in which the two could be related, nor does he understand implication, nor does he even know that some auxillary verbs can be turned into abstract nouns and treated as entities shorn of context. None of this destroys the distinction he does understand between 'you can eat a sweet' and 'you must eat your rice pudding'. Moreover the child would soon object 'I can't' if one said 'you must jump over the moon'.

The major difficulty about writing this sort of book is that managers are not naïve; they know very well the things that really happen. It would be foolishly patronizing to try and instruct them in the subject 'real life'. But they would in turn condescend to the author if they thought that this was his object. An eminent physicist (I am sorry to say I have forgotten which) has said that an intelligent child could solve the most abstruse problems of modern physics if only he could understand what they are about. This is presumably because pure intelligence does not grow, it is an innate ability, and because a child is not encumbered with the languages, structures and solutions which his elders 'know' — and which actually inhibit their discovery of novelty. That child could do the same for us managers, if he knew much about real life in business. We for our part do know, but we are constrained by our own experience as well as informed by it. In particular we have a managerial culture in which some things, distinctively modern, cannot be expressed although we know them.

For example, consider production control and management accounting — the topics to which I promised to return. Managers, I insist, know very well what these two are and will soon object if one says stupid things about them. And yet, because both are manifestations of modern approaches to relatively new dilemmas, there is no way of talking sensibly about them. They do not fit the vocabularies, the syntax or the concepts of traditional management; they do not fit the organization chart. The explanation is this: both these things 'belong' to general management and nothing else. But general management, except in the case of the General Manager, is split up into divisions. If some managerial activity fits none of the divisions, then it must report straight to the top. But, first, there are nowadays so many of these activities that this conclusion is nonsensical; and, second, the people who carry out these activities are relatively junior. Thus in a culture which accepts (say) half a dozen company directors, each very senior, and each in charge of one sixth of the boss's job, we suddenly find ourselves threatening to say that there should be (say) twenty new directors, all terribly junior ... It is absurd.

Hence, sensible chaps that we are, we do not say this. Instead, however, of observing that the reason for the trouble lies in the fact that these activities *inter-relate* the standard parts of the business, we try to squeeze them into one or another box on the organization chart. And here we are not so sensible; or at least we do not speak an appropriate language. Take production control. This is a means of satisfying customers by meeting delivery promises (sales) and of maximizing machine utilization (production) at the same time, well knowing that the two objects are incompatible, costing intervening. This is (what was just called) a modern dilemma because it is a function of the firm's size. The little business had the plant it needed to meet the orders it had. The big business tries to balance its vast plant with a potential order book of very high variety, and fails. In fact, the problem is so complicated that large firms rarely have much idea of the optimal order book to match the plant, or of the optimal plant to match the order book, or of the relative costs (which are costs of foregone opportunity) incurred by the infinite number of ways in which the gap can be crossed. Hence the importance of production control, which must find a solution, and whose solutions can make or break the business.

But where does the function belong? I have seen it (indeed I have *been* it) both under sales and under production, and in both cases the other partner, not to mention the accountant, was quite rightly dissatisfied. When you have only half the story, when you have a lop-sided loyalty, you cannot achieve a balance. I have seen this function under 'the office', under accounting itself, under engineering — in fact almost everywhere but the medical department. It will not sit still and be categorized. Because of this difficulty, I have actually ended up (while still very junior) reporting directly to the general manager himself for production control. At least this made sense, and it was the best of the bunch for the sake of the firm's efficiency. But in fact it was totally unworkable and could not last, because the boss could not give it time, whereas everyone else wanted to contest my day-to-day rulings with him as the next superior to me.

As an experience, by the way, this was considerable hell, and it certainly provoked thought about the company's organization chart — which could not contain a novel activity (as it then was). Reiterating: this was not because no thought was given to the matter, but because there was no answer. The language of the organizational structure could not express the concept. Today, things are no clearer — in so far as production control may be accepted by custom in a given firm as belonging to some niche, but frankly does not do the job very successfully.

In the case of management accounting, to quote the other example, we have a clear case of a line-staff confusion — as the very term implies. The idea behind this function is again to inter-relate parts of the whole; it says that there is an accounting activity which is not just a matter of recording cash flows and obeying the Companies Act, but which has to do with controlling the business. Therefore it belongs firmly in the general management sphere. If it is not actually placed there, managers up and down the line will say that the accountants appear to be making a takeover bid; if it is placed there it will look as if they have succeeded.

And so by all these routes, the arguments from arbitrariness to archaism, and from structural inadequacy in the orthodox model, we return to the basic contention: a new model is required which will actually work. Now the term 'model' has been slipped into this chapter already. People are beginning to appreciate the sense in which a company organization chart is, or at least is meant to be, a model of the real organization. They often get into difficulties however with a more elaborate use of the word.

Some people think of a model as a mathematical equation, others think of it as a theory, still others as an hypothesis, and yet others as a physical thing. The last group looks the least sophisticated, and yet these people have understood best. We talk about a model ship or a model railway; especially we talk about a working model. In these expressions four key notions are embedded. There is *scaling-down* in both size and complexity — a model of Shakespeare's birthplace, for instance, could stand on the table and would not be expected to incorporate miniature bricks in equivalent numbers to the building in

Stratford upon Avon. There is *transfer across*, whereby actual parts of actual things are represented again in their relative positions. And arising from this there is *workability*, by which I mean that the model can, in principle anyway, operate like the original. Thus a model train actually runs round a model railway, and it looks so much like the thing modelled that ciné films of models can be substituted for film of actual trains and successfully pretend to be real. That this can be so, although the engine may be driven by clockwork (and no real railway engine was ever so driven), introduces the fourth point. The model is a good model if it is *appropriate*. Someone watching the film just mentioned is not in the least concerned with how the engine is powered; but an engineering student who dismantled a model railway engine in a technical college and found an enormous coiled spring inside would not be impressed.

In general we use models in order to learn something about the thing modelled (unless they are just for fun). For example, we make a model of the contours of an aeroplane and test its aerodynamic properties in a wind tunnel, or a model of a ship's hull for testing in a tank. In both cases the shape is the appropriate feature to model. This shape is scaled-down, transferred across into a plastic (say) representation, and made to work in relation to the wind or the water. No one complains that there are no people inside, or even that there is no engine to power these craft — because these are not appropriate features of the situation. On the other hand, no one complains that these models are 'mere analogies' as long as the aptness of the model is properly defined. Now the criticism of the organization chart as a model of the firm is that it is not appropriate as modelling those aspects of the firm we most wish to understand — which have to do with control. In all fairness, the unfortunate chart did not set out to be that kind of model. The trouble is that, since this is the only model we have, people insist on trying to use it inappropriately. It is as if we poured paraffin into a plastic model of a jet airliner in the hope that it would fly.

It follows from these considerations that if we wish to think about control in the firm we should use a control system as a model. Control systems, as was explained at the outset, are the topic of study of the science of cybernetics. The trouble is that control systems of sufficient complexity to serve as adequate models of the firm are themselves so complicated that cybernetics does not fully understand them — except through models.

In other words, cybernetics is actually done by comparing models of complex systems with each other, and seeking the control features which appear common to them all. These invariant features — as it were the laws of control itself — certainly do exist. They can be invoked in the design of any controlling mechanism for any system, and we saw some of them used like that earlier, in Chapter 2 for example. But although fundamental 'rules of the game' are an enormous help, and although they are neither arbitrary nor archaic, they are not enough.

When we criticized existing approaches to managment theory as arbitrary and archaic a little while ago, we also found them lacking in structural adequacy. This third matter remains a problem, because natural laws have to be obeyed (they will be in any case), but they tell us nothing about design.

Suppose we were the architects of a building. We might know about the law of gravity, and that tells us for example that the edifice ought not to be designed leaning sideways beyond its gravitational axis or it will fall down. We might know about the second law of thermodynamics, and that tells us for example that the walls must be insulated or else all the heat inside will escape into the cold air outside. All this is true. But we are no nearer to settling the building's design, because we do not know yet what it is for or how it will be used. Similarly, we could set out here many statements about the things that can and cannot be expected to work in the management of a business, on the basis of cybernetic laws, but we should be no nearer specifying the basic design of its management structure or method of working.

Now if we can learn about shape from a model (as in the case of aerodynamics), or about stability from a model (as when testing a bridge design), why should we not learn about the structure of control in complex systems? That would mean deriving a model of a complex system in which control was already recognized as highly successful. Such a system could teach us about structure, surely, provided that the rules of model building were followed carefully. Scaling-down, transferring, and investigating workability in an appropriate description would be essential, but the cybernetician is used to doing this job. (There is quite a detailed account of how it happens in *Decision and Control*, see Bibliography.) Now we must decide which system to choose.

There is the system of animal ecology, for a start. It is attractive as a teacher of structural control principles because it shows how control may be exerted without any actual controller, simply by the balanced interaction of all the system's parts. We are not over-run by caterpillars; whole species are not (often) suddenly wiped out because they have eaten all their prey — and so on. Moreover, nature at large — the wind and the weather — is rather unpredictable; so we have a control system that can cope with many uncertainties. That should appeal to any manager. However, ecology is rather chancy — there *are* great droughts and great tempests which upset control so that there *are* plagues and famines. Besides, the system runs rather ponderously because it is not self-aware. Then we might take an artificial kind of ecology, within which there is a lot of awareness: the economic system of a country. This too maintains itself in some kind of balance, and includes many self-conscious elements. But we said that the control system to be modelled ought to be recognized as highly successful . . .

No; let us not be too coy. It can hardly be accidental that so many anatomical and physiological terms, descriptions and comparisons have already appeared in this book. The fact is that the firm is very like an animal (let us say a human) body. It has a head, where top direction resides. It has a trunk, housing the vital organs. It has limbs or branches, services, inputs and outputs of energy linked by a metabolic process, and so on indefinitely. The comparison is very obvious, and could be extended in a literary way at great length. But we are not interested in comparisons but in models, and we ought to be scientific rather than literary. Let us pick up some of the things we learned in Part I and apply them.

Control is integral and control is intrinsic. But see the sort of thing that happens in the firm. It is not sensible that one company director should be planning next year's work and another, quite separately, trying to authorize next year's budget — even if they are responsible to the same managing director — because the amount of duplication of work and confusion of intentions is enormous. This commonly happens, and of course the system is defended as this procedure demands. The settling of next year's activity is an integral exercise in which technological, commercial, production, labour, and financial factors are all profoundly implicated. Everything has to be settled at one go, by solving simultaneous equations as it were. The task is not beyond contemporary management science; but the effort will not be invoked if the organization is 'pointing in the other direction'. Even if the effort is invoked, experimentally, it will probably be frustrated by the local but powerful interests of a fragmented management. As to the intrinsic quality of control (as defined in Chapter 2) we do indeed find that the firm is self-regulating at lower levels in many ways. From the standpoint of senior management, that is to say, there are intrinsic controllers at work which do not, or do not normally, demand attention. But how is 'normally' to be defined? And who could deny that many senior managers not only attend to these implicit controllers but interfere with them and stop them working?

If we look at the body, on the other hand, we find that these same problems exist, and are actually and reliably solved. Our physical activity is wholly integral, and the many conflicting demands that are made on our internal resources at any given moment are being resolved into a smooth operation. Most of the control is intrinsic, in that the 'senior management', conscious cerebration itself, does not and in most senses cannot concern itself with the biochemical or electrical details. When rest is required, it can be obtained, and when violent action is urgently needed, the whole physical apparatus leaps into fully geared activity with a very rapid response time. Surely this is good management *par excellence*. How is it done? Can we create a model of this system which would compare with a model of the firm, so that the organizational structure of the firm can be adapted second-by-second with beneficial results?

The answer is that we can try, using modes of description learned in Part I — where it was already obvious that the basic attributes of a control system and the basic notions of control practice were quite general. We therefore embark now on the formation of a model management system which we know, first-hand, to be admirable and survival-worthy; the human nervous system.

Let us not undertake this effort, however, without some careful reflection on the foregoing arguments about the nature and utility of the model that we intend to construct. Could a *neuro*cybernetic model really tell us anything about running the enterprise: is there really a *brain* of the firm? There can be no interest in analogy at this point: a useful model (as already discussed) must be able to handle differences in scale, transference, workability, and appropriateness in convincing style. The rest of the book shall speak for its success in these terms, just as so many real-life applications have already attested to its potency in the diagnostic context. But there is something more to grasp quite firmly if the mistaken notion that we are dealing with an analogy is not to recur to the user of this work, with concomitant unease.

That is the concept of **invariance**, which first came up a few pages ago. It is a mathematical term, whereby it is said that one thing is invariant with respect to something else — that is, it does not change as the other thing changes. In a legally conducted business, the assets must be greater than the liabilities: this inequality is an invariant of all trading companies — it does not matter whether they are dealing in steel or soap. The opposite inequality is called bankruptcy, and that is an invariant too — it does not matter whether they are dispensing holidays or soup.

Our neurocybernetic model pursues and hunts down *organizational* invariances in large, complex, probabilistic systems within the methodology of model-building already noted. To take an example (which is fully discussed in Chapter Fourteen): how does such a system operate effectively if its components are unreliable? It turns out that there are invariant rules governing such a system, which may be derived from the theory of probability and expressed mathematically. It does not matter whether we are dealing with a brain or a firm.

If it does not matter, people ask, what was the inducement to use a neurocybernetic model at all? The answer to that is that the human enterprise is in a very unsatisfactory condition (see Chapter One): its record of failure is mounting in the face of environmental change, and no-one can be sure which aspects of organizational wisdom are conducive to viability and which to disaster. The human nervous system sometimes fails as well; but it seems to have solved many problems that the enterprise has not yet solved. It ought to be successful, of course, because of such long-term investment in its structure: and we should be ready to learn from those several million years of research and development.

CHAPTER SEVEN

Control physiology

The nervous system is not easy to understand, and few people seem to make much effort to understand it. If we wish to make a model of it which will illuminate the problems of management structure, however, the attempt must be made. I suppose the major difficulty is the fact that the brain itself is folded and refolded to be packed away in the skull. If we imagine a parachute that has been packed like this, but between the internal folds of which all manner of internal connections have been inserted, the snags attaching to an investigation are obvious. Any account must pull the folds apart, and doing that alters the relative position of important sites, and also disrupts whatever connections were holding the folds together.

Fortunately we are not really concerned with the geography of the system, except in so far as it helps. In some ways it does help, because we each own a nervous system. Thus it really is common knowledge that there is a spinal cord, contained within and protected by the backbone, and that nerves emanating from this cord run all over the body. Then, in some way or anc.her, there is a brain stuck on top, which looks rather like a walnut without its shell. There are many ways of cutting the whole thing up, and if anatomy itself were the key interest, we should have to try and make a true dissection. But physiology, which says how the control actually works, is the key interest, and we need only a rudimentary anatomy.

The spinal cord is literally the start of the whole business, which means that it is the oldest kind of nervous structure. In evolution it came first; the brain eventually evolved on one end. Quite elementary organisms, some of those without backbones, have nervous tissue which channels information around the body, and this means that afferent and efferent circuits are in being. In man there are thirty-one pairs of spinal nerves through which most of the body is innervated, and the cord itself provides a central axis of command.

Now most living structures, thanks to the way living tissue is built, are best regarded as tubes, and the nervous system is no exception. We learned in Part I to expect that the afferent part of a control system would end in a sensory plate, that a motor plate would originate efferent parts of the system, and that the two would be connected by an anastomotic reticulum. The tube that comprises the spinal cord is just like this, the two plates being bent round to form the tube. A slice *across* the tube therefore shows the sort of afferent-efferent response mechanism we have come to expect. Inputs come in at the back of the tube, and outputs leave from the front. For the moment we may forget about the vertical system running up and down the tube.

Indeed a great deal of control goes on in this way and using this mechanism — at a particular level, as represented by the slice. Especially, the reflexes we all know about (remember the knee-jerk reflex, if you have ever had a medical examination) work *across* the vertical command axis, input from the back and output from the front. Let us then speak of a lateral command axis, although there is no one handy channel like the vertical backbone through which to run all the nerves, which are disseminated all through the body.

But if this lateral command can operate at each appropriate level of the spinal cord, it is still true that bundles of nerves run vertically up and down the central command axis. Therefore we have an essentially two-dimensional system. This is one organizational secret of the body's ability to run affairs — a particular organ for example — autonomously (working laterally), and also to integrate that local activity into an organic balance (working vertically). Thus it matters to us to know what happens at the apparently mysterious moment when we run out of vertebrae at the base of the skull, and the vertical axis apparently runs into the walnut-like brain.

And now a little dissection is inevitable. The visible outside part of the brain that looks like a walnut is the cerebral cortex. Also, like a walnut, it comes in two halves — the cortical hemispheres. But here the resemblance ends. These hemispheres are also really tubes which are wrapped round something inside. They are very big tubes, and they are squashed nearly flat. Even so, there remains a space inside each, called a ventricle. The reason why they are so big is that the brain needs a large surface area, and the reason why the external appearance shows so much crinkling is partly because of the packing problem, and partly because of the internal connections mentioned before. The two hemispheres are connected by a great mass of cabling (the corpus callosum) running over the top of the 'something inside'. All this equipment is concerned with the brain's highest functions, with intellect. If we take it all away, we can look underneath.

The 'something inside' is like a fist, on which the cortex sits like a judge's wig. It is the brain stem, the oldest part of the brain, squeezed out as it were by evolution from the spinal cord. This, we said, is also a kind of tube, and what happens when we 'run out of vertebrae' is that the tube opens out in a series of swellings, which make up the brain stem. These structures are also convoluted, but again the ventricles appear wherever the tube is not completely flattened. Refer, quite briefly, to Figure 13 — just to see what it all looks like. The first swelling is the medulla, and the second the pons; to their rear is the fourth ventricle, the hollow part of the ascending tube. After this comes the mesencephalon, then the diencephalon, the space left of the tube here being the third ventricle. The sides of the diencephalon are the thalami, sometimes thought of as the brain's switchboards. Slightly ahead are the basal ganglia; behind is the cerebellum. The figure gives some idea of the layout, and shows the outline of the cortex itself within the skull.

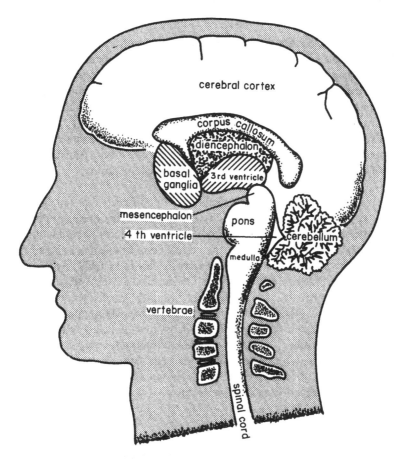

Figure 13. General layout of the brain

It is necessary to see something of this anatomy, because the brain stem is the continuation of the spinal cord. From it arise the remaining twelve pairs of nerves, the cranial nerves. When we talk about the brain in a colloquial way, meaning our powers of association, pattern-making, intellection, recall, foresight, and thinking capacity in general, we are referring anatomically above all to the cerebral cortex. It is important to know that this apparatus has no *direct* connection with the outside world at all — nor even with the body of which it is the brain. All information originates in receptors which make use of those thirty-one plus twelve pairs of nerves as communication channels. The whole of this information is then processed through the spinal cord and the brain stem, which — despite all its intricacy — can be thought of as the anastomotic reticulum of the old part of the nervous system. The specialized parts of the entire brain, of which some of the main ones were listed in the last paragraph, have evolved out of this reticulum.

The spinal cord is concerned with the lateral control axis, as was said before, and with passing on information about it to the brain stem. The brain stem also collects the data relating to the highly specialized senses (sight, sound, and so on) through its own — the cranial — nerves. Here all the major processing and switching of data goes on that is needed for controlling the body before thinking as such starts and voluntary action begins. To achieve this, the brain stem must pass on information to the cortex, and if we decide consciously to do something, the brain stem must receive the instructions, translate them into commands, and pass these down the spinal cord for action.

Briefly reviewing the role of the specialized computers of which we have spoken, we start with the medulla. This provides the key linkage between the cord and the brain proper, and a lot of the co-ordination of reflex action goes on here. Although what was called the lateral control axis uses slices through the cord itself to achieve much local control at that low level, this higher level of co-ordination is required to keep these intrinsic controllers integral. The medulla also contains the switching-circuits (called nuclei) which serve many of the cranial nerves. The pons carries the long fibres belonging to the central command axis, and also short transverse fibres needed to co-ordinate the two halves of the cerebellum. In this part of the reticulum some very remarkable information-filtering takes place, as will be seen later. In the mesencephalon, which lies next on this ascending rack, the so-called 'righting reflexes' are monitored. These keep the body in equilibrium — without them we should fall down.

Thus we pass on to the diencephalon, with its thalami, and the basal ganglia — sorting, switching, relaying between the lower and higher parts of the brain. These higher, cortical parts concern intellection — operating, as should now be clear, on data that have been very well pre-digested. This leaves the cerebellum, which is not quite 'in line' with the rest. It receives information from both above and below, which arrangement is necessary to its function of controlling skilled acts. These demand the co-ordination of muscles, and the information about them obviously moves up and down the spinal cord, plus the use of special sense-data (from the eyes, for instance) which are being mediated through the diencephalon. The cerebellum may also need input from the cortex itself, if conscious attention and an effort of will are involved.

Now these major parts of the brain were just called specialized computers, and the cybernetician can hardly fail to think of the whole brain as a computing system. After all, that is what it is, and it does act as a whole. But the specialized computers are known to be specialized, because the functions attributed to them fail if they are damaged. It is interesting to see, however, that specialized computers are not dotted around in the system — as they often are in management systems, each relatively isolated from the rest, each demanding its own information-capture procedure and producing its own localized output. What happens in the brain is that one stream of information is passed up the central command axis, having been collected on the lateral axis. The specialized computers lie on the track of this information flow, and éach of them undertakes three tasks — whether it is a slice through the cord, or a swelling on the brain stem, or a lobe of the cerebral cortex itself. We shall now tease out these tasks from the complicated operations of the living brain.

The first task is to inspect the information coming up, to see whether it is information which is appropriately dealt with at this level. If it is, two things happen. First, controlling action is taken; that is, messages are sent back down the central axis which evoke response in the body. Second, a modified version of the information that has been operated on (and the modification includes attaching a label saying that it *has* been operated on) is passed on — upwards. If, on the other hand, the specialized computer is not competent to take command action there are two alternatives. One is to pass on the information untouched; the other is to do this but to filter it as it goes. Now we could define a filter as a many-one variety reducer. So a filter must either suppress some information altogether, declaring it to be 'noise' (that is, irrelevant), or it must combine information in some way, so that only one thing is transmitted where more than one thing arrived. An example of filtering of the first kind is what happens when one concentrates on a particular conversation at a cocktail party, although other conversations are going on all around; or alternatively when one listens to a broadcast which is 'noisy' — many other stations are contributing snatches of music and foreign languages to the message one is trying to hear. Filtering of the second kind is like swallowing a thousand figures, adding them up and dividing by their number, and transmitting the resulting arithmetical average. This one figure then does duty for all the others.

In so doing this filter also suppresses information, one might say. For instance, the 'spread' of the original distribution of a thousand figures is not transmitted by the arithmetical average. But of course the mean value alone *may* be all that matters. Alternatively, let us suppose that any large sample of data input from a particular source is statistically distributed according to a particular curve (let us say the Gaussian or 'normal' curve). Then by transmitting the mean of this sample of a thousand, and also its variance (which is a measure of spread) we preserve all that is likely to be important about the stationary input pattern. Two figures instead of a thousand — and it sounds efficient. But suppose that the thousand are not randomly distributed with respect to time; they may exhibit a trend. In that case, and if time trends are important in this case, a few more figures must be transmitted by the filter. These will define the slope of a trend, or the amplitude and the periodicity of a regular wave, for example. The point is that a filter, like a model, has to be appropriate to its purpose. Given that it is appropriate, large economies in information flow can be obtained. A filter is a variety reducer.

A truly vital kind of filtering process in the brain stem is the 'arousal' mechanism. It is all very well for the series of specialized computers to go on dealing with information — sending down instructions, and sending up digested data towards the cortex. The whole system is perpetually bombarded with sensory input, and if all of it precipitated acts of consciousness we should quickly go mad ('to blow one's top' is a colloquialism which may derive from blast furnace operation but reads like good physiology to me). Thus it is that if we go into a room, speak to someone, and come out again, we have received a welter of sense-data which we simply do not want consciously to entertain. The filters must operate. And if a fly is buzzing round while we are reading, we want its presence suppressed too.

The risk we run by providing ourselves with all this protection is serious. If something happens which is actually dangerous, or indeed of special interest in some other way, we cannot afford to have the sense-data which recognize the relevant details filtered out like so much noise. Archimedes was killed during the sacking of Syracuse in 212 BC, despite the ruling of the conqueror Marcellus that he was to be spared, because (it is said) he could not be aroused from his mathematics by the threat comprised in the soldier who was asking his name. We should all die a dozen times à day on the city streets, for the same physiological reason, if we had no special filter for arousal. On the other hand, if the arousal mechanism becomes oversensitive, as it sometimes does when we are debilitated, we find ourselves jumping out of our skins at any sudden noise.

Now this whole business of arousal is apparently tied up with the whole business of filtering. We should not think of a filter simply as an inhibitor, whereby a lot of data is stopped or reduced. It can also be a facilitator — if it allows only certain kinds of message to pass through, and stops or inhibits the others. There seems to be no one site, there are no special-purpose nuclei so far defined, in which this alerting goes on; it is a function of the brain stem at large. We have thought about the special-purpose computers, we have recognized that they each contain specialized nuclei. What is left is what looks like an undifferentiated tangle of nerve cells and their nerve processes, in which these specialized parts are embedded. This constitutes an anastomotic reticulum, if we have ever met one, and indeed the anatomic name for the arousal mechanism is the *ascending reticular formation*. (Note the 'ascending' — an odd word to use in anatomy. The fact is that this filter is one-way.) This is, I think, one of the least well understood aspects of the brain, and in saying that the mechanism 'looks like an undifferentiated tangle' we do well to be cautious. Perhaps there are parts and specially dedicated circuits here too, which will one day be disentangled. Part of the difficulty is the staggering compression of the whole mechanism. We are dealing here with no more than a few cubic centimetres of brain fabric. In this fabric one researcher reckons to have distinguished forty-eight nuclei — sets of distinctive neurons — but how the system is connected remains obscure. At any rate, the point worth making will presumably remain: quite apart from specialized computers lying in serial order on the vertical axis of information flow, the transmission lines themselves are, by some device, activist.

Again there comes the emphasis on the brain as an integral though complex whole. No sooner do we dissect it, and nominate parts, than we are faced with activities going on in another dimension — in a plane different from that which we are seeking to describe. It is annoying not to be able to isolate a little arousal computer in the reticulum, but at least we can see how such a filter fits into the general scheme. When we were on the main track upwards, we knew that in this area of the brain stem the afferent input was being processed steadily towards registration in the sensory cortex. Because of all the filters which subdue and make sense of the afferent bombardment, we knew that some sort of watch would have to be kept for danger signals. To achieve this, signals have to be tapped from the ascending transmission lines and diverted through the filter, and this is just what happens. We have a little collateral system shunted from the main system, which must be described in slightly different terms from those which were serving well. If this makes the task of comprehension difficult, it also constitutes an important lesson.

There has to be a central command axis, and specialized controllers have to be integral with it — even if they are operating in a different mode. They all have three tasks to perform, we were saying, and now these tasks have all emerged and can be listed in the form of instructions:

1. Test incoming data and recognize any on which command action should be taken; take that action, and send on the original information, suitably modified.
2. Test and recognize any data which have to be filtered at this level, compressing, facilitating, inhibiting the ascending path.
3. Store a record of these transactions, in case details have to be retrieved.

The third of these tasks is, in the first place, a logical necessity. The path followed through an anastomotic reticulum cannot be retraced, because any signal passed from point A to point Alpha might have come not from A, but from B,C,D,etc. just as well (hence, as we saw in Part I, the adjective 'anastomotic'). So, should we need to look back, there must be storage sites along the route. Consider first the macro-situation. A page or two ago we went into a room, spoke to someone, and came out. What colour were the walls in that room? Everyone has had the experience of dredging his unconscious mind (as he might put it) for facts which he had not consciously registered at all. They can often be retrieved. But at the micro-situation level, it seems certain that each individual neuron must (that was the logical necessity mentioned) store at least its last state. If it does not, we cannot make the logic of neural networks undertake the simplest computation. Between the first, very general, remark and the second, very specific, lies the whole problem of memory. We know very little about it.

Surely it is almost incredible that the brain, with its ten thousand million neurons, should be capable of re-establishing all the states it ever had. Sums can be done to determine the dimensions of such a storage problem; suffice it to say that it looks daunting. And yet no one has managed to *prove* that the brain ever totally forgets anything and certainly there is much evidence to show that it can often retrieve information which it appeared to have forgotten. Feats of recall under hypnosis, or under drugs such as pentothal, or in dreams, or for no apparent reason, are often very surprising. But here again we are in 'the wrong dimension'. There is no memory *site* in the brain — unless perhaps every neuron has a long-term as well as a last-state memory; there may be memory *circuits* — facilitated pathways through networks of neurons, but perhaps we are again talking about something that goes on in another plane. For example, it is not absurd to postulate that the mediators of memory are biochemical; the whole memory business may be going on at the molecular level, residing, that is, in structures smaller than the neurophysiological structures under discussion. Some evidence for this hypothesis has been found in studies of learning made with flat-worms. A worm can be conditioned to make a given response to a stimulus; if conditioned worms are minced up and fed to unconditioned worms, it seems that the second lot acquire the conditioning themselves. Perhaps memory is served by all these devices and more. I repeat: we do not yet know. But for our immediate purpose it does not matter very much how data are stored, given that we know they are stored. The things that do matter are the anatomy and physiology of control.

We have seen the sense, now, in which all this is integral. We have gone so far as to call the whole nervous system 'a computer' — despite the recognition of specialized computers within the whole. The description of the brain as a computer caused a furore in the early days of cybernetics, when men such as Warren McCulloch used it with iconoclastic zest. People thought that their human prerogatives were being undermined. Yet in truth the description works; as to prerogatives, there is still plenty of mystery left in the human condition. The McCulloch description sounds something like this.

The brain is an electro-chemical computer, weighing about three pounds. It is slightly alkaline, having a pH value of 7.2 — a stable quantity, unless the subject is having a fit. It is highly structured, having a neural logic connecting some ten thousand million neurons. Because of the structure of the cortex, and the rate of propagation of nerve impulses, it has a typical cortical rhythm, a periodicity averaging ten cycles per second. Storage capacity is around 10^{12} to 10^{15} bits. The 'rate' of an individual neuron is about thirty microseconds (millionths of a second), and the brain as a whole operates in the milli-second (thousandths of a second) range. This, incidentally, is very slow by modern computer standards. Nowadays we talk about nanoseconds (thousand-millionths), and the latest computers work in the 500-nanosecond range. That is, they are already two thousand times faster than the brain. (So much for 'the speed of thought'.)

As to fuel, the brain runs on glucose at about twenty-five watts. The glucose is transformed to pyruvic acid, burnt to carbon dioxide and water using oxygen. Energy is stored in phospho-creatine, held constant (except for those convulsions again), and released as adenocine triphosphate — the same form of energy as powers muscle. The oxygen is of course provided by the blood, the circulation of which through the brain is about a quart per minute — one seventh of the whole circulation — without oxygen a neuron dies in three minutes. The twenty-five watts come in because this power is needed to heat the blood by one degree Fahrenheit.

Now it is easier to think about the brain as a computer than to think about the electronic computer itself as some kind of brain. This latter comparison was also made much of during the early days of automation, and was much criticized too. The programmed computer is not itself very brain-like; yet the typical modern computer configuration can be designed as an integral assemblage of specialized computers, and they can be arranged hierarchically. What was said in Part I about hierarchies of command, which have already been seen in relation to management systems, is now very much to the point. We can certainly envisage a central command axis inside the firm — indeed we can identify it in terms of men and procedures. If this were automated we should have an analogue of the spinal cord, collecting information and undertaking lower-level action on the lateral command axis. The ascending information would eventually reach the firm's central computer, where a part of the configuration would be needed to integrate the activities of all the branches and functions. This part of the configuration would be the analogue of the brain stem, and there would be a cortical-level part of the configuration, in which the role of consciousness is played by the senior management.

Between these two would come all the sorting, switching and relaying associated with the diencephalon and the basal ganglia.

We are confronting what seems to be a five-level hierarchy of systems contained within a major computer configuration. I say 'seems to be' because the choice of five (rather than some other number) is somewhat arbitrary. It looks as though it will pay to differentiate five levels, because of the major functional differences involved, and we do not want to differentiate any further than we must. All five systems are serially arranged on the vertical command axis of the firm, and they model the somatic nervous system of the body — which is what we have been talking about. The middle three of the five have so far claimed most of our attention and they are divided out of the cord and the brain stem. The cord itself is the lowest, the medulla and pons are grouped together next (jointly called, if it matters, the rhombencephalon). The third of these three echelons is the diencephalon, with the thalami and basal ganglia. This classification leaves out the mesencephalon, with its 'righting reflexes', and in terms of control theory, I see no reason why this should not be included with the medulla and pons — although it is always regarded as distinct by the neuro-anatomist. It is now time to look more closely at the outer pair of the five sub-systems: the lateral axis which mediates afferent and efferent information, and the cerebral cortex itself.

Before doing so, let us make a particular note that the specialized computer which links the third (brain stem) level to the fifth (cortical) level is what management people usually call a staff function. All the sensory nerves report to the thalamus; everything that the cortex gets is sorted and switched through the diencephalon and basal ganglia (our fourth level). In orthodox management talk this level has nothing to do with command. In our model it has everything to do with command: it lies smack on the vertical axis itself. This fact repays much reflexion. After all, are not those very senior 'staff men' and their officers commanders in disguise? What matters to the firm's top management is not so much 'the facts' as 'the facts as presented', and the presentation chosen can govern the outcome of even the most important and well-considered decision.[1] Just as the cerebral cortex is not in direct touch with peripheral events at all, but receives only such data and in such form as the subordinate echelons pass on, so top management should be presumed to be isolated from actual events. This is why I reject the orthodox line/staff dichotomy in management theory; it is chimerical. Moreover it is a soft option for any staff man who would rather not be overtly implicated in the decision process, which carries responsibility. A big advance in most firms would be made if the chief executive recognized his staff 'advisers' for what they are, and if they themselves accepted their role as commanders-one-down overtly.

[1] An example of this, in which a junior clerk unconsciously makes the decision (which his manager thinks *he* is making) as the direct consequence of the way he sets out tabular information, is worked out in the very first chapter of *Decision and Control*. (See Bibliography).

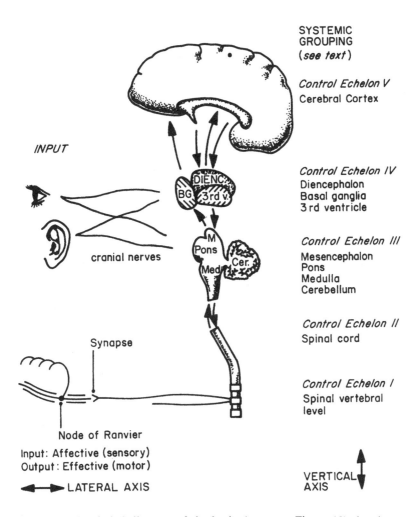

SYSTEMIC
GROUPING
(*see text*)

Control Echelon V
Cerebral Cortex

INPUT

Control Echelon IV
Diencephalon
Basal ganglia
3rd ventricle

Control Echelon III
Mesencephalon
Pons
Medulla
Cerebellum

cranial nerves

Control Echelon II
Spinal cord

Synapse

Control Echelon I
Spinal vertebral
level

Node of Ranvier

Input: Affective (sensory)
Output: Effective (motor)

LATERAL AXIS

VERTICAL
AXIS

Figure 14. Exploded diagram of the brain (compare Figure 13) showing
classification as five-tier hierarchy

Those of them who most adamantly claim that they are 'only' advisory often enjoy the real power they have but disclaim more than their openly powerful superiors. And that has its own dangers too.

In those archetypal (because so very ancient) organizations the army and the church we find the embryonic staff man. He serves the highest echelon, as the thalamic level in the brain serves the cortex. His power is very obvious to all juniors concerned. Consider the effect of the War Office machine on the Chiefs of Staff: what they know (afferent), and what they can actually manage to do (efferent), depend on the operation of the so-called 'administrative' machine. In the Catholic church the activity of the Roman Curia has likewise been seen to play a major part in command — although command is supposedly vested in a synod of bishops working to an infallible commander. It is just the same in industry. Why then should it be necessary to object to a stereotype of 'staff' which, it is alleged, is misleading? The answer is that in industry and government the ranks do not reflect the facts. Curial cardinals are princes of the church; 'staff men' are not, they masquerade as mere nobodies. This is not honest dealing. The diencephalon and the basal ganglia clearly, by their organizational positions, dominate the proceedings of the nervous system, albeit that the cortex itself is in command of volition. Equally, a general staff officer in the army carries rank — and, moreover, special insignia — to denote his peculiar relationship to the commander. Thus even a major, wearing red tabs, caries a distinction beyond his established majority and other, ordinary majors take due note of this. But in industry the accountant, the operational researcher, or the engineer, carries neither the highest rank nor the special marks of power. In this they are like the senior civil servant — even the civilian inside the war machine. Thus it is that this powerful role is overlooked, and the 'staff' notion is propagated. It is not often misunderstood by people lower down — they feel the effects. But it is often misunderstood by the senior management itself, who will be heard to pooh-pooh the misgivings of junior commanders in relation to 'the staff'.

With this parenthesis, we must return to the lowest of the five control levels: that of data-capture and initial processing. The body, just like the firm, is studded with receptors which register information. Some of this information is about the outside world, and it is captured by exteroceptors — receptors looking outwards. Of these there are first the telereceptors, which work at a distance. In the body, the eyes and ears are telereceptors; in the firm, whatever functions are responsible for examining markets, economic conditions, the credit-worthiness of customers and suchlike deserve to be similarly described. Then there are chemical receptors — serving the senses of taste and smell. Thirdly, there are cutaneous receptors, those in the skin, and they are of many types. Touch, for example, is sensed in three main ways. There is a kind of corpuscle (called after Meissner) just under the surface of the skin, inside which the nerve ending is coiled round in a special tissue. It responds to slight pressure, and a tiny electrical charge travels up the nerve. That message is analogous to any kind of data-logging signal in a distant production plant. There is another kind of corpuscle (Pacinian), buried deeply, in which the nerve ending is encapsulated in a laminated sac, responding to heavy pressure — and highly reminiscent of the engineer's load cell. But thirdly, and looking very like any of the sensitive antennae used by the firm to detect a delicate situation, is hair. The slightest touch, too light to fire the sensory neurons lying behind the pressure-sensitive corpuscles just mentioned, will disturb the fine hairs covering so much of the skin. (Consider a moving air current, for instance.) The hair follicle is ringed by a most delicate nerve plexus which is stimulated by the movement of the hair itself. There are other exteroceptors in the skin. In particular, there are capsules containing an intricate reticulum for detecting cold (Krause end-bulbs) and for detecting warmth (the Ruffini organs).

The interoceptors capture data relating to the internal states of the organism, and the firm has many of those too. There are the afferent nerves from muscle, which derive from muscle spindles attached to the muscle fibres themselves; these behave exactly like strain gauges. And if the production plant were made of protein instead of steel we should need many more strain gauges than we need in industry at present. In fact, this would be extremely convenient, because we should be able to calculate all aspects of the load on the plant by this means — just as the body does. the visceroceptors report to the brain about the viscera itself, as distinct from muscle. Here again are stretch receptors, and here again the chemical receptors and the Pacinian corpuscles we have already met. Here is service to a kind of superior production control function, which holds the internal economy in balance — as will be seen later. Finally there are the proprioceptors, which serve the so-called kinaesthetic sense, which has to do with bodily position *vis-à-vis* everything else. The 'labyrinth' behind the ear, with its three semi-circular canals, senses the position and movement of the head in space. It is the failure of these receptors, or their confusion, which makes us giddy. The muscle and joint proprioceptors report on the position of the limbs. It is the sixth, the kinaesthetic, sense which enables us to run upstairs in the dark — because we can programme our movements according to proprioceptive recollection.

All these receptors, and many more, are backed by roughly the same transmission system. What we call a nerve is essentially a bundle of fibres. A nerve fibre itself is the long thin 'process' of a nerve cell, the neuron, and the thread is called the cell's 'axon'. This is the conducting part of the neuron and is made of protoplasm (a gel) covered by a thin membrane. The whole thing is, in most of the transmission lines we are discussing, protected by the medullary sheath composed of a substance called myelin which can fairly be regarded as an insulator, since nerve impulses arrive more quickly through myelinated nerves — because they do not leak the charge. The sheath is discarded at the nerve endings — the receptors — and also close in to the spinal cord, after the signals carried have been relayed at the ganglia serving the central command axis. But the tiny elecrical potentials generated in the nerve need relaying along their journey too — we do not have endlessly long axons. Thus it is that a network of nerves passes on a signal from one neuron (with its axon) to another (with its axon), and the junction is called a 'synapse'. The nerve cell itself is a roughly diamond-shaped body, with the axon emerging from one vertex. From the other vertices other thread-like processes, called 'dendrites', emerge and wander through the tissue, eventually attaching themselves in large numbers to the cell bodies of other neurons. It is this interweaving which creates the anastomotic reticulum wherever neurons interact, and which provides the richness of logical structure which enables neural networks to compute.

Returning to the long axon itself, which is the transmitter part of the neural assembly, there has also to be a capacity to explode into a large number of nerve endings. Often hundreds of terminal processes will emerge from a single axon to innervate the receiving tissues. This need is catered for by internodes along the length of the axon, at each of which a special nucleus is located. The medullary sheath breaks at this point, and the hiatus is called the 'node of Ranvier'. These nodes occur every millimetre or so along the length of the fibre. The electrical potential which constitutes a nervous impulse seems to jump from node to node; at each one it is chemically regenerated and (in the electronic term) 'reshaped'. So the nerve is both excitable and open to being tapped at its nodes of Ranvier. A picture of nervous transmission lines looking like a submarine cable complete with relay stations along its length is useful, but there are complications. The explosion of fibres at the end of the line may indeed be compared to many telephone outlets or electrical points deriving from a single main cable. But at each synapse will be found an anastomotic confusion of connections, and as the lines approach the central command axis they burst into highly complex ganglia. Equally, the effector parts of the system, as the lines leave the cord on their way to innervate the viscera, often burst into even more elaborate networks, the plexuses, using the same structural devices as before. (It is, by the way, not at all easy to distinguish structurally between the affective and effective nerves, since they are often intertwined — and in some classic cases even share the same transmission line.)

This, at any rate, is a thumb-nail sketch of the way in which the lowest level of the system — which we have called the lateral axis — collects and disseminates information. That information, we already know, is passed on through three major levels of the central command axis, and finally, at the fifth level, it reaches the cortex. By this time, it has been argued, a vast amount of control action is already taken care of. But the cortex needs the input supplied by sensation too, and it also needs facilities for output which will initiate action. Thus it is that we distinguish between the sensory and the motor cortex: cybernetically they can be regarded as the ultimate plates of the input and output systems. They lie transversely across the middle of the head, one behind the other, and the rest of the great cortical mass, not to mention the relaying, sorting and switching systems of the diencephalon and basal ganglia, are their anastomotic reticulum.

The cortex, we said, has to do with intellect; it is the seat of consciousness. Its functions are incredibly complex, but they all seem concerned with one thing: pattern.

CHAPTER EIGHT

Autonomy

The word 'autonomy' is pure Greek; it might be freely translated as meaning 'a law unto itself'. So when we speak of autonomy, either in the body or in the firm, we mean that the branch or function indicated is responsible for its own regulation. It is necessary that large areas of any such complex organization should in fact be autonomous. If every aspect of the business, every smallest decision, had to be thought about consciously at the senior management level, then the firm would grind to a halt rather quickly. It is the same in the body and the same reasons apply. Both systems operate autonomic control, which is to say a level of management which does not involve conscious direction by the organism as a whole.

From the point of view of the whole organism, whether body or firm, the autonomic function is essentially to maintain a stable internal environment. We saw in Chapter 2 how central this idea, called 'homeostasis', really is to any viable system. Neither brain nor board could press on with prosecuting a deliberate policy if the internal organs were running amuck. The well-ordered production machinery must not overheat, whether in terms of men or machines; cost and quality must be kept within physiological limits, which is to say that they must vary within a range narrow enough for the health of the whole organism to tolerate; and stocks of inter-process materials must be kept small enough to avoid idle time. The company board expects that its autonomous internal management can cope with these matters, and the conscious part of the brain expects the same *mutatis mutandis* of its autonomic nervous system.

Now all these things can go out of control because of changes in the external environment, whereby some input is changed, or for purely internal reasons. For example, a change in the ambient temperature may so affect either the body or a machine (a refrigerator or an oven for instance) that *internal* controls — thermostats — must autonomically operate. Alternatively, some change inside the system, whereby the system's own temperature is required to alter, will set these controls in operation too. Whatever the cause of imbalance in the internal environment, at any rate, autonomic control must correct it. As was also shown in Chapter 2, the first necessity is to detect a change; receptors then alter their state, transducing the change into afferent impulses. These go to the control centre, are in some fashion computed with, and the necessary adjustments are made through the motor part of the system. This is the autonomic reflex. In the enterprise we are concerned with (what has in the past at least been) a middle management function. In the body, too, the control resides in the middle section of the spinal cord, known as the thoracolumbar outflow, or to use a more traditional and possibly more familiar term, the sympathetic nervous system.

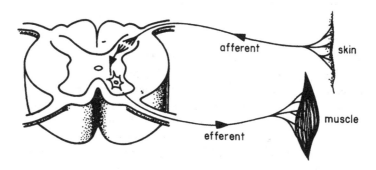

Figure 15. Familiar simplified account of the reflex arc, showing an intercalary neuron connecting input to output within the control centre

Figure 15 purports to show the workings of the famous 'reflex arc'. When we were at school we 'knew' how it worked, by shooting a message from some receptor (say in the skin) back to the spinal cord, whence emanated a message to a muscle. Thus if someone's leg is prodded — even though he is asleep and does not wake — his leg spontaneously withdraws. Similarly, when we were management trainees we 'knew' how a departmental manager exercised cost control. A receptor (probably a cost clerk) detected a 'variance', which is to say a discrepancy between standard cost as agreed and actual cost as incurred. An afferent impulse went in to the manager, who took a decision and sent a message to the effectors on the shop floor to correct the trouble. As a start, this account of the matter is not too bad. As we have seen, there have to be afferent and efferent parts to a control system, into and out of which messages are transduced by receptors and effectors respectively. In between there has to be a switching device of some kind. Moreover, we saw in Chapter 2 the sense in which such a circuit is best described as a negatively controlled feedback rather than as an emitter of instructions. And already the managerial comparison is clear, because the firm really runs itself and the manager intervenes 'by exception'.

Even so, this reflex arc explanation will not do, because it is too simplified. No element of control in an integral viable system is ever quite as localized, quite so self-sufficient, as this. In both the body and the firm we try hard to describe the way control works neatly and simply by classifying what goes on in a number of separate dimensions and according to a number of separate conventions. But a more thorough and less compartmentalized account is needed for real understanding in both cases. The nervous system relies heavily on varying involved forms of interaction between its major components, and what is survival-worthy in the organism depends largely on them. Diagnostically, for instance, this means that a pain in the arm is not necessarily to be treated with embrocation; it may well be a symptom of heart disease. And in industry, heavy costs in an office may result in a roomful of people being replaced by a computer, while the informational links used by the human beings are cut off because they were not understood. A managerial society, like a nervous system, relies heavily on intercommunication which does not at first sight belong to the sub-system under study.

Especially when thinking about automation, it is a mistake to regard the company's system of control and communication as homogeneous. Hierarchical control, whereby instructions are passed down the line, is not the only dimension of control. The point is very clear in the physiological model, from which we may learn. In the case of the autonomic reflex, corrective action cannot in fact be taken in one place without regard to its effect on other proximate activities. Managers at higher and lower levels on the central command axis, the hierarchical dimension, will either influence this apparently local decision or at least need to know about it. They already know about planned activity, because this originates in the brain (or the highest company control centre, the senior management). The main pathways up and down the central command axis are used to inter-relate the activities of the different departments and functions within the total plan. This is a sufficiently complex business, whether for the motoneurons of the spinal cord or for the different departmental controllers in the firm. But when it comes to the reflex arcs of the autonomic system, the local management is decentralized, and therefore the problem of communication up and down the system is not easy.

In industry, indeed, there is rarely any formal arrangement for coping with the problem. Take the case of two production departments, both of which are concerned with the manufacture of the same set of products, but each of which undertakes a distinct set of operations. The actual materials they work are passed back and forth between them. Now the plan to which they are working is agreed; it has been formulated in the central command axis, and each department is trying to work it. The manager of each department belongs to the central axis, so any major deviation from the plan, brought about perhaps by a change in the market, can also be organized centrally as modification. To effect the plan, each manager delegates part of the work to unde. -managers or foremen, who work peripherally to the centre. The way in which their activities are conducted includes, above all, the necessity to maintain the stable internal environment of the firm. They execute the plan in terms of a balanced autonomic activity, involving the sensible use of manpower, the proper loading of machinery, the intelligent manipulation of stocks, the control of maintenance, the observance of quality standards, the exercise of an appropriate degree of inspection, and a great many more aspects of life which must be watched. What the peripheral commanders do is certainly monitored by the departmental office. The information which comes to them passes on to the centre, where constant minor adjustments to the general plan have to be made to correct the misalignments which real events are creating on the shop floor. An appropriate change in plan is made, and the message returns demanding action from several activities which must work together to effect the change.

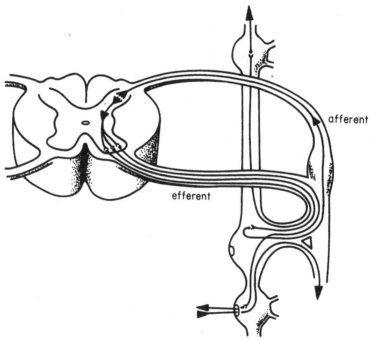

Figure 16. More elaborate account of the reflex arc, showing role of paravertebral ganglionic chain

Look now at this new diagram of a reflex arc, which shows more of the detail than we saw before. Both the afferent neuron, which transmits the input information about the misalignment, and the motor neurons, which give effect to the change in plan, lie outside the central axis. The major motoneuron inside, which is part of the hierarchical command system, has actually made the decision — autonomically. This reflex models the industrial reflex perfectly well, even to its mode of working. For the afferent neuron fires towards the central column only after it has noted sufficiently significant information about the process it is sensing to carry it over its threshold. Similarly, the central motoneuron will not fire until its threshold is also exceeded. And indeed, this will not in practice be likely to occur (in either the body or the firm) unless several sensory inputs, relayed by several afferent neurons, report the need for a change in the plan.

A difficulty is now reached in the example from industry which was being worked out. Although the central departmental office (and therefore in principle the departmental manager) knows about all the multifarious changes to the plan which have been approved for action in the peripheral locations, it (or he) can hardly transmit the whole of this information up and down the central command axis. For if all the managers in the line keep everyone else informed in this degree of detail, the major planning networks will become overloaded. Nevertheless, as was noted earlier, the changes wrought in stabilizing the internal environment in relation to a single section will turn out to have some bearing on other sections belonging to other departments. A good deal of analysis of actual information channels in industry reveals how this problem is generally handled in practice. As was also remarked earlier, there is rarely a formally acknowledged arrangement, but all concerned know how the system works.

What actually happens is that the under-managers or foremen who are responsible, through their clerks, for the afferent input which sponsors change, and who are also responsible, through their chargehands (for instance), for the efferent output which effects change, are in direct communication with each other. There is a complete society of peripheral management, which operates for the most part at the social level, and whose control language is not hierarchical in the sense of line command, but informational. Thus, long before any news about the progress of a batch of production that has been held up could possibly reach another department through the central command axis, the second department knows. In fact, the news will quite probably never become disentangled from what is going on in the affected departmental headquarters, because all concerned know that what is going on peripherally ceases to be news by the time it can be uttered through these channels. I have collected scores of examples of this. Sometimes, very often perhaps, the foreman in the related departments make it their business to keep in intimate touch. Maybe they walk across the road and drink tea together; maybe they telephone: 'You'd better know, Charlie, that ...'. In a few extreme cases, it was not possible to discover how the messages were transmitted — but transmitted they certainly were.

One case in particular remains vivid after many years. This was where the productivity of one department, measured by comparing actual against planned outputs in elaborate detail, varied inversely with the amount of stock accruing in its servicing department twenty miles away. The time-lag on this servo was very much less than it would have been under any official system, because it worked on a shift (eight-hour) phase — whereas it took at least three days to obtain and evaluate proper measurements, even when a team of scientists made a special investigation. This peripheral communication system, which is parallel to the vertical command axis, deals in a different dimension of control from that of volitional command. The people concerned in it have neither the knowledge nor the opportunity deliberately to reshape plans that have been formulated as a matter of intent. They do have the power to apply feedback. The difference is important for this reason. If under-managers are regarded as extensions of the central managers, and their jobs are regarded as being of the same kind but embracing more detail, then the whole control system becomes admonitory instead of self-regulating. In particular, when the systems analysts move in to undertake studies aimed at improving control, the whole system may become over-centralized; at worst, the informal links between peripheral under-managers may be cut. This can happen through a total failure to understand how the system really works; I have seen it ruled that such 'unofficial' interaction must cease, on the grounds that the central authority was being abrogated. In the limiting case, where the departmental outstation is fully automated, there is no possible way in which the social link can be maintained. Computers do not just happen to develop the trick of shouting to each other across the void, as human beings always do.

Perhaps all this partly explains why some managers are so very cautious about automation. They suspect that some such breakdown in communications will occur, but they do not like to say so. They know full well how important social communication in their system is, but they are guilty about it, and feel they ought to have been capable of setting up a 'proper' control organization which did not have to rely on such (apparently) casual arrangements. This view arises only because the managers do not see the peripheral controls as different in kind from their own. They do not see the difference between volitional, command information, and autonomic servomotor information.

The neurophysiological model makes the whole business plain. If we ask how the peripheral ganglia interact without (or, better, in addition to) going into the central command axis, we find an immediate neuroanatomical answer — the sympathetic trunks. These link together the peripheral ganglia, as may be observed in Figure 17. It is these paravertebral ganglionic chains which really govern the stability of the internal environment, for they are the feedback regulators and integrators. In an earlier chapter we saw how a command circuit transfer function turns out to be dominated by its *feedback* transfer function, and in this sympathetic structure the two-dimensional nature of the control is fully revealed. Incidentally, in an electronic circuit the 'gain' of the system (its capacity to amplify signals) is likely to be variable — in mixing together the various flows of information for different control purposes, some signals may need to be more emphasized than others. In the social system, when the under-managers are communicating for instance, there is a clear analogue of this. People manage very well to grade the relative importance of messages — in the simplest case by shouting, and then in progressively more subtle ways. Notes are labelled 'urgent'; oral sentences are prefixed 'don't forget this one', and so on. In the physiological system, from which this model is drawn, there is also an analogue of variable gain. It is provided by the endocrine system, which changes the bio-chemical conditions in which the neural circuits are operating. Thus the release of a powerful hormone such as adrenalin changes the rate at which the command system responds.

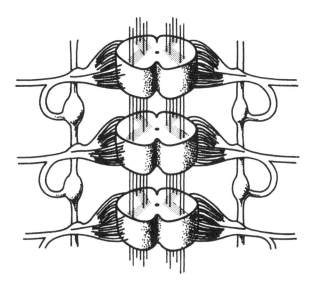

Figure 17. Exploded diagram showing the way in which the vertical and lateral command axes are linked, and the arrangement of the paravertebral sympathetic trunks (compare Figure 16)

The more the neurophysiological model is studied in detail, the more astonishingly accurate does it seem to be in reflecting what happens in the firm. Here is just one example of such a correspondence, which occurs at a level of finer detail than we have yet described or drawn. Attention has already been directed to the risk that when a computer, or some other specially engineered control system, replaces a local management centre, then the unofficial connections between this office and other offices may be cut. I called this a risk because the connections are important, yet if the systems analysis has been correctly done no harm will result. In fact, one of the key problems for scientists installing such systems in industry is that the connections they *wish* to cut are not always successfully cut. For example, a sub-office (controlling a section of a department) may acquire a well-designed production control system, and the old-fashioned system it replaces is discarded. The foreman in charge then operates the new system. But some of his charge-hands, lacking confidence in this manoeuvre, are subsequently found to have retained personal systems of their own. They carry little books of private information, and try to run their groups of machines from those. Surgeons have encountered a precisely similar phenomenon when performing trunk sympathectomies. When the sympathetic ganglion is removed, the surgeon does not expect the feedback circuits involved to operate any longer — but sometimes they do. This is because there are sometimes intermediate ganglia trapped between the spinal cord and the sympathetic trunk, formed by groups of cells which were arrested during embryonic development in the course of migrating from the neural tube towards the true sympathetic ganglia. They remain half-way down the routes shown in the diagrams (called the *rami communicantes*), and proceed to relay messages from there.

But it is time to leave the thoracolumbar outflow from the spinal cord, which we called the sympathetic nervous system, and to consider the second part of the autonomic system. This is the craniosacral outflow, which gives rise to the parasympathetic nervous system. It is remarkable, and keenly interesting to the cybernetician, that this part should be markedly different in almost every way from the sympathetic part. It is not always easy fully to distinguish the two in terms of anatomy, because the body (as usual) really is immensely complicated; but the outline of this control circuit is clear enough.

The system so far described is organized, in the cause of maintaining a stable internal environment, primarily to obtain a balanced mass response from the whole organism. The target is a general homeostasis. But in addition each major site of internal activity seems to need a more localized, more specific, kind of control which nevertheless cannot be obtained locally. That is, although more action is called for in the vicinity of some particular location, the information required to procure it is highly centralized. If the sympathetic system is, as it were, a middle management function, then the parasympathetic system is a senior management function. This is not to say that the top echelon is corporately involved; we have not broken through to the level of consciousness, still less to volitional control of the organism. But we are talking now about information and direction deriving from high up in the command axis. In the body, the system originates so far up the spinal cord that we are really into the brain — its stalk or core. (There is a second part, the sacral as distinct from the cranial outflow, right at the base of the spinal cord, but it may be thought of as a part of the higher-level system which is sited for convenience near the lower part of the body it serves.)

Now what is so interesting is that most organs of the body receive a nerve supply from both the sympathetic and the parasympathetic systems, and that the effects the two produce on site are largely antagonistic. Moreover, the chemistry of the two systems is largely different. If another slight over-simplification may be forgiven, the sympathetic system works mostly on adrenergic impulses, while the impulses of the parasympathetic system are cholinergic. The former word implies the use of an adrenalin-like substance, while the latter derives from the Greek word for bile. In short, the chemical transmitters which operate the two systems (norepinephrine and acetylcholine respectively) are quite distinct. In any given situation they seem to produce counter effects. Typically, the adrenergic impulses increase heart activity, while the cholinergic impulses decrease it. On the contrary, the adrenergic set inhibits, contracts or constricts many other parts of the body which the cholinergic set stimulates, relaxes or dilates. Note, then, that when it comes to adjusting the variable gain in autonomic feedback circuits, the sympathetic and the parasympathetic components of influence will respond differently to drugs or hormones. This is clearly vital to the task of obtaining discriminatory checks and balances between the body's organs.

Activities in the autonomically controlled part of the organization, then, are controlled by two masters. They are morphologically and biochemically distinct. They are antagonistic to one another in their effects, and it is the 'trimming' of one influence against the other which produces (at least one kind of) the balance required to maintain a stable internal environment. Now whatever pundits may say in terms of organization theory in industry, exactly the same situation arises there in practice. 'One man, one boss' may be the cry; one activity responsible to one manager may be the theory. The practice of industry is precisely different — stability is maintained by checks and counter-checks. A particular example will be examined a little later. Meantime, take a closer look at the parasympathetic system.

There are twelve pairs of nerves connected with the brain, which are called the cranial nerves. The first, second and eighth have to do with the distinct sense of smell, sight, and hearing. Three more, the third, fourth, and sixth, deal with the intricate muscular control of the eye — the eyeball and the pupil. The fifth and seventh nerves innervate the face, and the twelfth the tongue. The ninth, tenth, and eleventh nerves deal with the internal organs in the stomach, heart, lungs, and so on, up to the back of the mouth. The cranial parasympathetic system is distributed between the odd-numbered nerves, plus the tenth or vagus nerve.

In so far as the model has discussed mainly autonomic control of the internal organs of the body, it is most natural to consider the tenth nerve (to which the eleventh is accessory) here. The tenth nerve which carries by far the greatest number of parasympathetic fibres, innervates the entire viscera. It roves or wanders about the whole body space, hence its name from the Latin: vagus. It derives from the medulla oblongata, to which it is attached by eight to ten rootlets. The medulla, as Figure 14 showed and Figure 18 repeats, is the 'lowest' part of the brain — an extension and swelling of the spinal cord. The nucleus of the vagus nerve lies inside the medulla. There are specialized parts of the nucleus for the afferent and efferent functions of the nerve, and there is a distinguishable zone for the fibres dealing with the heart. The nerve descends from the medulla into the body down two great branches, to the right and left, and thence to the locations of all the organs which we have earlier seen as at least partly controlled by the sympathetic system. In fact, it is the antagonistic action of the parasympathetic system which completes that control.

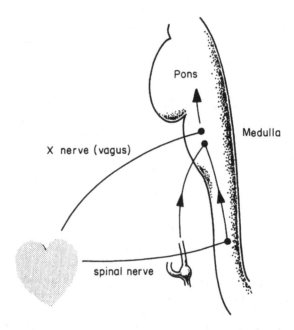

Figure 18. The respiratory centre in the medulla connecting to the heart. Note the dual ascending paths (compare Figure 16)

Despite all the complexities which make simple accounts of autonomic control both difficult to formulate and likely to be over-simplifications, we do basically understand how it all works. The self-regulating properties of the eye pupil, of the mechanism which governs sweating or of the control of the urinary bladder, may all be understood in terms of the primary system so far described. And it is important to note that the control engineer would not find it possible to regulate comparable artificial mechanisms within industry without using the antagonistic controllers, the feedback systems, and the parallel circuitry which has been neurophysiologically described. If this is indeed the case, one might wonder how the model itself can be useful in the firm. The answer is that the control engineer is not normally concerned with so many mechanisms which are all interacting, nor with the kind of transfer function found in an anastomotic reticulum. But the management scientist is. Thus for him the model provides the bridge between the practical problems of control in the enterprise, and the apparently too simple, too analytic, too demanding computable models of servomechanics.

In engineering, for example, it surely does not often occur that there are *two* control centres governing a particular activity, one of which is especially concerned to stimulate and the other to inhibit. A competent engineer, who has access to the process involved, will assuredly coalesce these functions in a single control centre within a machine. Yet in management the tendency of a somehow *basically* inhibitory centre (such as an admonitory financial director and his staff) or of a somehow *basically* stimulatory centre (such as an enthusiastic development division) to fall victim to ungovernable positive feedback often occurs. Human beings and social groups which are really effective tend, that is, to parody themselves. What began as financial prudence ends as a kiss of death; what began as innovatory keenness ends as profligacy. Hence it is altogether normal in management (in contradiction to some textbook utterances) to find that control of some function that is vital to the enterprise is not after all the province of one decision-taker, but of two. Theorists say it must be wrong, and still seek explanations for this dire condition in 'company politics'; they try to arrange matters so that authority resides with responsibility in one centre. But they themselves are wrong; twin centres of different tendency may turn out to be one of the necessary consequences of having a control system which is not fully specifiable.

This organizational mode may be studied in the model that is most vital to all functions, the beating of the heart. The sympathetic control feedbacks operate here, just as described earlier. Autonomic sensory information about the heart goes straight into the spinal cord. But the other sympathetic channel is used too — the same information rises up the sympathetic trunk. The fibres involved in both circuits reach the medulla, where there is a control centre. Any increase of pressure in the right atrium of the heart, or in the veins that return blood to the heart, is registered by the system and results in increased heart rate. Thus, the control centre in the medulla is concerned with stimulation. But any increase of pressure in the left ventricle, or the arch of the aorta, or the carotid sinus, is registered by receptors belonging to the parasympathetic system — indeed to the vagus nerve itself. The impulses arrive in the dorsal nucleus of the vagus, which we have already seen also lies in the medulla, and they result in a reflex slowing of the heart. The point that was being made is that this inhibitory cardiac centre is separate from the first (the stimulatory) centre, being located slightly above it. See again Figure 18.

Such a mode of organization is, even so, rather unusual. There are other and more complicated autonomic control systems which after all coalesce the antagonistic impulses, as far as we can tell, in a single centre. An example is the control of respiration. Breathing is a complicated activity, and it must not falter — waking or sleeping. Again we find that the relevant autonomic control centre lies in the lower region of the brain, where the sympathetic and parasympathetic systems are close together. The mechanism for heart-beat control, just discussed, turns out to be embedded in a respiratory centre (shown on the last diagram); it actually lies between the pons and the lower apex of the fourth ventricle. It is part of the reticular formation of the brain stem, where the switching circuits offer the very best example of the anastomotic characteristic discussed earlier. It is worth examining how this system works.

The body uses various fuels derived from its food — most of them are sugars — and oxygen, circulated by the blood, is needed to burn them. Carbon dioxide is the most important waste product resulting from this combustion, because it must be disposed of quickly; the other main by-product is only water. Considered as a sugar-furnace, the brain needs fantastic supplies of oxygen. A neuron will die in about three minutes if it is deprived of oxygen, and there are ten thousand million neurons to supply. This entails a blood flow through the brain of a quart a minute, a seventh of the entire circulation. The lungs are the oxygen-acquiring plant, which is driven by motors — the muscles which expand the chest. The system is like an AC system on a slow scale, because the motors are switched off to collapse the chest and expel the air in the lungs, and must switch on again to start a new cycle. Given that this system is working, however, we need autonomic controls to adjust it according to the state of the internal environment. Clearly the feedbacks involved in doing this job must take account of the amounts of oxygen and of carbon dioxide which affect the energy system continuously in relation to the effort which the body is undertaking.

Basically, the story is familiar. Receptors are needed first of all. There are chemical receptors which measure changes in the two key gases found in the blood, both in the carotid sinus and the aortic arch. They are small glandular structures with many sensory fibres. There are more chemical receptors in the medulla itself, but they respond only to the carbon dioxide content of the blood — and indirectly at that, because they are not in contact with the arterial blood itself. Instead, they infer the required measurements from diffusion of carbonic acid which has reacted chemically with the salts of other acids. Thirdly, there are afferent signals deriving from the mechanical action of the chest, and from receptors in the airway walls. All these receptors transduce information through parasympathetic nerves to the brain centre. The effector part of the system works through motoneurons in the spinal cord which operate the muscles of the chest, having been fired by impulses travelling down from the anastomotic reticulum of the respiratory centre itself.

The feedback structure is in principle perfectly clear, but from the control-theory point of view there are many complications. The elaborate chemical analysis system in the medulla involves computing which takes time, just as the chemical diffusions which reflect the general activity of cells throughout the body take time to reach the medulla. Bayliss[1] regards the former as imposing an exponential delay on the whole Servo, and says that the diffusion delay will be from five to fifteen seconds. There are other difficulties in analysing the servomechanics of the system, but they have been elucidated by Priban and Fincham, one of whose illustrations is shown here.[2]

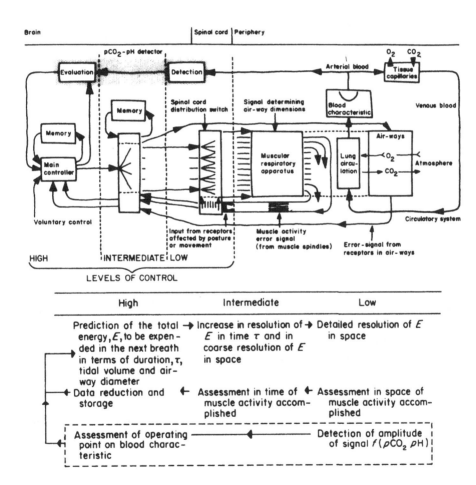

Figure 19. Priban and Fincham's account of the organization of respiratory control

[1]*Living Control Systems.* See Bibliography.
[2]*Self-adaptive Control and the Respiratory System.* See Bibliography.

These authors show that the respiratory system is concerned to do something more than regulate an operating system. It is true that a chemical control, a muscle control, and an airway control are all necessary. In a business (using the model) it is likewise necessary to control the flow of material, to control plant, and to control the flow of cash. Moreover, it is necessary that all three functions should be controlled in combination, so that the organic system of body or business operates in an internal harmony. But, say Priban and Fincham after making their servo analysis, the control of respiration is also organized to work at minimum cost. This is achieved by ensuring that the ventilatory gas exchange and the metabolic gas exchange are equal. The mechanism by which they see this being accomplished has three levels, and these levels exactly parallel the planning activities of senior, middle and junior management in my own analysis of autonomic control in an industrial enterprise. Furthermore the mechanism works by a precise technique which I have often installed to control physical production.

The highest level of control defines the total effort to be expended and the time over which it is to be dissipated. 'It does this by evaluating the optimal predicted activity of a breath with the actual activity in that breath. The result is the prediction of the next breath in terms of energy and time.'* Now the ratio of optimal to actual activity in industrial production is a measure of productivity, and in industrial practice I have familiarly used that ratio as a planning tool (we shall meet this again in Part III). It is possible to keep the ratio under continuous surveillance, and to adjust the future of the system to its immediate past. So, whether we speak of respiratory control in the body or production control in a works, we are operating on the same cybernetic principles which apply to all adaptive systems.

The next two levels of control are concerned with interpreting the higher-level instructions into more detailed patterns of activity. They are also responsible for initiating the feedback signals which enable the higher controller to make predictive plans. In so doing, the feedback data 'are reduced at the low and intermediate level controllers so that only the significant information about the accuracy of the prediction is fed back to the main controller'.* Again, this exactly parallels the industrial control system already mentioned. So does the systematic improvement facility built into the respiratory controller, which feels its way into the future by the criterion of maximizing the productivity function which is the measure of effectiveness in both systems.

So this is autonomic control, which takes a basically operational system and a basic set of instructions for granted, and then proceeds to keep what is happening in balance and in economic health. Note that its activity by no means precludes intervention from a much higher level in the brain, where

*Priban and Fincham, op. cit.

consciousness may take over control if it wishes. My respiration continues autonomically; but at any moment I may decide to hold my breath or to take a deep breath. If I do so, the autonomic system must subsequently cope with the consequences when my conscious intervention has ceased and I am thinking about something else. The same is true in management, and in the next chapter we shall study more closely the consequences of these neurophysiological and control-theory insights for the business enterprise.

CHAPTER NINE

Autonomic management

In the last two chapters we have been tracing the physiology of a control system in terms of a model of the human nervous system, taking in just enough of its anatomy — which is to say its structure — to make sense of how it works. The relationship in which this control system stands to the control system of a firm has been borne in mind, and illustrated generally. In this chapter we shall try to sharpen the focus of the whole picture by saying just how a firm organized like this would work.

But what firm are we talking about? What is this model supposed to be a model of? The answer is simple, but it must be clearly grasped — otherwise there would be a good deal of confusion. We are talking about the control of a (that is to say *any*) viable organism. Thus the firm may be small or large. If the firm is small, and suppose that in the limiting case it consists of a one-man-band, then all the functions we have been discussing will be condensed precisely into the one man. It was mentioned before that there is a mathematical account of the model building process, but from the mathematical point of view, by far the most elegant and satisfying model of anything at all is in fact itself. That must sound odd to anyone who hopes to use a model for purposes of elucidation, but it does at least provide a valid and substantial starting point.

If a man *is* the firm, then he is using his own nervous system to run the firm. If two men go into partnership, then they are likely to divide the functions of the firm between them. Suppose that one of them makes things, while the other goes out to sell them. We can see the sense in which the first man has all the interoceptors — he is the one who knows about the state of the machinery he is using, the rooms he is working in, the heat, the light, the raw materials, work in progress, and available finished goods. The other man has the exteroceptors. He provides the interface with suppliers and markets, and brings back information about the interaction of the firm with the world outside. How do we now see the ascending hierarchy of computing systems which constitute the brain of this firm? Undoubtedly these two men will talk together, and if the partnership is a good one they will mutually decide on the filtrations, on the control actions at every level, and ultimately on the firm's policy.

If the firm is now enlarged to a sizeable business, in which several hundred people are taking part, the position is not so simple. We shall, in any orthodox business, discover that the whole organization has become fragmented. Among the work people, this is unexceptionable (we have the analogue of the body's organs, each performing its appointed task). But control is vested in management, and the likelihood is that management has become fragmented too. Instead of the main stream of ascending information passing through a hierarchy of computing systems, we shall find information going up, as it were, in species of information — that relating to production, to costs, to sales, and so on. And the heads of each of these functional divisions, each of whom is probably a director of the firm, now have the task of communicating, of shouting to each other across the void. This task they will find rather difficult. Because once the firm grows to any size, the intimacy of what used to be a partnership is lost. The people simply do not have sufficient time to do as much talking as information theory would calculate they need to do if complete harmony is to be established.

After all, if I want you to know *in complete detail* what I have been doing for the last hour, then I shall want exactly one further hour to explain. If I have ten colleagues, and cannot see on average more than two of them at once, then I shall need five hours to explain my one hour. It is just an application of the law of requisite variety. If I can afford no more than ten minutes in explaining myself for every hour worked, then I shall devote two minutes per pair of colleagues, and there will be a ratio of 30:1 in the reduction of variety between myself and them. Some lethargic managerial societies seem to work quite smoothly on this basis, for the very simple reason that for them this turns out to be also the ratio of clock time to useful working activity. But a man who really is doing an hour's work in every hour is bound to lose in intelligibility. Next, we must note that this applies in the best of all worlds — one in which people love each other, and are completely determined to share their understanding. But human nature is not like this. Even the most willing of us finds himself antipathetic, in varying degrees, to some of his colleagues. Even the most innocent of us occasionally succumbs to political motives which make him a deliberately poor communicator.

The conservatively minded business men among us will have none of this somewhat ruthless analysis. There is no need, for goodness sake, for me to tell everyone else in detail what I am doing. I am paid to do my job properly, and all that anyone else needs to know is what I think they ought to know about the results of my work. And yet this is just the trouble. A viable organism works as an integral whole. A typical business is integrated too late, and too little.

Anyone of experience and perception who analyses last week's business exprience in his own firm is going to appreciate the point. People have ordered supplies that were there all the time, or that are no longer needed. People have taken a particular direction in a given matter because of a circumstance which is much outweighed by another circumstance of which they were unfortunately ignorant. If we could stop the business this week to analyse what happened last week, we should all be sadder but wiser.

I have never forgotten my first traumatic lesson of this kind, where the integration broke down at the very fundamental level of the external and internal receptors. The exteroceptors reported an order for a single sheet of metal of a certain size. The interoceptors reported a works capability slightly less than this specified size in each dimension — width and length. Managerial integration of the two inputs broke down, because the management was fragmented (in an entirely orthodox way) between a relevant sales manager and a relevant works manager. You might expect that the former wanted to satisfy the customer and to put pressure on the plant, and that the latter would want to save himself from attempting the impossible. Not a bit of it; — perhaps the two nervous paths crossed over as they do in the optic nerve! At any rate, the sales manager told the customer that the plant could not cope; the works manager found out and was extremely angry. He insisted on taking the order, and tried at least a dozen times to discharge it. But the body *did* know its limitations, and the sheet was not made. After unconscionable delays and endless prevarications the exteroceptors began to hum to such purpose that the whole arousal mechanism was set in motion. Senior management became involved — which is to say that the firm's consciousness awoke to what would normally have been an autonomic process. When this happens in the body we can be sure that consciousness will begin to interrogate the whole situation, demanding new facts, and that is precisely what happened. It was very soon discovered that the customer had calculated the size of the sheet as a very large multiple of the tiny squares he proposed to cut the sheet into when he got it (he was in fact stamping ashtrays). Thus is proved possible to meet his needs immediately by piling offcuts of the appropriate metal into the boot of a car and driving them to him.

There is a huge number of examples of breakdown in the control system of the firm from these causes, most of which are far less risible and far more serious. Indeed the most serious examples are perhaps the most common, and they have to do with the firm's major policy. Capital investment in plant is going to be decided by production people who think they know what the market requirements are. This is because the marketing people keep telling the production people what they want. But the marketing people do this on the basis that they know what the production facilities are. And so, quite typically, there is a chicken-and-egg problem which only the managing director or the board itself can solve. Unfortunately, these people are likely to see the problem which only the managing director or the board itself can solve. Unfortunately, these people are likely to see the problem as a battle of influence between the two protagonists, and they may well fail to notice that an integral solution — one which looks to the viability of the firm as a whole — will give a completely different answer.

In real life the position is much complicated by the viewpoints of other directors. For instance, the financial director may be wholly obsessed with an orthodox professional analysis of the situation; if so, he will be talking a language that has to do with replacement costs and investment allowances — a language which may be conducive to the inevitable perpetuation of the existing state of affairs. He may be supported by an engineering director, thinking in precisely the same terms. The firm that is most likely to break out of these endless loops is one in which the managing director has provided himself with a first-rate operational research group. If these people are left to acquaint themselves with the nature of the business and to make integral analyses of the firm's viability, they may well succeed in providing the linkage between the separate fragments which is required. Unfortunately, domestic OR groups are typically encumbered with problems fed to them by the fragments. That suits them because it justifies their existence in the eyes of the individual board members. But if a production manager commissions an operational research study of what he takes to be a production problem, he quite certainly expects a production-orientated solution. He does not want the OR group to start talking to him about sales policy. And so on. On the other hand, whoever has to answer to the board for the cost of the OR department is not at all happy that they should be working away on what appears to be 'nothing in particular', and therefore he encourages the group to devote itself to assignments allocated by the sectional heads.

Although, as will be seen later, the general purpose OR group is required, it is still rather absurd to lay the whole onus for the integration of the business upon it. This needs to be done by an anatomy and a physiology designed to this very end. We saw in Chapter 1 how it comes about that businesses do not actually have well-designed control systems, and hitherto no one could blame them for we did not have the information-handling capability to do other than we have traditionally done. But today we have that capability, thanks to electronics. And this is why computer systems are needed even in relatively small businesses — because we soon run out of 'partnership' information-sharing capacity in human terms. Thus it happens that what looks like a business that is too small to afford a computer is in fact too large not to afford it. It does not follow that the firm must have a whole machine of its own, because it may hire terminals fairly cheaply that are connected to a time-sharing service. Moreover, as the capacities of microprocessors become properly understood and exploited, necessary computing functions will become disseminated all over the firm. At that point, it is predictable that it will soon be a status symbol *not* to own a computer. At that point also, this neurocybernetic model — which offers the blueprint whereby these microcomputing facilities need to be *interconnected* (as indeed they are in the nervous system) — will predictably come into its own, not merely as a diagnostic tool, but as a circuit diagram.

As long as computers are regarded (see Chapter 1 again) as 'sophisticated', and more particularly as long as they are typically used to do the wrong job, they are an extravagance. It is a matter of priorities. It might well be better to spend what, in existing circumstances, sounds like an appallingly large sum on a correct application of computers than to do anything else. But it does have to be a 'correct' application. And by that rather silly adjective, readers will now more readily understand, is meant an application which provides integral control. At present, a firm must tackle this task virtually from first principles, and from within. This is because neither the computer manufacturers nor the consultants who advise on computer applications have made any effort to design a systematic package for controlling the firm. They seem to think that every company is different. And so it is — but not in every way. I consider that it would be possible to produce a quintuple-hierarchy system of mixed analogue and digital hardware, together with a mixed command and tracking language software, which would give any firm a flying start in tailor-making (as it eventually must) its own control system. The possibilities have been open for many years, and once again we must consider the introduction of microprocessors — since they make the outcome an inevitability. As argued in Chapter One, the delay has been due to cost: not because it has ever been excessive, but because it has permitted monopolistic control. That constraint is now lifted.

What is true of the small business is *a fortiori* true of the large business. The really big firm is an amalgam of smaller firms: there are divisions, subsidiaries, and so forth. If the human brain is beaten in the attempt to control a firm which is at least ostensibly *one*, then how much more difficult is it for the holding company of a large corporation to operate sensibly. Yet here again we are dealing with something intended to be a single viable organism. Just as there were competing claims and competing views of the world in the smaller firm, because of the fragmentation into production, sales and so forth, so there are competing views between whole companies when they are formed into a giant corporation. Unhappily, the directors at (let us call it) group level are still constrained by the three-pound computers in their skulls — just as is the head of the small business, or the one-man-band himself. I often think that if a scientist were to arrive from Mars and study our organization charts, he would inevitably conclude that the managing director of the corporation must have a brain weighing half a ton. That is to say, we organize ourselves in a way which the law of requisite variety, and information theory in general, cannot justify — unless the size of people's heads increases exponentially with their seniority. Unhappily this is never true (except perhaps in a metaphorical sense).

So the question: 'What is the model a model of?' is answered by: 'a viable organism' — regardless of its size. This is an interesting invariant of the model's application, but it does (as I warned) lead to confusion unless we are careful. The warning is this: Before anyone starts thinking about a business in terms of this model, he must clearly decide how the model is supposed to fit. If he looks at the actual organization, he finds some parts of it to be conscious, some parts autonomic, and so on. The point is that which parts are which varies, depending on the application he tries to make. If we consider a giant corporation as a viable entity, then the main board alone can possibly be allocated a conscious role. The boards of subsidiary companies are, from the standpoint of the holding board, centres of autonomic activity. But this does not prevent our moving into one of the subsidiary companies, and treating that as a viable entity. If we do, it will mean that our control system is aimed at obtaining survival-worthy policies for that company as if it were isolated. In that case, it may 'go to war' with its associate companies — and then the main board will have to sort the matter out.

From the point of view of the management scientist, at any rate, he will apply his model where he is paid to work and to apply it. To drop yet another stage, for instance, it is quite common for the operational research man to be pegged at a departmental level — within a company, within a larger company, within a corporation. There is then nothing to stop the OR man from using an organic control model within the department — if it seems worth the effort. But the onus is on senior management to have these things rightly applied. I have seen it happen that one department was made so effective that a gross imbalance within the company was created, and that one department was virtually controlling the firm. From our point of view, at any rate, we can do no more than acknowledge that the model *ought* to be applied to the major entity with which we have to deal. If the Prime Minister is reading this, she will realize that the model should be applied to the country. British Prime Ministers, however, as each memoir in turn shows, prefer reading that rehearses the past, rather than reading directed to the future (over which, supposedly, they have some influence). This is not the case with some other countries — as Part IV shows.

Consider then a firm, that integral organism, with a vertical command axis consisting of five hierarchically arranged computer systems (which long ago we numbered as the control echelons one to five). And consider a subsidiary of this firm, whether it be a whole company or a department, as analogous to a limb or an organ of the corporate body. This is connected to the vertical command axis — at the level of System One — by a lateral command axis. The subsidiary (call it B) sponsors action, and the action is designated in the diagram shown at Figure 20 by the wavy arrows. What is going on in this subsidiary must be communicated by System One to System Two, which it will be remembered is the analogue of the spinal cord. In the diagram just one

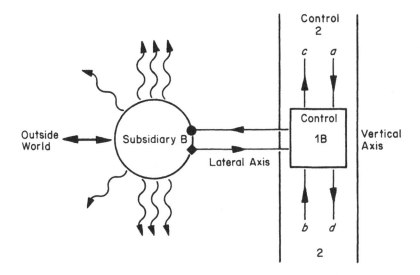

Figure 20. A firm's subsidiary has its own relations with the outside world, its own management problems within the corporation and its own control system embedded in the large one

'vertebra' of System Two is shown — it is the System One command centre itself. Because the subsidiary is part of the corporate whole, its activities are to be sensed by interoceptors — and these are designated by the black diamond in the diagram. Information is fed along the lateral access to the intersection of Systems One and Two, and the response is fed back to the subsidiary. Instructions for this subsidiary arrive at the appropriate System Two vertebra called System One from the higher-level systems down the line marked a (and those designated for lower action pass on down the line marked d). Data about the activities of other subsidiaries intended for higher control levels are coming up through the transmission line marked b, where it joins new information from this centre, and proceeds onwards up line c. For the moment we shall look at the control loop of System One itself.

It is not in the first place very difficult to devise arrangements which will inform System Two of the subsidiary's activities, through its own System One control activity. Wherever computers are used a mode of transduction has to be found, and usually it takes the form of a card-punching department where the vital statistics of the subsidiary are converted into cards or tape which the computer can read. This is a satisfactory form of transduction for interim use. But it imposes an inevitable delay, and it entails human selection and condification of information. Ideally, we want what is going on in the subsidiary to register itself automatically in all levels of the corporate control system. And therefore System One needs a set of transducers which are analogous to the interoceptors of the body. For a good many kinds of data this problem presents little challenge. For example, wherever production machinery is used, there will (these days) be electrical circuits. These can quite readily be tapped and transduced. If a production machine is actually producing, then the moment when production starts and finishes can be recorded in real time. The rate at which production is going on can also be measured and fed to the control.

Difficulties begin when the machinery is at a standstill, because the control system undoubtedly wishes to know the reason. This may have to be fed in manually according to a code — but that has often been done. Control also requires to know what is being produced, details of order numbers for example, and who is manning the machine. Again all this can be arranged without much difficulty. Perhaps the most readily implemented solution is to use detailed job cards issued by the computer, validated by the foreman, and read back by the computer itself. In short, there are no overwhelming technical problems involved in this transduction, and there is a lot of proprietary equipment on the market which will help. Photo-cells, infra-red cells, load-cells (so like the pressure-sensitive cells in the skin) all provide valid input transducers.

Now the vertebra of System Two, which is the System One controller of subsidiary B, has a set of basic instructions received down transmission line a, together with moment-to-moment amendments and special instructions, which it stands ready to match against the transduced input from the subsidiary. And there lies the critical point. System Two has an initial plan for the assemblage of subsidiaries, and this particular vertebra (1B) has an initial plan for subsidiary B. Thus the 1B controller is able to compare actual performance with this plan as it occurs, and also to modify the plan on receipt of new instructions as they arrive. There is a vast number of reasons why activities in the subsidiary should at all times fail to accord with the original intention, and therefore adjustments have to be made. It is the primary task of System One to compute such adjustments quickly and feed them back to the subsidiary. This is a reflex control action, and it has everything in common, from the point of view of control engineering, with the task of guiding a gun on to its target. The mathematics of the whole business are well known. The process is governed by a set of transfer functions, many of them concerned with negative feedback, of the sort described in Chapter 2.

We ought at once to take note of a very special fact. Thanks to predictive techniques of modern statistical theory, it is possible for the controller (1B) to *anticipate* deflections from the plan and to begin modifying its instructions in advance. There is a sense in which this is obvious and a sense in which it is very surprising. Because we can, within certain limits, measure trends as they occur and compute the probabilities that they will continue, the anticipatory faculty is obviously possible. It happens all the time in servo-engineering, and it happens on the macro-economic scale in marketing. For example, small quantities of a product are at first released to the market. The rate of sale is established, and various measurements are made on the probable effect of advertising, premiums, offers, and so on. As the accelerative effects become known, and as decisions are taken as to the investment in them that ought to be made, the rate of production and distribution of the product is modified to suit a constantly adjusted forecast. All this is rather familiar. But what is surprising about this facility considered as a basic tool of management is that, for the very first time, we are looking at the facts before rather than after they occur. The very best accounting system in use today remains historical in character, though many will object to the pejorative word. Noble attempts have indeed been made to speed up the responses of accounting systems. But history is still history, even if it is recent rather than old. There are many businesses that cannot establish what has happened until months later; even the best organized businesses must wait until data have been recorded and analysed. So there is a lag, and even yesterday's figures or last shift's figures tell us only what we ought to have done today, or this shift, when it is just too late. It is worth making a tremendous effort to burst through the barrier marked 'now', and to make managers concern themselves with what *can* be managed — namely the future, however near — rather than peruse a record of what can be managed no longer — namely the past, however recent. We may learn from that past record of course, but we cannot influence it in retrospect.

This, then, is what the lateral axis, System One, has to do. As we have recently seen, it is also what the lateral axis in the human body has to do. The task becomes impossible if any of the following features of the system are missing. There must be an initial plan. There must be a constant updating of that plan on the central command axis — otherwise the plan is no longer calculated to meet the needs of the organism as a whole. There must be *immediate* recognition of the actual state of affairs; otherwise time-lags are introduced which (the model from control engineering reveals) will send the reflex loop into uncontrolled oscillation. There must, finally, be a way of commanding the subsidiary to update *its* plan to meet whatever difficulties are encountered. It is surely true that the emergency action which the local management is compelled to take in a subsidiary under an orthodox company control system is usually not the best that could be taken from the overall, corporate point of view. There is simply no reason why it should be, because the local management has only the local facts to go on. In an extreme case it may of course start telephoning — but here again it will run into the constraints of the law of requisite variety. Men simply cannot telephone all the other men in the company who may be quite seriously affected by an emergency decision every time there is a slight departure from plan.

Well, System Two can cope with some of these problems. It exists to provide a local interaction between the Systems One of all the subsidiaries. In Figure 21 we see that analogue of the spinal cord, wherein are situated all Systems One;

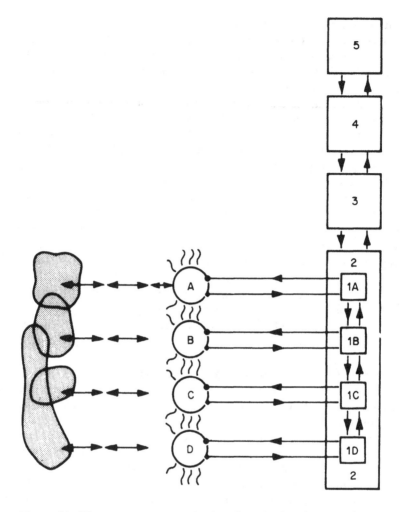

Figure 21. The corporate control of a firm having four subsidiaries, A,B,C, and D, each trading with the other three and with the outside world

and we see moreover how each System One is put into communication with its fellows in order to obviate logical contradiction. all of them must act in concert on the descending line *a* which is giving the orders.

But a mere lack of contradiction between System One controllers is not enough. The snags begin to arise when the control process (Systems One embedded in System Two) is conceived as a dynamic activity. This is where the autonomic system itself comes into play. We have already seen in Figure 21 how System Two forms an analogue of the spinal column. In Figure 22 the neurophysiological autonomic system is added. On the right of the diagram is the analogue of the sympathetic trunk, which links together the vertebral nodes of System Two. On the left of the diagram is the analogue of the parasympathetic set of nerves. We saw something of the behaviour of both these regulatory devices in the last chapter. It is this System Three which controls the stability of the internal environment of the firm, and this it does by providing feedback. Each organ of the body, which we have called the subsidiary of the firm, would be isolated on its lateral axis if it were not for the arrangement of each organ's own controller into a cohesive set of such controllers — which we have called System Two. But System Two itself would hunt about aimlessly if it were not monitored at the higher level of System Three.

Consider first production in the firm, and assume that each of the subsidiaries has a role to play in manufacturing the firm's major set of products. Then, for example, subsidiary B manufactures an output, some of which indeed may be dissipated as directed sales to the outside world (as shown in Figure 22), but some of which is passed on to subsidiary C for further processing. Thereafter, some of this output will be passed on to subsidiary D and so on. Suppose that something goes badly wrong with the production programme in subsidiary C. Its controller, 1C within 2, will attempt to adjust the C plan accordingly. But this may very well be locally impossible, in the sense that the contract to acquire supplies from subsidiary B may have to be varied, and the contract to make various deliveries to subsidiary D cannot be met. Controller 1C within 2 must inform controllers 1B and 1D, and all three of them will try and change their plans to suit each other. Needless to say, the trouble may reverberate from B to A, from D to E, and so on.

The autonomic system (sympathetic) in the right of the diagram is monitoring all this. It uses a higher-order language than System Two, because it has to discuss System Two's behaviour. If its job is to stabilize the production environment of the firm it must supply feedbacks at the various levels which will tend to damp down the oscillations caused by the replanning adjustments. Even so, what is now going on is a frenetic activity, and one would see this again in the case where the higher control centres in the firm called for a major productive effort in order to meet some kind of crisis. If that happens, all the subsidiaries will know about it (look at the diagram). Their System One responses will go straight into the System Two computers, where they will be locally rationalized, and be passed on to the control centres of System Three through the central (somatic) system. But the same information will also rise up the sympathetic trunk, and will reach the control centre by another route. The stimulatory feedbacks work here so that there is a right-hand loop of *excitatory* activity going on which is trying to meet the call of the leadership.

But suppose all this leads to too much strain in the subsidiaries. There are many ways of monitoring what is happening there to protect the firm from

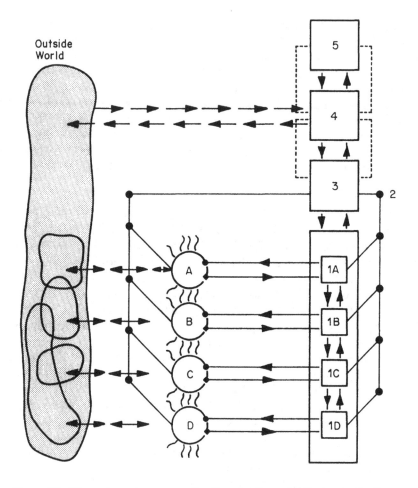

Figure 22. The automatic system of a firm having subsidiaries A, B, C,
and D

risk. Productivity indices measuring the rate of production may rise above the
upper control limits normally in force; the level of overtime worked may rise
dangerously too; inspection procedures may become unstable, because
everyone is in too much of a hurry. Such signs of undue pressure will be
registered in the autonomic (parasympathetic) network, shown on the left of
the diagram. These data too will be fed up to the control centres of System
Three. The result must be to damp down activity, in the cause of safety, so that
an *inhibitory* loop is going on round the left-hand side of the diagram. It is then
up to the autonomic system as a whole to balance the excitatory and inhibitory
pictures to produce an overall internal stability. And it is certainly up to
System Three to report upwards, through System Four to System Five —
where the policy was formulated.

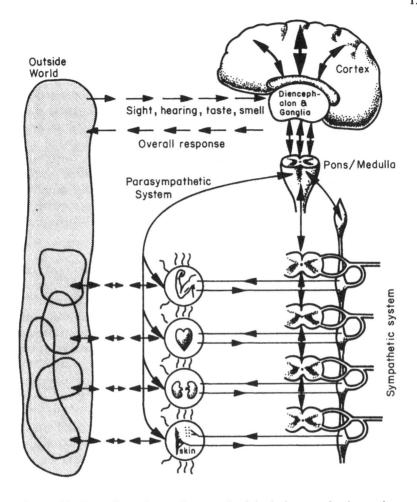

Figure 23. Two dimensions of neurophysiological control: the main vertical command system (somatic) and the sympathetic and parasympathetic systems (automatic)

This account is directly comparable to the account of control of the heart or of respiration given in Chapter 8. It will be useful to refresh our view of the basic neurophysiological method by looking at Figure 23 and comparing it with Figure 22.

Now consider. I personally may formulate a policy, using my cortex, to run for a bus. I do this on the basis of estimates of distances and speeds, and a rapid forecasting calculation which suggests I may be able to manage it. My body goes into action. Relevant organs, for instance my heart and my lungs, are instructed (System 5 to 4 to 3 to 2 to 1) to increase their activity drastically.

The autonomic system, number Three, sits in the middle of the procedure monitoring the effects. The right-hand loop, the sympathetic, supervises the interaction of the organs and the flow of adrenalin. But the left-hand loop, the parasympathetic, is watching for signs of strain. It may well be that I am physically incapable of catching this bus. The inibitory loop operates to save me from internal physical disaster. Even so, System Three has got its work cut out to hold my internal environment stable, and the next level of the hierarchy must take a hand. The general output of the vertical axis so far is again monitored and switched by System Four to inform the cortex, where the plan was formulated, that matters are getting out of hand. And here we see the topmost computing sub-system of all engaging in exactly the same type of monitoring process that we saw at the lowest level. There was a plan; inputs are arriving indicating that the plan cannot be maintained — and therefore System Five must alter the plan.

This time, of course, it is not possible to call on further reserves by passing the message higher up the chain. We have reached the limit. and this is the peculiar role of consciousness for the human being. We say that we *decide* to let the bus go. In computing terms, the brain has re-evaluated the original plan against a set of modifying inputs, and determined a mismatch. It is exactly the same in the firm. The board deliberates on the strength of the information it has and formulates a plan — say one calling for a major company effort. This is a System Five activity, suitably fed by all the available information arriving from the exteroceptors and the interoceptors through System Four, where the staff work is done. It is System Four also which will re-sort the top-level decision, and relay its consequential commands down the vertical and along the lateral axes. System Three, the autonomic, will try to see that this plan is implemented. As long as it still appears possible to carry out the board's instructions *within physiological limits,* System Three will continue the task, continually reporting upwards as well. If the plan turns out to be impossible after all, it is up to the board to down-grade its original intention.

In all such activity of the firm, with its quintuple-level controls, the constant contrary pulls of internal and external motivations may be observed. If the internal motivations are loosely equated with production and the external motivations with sales the point is well made. There are clearly two criteria in action here, one seeking to maintain the stability of the internal environment, and the other the stability of interaction with the external environment. That is, the production director is supposed to maximize the use of his assets, and the sales director is supposed to satisfy his clients. From the production man's standpoint, the task is to make the things he can most easily make in the most balanced way, thereby minimizing costs and maximizing outputs for a given set of capital assets and material and human resources. The sales director is in principle willing to place any kind of strain on the internal organism in order to achieve a profitable sale or to open up a profitable market. There is no reason whatever, despite the pre-established harmony of the natural universe, why these two objectives should coincide. Normally they will not coincide exactly, although it may be noted that *in general* lower costs enhance the chance of sales, while an active market provides a degree of production freedom.

The major control task in the firm, as far as its existing activity (which we began by calling technology A) is concerned, is to bring these two into accord. Sometimes production will have to make a concession (if costs go up through using a somewhat inefficient production route in order to meet a delivery promise). Sometimes sales must make a concession (it has to take a longer delivery promise on some items in order that the cost of overtime should not exceed all bounds). If full-scale scientific method is applied in the firm, we shall find that System Three is the centre of a major resource-allocation procedure. Linear programming techniques, or better still dynamic programming techniques, belong at this level — and operate to this end.

Well, that is what control systems are for. The quintuple hierarchic system envisioned here is supposed to do it as efficiently as possible. So far we have discussed, from a senior (that is, corporate) management standpoint the three lowest levels of the five. They constitute autonomic management, a name chosen from neurophysiology rather than business lore to designate what must happen within the firm to ensure its internal stability without much top-level intervention. It has been tried in the body and it works.

CHAPTER TEN

The biggest switch

We have arrived at the point where the internal stability of the organism is ensured by the three lowest level systems — a control apparatus summed up as far as this is concerned by the term autonomics. And we have seen how this set of systems is fed by a vertical command structure originating intentions (as distinct from reflex responses) within the 'thinking chamber' of System Five. The final part of this book will deal with that fifth-level global operation of the corporate body. This leaves the problem of System Four, which is the great linking mechanism between volitional and autonomic control. It is the biggest switch of the whole organization.

A switch is a device, or a whole mechanism, which transfers signals from one part of the system to another. We have already met many switches, in both the physiological and the managerial aspects of this book. They are not simple flick-over devices, such as those which operate the electric light, in either of these contexts. We examined their nature rather carefully in Part I, and called them algedonodes. At that time, we were looking at artefacts made up of wood and brass strips. Now we are ready to pick up the story in terms of neurophysiology.

The many receptors which activate the nervous system, like the receptors which notify machines, men, and managers of change, are themselves switches of some kind. These receptors are attached to some sort of input cable — which they make alert, or along which they propagate a signal. When this cable length runs out the input signal would be extinguished if it were not switched into another cable length. As we have seen, the neurons in the body work like this, passing the signal on from one nerve cell (plus its cable length, the axon) to another at a synapse. We need to look a little more closely at all this switchgear.

Engineers and computer men may think of a switch as a device which passes on, and very likely amplifies, a signal. That is, the arriving signal *excites* the system beyond the switch. In the body this happens too, but the second possibility arises that the signal will *inhibit* rather than excite. This is an extremely important mechanism, because of the problem of overloading which would otherwise clog all the channels and switches further on. Much earlier we saw that the theorems of information theory require a greater capacity in the channels than the variety of the input system. In the body, this law is obeyed — indeed there is ample provision to meet the point. The maximum rate of discharge of receptor organs lies in the bracket of 100-200 pulses a second. But the nerve channels themselves can cope with 300-400. Even then, we cannot afford to excite the entire nervous system with every input. Thus whenever data transmission occurs in the nervous system there is a dual mechanism, in which excitation is balanced against inhibition, rather than a single firing device as might be supposed. The same is certainly true in management, where more input signals may well be extinguished than are transferred and amplified at any switch. But it would be a mistake to think of this as a 'go/no-go' device. There is a more subtle mechanism here, as there was in the algedonode.

Consider the most typical neurophysiological switch, the synapse. There is an actual gap, called the synaptic cleft, which has to be bridged between one neuron and the next. In excitation it seems that the action potential — the electrical bleep traversing a nerve, which may be traced on an oscilloscope — arrives at the cleft, causing the release of a transmitter chemical which crosses the gap. This substance depolarizes the membrane on the other side, regenerating the action potential in the second fibre. But another fibre, working to the same target neuron, may release an inhibitory transmitter. The effect here is hyperpolarization, which offsets the effect of the first, excitatory, impulse. Alternatively, the inhibitory message may be *pre*-synaptic; it hits the excitatory fibre itself, and nullifies (or at least reduces) the discharge of the excitatory transmitter. However the network of dendrites carrying these alternative messages is arranged, the effect on the neuron across the synaptic cleft is some kind of summation of them all. Whether the neuron changes state or not depends on an electrical threshold which, by this summation, is or is not exceeded, just as happened in the algedonode.

So a synapse, or for that matter any other switch, such as a receptor or an effector, or a complex affair such as a ganglion, works to a threshold — and that threshold is chemically determined. The levels of potassium and sodium inside and outside the cell membrane, in particular, determine at any given time what the threshold is. Thus does the threshold change. In fact, the whole mechanism (which is only recently at all well understood) is very beautiful, and the scale on which it works is almost unbelievably fine and precise. Surely it is worth a paragraph of digression, just for the joy of it.

The synaptic cleft, which is the gap in the switch, is only 200 Angström units wide — and an Angström unit is one ten-millionth of a millimetre. The synaptic knob itself, where the nerve impulse arrives, contains tiny vesicles of the transmitter substance mentioned — and one or two of these vesicles burst when the electrical pulse comes in. The little package of transmitters is so tiny that it contains perhaps only 10,000 *molecules* and that is enough to change the permeability of the membrane on the other side of the gap for just about a thousandth of a second. It is long enough to let the ions (which are charged particles) through the membrane, where they determine whether or not to regenerate the impulse in the second length of nerve. Now the pores which let the inhibitory ions through are (obviously) very small — they are in fact 1·2 times the diameter of the hydrated potassium ion. The mesh is very accurate indeed. Ions of 1·14 go through; ions of 1·24 are blocked. This means that sodium ions (which are excitatory) cannot get through, because they are too big. It is fascinating to know that the pores of inhibitory synapses are always of this same size — as determined by the size of the ions — regardless of species. They are the same for the whole vertebrate kingdom, and it now turns out that the same mechanism works for molluscs too. On the excitatory side, as may be expected, the synapse membrane pores are twice the size — so the sodium ions go through freely. Finally, and assuming that the net effect of excitation and inhibition is indeed to regenerate the impulse in the next nerve, these tiny chemical changes are sufficient to amplify the transmitted impulse a hundred times.

Here is an algedonode *par excellence*. It is analogous to the managerial switch which provides a 'go/no-go' answer, but whose decision is governed by a conflicting set of excitatory and inhibitory inputs, and a threshold value which is variable. It is *not* analogous, however, to any formal management information system, computerized or not, that I have ever seen. But it should be. Groups of human managers work in just this way.

We speak about selective changes, depending on conditions in the locality of particular neurons, or particular management groups, in applying our cybernetic model at this level. And yet there are more general, possibly quite general, ways known to the body and to the firm for changing the activity of the nervous system — upwards to excitability, or downwards in depression. The hormones themselves (and the transmitter substances are hormones) may be supplied more or less plentifully. But drugs especially of every kind have elevating and depressing effects. These are easily recognized in behaviour, but they are initiated on a micro-scale — precisely by intervention at the switches. They are threshold-changes of the algedonode.

Nicotine, for example, is a ganglionic stimulating drug, and smokers enjoy the excitatory effects. But, as with so many physiological mechanisms, the picture is very complicated. This is basically because the pharmacological effect of drugs varies on different parts of the nervous system, and because simultaneous changes in threshold in all manner of physiological switches often produce a total effect which works in a contrary direction. See how this works with nicotine, and bear in mind the counterpart mechanism in human groups.

Nicotine excites the sympathetic cardiac ganglia and paralyses the parasympathetic component to produce the typical rise in heart-rate that smokers know. But in another phase it may stimulate the parasympathetic and paralyse the sympathetic to produce a slowing effect — in nicotine poisoning, and perhaps in death. Threshold, complex networks, dosages — all affect the situation, and this is why it is so difficult to prescribe treatment to correct elation or depression in patients who show either symptom to excess. What is meant by 'another phase' in the penultimate sentence is perhaps best understood by considering alcohol. In the long run, this — our 'socially acceptable' — drug is going to lay you out; it is a depressant. But its first-phase action is to excite. This is a behavioural outcome and a behavioural paradox. Inside the body the effects are consistent, and there is a no systemic paradox. This is because the excited state is produced by the *depression* of *inhibitory* systems. It is an important point; the physiological result is exactly like the grammatical result of using a double negative.

In general, the activity of the whole body may be excited by pharmacological intervention at the switchgear, so that people become excited, or more excited, or positively euphoric. Beyond that state come tremors, and then convulsions. Alternatively, depressant drugs bring sedation, or tranquility, or trance — and beyond that a state of general anaesthesia, and then coma. Death may result in either case at the end of the line, and that would be quite explicitly because the interference is so gross that the stabilizing mechanisms already discussed can no longer work.

This is the way that the basic switchgear operates. As was said just now it represents a set of mechanisms which we understand how to copy (witness the algedonode), and which *is* copied, rather closely, in human decision-taking, especially by the social group. Yet it is not reduplicated in automotive systems driven by computers, although that would be perfectly possible. What may not yet be possible, and this is something to which we ought to be alert, is to understand (let alone reduplicate) physiological control mechanisms which are not straightforwardly mediated by the nervous system as described. No one yet knows whether there really exists a set of phenomena such as are usually bundled together under the term 'ESP'. Extra-Sensory Perception may be a reality; but 'ESP' must turn out to be a misleading term. If we *sense* something, then there must be *sensors* — we cannot by definition sense something extra-sensory. Still, we should not be captious; the term obviously relates to a supposed mechanism outside or beyond receptors which we do know are there — and even so cannot fully account for. These are the sensors which deal in external chemical messengers.

We know most about this mechanism in insects, for it seems that chemical messengers, rather than Maeterlinck's 'spirit of the hive', make insect societies work. If I questioned the possible existence of chemical messages flowing within a managerial group, I should be oddly regarded. One thinks in terms of cigars and after-shave lotion, rather than the smell of decision in a board-room. And yet it is common folklore that animals 'smell fear' in human beings. There is now scientific backing for this — and more besides. Consider a brief note on the work of Dr Wiener. It relates to rats rather than men, but they are higher animals, and the evidence is pretty striking.

When thirty female rats are put together, without males, in a cage, their entire oestral activity is wholly upset. The normal cycle (five days in a rat) is chaotically deranged, and there are pseudo-pregnancies. But everything returns to normal as soon as a male joins the cage. A genuinely pregnant rat closeted with a male other than the 'father' for a quarter of an hour a day soon resorbs the embryo. That all this happens due to the smell receptors is established. The presence of male urine alone will cause resorption, but if the female olfactory bulb is excised nothing happens. Olfactory sensors, however, do not account for the whole behaviour. Equally, we humans may well *receive* olfactory impressions during a board meeting of which we are not conscious, and of whose subsequent passage through the neural anastomotic reticulum and ultimate effects we know nothing at all.

With these passing thoughts, which are included to show how nature deals with its problems of generating requisite variety, let us return to the mechanisms we better understand. Recall how we have located typical algedonodes, which are theoretical structures of our own invention, at various levels in the total system. Receptor end-organs themselves, synapses further up the line, ganglia with their own thresholds, and the great reflex centres inside the spinal cord, all these — like the logical elements, the neurons, of the cortex itself — seem to operate as algedonodes. The biggest switch of all, System Four, seems to operate like this too, but it is incredibly complex.

Perhaps the best way to tackle this is in terms of the excitation and inhibition which we know we must expect in any algedonode. For some version of this pair of antithetic influences in the switch is necessarily required to cope with the concept of conditional probability and the mechanics of the changing threshold. The important point is that this pair of influences exists in a different dimension from that which carries messages (we saw all about metasystems in Part I, and have watched them in action throughout the hierarchic structures described in Part II). That is why we called the cybernetic paradigm of the required switch an algedonode, meaning a pain-pleasure modulated probabilistic switch.

Clearly neurophysiologists themselves would not care to have the pain-pleasure circuits (which have their own nerves) mixed up with the inhibition-excitation biochemistry of the synapse (just discussed); still less would they equate either mechanism with the sleep-arousal controls to be mentioned next. Then what is my excuse? I want to distinguish sharply between the way in which the body achieves results and the logic of the results it achieves. Neurophysiological descriptions in this book are there because they are interesting, and we can learn from them. The whole point about cybernetics as a science is that it should abstract the laws behind the control system it studies, and make them generally available. When I call the algedonode a cybernetic paradigm, I mean that it is a theoretic mechanism which accounts for the body's switchgear, and that it can be modelled in a management information and decision system under automation. Now the messages passing through an algedonode are either to be 'toned up' (perhaps to the point of acceleration and the whizz-bang declaration of their indomitable existence) or 'toned down' (perhaps to the point of extinction). In the paradigm, this means raising or lowering the conditional probability that the switch actually transmits the message. This is the effect of excitation-and-inhibition, as it is in another situation of pleasure-and-pain.

So is it also true of the waking-and-sleeping modes of the entire organization. There are kinds of wakefulness; there are kinds of sleep; there is, in general, attention-and-inattention. Now the cerebral cortex, or the board of the firm, or the cabinet of the government, is busy thinking. Therefore it does not wish to be disturbed. Therefore not too much information needs to flow up the vertical axis to engulf it. If it is actually asleep (which may be quite a useful analogue of its doing something else altogether, such as 'unwinding'), it will turn over the whole organism's operation to the autonomic system. It will effectively stop short at the third level up — System Three is in command. Neurophysiology has much to tell us about this.

In brief, it is that System Three, from the corporate standpoint, is a naturally sleepy or inattentive controller. It is wholly alert *downwards* — all those autonomic functions must be attended to. But its own major controllers of corporate, that is *upward*, awareness are essentially inhibitors. If this were not so, the higher levels of control would be inundated with information about the big toe and so forth — information quite unworthy of strategic or policy-level consideration. Well, System Three almost overdoes it, because of the sleep centres in the pons and medulla. These, called the 'raphe nuclei', are sited on the midline of the brain stem. Without their systems of neurons (packed with serotonin) we would suffer from perpetual insomnia. So, if we continue to conduct our control analysis upwards, we are likely to shut off the higher centres (Systems Four and Five) by going to sleep.

The same phenomenon, as usual, may be observed in management systems. The results of delegation to autonomous units, even when these are re-centralized in corporate committee structures at the autonomic level, are ignorance and complacency at the top. Many managing directors, prime ministers, presidents and dictators have found themselves cocooned in this way, cut off from meaningful activities. The organism is carrying on quite cheerfully on its own; the higher authorities are doing something different altogether; the enterprise as a whole is asleep. If the neurophysiological analogy holds, as a matter of fact, what the top brass is doing is (probably) dreaming.

It is, I think, quite helpful to regard this as a natural state of affairs. This means to say that all is well with the organism except that it is asleep — therefore the problem is to awaken it, to alert it, to arouse it from somnolence to activity. If we think of the organism (body or firm) from the top down, then the 'natural state of affairs' would be frenetic activity. The problem of stopping the autonomic system from going crazy as a result is perhaps conceptually more difficult. But either way, thinking about it upwards or downwards, System Four has to do the switching.

The positive solution which the body has found is a special and definite arousal mechanism which alerts the higher brain centres to quash the upward inattentiveness natural to System Three at the lower brain levels. This is the ascending reticular formation, an anastomotic reticulum which carries the vital management-by-exception information up through all the autonomic controllers and the sleep centres, and out through the highest structure of System Three — the mesencephalon. At this point the Biggest Switch must operate. Is the arousing of the cortex, of the higher management, to occur or not?

The neurophysiological answer to this question is immensely complicated — and perhaps this is in itself the most important lesson to learn. *There are many routes to the cortex.* We have seen how the main route, bringing sensory information straight up the afferent input system to the sensory cortex, tends to be inhibited by many systems — so that we are not driven crazy by an arbitrary bombardment of stimuli. Then there is an obvious risk that vital arousal information will be suppressed. Now the ascending reticular system receives collateral fibres from the afferent input system — which means that the higher centres again stand to be alerted by information that has already been filtered out by the major sensory filters. This collateral information seems to be distributed around the brain in a variety of ways, impinging on the cortex from various directions, having been re-filtered by various systems. The keen importance of a multi-criteria examination of available inputs claiming managerial attention receives the brain's testimony in this way.

The hypothalamus is the floor of the third ventricle, and very much the link between the third and fourth systems of the model under discussion. It is the highest element in System Three, or the lowest element in System Four. We met the hypothalamus before; it is a major mediator of homeostasis, and therefore the most senior regulator of the autonomic system. Moreover, the hypothalamus exerts a major influence on the endocrine glands — and this has much to do with what we normally call 'the emotions'. There are other features of the cerebral map in this area which are involved in the whole business of arousal. The hippocampus is heavily implicated, and so is the mamillary body. All these structures are closely packed in the centre of the brain, and there seem to be many feedbacks between them. (Remember from Part I that control mechanisms in general become functions of their feedback rather than their input as soon as the regulators begin to operate.)

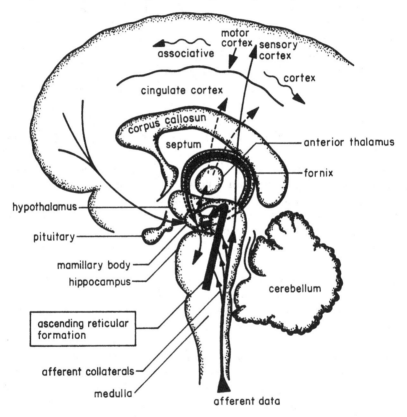

Figure 24. The brain's handling of arousal information by systems distinct from ordinary afferent input (compare Figure 13)

At any rate, the arousal information carried by the ascending reticular system eventually reaches the cortex (if at all) through the complex mediation of System Four. In the brain it is switched through the structures just mentioned, through the anterior thalamus, and on up through the cingulate cortex which lies below the cortical surface level and above the corpus callosum. Check through the route in Figure 24. The idea is not to learn the names of the parts, but to understand the necessary *richness* of the mechanism. There are many many lateral channels in the cortex, so this information can be (as it were) 'reviewed' by circuits handling both conditioned and unconditioned behaviour, 'compared' (as it were) with other information by what is known as the associative cortex, or mobilized for direct action — such as fight or flight — by the motor cortex itself. This is the command centre of volition, the part of the brain at the highest level that triggers action using the descending command chain of the vertical axis, right down to the body's extremities.

So our biggest switch of all really has a great deal to do. It is right on the vertical command axis linking the thinking chamber of the whole organism to its corporate embodiment, and constitutes a ramified collection of algedonodes for switching *downwards* all of the volitional requirements of the brain. Equally it switches *upwards* all of the information required by the cortex to run the body — including appropriate representations (duly filtered) of autonomic function which is itself commanded from lower down. Next, it captures all data relating to the environment through whichever senses, filters them, and redistributes relevant information both upwards and downwards for use by all the other control echelons. Finally it operates what we have called the algedonic system itself — the pain-pleasure, wake-sleep arousal mechanisms, which have their special nerves and their collateral channels distinct from the normal afferent and efferent pathways.

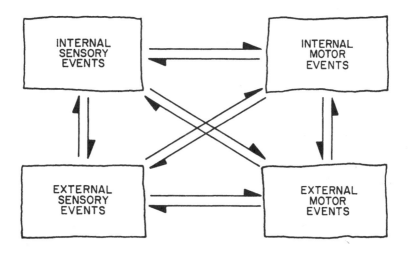

Figure 25. Every corporate management (of the body or the firm) must maintain continuous compatibility over all six couplings of these four major areas of concern

In *Principles of Self-Organization* (proceedings of a cybernetic symposium held in 1960 — see Bibliography) I offered a mathematical model of this arrangement, and tried to show how it is applicable to the operation of the firm. The model depends on the following key notions. Both the sensory and the motor activities of the brain (which, remember, have their highest — that is, System Five — representation in distinct and different locations of the cerebral cortex) handle accounts of both internal and external events. Organisms, whether bodies or firms, maintain a clear distinction between all four groups. To muddle internal and external affairs, or to confuse passive sensibility with sensations of action in regard to either, means a major pathological condition. Then the switching centre at the thalmic level (here called System Four) has an over-riding task — to match, without confusing them, the current state of all four groups. Contemplation of Figure 25 will show the sense in which all six possible couplings of the four groups of brain activities must be internally compatible if the organism is to operate integrally in relation to the changing states of the world.

In Chapter 2 we discussed the nature of ultrastability, which is just the concept needed now. It was devised by Ross Ashby specifically to explain, also in mathematical terms, the nature of physiological homeostasis. And that is the problem we are considering here. Putting the matter in its simplest form, we consider just one coupling of the sort depicted in Figure 25. There is a set of states which each of the two groups of activities may take up. Since each group is itself a highly complex organization, involving huge numbers of events, and since each event might take on any one of a huge number of forms, we have a typical system of proliferating variety. A *state* of the system is defined as a particular allocation of forms to events, given a particular configuration of events. Taking the first of the two systems then (and large, ramified, and proliferating though it be) we may picture its state at this precise moment thus:

•

This dot stands for a unique state of the whole, which is to say that everything characterizing the system ·has been specified. A different state would be specified by a different dot. Thus we may imagine a system with a phase-space comprising millions of dots, i.e. any state possible in the system has a dot which represents it. Suppose now that a change is effected within the system. Then the systemic state will be indicated by a new dot which (we may imagine) lights up, whereas the dot previously lit up goes out. Then the apparent movement of light from dot 1 to dot 2 will be the *trajectory* of the state-variable of the system.

Every event changes the systemic state, therefore there is a continuous trajectory. But we may distinguish between states which support homeostasis within this one system, and those which do not. Then let us collect the dots representing the stable state into a group and enclose them in a circle. Now the trajectory of the state-variable ought to describe a movement *within* this circle. If the trajectory moves outside, then the system is out of homeostatic control.

When two such systems are coupled together, the concept of their *joint* homeostasis (which is the equilibrial condition of the metasystem comprising the two systems) may be invoked — and a meta-control operation may be envisaged. It works as a self-vetoing system, and is depicted in Figure 26. We suppose firstly that each of the original systems is operating under local homeostasis, so that the trajectory of each state-variable is within its own circle. Then the messages travelling down lines A and B do not attempt to define the state of each system from moment to moment (the channels could not have requisite variety); they simply say 'homeostasis'. This means that wherever one system impinges on the other, it recognizes a match which is normal to their coexistence. In the diagram, a few of these matched states are indicated by thin lines.

Well, this allows the two systems to communicate with each other about apparently elaborate states of affairs without disobeying the law of requisite variety, and without offending against the theorems of information theory where channel capacities are concerned. What the mathematical model really proposed was that each system could *learn* about the other, not in terms of understanding all about it, but in terms of recognizing it *as being in normal operation*. Then what is to happen when one of the systems is not normally operating, when its own trajectory leaves a homeostatic state, and when — consequently — a mismatch occurs between aspects of the two systems which impinge? The answer is that each system acts (having of course requisite variety) as controller of the other.

This act of meta-control is supposed to work like this. Instead of the A message declaring 'homeostasis', the A message reads 'non-homeostasis' as soon as the trajectory in A leaves its circle. This message causes the second system to change its own state, in a way indicated to A by changes in the relationships of events common to both systems. The effect of this change on A (the two systems being coupled) is to cause its state to change again, and therefore to alter the trajectory in A. This process is iterated round the meta-control loop for as long as it takes to get A's state-variable back to 'homeostasis' and all is still again.

The first thing to note is that the restabilization of A under B's meta-control may take a very long time. Indeed, if A goes a little wild as an internal system, it may be losing control of its own homeostatic equilibrium at a rate faster than this apparently random technique of trial-and-error government can operate to restore equilibrium. The analogous situation in the firm, and particularly in national control systems, should be thought about. The second

146

difficulty is that in changing its own state, as a means of supplying A with control variety, B might inadvertently knock its own state-variable out of its circle — thereby losing control of its own internal equilibrium, and originating a 'non-homeostasis' B message. Then both systems are out of control — a classic *hunting* situation.

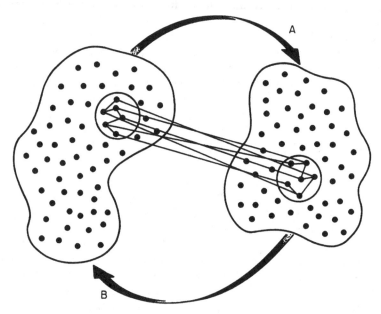

Figure 26. Ashby-type self-vetoing homeostasis operating between any two areas of Figure 25. Each dot represents a total configuration of the system; dots contained in circles represent satisfactory states. The two systems are in equilibrium, because the trajectories of each (thick lines) remain within the circles

Ashby's original theory of the homeostat appeared vulnerable to these two possibilities. I personally spent many years experimenting with the problem in three sorts of system. Firstly, there was the mathematical model (the sort of thing called a 'paper machine'). Next there were actual machines devised for the purpose (a bit like the wood-and-brass machine of Part I). Thirdly, there were social systems within the firm. In all three manifestations, the problems seemed to revolve around learning. There is never requisite variety, never adequate channel capacity, and never enough time, to reach homeostasis at this meta-control level simply by inducing variations, although *formally* the process ought to work in the end. I learned how to modify all three experimental approaches from the study of Waddington's work in genetics — for evolution has exactly the same problems in the rate at which adaptation can possibly occur. Random mutation, as first proposed by Darwin, ought to work; but again my calculations (see *Decision and Control*) showed that such an evolutionary mechanism was short of variety, of channel capacity, and, above all, of time. Despite the aeons of evolutionary time available, there does not seem to have been enough to evolve the well-adapted creatures alive today by a simple mutate-and-see-if-you-survive evolutionary kit. There has then, to be a further mechanism to do with the facilitation of survival-favourable trends and the extinction of time-wasting, if not actually damaging, development circuits.

Where Waddington spoke of an 'epigenetic landscape' in his evolutionary theory to deal with the problem, I inserted the algedonode into the theory of the anastomotic reticulum.[1] In both cases the idea is that the movement of a trajectory (as here defined) changes the conditional probabilities along its path that this path will be used again. The criterion is of course the speed of success in adaptation — what engineers might call minimizing the relaxation time of the system. If the trajectory can find a natural return route to its circle, then this pathway will in future be facilitated. If it moves into an area of its phase-space from which return proves to be dangerously difficult and lengthy, then the probabilities change so that it is less and less likely to enter that area again. This means that the apparently unstructured phase-space of the system, to which we have so far admitted only one organized component — the original circle — will gradually grow in organizational structure, for other sets of dots than those indicating homeostasis will be grouped together in a self-organizing way and will be marked — designated — by their routes 'home', and the difficulties to be expected in realizing them.

These notions were incorporated in the 1960 mathematical model, and various experiments with machines and in firms were conducted too. The idea is to use the biggest switch to run this system across all six couplings of the four main groups of top-level control activity (remember Figure 25). Thus each group is held in control by the other three, and there is a matching process across the six couplings tantamount to a learning process which happens in synchrony. More follows on this topic in Part III. Meanwhile, there is one thing more to add.

In so far as the algedonodes really work, in so far then as the individual systems rapidly converge on both internal stability and corporate ultrastability, in so far as recognition and matching occur, so that organization extends across the intervening anastomotic reticulum, the whole switch is in danger of losing its flexibility and selectivity. It will become set in its ways. We see this happening in every kind of social situation: it leads to stereotyped behaviour, to taboos, to a lack of adaptivity as an outcome of too facile an adaptation. We know about it within evolution, too, in the over-specialization of species which leads to their becoming extinct. We see it in the firm which 'really knows its business' to the extent that it can no longer recognize either the new technological challenge or that the business is changing.

[1] *The Strategy of the Genes.* See Bibliography.

Then return to the brain from which this model is drawn, where we can at once see the point. For we actually said that the brain would be sleeping as a result of all this filtering and self-regulation; we also said that it would become inattentive as a result of too much organizational delegation and self-organization. We have also learned that the answer lies with a collateral afferent system, a special development of algedonic filters, and a multi-path redistribution of arousal messages to System Five. It was called the ascending reticular formation, and it is the core of System Four.

Now we may ask how this arousal system actually works. It is not difficult to perceive a formal managerial analogue for the ascending collateral pathways: we should need to siphon off information from standard reporting systems, and to process the data through special statistical importance filters as described in earlier chapters. Instead of collecting aggregate information about the parts of the company for further aggregation directed to the simple presentation of a company over-view at the top, we should be highly selective. The aggregation arrangement must continue in some form, of course, as it does in the body — and must in the firm to meet the requirements of general management and indeed of the Companies Act. But the arousal system would measure statistical non-conformity, on the basis of probability theory, at the source of the trouble wherever it occurred. Synapses would then pass these special data on, acting as algedonodes at every stage, until System Four operated in its biggest switch capacity to alert the appropriate people or bodies within top management. These would themselves need to be specially organized to handle arousal input. They would have special powers . . .

To do precisely what? How do the ascending reticular system and its fifth-level reactions in the cortex change things to obtain a radically new mode of behaviour in the body? The answer comes in two stages. First of all, they must intervene quickly and drastically in the tonicity of the corporate body. The tone of the body or its organs is a measure of its tension, and therefore of its preparedness to act fast. When we sleep, muscle tone falls off so that limbs are limp and the musculature at the back of the neck is flaccid. Alerting the organism means an immediate pumping up of tone, again by a special arrangement whereby hormones are made available to activate all the feedback loops which are concerned with attentiveness, to change the thresholds of synapses and neurons, and so forth. In management situations we can see what this means, but we know that the speed of response is mostly far too slow. In the production context, an activating system usually works well in the presence of something like catastrophe. After all, if expensive and dangerous plant has blown up or fallen down, men and managers will be called from their beds. In the ultimate survival situation for a board of directors, too, such as a takeover bid ruthlessly advanced, action may be taken very quickly. Short of such bizarre threats, however, the arousal mechanism in managerial and government situations of algedonic character may take months to become active. It is mostly too late, and formal procedures are needed to change this situation. What this amounts to is that there *is* an arousal system in management, but that its thresholds are fixed at such high levels that action is triggered only when the emergency is nearly over for good or ill.

Then the second part of the answer is to note the real meaning, at the abstract level of cybernetic thinking, of a change in tone as drastic as all this. It is a *reprogramming* of the control system. That means a switching out of one control mode and the switching in of a different one. It is too facile to say that various activities in the corporate government must be increased, that reactions will be faster, that there should be more adrenalin or less inhibition: all these comparatives propose a change of rate. That concept suffices when we think of the need to adjust on-going behaviour to changing circumstances. But in arousal, and in general algedonic situations, the rate of change involved is so steep that it is more convenient to think of it as a step-function. Now if that entails reprogramming, there is clearly no time available to embark on experimental programme modifications. There needs to be a separate programme all ready, which can be selected in short order and used.

Observable changes in the electrical activity of the brain at the moment of arousal support this description. Moreover, what has been learnt by control engineers in the context of elaborate systems, particularly in space science, supports it too. The guidance system which successfully carries a rocket on a space cruise is switched out when the voyage nears its end, and a terminal guidance system is switched in. More closely analogous to the subject of this discussion would be a 'crisis' programme switched in to supersede a 'normal running' programme in any piece of automation, however humble. There are many examples. Think for instance of the prescribed drills left behind by manufacturers for intervening in the control system of a central heating installation or even a motor car. They are artefacts of ascending reticular performance.

Probably the most obvious analogue of these arrangements in management is found in civil government as a precaution against emergency. If an epidemic reaches certain proportions a 'yellow warning' or a 'red alert' may be issued — precisely to reprogramme the medical services to deal with an atypical state of the system. We must consider in the next part of the book how to build such arrangements into Systems Four for quite general management purposes.

THE USE OF THE MODEL

Summary of Part Three

As before, it would be a good idea to recapitulate on Part Two by reading the summary which began it, before starting this analysis of the next piece of text. Of course the second summary incorporates advice to read the first *summary.*

The aim now is to exploit the model and our understanding of it to say as much as possible as crisply as possible about the regulation of that viable system — the enterprise. In a way this is the start of the book, for this Part contains the whole (just as we have learned to expect). But it seems likely that a reader starting here, without sharing in the insights of the model or the creation of the language in which to think about it, would have no more than a vague idea of what it means.

Chapter Eleven begins by laying out the corporate model as developed, using as few lines as possible. As we look at Figure 27, however, we should feel supported by the richness of the concepts which went into its gradual development. Just as drawings conveying optical illusions compel us to see first one meaning and then another in the picture, we may see here the living body with its unceasing flow of regulatory messages suddenly replaced in the mind's eye by the firm in all its activity. Anyone used to other kinds of organization, who has been thinking about the relevance of the model to them while reading, should be able to switch in mental pictures of those other viable systems too.

We go on to work out some rules for the operation of the system from the Divisional point of view, noting the main danger points, and then ask how to quantify the messages which say what is going on. Next, in Chapter Twelve, come similar notes on the operation of the whole system: One-Two-Three. All this should by now be easy to understand, because the pieces of the cybernetic jig-saw are being slotted into place over a 'crib' — the picture of the firm as we know it already, which in so many ways actually works (although it is not usually described) like this.

But in Chapters Thirteen and Fourteen the reading experience is likely to be very different. They deal with Systems Four and Five respectively, and in both cases I am proposing very novel ways of interpreting the cybernetics of the model in terms of the firm. There is good reason for this. In most firms System

Four is a fiasco — because it is not recognized for what it is or what it should be doing, and because the capabilities of management science and the available computing technology are not understood. So I have invented this version of a company's System Four, as guided by the model. The examples given are exceedingly simple, but they actually work. Simple or not they have proved to enrich the understanding of those few who have actually used them.

As far as System Five (Chapter Fourteen) is concerned, where we finally reach the top direction of the firm, I have no treatise to offer on the total role of general management. This book is firstly about the structure *of organizations — and when one has identified the suite of rooms 'where the buck stops' there is no more to be said about that — but secondly it is about the* process *of regulation. The most important change that has come over the process of top direction in recent years is the replacement of autocratic by collegiate authority. On this matter there is much to say, and two new cybernetic models are developed.*

The first is a brain model of the 'college' itself. This draws on neurocybernetics at a different level from neurophysiology (which is why this part of the total model is not in Part Two). The model is drawn at the level of cells — the neurons of the cortex — and it offers a quantified insight into the process of obtaining reliable decisions from unreliable elements. (Let's face it: managers are not machines for pumping out correct answers, and neither in fact is the neuron.) The second model comes from information theory, and offers a totally new approach to the monitoring of complex decisions — while they are being taken by a group such as the first model considers. This second model is almost impossible to understand at all clearly without a fully worked out example, so I have included one, which is as simple as I could make it. But the technique is meant to handle very much more complex problems indeed than this one, and so it has in practice.

The final chapter (Fifteen) is very much a ... final chapter. I mean that it tries to say some exceedingly important things which could be understood only by someone who had read the whole book to this point — and it therefore sounds a bit metaphysical. I would like to convince you that it is not really so; if, therefore, you get that far, please try to take the last hurdle before embarking on the case history of Part Four.

CHAPTER ELEVEN

Corporate structure and its quantification

Now this book can really begin. In this chapter, I set out to say as simply as ever possible what I think any organization should look like. In Part I we considered the concepts and terms which would be needed to describe an organizational model. In Part II, we used these basic notions in formulating and discussing the nature of that model. Now all of that is taken for granted, and we may be bold enough to say how organizations work.

What follows is not put forward as a final prescription for organization, in the sense that responsible people ought to have it dispensed in their own institutions — and then just take the medicine. Quite the contrary; it is contended that all viable organizations are really like this already. Therefore the value of the model is to make clear how the organization actually works, as distinct from the way it allegedly works, so that it may be streamlined and made more effective. I usually find that a thoughtful and respectful consideration of the viable organism that is the institution clearly reveals all the structural features which we have discussed. There may be accretions and elaborations which can be trimmed away; much more likely, however, some of the key features of the model may exist in no more than a rudimentary or even vestigial form. This risk applies particularly, I have found, to Systems Two and Four. Beyond these structural considerations, we need to consider the effectiveness of the information flow — and particularly the nature of the filters and the relative time-lags around the separate organizational loops.

In short, the model is intended for use as a *diagnostic tool.* We map the extant organization onto the model, and then ask whether all parts are functioning in accordance with the criteria of viability, as these have been set forth in neurocybernetic language. It has to be remembered, however, that the mapping does not result in an organization chart — at least, not in the sense recently criticized. It is a mistake to imagine that each department of the extant organization should be allocated to a box or a flow-line in the model, as being 'roughly' its most obvious cybernetic home (and some people have done exactly this). Many activities of the actual firm will be found to be playing a variety of roles in terms of the viable system, and that is perfectly satisfactory — so long as the sum of their various contributions adds up to the cybernetic function that is required. This is where the trouble is normally found. *Someone else* is doing the job that is cybernetically required; but this someone else is not doing that job after all, because *someone else* is doing it — and so on. Thus although there is no point in asking the enterprise to change all of its organizational terminology into this language, merely for the sake of erecting a bronze engraving of 'a cybernetically organized company' in the foyer, it does sometimes turn out to be helpful to bring established departments and their interconnexions more into line with the cybernetic model. What the firm decides to do about this will largely depend on the diagnosis itself, and that is a matter of strictly local relevance.

But the model of the viable system, which is finally presented in Figure 27, is not of local relevance. It is perfectly general. It may be compared at once with its neurophysiological counterpart in Figure 23, and with the idealized (content-less) chart at which we arrived in Figure 22. The very first thing worth noting is the essentially metasystemic character of the five-tier hierarchy, with which by now we are familiar, together with the very powerful metalogical circumstance that the organization of each operating division of the whole is a microcosm of total organization. It has been stressed *passim* in this book that the whole is always encapsulated in each part, and that this is a lesson learned from biology where we find the genetic blue-print of the whole organism in every cell. This means that, in Figure 27, the whole of the chart is reproduced within each circle representing a division, and of course this means in turn that (if we could write or read that small) the whole chart would be reproduced in each division of each division — which is to say in each little circle within every big circle. And so on indefinitely. It is this recursive characteristic which makes this chart a competent chart for *any* organization. Cybernetics has learnt the trick in theory from formal logic and in practice from genetics.

It needs to be noted, however, that this depiction of recursivity (the re-embodiment of the entire chart within each circle) is a graphical device alone, intended to bring home to the reader what in principle the notion of a recursive organization *means*. Clearly, the five systems shown ringed by each circle do not all belong to the 'operational' element of System One, which are what the circles actually depict. In particular, Systems Three, Four and Five at this second level of recursion necessarily reside in the square 'management' boxes, and not in the circles themselves. As remarked: this is a graphical device (the full logic of interconnectivity between recursions may be consulted in *The Heart of Enterprise*). But the meaning of the graphical device ought to be clear: the confusion of recursions is assuredly a hazard of managerial cybernetics.

In following the ensuing commentary, then, the reader is asked to decide in his own mind what large organization the total model is meant to represent; what

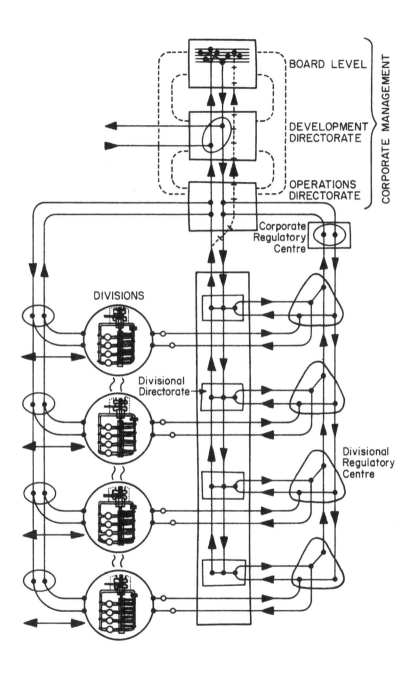

Figure 27

count as its 'divisions', and what smaller organization counts as a division of this division. Finally, he ought to have in mind a notion of what institution the organization of which he first thought is itself a division. That is to say, when we know the institution which Figure 27 is supposed to depict, we should draw a large circle all round it, and imagine the whole of the chart reproduced once again to a size which would fill the room. The intellectual exercise involved in this recommendation offers the one chance I know that we shall be able to attain and to maintain a proper perspective on any one application.

To take the simplest example, let us suppose that we work for a large corporation. Figure 27 is a model of the corporation's organization and each little circle in Figure 27 models a division of the corporation. Then each tiny circle within the *divisional* model represents a company. The undrawn circle around Figure 27 makes it — the whole corporation — a division of an industry, which is in its turn organized on the lines of another, and metasystemic, Figure 27.

All of this quite necessary exegesis reveals that there is no point in undertaking a further discussion of the divisions themselves, of which four are shown in the diagram. This is because any such discussion would at once embark on the nature of the divisional organization; and that discussion would turn out to be precisely the same discussion as we shall have now about corporate organization. Please note the absolute symmetry of this organizational logic — once the metasystemic hierarchy is accepted as a conceptual model.

This notion really is very important, and it is insisted upon at this moment because managers so rarely accept it. The manager in a given echelon seems in practice to think of both the echelon above and the echelon below as in some way utterly different from his own. It is not. It is exactly the same. What makes it *look* different is the relative seniority of the three interlocking systems. But suppose, to make the point as clear as possible, that we were actually discussing the nature of 'the threefold'. We might say that a unit may be divided into thirds, and each third divided again into thirds. Then if we begin to discuss the nature of 'a third of the whole' by looking closely at one third of the whole, we should merely find that this third is divided into thirds. It is in this sense, and for this logical reason, that we cannot discuss the internal nature of the divisions depicted by Systems One in the chart. But we may make a few basic assertions about divisional *control* — which should already be self-evident to those who have read the first two parts of the book.

Notes on the Divisional Role in Corporate Organization

A division is run by its directorate, shown on the diagram as a square box on the vertical command axis. A division is essentially autonomous. That means it 'does what it likes' within just one limitation: it continues to belong to the organism. According to our analysis, this one limitation imposes precisely three practical managerial constraints. These are:

(i)   Operate within the Intention of the Whole Organism

The objectives of the total organization and the intentions these entail are communicated down the vertical command chain from System Five, and accountability is depicted in the diagram by the ascending lines on that axis. These objectives and instructions must, at the very least, be explained carefully to the divisions; preferably the divisions should participate in their formulation. This is to talk about the psychology of the system (and not its logic), and a whole corpus of knowledge in behavioural science exists to help decide how this should be done in particular enterprises. As to the logic, however: never forget that the division is short of a metalanguage. Thus corporate objectives *cannot even be expressed* in the language of System One. It follows that divisional people must first identify themselves with the corporate enterprise, and learn to speak the metalanguage, before they can understand the issues. Contrary to the blithe assumptions of some optimists, they are often unwilling to do this. In that case a divisional potential to influence the intentions of the whole organism still exists, but the methods open to it are exhausted by;

(a) the degree of facility with which it obeys vertical instructions, as transmitted down the vertical command axis (monitored by System Five);
(b) the degree of pleasure or pain it experiences in so doing. We expect this to
be transmitted by the collateral information distilled from its report on
accountability through the algedonic route specially marked by crosses in
Figure 27 (monitored by System Four). In any human organization this
takes the form of direct calls for attention made by System One people on
System Five people, which must pass the filter of the secretariat in Four;
(c) its autonomic report information separately presented to System Three.

Danger points. The distinctions drawn here are not at all obvious, and misunderstanding them is the main cause of dissension between the periphery and the centre in almost all large organizations. The misunderstanding arises from the fact that, according to our cultural conventions, there are people — that is to say, named individuals — inside the division who undertake corporate roles as well. This means that a divisional chief executive, for instance, who *in logic* (see above) cannot understand corporate objectives properly, may well be a member of the board which operates System Five. He therefore helps formulate the intentions which he himself later receives in another capacity as 'incomprehensible' instructions. Every important individual in the total organization, including the divisional chief executive himself, may freely and often acknowledge the duality of his interests. But (such is human nature) it is rare indeed to find that all parties to a corporate decision fully understand at any one time who is adopting which role. This fact may well be the predominant basis of managerial confusion throughout contemporary society.

(ii)   Operate within the Co-ordinating Framework of System Two

The divisional directorate must accept the existence of other divisions, on whose interaction the corporate synergy depends. Divisional chief executives themselves are incapable — again in formal logic — of taking account of this fact. This is quite simply because they have their own 'corporate' organization to run within their own circle, and there *can be no formal method* by which in their eyes adequate account may be taken of this point. True, there may be a committee structure dedicated to collaborative ends, and once again individuals may (because of their dual roles in the organization) understand some of the issues. But, in practice, the divisional chief executive must be dedicated to the effective running of his division, *as if* his division were expected to overthrow the others — in the competition for capital, for example. It follows that a measure of control must be vested in a corporate regulatory centre (see Figure 27) charged with effecting the purposes of System Two.

Danger points. It is difficult enough for the divisional chief executive to maintain the duality of his roles within System One and (probably) System Five. To accept the regulatory action of a relatively junior control echelon at the corporate centre is — in psychological terms this time — anathema. It is bad enough, feels the divisional chief executive, to accept 'instructions' from above (System Five) *given that* this same man is party to such policy formulating in his other role. But the System Two regulatory action is nothing more nor less than 'gross interference by people who do not know what they are talking about'. Unless this problem can be overcome, then cybernetics safely predicts that the organization will go into a dramatic oscillation.

(iii)   Submit to the Automatic Control of System Three Itself

The internal homeostasis of the corporation is not simply a matter of preventing oscillation (which is a System Two undertaking). If corporate synergy is to be achieved at all times — which is to say, throughout current operations — then sometimes the needs of one division must be sacrificed, not to the needs of the corporation, which is another point dealt with under

System Five, but explicitly to the needs of other divisions. (The difficulties implicit here are well exemplified in many large organizations by the problem of transfer prices.) It follows from this objectively 'obvious' constraint that a division may even be asked by the others to go into liquidation. Why not? It may well be inimical to the optimal behaviour of other divisions simply as a matter of practical day-to-day operations, and regardless of the role of such a maverick division in a perfectly viable long-term corporate plan. There is a conflict of values here which can be resolved, in logic, only at the top.

Danger points. However — I say again, however — the very possibility that this demand for dissolution or contraction might happen to any division of the corporation constitutes an omnipresent threat in the minds of many divisional directorates. They therefore often act as if they were threatened with extinction, and become agressive to fellow divisions when all the evidence shows that they ought to be co-operative.

It seems ironic that we should say: 'we cannot discuss the division, because it is no more nor less than the whole in microcosm' — and then go on to say many things about the divisional role in the enterprise. The reason for this apparent inconsistency is the chief lesson worth learning, and it emerges from the notes under each of the three 'Danger Points' headings above. To the divisional chief executive and his divisional directorate it is *always* true that things are not what they seem. This is essentially because of the duality of roles — on which comment has already been passed. But even if we were to forbid divisional chiefs from participating in corporate endeavours, the result would be the same. This draws attention to a weakness in our model: the units of the body politic are themselves *self*-conscious. Therefore, even if the people concerned at the divisional level are excluded, quite formally, from corporate management, nothing on earth can prevent them from deliberating on the nature and behaviour of the corporation as such.

It is as if the heart were given a little mind of its own, with which to ask whether the whole body were behaving so badly that it — the heart — might end up with coronary thrombosis. Just think what a threat this suspicion would constitute to the heart as a major organ of the body. Before long it would come to suspect the liver and the kidneys of unthinkable perfidy — whereas those blameless organs were without fault in submitting to the three constraints constituting their own autonomic limitation. This is a thought-provoking reflection. The psychiatric problems of organs endowed with self-consciousness would be legion.

Thus in some ways our liberal-minded and culturally sophisticated attempts to involve divisional managements more and more in corporate policies may be asking for trouble. But please do not take the remark too seriously; given that divisional directorates comprise people, there is probably no doubt that maximum participation offers the best solution. If these head-scratchings reveal anything at all it is that participatory management (divisional *vis-à-vis* corporate) may raise more problems than it solves, and does — at the very least — depend heavily on the full-time awareness of *all* concerned that their roles are indeed dual. This means that what the cortex self-consciously knows may be death to the autonomic system — a most unphysiological state of affairs.

Notes on the Measures of Achievement

The dynamics of this whole structure depend on the quantification of its performance. Hitherto business has used the measure of money: cost and sales price, the direction and rate of cash flow. Thus we have come to identify the quantification of business activity, in the corporations we already know, with the cost-accounting function. This is because cost accountancy provides a *lingua franca* by which the disparate activities of unlike divisions may be compared and aggregated. There is no reason why this should be so, beyond its historicity and (alleged) familiarity.

Secondly, in so far as there is an observable trend in the corporations we already know, it is toward the construction of massive data bases within divisional centres, on which it is claimed corporate management will be able to draw for every purpose under heaven. This development has been attacked in previous chapters from many angles; people are already finding it inoperable and certainly uneconomic. But the most important argument against the approach is that it rides on hidden premises about computational capabilities which cannot be fulfilled (as was argued in Chapter 3). Then what should we do?

From the corporate standpoint, divisional performance is about *both* short- and long-term viability. The notion that cost should be minimized or profit maximized within a fixed epoch leaves right out of the count other factors which are vital to the future viability of the business contained within the division. They are the latent capabilities of the firm, which may be built up and metabolized by wise management, or squandered recklessly by stupid management — without in either case procuring a change which is reflected in costings. For costings are short-term control instruments, and will not detect the mismanagement of latent resources. By definition, this mismanagement will not be detected until it is too late (through the financial accounts, no doubt) although it is happening *now* — and ought to be checked.

We need a measure of achievement which is both less 'loaded', in terms of the emotional appeal of profits, and which is also more comprehensive, in terms of the real resources at risk. The measure must none the less be expressed in a common metric for the whole corporation. If money is not the unit, then we must think in terms of pure numbers.

There is a classic measure of productivity which can be extended. It expresses the ratio of what is possible to what is actual. Thus if a typist *could* type 100 pages in a given time, but types only 50, then her productivity over the period is clearly one half. 0.5 is a pure number. Now we may deal with the problem of incorporating latent resources by a slight elaboration of this theme, which requires us to define three (rather than two) levels of achievement. They are:

actuality: This is simply what we *are* managing to do now, with existing resources, under existing constraints.

capability: This is what we *could* be doing (still right now) with existing resources, under existing constraints, if we really worked at it.

potentiality: This is what we *ought* to be doing by developing our resources and removing constraints, although still operating within the bounds of what is already known to be feasible.

It would help a lot to fix these definitions clearly in the mind.

Now of course we may project our future plans on the basis of any one of these notions of achievement, or indeed have three sets of plans which separately employ these three criteria. Again it will pay to assimilate the following definitions. Planning on the basis of actuality I call *programming*. Planning on the basis of capability I call *planning by objectives*. Planning on the basis of potentiality I call *normative planning*. The first of these is simply a programme because it accepts the inevitable shortcomings of the situation, and does not admit that anything can imminently be done about them. Programming is a tactical ruse. We move to genuine planning only when we set new objectives and try to achieve them. This is the strategic planning level. Normative planning sets potentiality as its target — and incurs major risks and penalties, although it also offers major and perhaps decisive benefits. But, however we plan, what really matures is always called actuality, and the measures of achievement proposed relate capability and potentiality to whatever may be actual at the time. Here are some more definitions:

productivity: is the ratio of actuality and capability;

latency: is the ratio of capability and potentiality;

performance: is both the ratio of actuality and potentiality, and also the product of latency and productivity.

These relationships are laid out in Figure 28.

The behaviour of ratios is a strange phenomenon, and Figure 28 repays a good deal of contemplation. If full achievement is to be read as unity (that is, 100 per cent), the smaller of the two raw measures must always be the numerator and the larger the denominator. It is not possible to write down these pairs of terms as one 'over' another, because which way up the fraction is written depends on the measures one is using. Potentiality is *always* better than capability, which is *always* better than actuality. But if we are talking about profit, for example, 'better' means 'more', whereas if we talk about the number of men required to do a job, 'better' means 'less'. The second point to note is that the overall measure of performance is determined by the ratio of actuality and potentiality, as being two extremes. This means that capability is floating between them, and can change without affecting either.

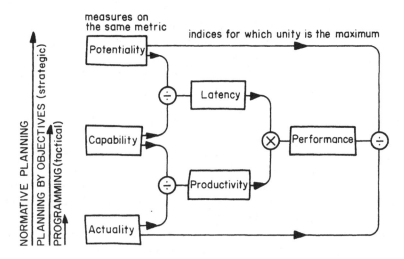

Figure 28. Three measures of capacity generating three measures of achievement

Consider then the question of what happens to the achievement indices when we go on doing what we have always done (note: nothing changes in the cost report), when the ultimate possibilities remain the same (note: nothing changes in the corporate view of R & D), but where divisional management acts to change the capability. This it may do by undertaking work study of processes, negotiating new agreements with the unions, raising the morale or improving the quality of managers, and so forth. Clearly the overall performance index does not change. What happens is that the latency measure improves (because capability is approaching potentiality) and productivity is lowered. But if potent management can in these circumstances improve the *actual* performance, as obviously it should, all three measures of achievement will rise.

These are the kind of measures that we need, and they may be applied in general to divisional performance or in particular to individual activities. They

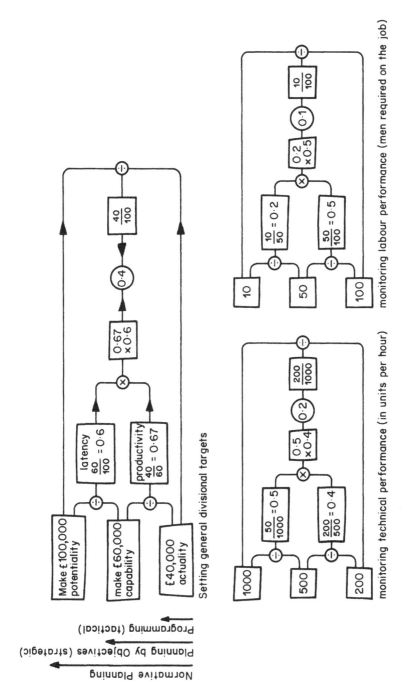

Figure 29. A miscellany of applications using the same achievement measures (see Figure 28)

may be applied segmentally to various aspects of work — to the effort of the labour force for instance, and to the technological capacities of plant. In that case these segmental indices may subsequently be multiplied together to provide an overall performance measure, which is consistent with its direct computation from the raw data. However it is done, and indeed the doing may involve work study and operational research on a considerable scale, the resulting measures are simple and easy to use. After all, all three measures of achievement should be rising.

Here we finally detect the manager who is doing most these days to wreck industrial enterprise. He is the irresponsible cost-cutter (note: this does not say that cutting costs is irresponsible). The manager I speak of raises productivity (and hopefully profits), and thereby acquires a marvellous reputation, *not* by increasing actual achievement but by lowering capability. This he does by squandering his latent resources. He cuts budgets, he 'lets go' valuable men, he fails to implement research results should this involve the slightest effort, expenditure or risk. Thus he triumphs as a tough, practical man. In the orthodox scheme of reporting, no measure will reveal the damage he is doing. There is no element in either the profit and loss account or the balance sheet which declares him to be murdering the company's reputation in markets for products, for supplies, or for staff — which may well be needed in a few years' time. The proposed indices do reveal this. Consider what will happen in the case quoted. The manager's productivity will be seen to increase, for indeed it does increase, and that doubtless means that this year's profits will rise. But his latency index will deteriorate and so (probably) will his overall performance. So keep your eye on profits in a few years' time.

Figure 29 details a few quite dissimilar applications of these achievement measures. The examples demonstrate the versatility of the scheme, which could be applied to any endeavour — given suitable definitions of the three initial terms. Here again it is a useful exercise to contemplate each of the examples in turn, working out for oneself what are the consequences of various possible actions.

There can be no argument about the numbers used to measure actuality. There will be severe arguments about the other two sets of numbers. But if we use good operational research it becomes possible to gain agreement that the numbers used are sensible — and the process of investigation and discussion is itself highly beneficial. What matters is that capability and potentiality measures, though somewhat arbitrarily fixed, cannot then be arbitrarily changed. Hence although the absolute values of the productivity and latency indices provide only approximate assessments, movements of these indices over time provide the information that we really need.

CHAPTER TWELVE

Autonomics — systems one, two, three

The principles of an autonomic system were discussed at length in Part II. Essentially we are dealing with the evolutionary answer to the bogus dichotomy of centralization versus decentralization. As in the previous chapter, I shall take the whole of that earlier discussion for granted.

We need to know first of all how System One really works — in the eyes of the corporation. Remember that it has to control a division, in response to policy directives and over-riding instructions from above, in reaction to the direct demands of the external world upon it, and in awareness of the needs of other divisions.

There has first of all to be a divisional directorate, which was depicted in Figure 27. It lies on the vertical command axis, reports to the corporate management from which instructions are received, and is responsible for managing the division. Essentially this means that it in turn controls activities in a 'line' sense; but from the corporate standpoint this responsibility is routine. What really matters is that the divisional directorate assumes responsibility for programming, planning by objectives, and normative planning throughout the division.

Its management tool is the divisional regulatory centre (marked in Figure 27 with a triangular symbol). Here the monitoring and filtering functions for input data, and the strategic planning and tactical programming functions for output data, jointly reside. (Then this part of the *corporate* System One constitutes the *divisional* System Three — the operations directorate of the division.) This organ, the regulatory centre, explicitly models the spinal ganglion in relation to the vertebral segment of the cord.

Notes on the Operation of System One

In view of the arguments advanced in the last chapter, we shall take it that basic information about performance is to be generated for corporate use in terms of pure numbers — the achievement indices. At once an opportunity occurs to classify divisional operations on a better basis than is normally attempted in orthodoxy.

People normally classify activities according to their manifest appearance to the world at large. They may be classified by their location, by the nature of the processes they employ, by the nature of the things which they produce, by the sort of people who undertake them, or even by the geographical destiny of the output. But since management is interested in efficiency, and since a particular measured level of performance now attaches to each of these activities, a more managerially sophisticated and practically useful classification system may be developed.

What matters to management about two entirely different products is not whether they look alike but whether they are profit-earners or not. Two very similar-looking products may perform quite differently; two dissimilar products may display the same performance. Then we should use the pure numbers we have generated to classify what is going on in the firm by these measures of achievement.

The tool to use here is applied statistics. Assume that pure numbers are now flowing out of the division, and along the input line to the divisional directorate. It is a function of the divisional regulatory centre to cause these numbers to fall into convenient heaps (technically: Gaussian distributions), whereby probability theory may be used to determine to which family of performance a particular number belongs. There is no prior judgement here from historicity, nor from manifest appearance. The criterion is straightforwardly the shape of the 'achievement profile', determined by the absolute value of the performance index and the balance within that index of its constituent latency and productivity.

All this is very easy to arrange on a computer, because there are simple and robust tests for statistical normalcy, and extremely familiar tables of the integral under the curve of the two tails of the normal distribution. Technical note: the ratios, which have an upper bound of unity, cannot be used as raw data immediately for these tests, because they generate skewed distributions. Some adjustment will be necessary: I have always found the inverse sine transformation of the raw score to be quite effective, but there are other possibilities. However, this is a matter for the statistician member of the implementation team. We need not be delayed here by considerations of technical detail.

The point is that we should no longer classify the firm's activities according to convention, apply cost measures to these activities because they are the only measures we understand, and then aggregate the answers. We should instead apply the measures of performance we have designed to the activities, and demand that the information system classifies the operational world on our behalf. The brain does this for us in ordinary life through its pattern-recognition capability, and produces the classification by manifest appearance with which we normally wish to work. As managers, however, we are seeking to detect other patterns — those of significance to the business — and that means classifying by achievement.

The input to the classification machine at the divisional regulatory centre consists of raw data emanating from divisional operations. These data need to be collected and organized ready for processing, and then passed on to the divisional regulatory centre. This is a synaptic function, and it is depicted in Figure 27 as a very tiny circle on the input transmission line. The synapse itself is shown in the more detailed drawing of Figure 30, depicting System One — it is Step 2. Initially, the whole of the data will be collected so that the classification system may be created. We shall need to store quite simple models of potentiality and more complicated models of capability which have been evolved by operational research. Then, as data about actual operations flow in, from Step 1 transducers and through the synaptic Step 2, we shall need to compute the achievement indices — and arrange them in statistically homogeneous groups (Step 3). Thereafter, however, it will be necessary to transmit only organized samples beyond the Step 2 synapse — for checking against the population characteristics of the group.

Here we encounter the first filtering process of the divisional regulatory centre. This also is based on the application of very easily handled statistical techniques — exactly like those used in Quality Control applications. A set of activities belonging to Class X builds up a data potential at the Step 2 synapse, and (on reaching an intensity threshold) fires the whole sample into the regulatory centre. Here (Step 3) the data are applied to stored models, and the appropriate achievement indices are formed. These values are compared with the stored parameters of the appropriate achievement group (Class X), to see whether any statistically significant information has been evolved. If it has not, the filter suppresses the information. If it has, the filter passes it on.[1]

The regulatory system as so far described is capable of detecting the movement of members of the population out of that population and into another; it is capable of detecting movements in both the mean and the variance of the population itself as a time trend; and (practical experience shows) it can do both these things long before human observers have detected any significant change. Thus the classification system is made continuously adaptive to the events of the real world, and the divisional directorate is simultaneously alerted to any change that has occurred (this is Step 4 in Figure 30).

[1]A detailed account of the cybernetics of this whole process is given in Chapter 13 of *Decision and Control* (see Bibliography), together with an historical case study showing the results achieved.

170

Key to corporate system one
A. Directoral function to receive over-riding corporate instructions.
B. Directoral function to report back.
C. Normative planning function (divisional Systems Four and Five).

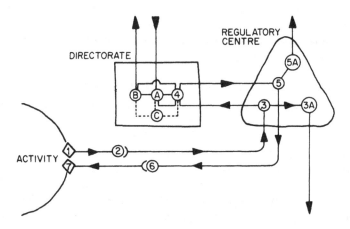

Operations control (divisional System Three)
1. Sensory transduction (codifying actuality on continuous basis).
2. Input synapse (transmitting samples at given threshold of intensity).
3. Achievement monitor (calculating, classifying, filtering indices).
3A. Information relay to other divisions.
4. Directoral function to respond (endorsing routine, initiating special action).
5. Continuous planning (strategic) and programming (tactical) generator.
5A. Information relay to corporate regulatory centre.
6. Output synapse (transmitting programme).
7. Motor transduction (determining action).

Figure 30. Organization of divisional management — System One

Here is the managerial trigger of the reflex arc which responds to the sensory input so far classified, monitored and filtered. To understand what happens next (at Step 5) it is vital to realize that basic procedures for controlling activities are already settled. For example, we know the process routes for all products, or we know the list of retailers on whom salesmen must call. The purpose now, therefore, would be wrongly regarded as the 'creation' of a plan and a programme, because they already exist in shadow form. Rather Step 5 is a dynamic process of adjustment, which *selects* particular plans for implementation, and *quantifies* the required programmes in a feasible form for the present epoch.

Planning therefore consists of the arrangement, within these known procedures, of a number of building blocks which are forecast actualities. Note that the directorate may gear itself to normative plans, and also (particularly in collaboration with other divisions) strive towards those harmonious and synergistic relationships which will raise the whole level of actual achievement to the level of capability. But in the short run, in responding at Step 5 with motor output to a sensory input, the governing required must needs be based on an accurate assessment of what will actually happen. It is now clearer than ever why the provision of massive data bases will not achieve these ends. Every possible variant on every possible programme cannot be evaluated in advance, and cannot be stored; that is our standard argument. Still less, we can now see, would it be possible to update all these features from epoch to epoch in the light of whatever time trends were affecting productivity. The alternative is to generate the quantities required, as they are required, by the following method.

There is a general model of capability in store, which was not too difficult to construct nor too expensive to record — because it is idealized. We may then select the required features of our programme from this model, just as if we intended to issue an idealized programme based on capability. But before putting the building blocks of the programme together, we adjust or weight each item by the reciprocal of its current productivity index.

For example, suppose that the time required to do a certain job comes out in capability terms as two hours. If the mean productivity currently attaching to the class to which this item belongs is one half, then the forecast actual time for use in the programme will be four hours. Now suppose that, as a result of turning this particular set of programmes into an activity, the division succeeds in effecting radical and permanent improvements in its methods of production. This will be detected in the next epoch, and Steps 2 and 3 of the sensory input will detect and measure the change. To take an extreme case, suppose the productivity rises from a half to four-fifths. The filters will at once alert the directorate, which (assuming it can satisfy itself as to the change) will approve the new coefficient at Step 4. That means, that in this next epoch, Step 5 will be computing the same element in its programme as follows. The basic model of capability will continue to supply a time of two hours. But now this will be multiplied by the reciprocal of four-fifths instead of a half, and the forecast actual time will emerge as $2 \times 5 \div 4 = 2\frac{1}{2}$ hours.

Here is what is happening:

$$\text{actuality} = \text{capability} \times \frac{1}{\text{Productivity}} \qquad \text{...we said}$$

$$\text{Now Productivity} = \frac{\text{capability}}{\text{actuality}} \qquad \text{...by definition}$$

$$\text{So} \quad \frac{1}{\text{Productivity}} = \frac{\text{actuality}}{\text{capability}}$$

So what we said amounts to:

$$\text{actuality} = \frac{\text{capability}}{1} \times \frac{\text{actuality}}{\text{capability}} = \text{actuality again.}$$

As we saw in Figure 29, the productivity equation, depending on the measurements used, may be 'the other way up'. But in that case, the rest of the above argument is also inverted. It makes no difference. In either case we are confronted by a circular argument, an algebraic tautology. It must be right, then, but why undertake it? The answer is: *ease of control*. We are taking actuality to have one constant and one variable component. The constant is easy to store; the variable is easy to control. To try and handle the whole thing in one go would take us straight back to the massive data banks which have been repudiated.

Programmes for action within the division, continuously generated in this fashion at Step 5, will be assembled for issue to the operating centres as required at the synaptic Step 6. As a typical example of this Step, we may think of the preparation of a complete shift's work of job cards, which will be transduced into a production shop (Step 7) by whatever means is customary for their distribution.

It will be appreciated that the approach we are using decouples the control variables (which are pure numbers) from the managerial parameters of the system. These parameters may be expressed in terms of machine occupancy, time taken, number of men employed, and so forth as required — and as determined in advance by the general idealized model. In that case, we should treat the cost variable in precisely the same way. Actual costs may be associated with every resource used at the idealized (capability) level. This means that the model can at once generate an idealized cost for which a given activity *could* be undertaken. But the components of this cost will each be modified (along with every other feature of the activity) according to the appropriate productivity classes which become invoked in the programming process. Hence we shall generate forecast actual costs for all activities *as a by-product*. Moreover when the work has been completed, we shall of course be able to generate an historical cost from the final measured productivity which the specific activity, in the event, procured.

Notes on the Operation of System Two

System Two is the metasystem subsuming all Systems One. Throughout this book its existence has been diagrammatically indicated by the tall thin rectangular box drawn round the column of boxes which are themselves the System One. However, the mechanics of System Two are found in the interlinking of the divisional regulatory centres, and in the corporate regulatory centre, as shown in Figure 31. So it would be correct, and even helpful, to think of System Two as an elaborate interface between Systems One and Three. It partakes of both.

The need for a System Two was explained at some length as being the only means whereby uncontrolled oscillation between the divisions could be prevented. Consider now exactly how this works. An example from any kind of operation will do, since all operations are measured and monitored in terms of achievement indices. Suppose that Division B receives a raw material from Division A which is, for A, a finished product. Note that the physical stuff will be transferred from A to B down the squiggly pipeline which joins their two circles in Figure 27. The requisition of the raw material, however, and its acknowledgement, progressing and invoicing, are all information transfers which will occur on the vertical paravertebral chains shown in Figure 31.

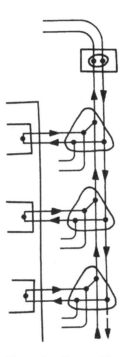

Figure 31. System Two

How, first of all, is the 'requisition' placed? In most firms, an actual internal order for the raw material is originated by B and sent to A. Yet in most instances (although one can think of exceptions) this is a silly procedure, a ritual which people think must be undertaken for the sake of sound accounting in the office. It is contrary to the notion of *continuous* planning and control developed throughout this book. In fact, Division A knows very well that a volume of this particular raw material flows to Division B, and it currently produces what B currently consumes — unless, that is, an interdivisional stock of the stuff is held. In that case, more complicated rules may be used to govern A's output to suit B's input. But in general, and over a period, actuality is the same for A as for B in relation to this material. If it were not so, the stock (or queue, as we call a stock we do not like) would become infinitely large, or else B would have idle capacity for lack of supplies.

Then we start with the notion of a material flow which, however governed to suit the two divisions, is understood to exist and to be adjusted to B's actuality — which varies with its own order book. Here we have a simple error-controlled feedback system. Now suppose that for complex reasons A's capability falls. Its productivity will then be affected. Suppose it is so affected that the measure of achievement for the production of this material leaves its statistical achievement group. In Division A this will be detected at Step 3, and a replanning process will take necessary action through Steps 4, 5, 6, and 7 to make sense of the production programme. The directorate will be alerted, so that its members (the B and C functions of Figure 30) do what they must do to investigate matters — hopefully to restore productivity to its former level.

The next question concerns the impact of all this on Division B, whose supplies are now in jeopardy. In an orthodox system, it is a moot point whether or when B will be officially informed. The supplying management may be too proud, too optimistic or too forgetful to alert the consuming management. If not, what is actually to be said? 'We are having a bit of trouble in the annealing, old man,' will alert Division B, whose managers will then try to discover what this remark means. Will the material be late, and if so, how late? How much stock is there? Should they go outside for supplies? And so on.

Now complicate this example one little bit. Suppose that not only Division B, but Divisions E, F, and G also use A's product. Perhaps B could borrow from the E, F, or G stocks. But these divisions are threatened too. Suddenly we are in a competitive situation instead of a collaborative one, and experience shows that this is where communications break down. For an element of gamesmanship is introduced into an already complicated situation. The fact that all of this can happen (has happened, often happens) leads to a new result. The consuming divisions adopt a cautious policy about their stocks, and try to build them up; the financial authorities become alarmed (the performance of investment is being adversely affected), and they intervene; meanwhile all concerned devise rules and procedures for handling the situation which are supposed to be fair, supposed to be collaborative, supposed to be optimal. But by now people are playing poker with the situation; trust is lost, informal rules are adopted at the divisional level which are intended to secure local satisfaction ... and oscillation has set in.

The intention behind System Two is twofold. First, the change in productivity in Division A is automatically relayed to the other divisions by Step 3A. The change notified is neither fuzzy nor emotive: it is a statistical statement couched in achievement numbers. The regulatory centres in other divisions can immediately evaluate the effect on their production plans and programmes, and look to the performance measures of their own stocks. Secondly, the corporate regulatory centre, receiving all this information, is enabled to take a higher-order view of the total consequences. It will report to System Three, which (be it remembered) is on the vertical command axis — and can take managerial action invoking, if necessary, the authority of System Five. The corporate regulatory centre, it can be seen, is acting *vis-à-vis* System Three very much as the input synapse on the horizontal command axis acts *vis-à-vis* System One.

Perhaps the main point of this whole arrangement is its automatic simplicity, and therefore its speed. The message that 'something has changed, and like this' goes simultaneously from the divisional regulatory centre to (i) the divisional directorate, (ii) other regulatory centres, and (iii) the corporate regulatory centre — whence onward to System Three if required. The job of the divisional directorate is first and foremost to discover what went wrong, what made this happen, and to devise measures to put it right. Meantime, everyone else has other fish to fry. The change is, for this epoch at least, a fact, and one which must be coped with. So the divisional regulatory centre has re-programming to do. The other divisions have consequences to draw, and reports to make quickly to the corporate regulatory centre. That centre itself has to take fast corrective action, either through its regulating machinery, or (if managerial prerogatives are involved) via System Three and the command axis.

Contrast this with the orthodox procedures with which we are acquainted. The matter is not referred to the corporate level, if it ever is referred, until the oscillation has set in. This generates a difficult problem in terms of control theory, quite apart from human attitudes. But by the time these too have degenerated into suspicion and defensiveness there is an appalling management problem of a social and psychological sort as well. Small wonder that these fundamental oscillatory mechanisms in the firm (and in government and society at large) prove so very damaging. They are a curse of our age — because our age has produced so many large-scale organizations without a System Two. Most of the successful ones I have observed have been entirely unofficial and largely unrecognized.

The corporate regulatory centre, then, is both a monitor and co-ordinator of divisional centres, and also an input filter on the path into System Three, to which we now turn.

Notes on the Operation of System Three

Here is the highest level of autonomic management, and the lowest level of corporate management. Its function is primarily to govern the stability of the internal environment of the organization. The neurophysiological model of the process was advanced in Chapter 8, and its managerial analogue was discussed in Chapter 9.

There are three kinds of information system converging on System Three. The first belongs to the vertical command axis. System Three is part of corporate management, and therefore a transmitter of policy and special instructions to the divisions. It is also a receiver of information about the internal environment, which it handles in three ways: 1. as a metasystemic controller *downwards,* 2. as the most senior filter of somatic news *upwards,* and 3. as an algedonode. Secondly, System Three is the only recipient of information filtered upwards from System Two — the mechanics of this process have just been discussed. Thirdly, System Three handles the parasympathetic information circuits which are antithetic to those of the sympathetic (System Two) circuits.

The first task now is to examine this third informational component more carefully, and this is done in the recollection of earlier explanations. The key to an understanding of the parasympathetic component of the model (the left-hand chain of Figure 27) is the limitation of the sympathetic (System Two) component. All along we have insisted on the on-going nature of routine control. We do not suppose that a firm is virgin territory, over which we may trample — making plans — ready for the day when something will happen. The firm is happening now; the firm's activities are well understood; its regulators at System One and System Two *are* regulators, i.e. they are error-controlled feedback servos. It follows that there are models of standard behaviour enshrined in the control mechanisms we have so far discussed — they are the paradigms against which 'error' is measured.

From the viewpoint of corporate management, however, and in this case of System Three, such paradigms assume too much. They take no account of the external environment of the organism as a whole — only of the external environment of their own divisions. They may be regulators of *local* homeostasis, then, but System Three is the only competent regulator of *organic* homeostasis, since it alone has a System Four input. What we have so far (Systems One and Two) created, it follows, is a way of handling divisional control, and a way of handling interdivisional interaction — on the assumption that the divisions between them know all there is to know about the adaptation and growth of the total organism. This they do not.

In fact, it is easy enough to propose examples of total behaviour which (because they are novel, heuristic, evolutionary) cannot be adequately represented within System Two, with its paradigmatic models, although they may be communicated to System One by the direct somatic system. Divisional directorates will understand these latter messages, of course, because they are themselves masters of the company's operations. The trouble is that their local regulatory centres are not organized to handle what is not routine. In particular, they are not organized to represent — to attend to, to measure, to transduce — other than what locally happens. This is a problem of requisite variety.

The answer, learned from the autonomic nervous system, is a direct parasympathetic access to the divisional operations themselves. There, under the local supervision of the divisional directorate, antithetical modes of control may be established. These are antithetical precisely in the sense that they handle aspects of affairs not handled via System Two. Remember the cholinergic and adrenergic chemistries of the parasympathetic and sympathetic systems. The distinction between them is not absolute, any more than our diagrams are absolutely correct in dividing the autonomic system as a whole into quite separate parts. But the main architecture and chemistry is clear — and useful.

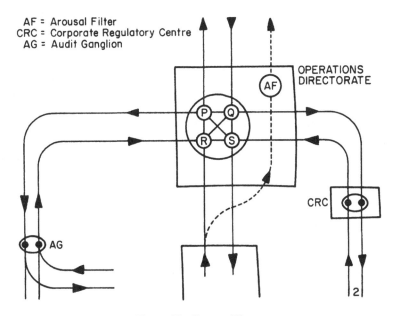

Figure 32. System Three

Looking at Figure 32, we see how system Three is intended to work. Routine information about internal regulation is always available from the corporate regulatory centre. Point S constantly receives filtered news; point Q may request any further data generated by System Two. The complex Q-S is filtering information down to the divisional directorates, while the complex R-P is filtering information up to the senior management. The entire complex P-

Q-R-S is the machinery for controlling internal homeostasis; point P is enabled to interrogate divisional operations themselves, which respond to inquiries at point R.

All of this is a corporate management structure, which constitutes the operations directorate of the firm. Since the R-P complex is intended to report upwards, its right to information should be carefully noted, and the role of its direct access (parasympathetic) channels must be properly understood. Remember: somatic information ascending the main vertical axis will be *divisional* information, coalesced to be called corporate information — for no better reason than that all the divisional operations taken together apparently exhaust the corporation's operations. The information ascending through the corporate regulatory centre is already more than this — it is genuinely about the synergy of the divisions. However, its limitation is its stereotyped nature; the structure of its mechanisms is paradigmatic. With the third type of reporting, both problems are overcome. Point P is instigating a kind of internal audit (though not simply financial, nor even necessarily office-based). This is a corporate activity, having short-term synergistic objectives (the Systems One have not) which are paradigm-free (and System Two is not).

In the diagram, the acquisition of information in this form is seen as mediated through special ganglia — centres which do not merely transmit information, but process it too. Thus each division has its own audit ganglion, reporting to the operations directorate, and dealing wholly with the corporate synergy. These ganglia will be brought into action solely for this synergistic purpose, and because every other kind of reporting upward must always fail to comprehend the information needs of System Three which arise beyond the pre-arranged routines of Systems One and Two.

This book deals nowhere with the established techniques of scientific management in any detail, but we should observe in passing how most of them will be applied by a competent System Three. The P-Q-R-S complex is ideally placed to use every kind of optimizing tool in its direction of current operations, from inventory theory to mathematical programming. A dynamic, current model of the firm's internal working must in fact emerge at this level, and offers the ideal management tool for the control of internal stability.

The final point to note about System Three is the existence of the arousal filter which models the reticular formation of the brain stem. The collateral fibres feeding the algedonic system are clearly shown in Figure 32, and the purpose of this system has been dealt with at some length already. We shall return to it when we reach the algedonode in System Five.

The arousal job at the third level is in fact the usual filtering job. Statistical criteria must be established to ensure that ascending algedonic information on the vertical axis, of whatever kind, is not simply absorbed by the P-Q-R-S homeostat in the performance of its own function, for it would then be lost in the upward reports from point P — which, after all, will be about the effective functioning of the homeostat and not about discrete internal events. Those are the ones we seek, algedonically, to monitor.

Notes on the Problems of Systemic Interfaces

There are evidently three interfaces between the three systems so far considered. The systemic interaction between Systems Two and Three presents no special problem since each is managerially controlled by the same authority, the corporate operations directorate. But Systems One are managerially controlled by chief executives of autonomous divisions, to whom the principle of accountability applies. They accept the policy-making of the corporation, which impinges on their activities down the central command axis. But their reaction to other kinds of 'interference', at the interfaces between their own Systems One and the corporate Systems Two and Three, may be very different.

Here then is a major snag; it is the hoary old problem of central control, written in a new form. Let this much, however, be clear at once: the snag is endemic to large-scale organization — it has not been invented here. All the cybernetic model has done is to identify the precise nature of the snag. It apparently has two components.

Firstly, there is the One/Two interface. This has to do with recognizing that there are other autonomous divisions than my own, and that they have rights as well. Especially, these others have the right not to be undermined by me, however pure my own motives are. Secondly, there is the One/Three interface. This has to do with recognizing that my own autonomous division is part of a corporation, and that it too has rights. Especially, sad as it seems, the corporation has the right to inhibit and if necessary to liquidate my autonomous division. The first component is about interdivisional collaboration; the second is about corporate synergy.

The problem will not vanish because of cybernetics. It will not be resolved by shouting. But there is a temporary solution: to declare roundly that the divisions are *not,* after all, autonomous, and that the firm has been wholly centralized. Then divisional executives who cannot stomach this edict resign, and for a while the monolithic firm runs on. It does not work; the whole of this book is dedicated to showing it *cannot* work. So the pendulum swings. The next temporary solution is ready-made: to declare roundly that the firm has been wholly *de*centralized. Then those who have been working at the centre for synergistic policies see that their work is doomed, they resign and for a while the fragmented firm runs on. This does not work either. It cannot work. The pendulum must either swing again, or the corporation blows apart in a series of takeovers.

There is no solution to this problem independent of common sense. (Pathetically enough, collaborative common sense becomes scarcer the higher one goes in an organization — for psychological reasons which are not obscure.) Cybernetics identifies this problem, and specifies where it lies. Cybernetics illuminates the problem, indicating the solutions towards which nature itself has evolved. Cybernetics provides a language sufficiently rich and perceptive to make it possible to discuss the problem objectively, without heat.

There are people (whom the gentle reader will not know) who find it much more fun to fight it out across the spurious frontiers of their own ambition.

CHAPTER THIRTEEN

Environments of decision — system four

Notes on the Context of System Four

We have set up the three-tier autonomic system intended to maintain a homeostatic internal balance, and even to optimize performance within an accepted framework and under established criteria. The successful operation of that autonomic system is dependent, *inter alia,* on a steady stream of appropriate instructions descending the central command axis from System Five. The environment for decision at this top level, then, includes representation of the autonomic condition, together with filtered information ascending the central axis. Both sorts of input to System Five are mediated by System Three but, as we have seen, they are switched by System Four.

Yet there is a second major component of input to top-level decisions: information about the environment set by the outside world, the total environment of the organism that is the firm. All indications of relevance here are collected by System Four as direct input from the outside world, and they too are switched into System Five.

These remarks are so far a commentary upon the elementary mechanism depicted as activating System Four in Figure 27. The time has now come to elaborate this story — which we cannot do, as in the case of the lower-level systems, simply by enlarging the box labelled System Four and taking a closer look at its contents. In the first place, we have already stated the key features; but secondly, the way in which the switching is undertaken on behalf of the higher management which this system serves varies enormously. One possible approach to the design of the practical operation of this biggest switch is the topic of the rest of this chapter. But first let us examine the context, within System Five, of the System Four design we must undertake.

In Figure 33 may be observed a simple enlargement of the box labelled System Four, which is the development directorate of the firm, and its connections with System Three. But System Five is now depicted in a new way — a way determined from the System Four standpoint.

It will be noted at once that a perspective drawing of the box labelled System Five has been substituted for the familiar planar diagram. All the ascending information assembled and switched within System Four is being registered in a sensorium, while the descending information is originated by a motor cortex. This is a brain-like figure, and it is worth comparing with Figure 7 where, long ago, we first met the anastomotic reticulum. Now both the sensory and the motor representations of the real world in System Five are generated by the activities of System Four, and the meaning of the irregular figure twice reproduced in the organizational box is precisely that it constitutes a representation of the same irregular figure in the external world. Were it not so, the organism would be in a state of hallucination. Its account of the world outside, and its account of its own attempt to match that world, must both actually coincide with it to a significant extent. Otherwise the organism has 'gone mad'.

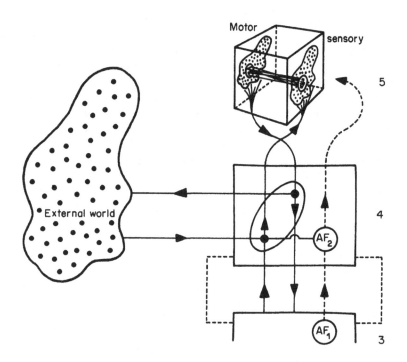

Figure 33. System Four

Next, the nature of the connection between the sensory and motor halves of the brain is the same as we met in Figures 25 and 26 — which ought now to be consulted. At last the story of the central command axis is complete. We have closed the homeostatic loop between sensation and action, between affect and effect. Here, at the very highest organizational level, is the firm's final attempt to say that what it does is derived from what it knows, and that both halves of this homeostat jointly constitute a mechanism for surviving in an outside world which it understands and with which it interacts.

This puts the process of effective corporate planning in its true light. System Five attempts at all times, with the service of System Four, to adjust its output to its latest input — and of course to the prognosis of change which the input sensorium is able to generate by rapid-time simulation (which is called foresight) in other parts of the cortex. But this is a topic for the next chapter, when the more subtle forms of System Five behaviour are discussed. We need to remember here, however, that a corporate plan must continuously abort, for unless that plan is continuously aborting, how shall sanity (the match between the world and the firm's notion of it) be preserved?

Apart from this, we need only to note the existence of one further mechanism. It is the one which we have kept in mind throughout these hierarchic descriptions: I mean the algedonic input, which has special channels of its own, depicted by the dotted line ascending from System Three. We observe a second arousal filter in System Four, which incorporates the new external information in the ascending stream. And we also observe (in the wandering arrow) what amounts to a potential danger signal, waiting to pounce on the smooth operations of the sensory-motor homeostat.

Notes on the Corporate Model in System Four

Remember that there is always a System Four, even if it is not identified in quite the form specified here. It will always be found as that set of activities, maybe disseminated, which feeds the highest level of decision making. We may then say that System Four *must* contain a model — some model — of the corporation.

There is no doubt also that this model may be disseminated, in separate chunks of cognition around the firm, rather than being cohesive and well formulated. Certainly, no one may think of it, or refer to it, as a model, but it must be there. If it were not, the senior management would have no idea what sort of firm they were running. Their idea of the firm, to put the matter in its least scientific terms, would be this model. Let us try to make a more scientific version of such a model explicit in a diagrammatic form which would be recognizable to a businessman.

184

Suppose a corporation intends to set up a new company as a subsidiary. The sources of capital are twofold. Money may be available from the corporate surplus, which is to say from the profits of other companies within the corporation; secondly, money may be obtained by borrowing. The new firm will process this capital input, according to its commercial plans, and produce two kinds of output: earnings and depreciation. Between them, they constitute the cash flow of the new company over any given epoch. This is in turn divided into three: tax, the dividend payable to shareholders, and capital usable by the corporation for other purposes. Again, still simply, this latter resource has two sinks: re-investment in the new firm itself, and money apportioned to other corporate needs. All of this is shown in Figure 34, where time is unfolding from left to right.

The little diagram shown in Figure 34 is of a kind often represented to businessmen by their advisers. But what happens to this 'corporate model' at the end of the first epoch, when re-investment occurs? The diagram we have been given is no longer of any use — because the re-investment itself has run off the page on the right-hand side. Thus it is that the picture has to be redrawn for a second epoch; for there is a new input on the left — the assets generated by re-investment. And indeed, as the new business settles down into some kind of equilibrial behaviour over the years, yet a third diagram will be needed. In this, *most* of the input will derive from the output.

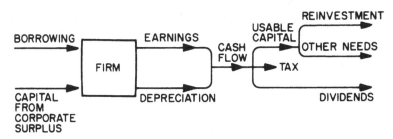

Figure 34

All this means to say that we do not have a very effective corporate model. The three pictures are satisfactory as far as they go, but clearly they do not represent the total dynamic of the business. If they did, there would be no need to reconstitute the entire picture every time the business changed its habits as a consequence of its growth towards maturity.

We can immediately do better, if we consider the firm as an adaptive system. Re-investment is now a feedback loop operating on a time cycle which may be studied in terms of the control engineering concepts put forward in Chapter 2. A decision to re-invest passes round the system as a 'blip': it is a step function.

The lagged return on this investment is a smooth function over time, generated by the total behaviour of the business, which may now be considered as a high-gain integrator. This means we are making synergistic use of our assets, and amplifying them. Figure 35 shows the new version of Figure 34.

Now we can see the control loop which governs the reinvestment of funds. As usual, it assumed that there already exists a basic plan that will generate this investment; what matters is that we should be able to monitor its performance, so that the plan may be *continuously adapted.* There are two very important cybernetic notes to make about the situation now depicted.

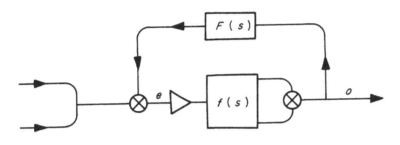

Figure 35

Firstly, because we are now considering a dynamic situation with appropriate feedback, the model is adequate for all stages of the new firm's growth. At the start, no feedback exists, because no operation exists. It follows that the entire input capability must come from outside the system, just as was seen in the case of Figure 34. Now the firm (still depicted as a high-gain integrator) operates on this input — that is, it performs the operation *f(s)*. As outputs (in terms of cash flow) mature, the re-investment loop is activated — in accordance with the plan made at the start. But what the model is now telling us very clearly is that any rigid plan, however well conceived, will not produce the goods unless it is continuously modified. That is because the operation *f(s)* is subject to external perturbation (not shown in the diagram) as well as to the perturbation of its own basic input. And if we require a steady (or, better still, an according-to-plan) output, then a highly ingenious mechanism will be required on the feedback loop itself to modify correctly the error signals. This mechanism is shown in the box marked *F(s)*. It is precisely the corporate planning function of the enterprise.

The second point may be understood from a recapitulation of the original discussion on feedback systems in Chapter 2. We saw there (consult Figure 8) how, in a high-gain situation, negative feedback comes to dominate the input signals. This is why the new diagram in Figure 35 does not have to be redrawn for a firm which is just starting, a firm which is gathering momentum, or for the mature business. The whole process is governed by the dynamics of the servomechanism we have already drawn. At the start, nothing happens on the feedback loop — everything is governed by the input i. In the second stage, the error signals (processed through $F(s)$) begin to modify the input via e. Much later, the perturbation of i ceases to matter at all because the feedback itself is now dominant.

If we take these two points together, we can see how the complex process of re-investment in the business conditions its survival. Businessmen know about this very well, although it is often convenient for them to pretend they do not — and to take a short-term view. Secondly, the activity which represents the feedback transfer $F(s)$ is corporate planning. This is the very adjustment activity which modifies, or continuously aborts, the plan enshrined in the operation on i of $f(s)$. Moreover, this so-called planning process is not at all a matter of sequentially aborting every plan which the management supposed itself to have underwritten.

The statements in the last paragraph can be read as banal. Alternatively, they are explosive statements. Certainly the world of business knows that re-investment is necessary, and certainly it knows that plans are subject to modification. So much for what is banal. Now take a look at the dynamite. The image of the firm 'in the City', with the financial journalists, and hence with the shareholders, is settled in the main by the absolute value of the output. Comments may be passed on the extent to which this output, if unfavourable, is as a matter of fact geared to long-term intentions — and this is an attempt to measure the effectiveness of the whole managerial control system. But it is easier for commentators to play down the importance of the company's long-term plans, and to make snide (and rather gastronomical) comments about 'pie in the sky' and 'jam tomorrow'. It is also, in the second place, true that commentators will usually observe the process of reinvestment as a recognition of the need to 'plough back profits'. But they know nothing of the intricate corporate planning processes going on in the box marked $F(s)$. It would be amiable to say that this is because such information is one of the firm's best kept secrets; it would be more truthful to say that this corporate planning work is simply not being done.

Before exploring further the nature of the corporate planning function which continuously aborts it seems necessary to enrich the model a little. So far, management has been seen as a regulatory activity necessary to control earnings at a level above some minimum necessary for security. But it has a second regulatory function: to control the match between product attributes and market demand. The first kind of regulation is performed in the face of perturbations introduced by the environmental economy, both of the nation and of competition in the money market. The second is performed in the face of market perturbations, which may be due to the aggressive marketing policies of competitors, but which are fundamentally caused by the rate of technological innovation. The management organization of System Four ought to consist of an institutional embodiment of the two major control loops associated with these two kinds of regulation. Usually this simply does not exist.

In Figure 36 appears the minimally richer model required to explain these points, and to draw some major conclusions about the control parameters of *F(s)*. This model is derived from work done by my colleague R.H. Anderton, and it indicates both major kinds of regulatory activity. Note how earnings generate future earnings, and how this flow is 'pumped' by the market and its demands. Revenue is shown as generated by the match between existing product attributes (including price) and the demands of the market, as conditioned by the economic climate and available technological alternatives for satisfying the same basic needs. Investment funds are seen to be divided between product improvement (A), product innovation (B), and the potential operating efficiency (C). These three factors, which it is open to management to control, represent capabilities of the firm between which investment choices must be made. According to this model, there are only two more control parameters in the entire system worth considering. One is the responsiveness (inertia) of the market (X), and the second is the power to borrow money (Y) — both of which are conditioned by other kinds of managerial action.

The value of any cybernetic model, however simple, of the firm derives from its dynamic characteristics. The model used in System Four is no exception. It facilitates the examination of corporate plans on the indefinite time-base which invalidates so many static models of the corporate economy. For there are no crucial dates in the development of the firm, except those specified by convention. It is sad to see the whole process of corporate adaptation geared to the purely conventional annual statement of accounts and the chairman's address. Consider, for example, the marked difference which is bound to exist between the time constants of the three investment channels A, B, and C (product improvement, innovation, and better performance). Secondly, there may well be a sluggish (long time constant) output response to certain kinds of fast varying input — because of the complexities of the total system which damp down the initial oscillations. There may also be amplifiers in the system which increase the amplitude of dangerous oscillations that ought to be damped. It is the task of System Four to study all these phenomena through its models, and it ought also to monitor managerial action as being itself a generator of oscillation. For one thing is sure about a system of this sort — it is that the control target of steady response, which entails steady profit making and steady growth, can be achieved only relatively. The important outcome of regulation is, as we learned from our study of homeostasis, to hold critical response variables within *physiological* limits.

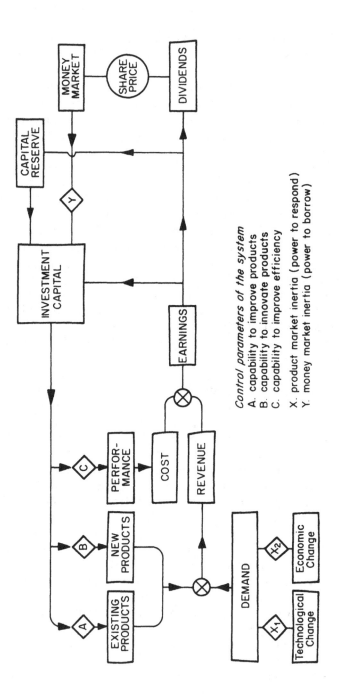

Figure 36

Now take a look at the way Figure 35 is enriched in Figure 37, as a result of thinking depicted by Figure 36. The five control parameters of the system (A, B, C, X, and Y) are now gathered into a box of control settings through which the feedback can operate. (Note that every line on the diagram should be drawn as five separate lines, one to each control parameter — the diagram has been simplified — because each has its own characteristic time constants.) In addition, there is now a 'feed-forward' loop, which activates the kind of model shown in Figure 36; the predictions of this model are compared with real-life outcomes to generate the feedback that activates the corporate planning return loop.

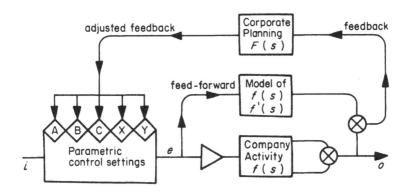

Figure 37

All this assumes that two kinds of basic regulatory mechanism have been isolated, as remarked before, and I do not think that this is as arbitrary as it may seem. When we consider the firm as an organism operating in an environment, and contemplate the intrinsic nature of business itself, it does seem very clear that both the money market and the product market must be satisfied. There are other interests to satisfy too — no doubt job-satisfaction and the monetary requirements of the labour force are critical. But such demands on the system might best be regarded as constraints rather than major homeostatic loops of the total ecosystem — particularly because the firm's response to the first two greatly conditions the climate in which the rest of the managerial responsibility will be discharged.

Anderton, who has experimented with various computer-driven versions of System Four models, has deduced one lesson about these two regulators which is highly disturbing. There is a very sensitive (that is, high-gain) relationship between product match and revenue performance. Now the means available to management for handling this sensitive area are the three investment control parameters A, B, and C. Their relative importance and relative effects are

190

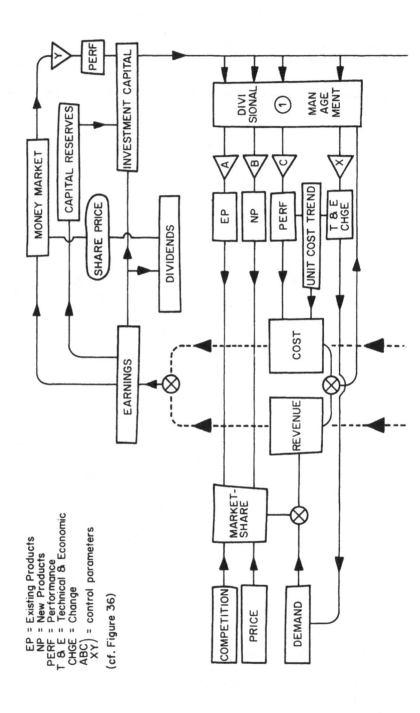

EP = Existing Products
NP = New Products
PERF = Performance
T & E = Technical & Economic
CHGE = Change
ABC) = control parameters
XY)

(cf. Figure 36)

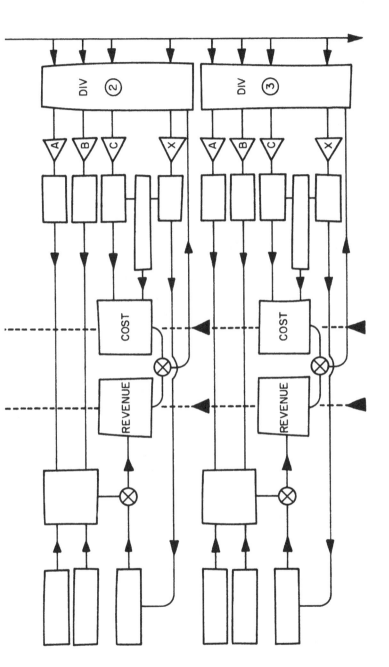

Figure 38. A System Four model of the total system (pen recorders read any group of flows — say demand, market share, earnings — and project them over next ten years)

hardly understood — particularly in terms of the people (who are not line managers) who will respond to their manipulation. Most talk about the management of change and innovation is about *either* economic viability *or* about human relationships as illuminated by behavioural science. Anderton's case is that we have not really seen the intersection of the two major ecosystemic control loops as occurring exactly in the same domain. Moreover, he says, there is a largely unrecognized coupling between the two loops which is *de-stabilizing*. This is surely a remarkable inference to draw from a simple theoretical model, but it invites profound reflection. To speak personally, it has illuminated much in my experience of actual business problems which was hitherto obscure.

As has been remarked before, there is an infinite number of possible models of the corporation, any one of which would count as a tool of System Four. In Figure 38 an attempt is made to map a considerable extension of the model in Figure 36 on to the corporate structure as we have learned to know it in this book. But please beware. The diagram at Figure 38 is not an *alternative* to, nor even an *elucidation* of, Figure 27. It is explicitly the diagram of a model of System Four. The reason why it looks like the total figure is that System Four must in some sense mirror or map the totality it serves. That is, we are dealing with a recursive logic, one which turns in on and duplicates itself.

Notes on the Operation of the Development Directorate

The development directorate will consist of people, and may indeed involve the activities of a large staff. For, in managerial terms, the development director himself must exercise control of all those functions needed to acquire information (therefore, for instance, marketing research), to evaluate information and propose solutions to policy problems (therefore, for instance, operational research), and also actually to implement whatever adaptive planning processes may be agreed with System Five that affect the whole corporation. This may lead to his exercising control over the research and development function; it will certainly give him a right of access to all ascending information from the autonomic system — and that may well include responsibility for its very design. Responsibility must lie somewhere after all, for governing the total information system and for the command structure of the corporation.

None the less, our primary concern has to be with the physiological role of System Four as 'the biggest switch'. We understand its central place between Systems Three and Five, at the conflux of information between the central command axis and the outside world. We know what it has to do, and the kinds of techniques available to these ends. But precisely how is it to operate?

For the first time in this book we shall look beyond anything that has yet been achieved, except in embryo. The real nature of System Four has never before been exposed, and therefore never organizationally consolidated. Bits and pieces of what we should now call this organizational unit certainly exist in every corporation, but because they are disseminated throughout the corporate structure, under different bosses, their interactions with senior management have never been properly codified. The head of operational research, for example, gets along as best he may, 'selling' his activities in an *ad hoc* fashion. If there is a corporate planning unit (which there ought not to be) it will often be found on the end of some organizational limb, immersed in its models, and wholly frustrated by its inability to influence the mainstream of managerial thinking. All of these units, which in terms of our model are all aspects of System Four activity, lack a means of communication with either the board or the operations directorate which goes beyond formal committee work, the production of reports, and informal conversation. In the first context, they are suddenly an enemy, seeking to interfere with what management is trying to do. As to their reports, they are not read. The third mode of interaction, the informal, is by far the most effective, but it is open to all manner of accusations of a political nature. Many large organizations are well nigh in despair about these problems. Successful outcomes seem to depend exclusively on the personalities involved.

There is just one clue in management history as to how the whole big-switching capability can be made to work in practice. The origins of the technique in Britain seem to lie in the information overload produced in the conduct of World War II. Think of the conduct of a large-scale battle, involving forces by land, sea, and air. Many units were committed, many of them highly mobile. A continuous stream of reports arrived at headquarters. From the fluid pattern of circumstances established by these reports it was necessary to make decisions — especially as to the commitment of resources. Now all of this is a close parallel to the situation described in this chapter.

The answer was the 'war room' — a large operations centre equipped with relief maps spread out on tables, on which incoming information could be depicted by the movement of counters. Girls were deployed, like croupiers, to switch the counters around. The senior management, operating on a balcony, surveyed the entire and changing scene without respite.

Some attempts have been made to model this operation in modern businesses, using electronic displays of data in place of the maps. Most of these seem feeble by comparison with their progenitor, perhaps because they lack verisimilitude; they also lack the speed of response associated with battles. The contemporary activity which most resembles the original war-room control centre is surely Mission Control in the Space Centre at Houston, Texas, where the real-time command of space operations is conducted.

To say that one wishes to see a control centre of this kind, updated technologically via computers, established in the corporation (or for that matter in government) is a bold statement. Clearly a move in this direction would involve an almost total change in the conduct of managerial affairs at the most senior level. To my mind, however, some such dramatic change is desperately needed, and the existence of this forum is consistent with all the teachings of the management cybernetics argued here.

I will spare the reader 'knocking copy' about established forms and practices which stifle both intuition and initiative and which produce such lags that corrective action becomes precisely out of phase with the performance it is meant to correct. But I do this on condition that he will bear in mind the horrors of it all, some of which have been made explicit in earlier chapters, but most of which he will in all honesty know more certainly from his own experience. For unless the point is taken that *something has to be done,* the upheaval imposed by the remedy (however attractive it may look in its own right) will seem too much.

I propose a control centre for the corporation which is in continuous activity. This would be the physical embodiment of any System Four. All senior formal meetings would be held there; and the rest of the time, all senior executives would treat it as a kind of club room. PAPER WOULD BE BANNED FROM THIS PLACE. It is what the Greeks called a *phrontisterion* — a thinking shop. Let us review what it might contain.

First of all there would be a large, dynamic electrical display of the corporation, in terms of an animated Figure 27. There would be flow lines on this figure proportional in width to the standard amount of flow — whether of materials, cash or profits. The flows would move on the diagram at appropriately differential rates. Changes in the system which were signified by information passed through the many filters discussed here would at once be notified on this board. The algedonic information especially would be signalled appropriately — that is, if necessary, with flashing red lights and the ringing of bells. There is no reason whatever to think that the production of such a continuous display presents any technical problem whatever. If the work has been done to establish the kind of model developed here as the brain of the firm, we are now faced simply with a display problem equivalent to any of those solved daily in every major industrial exhibition in the world. Of course this display equipment must be fed by the output of the electronic computers which are calculating the data needed for routine management purposes. But they are there and doing it in any case.

The next set of displays would enable the occupants of the room to call forward further information if they needed it. And here I at once (and for the nth time) repudiate the notion which is commonly propounded that it should be possible to have access to any data bank in the corporation and obtain a long set of figures on a cathode ray tube. This is silly. There is no need for it; we must give up our preoccupation with digits. *There is more to quantification than numeration* — an aphorism which I am sure would become famous if I could find a more elegant form of words in which to state it. The fact is that the human brain is singularly incompetent in the matter of handling figures.

Consider the following situation. You are trying to judge whether a piece of furniture will fit into a particular alcove. Try to estimate the length of this sideboard in feet and inches. The likelihood is that you will be anything up to 20 per cent out in each estimate, and therefore your 'calculation' as to the possibility of fitting the furniture in will be a nonsense. No; the best thing you can do is to *guess* whether the piece will fit or not. Except in the most critical cases you are likely to be right. More dramatically still, as a second example, think of yourself successfully dodging across a major traffic flow in the heart of London. Then contemplate your chances of survival if you were attempting to calculate the manoeuvre in terms of distances and relative speeds ...

In short, everything we know in psychology about perception, pattern recognition, and (in general) awareness of the state of affairs, says that we should try to reach our judgements in terms of relative size and shape, relative colour, relative movement. When we draw graphs and histograms we pay attention to the first of these desiderata — but even then, having reached the judgement as a matter of fact, we hasten to make it look 'respectable' by quoting rows of digits. But our control centre would leave the handling of digits where this kind of work belongs: inside the computer. Managers would be trained to deal with other kinds of display, essentially graphic, but depending profoundly on relative movement — a mode of communication so very well understood in all biological spheres that it is well nigh incredible to find it not exploited in the sphere of human affairs.

So much for accounts of what is actually going on, and the retrieval of in-depth information where required. To recapitulate: the first wall of the room displays an animated, quantified version of Figure 27. The second wall is used for the display of memory — it handles the need for recall and reconsideration. Now by far the most important part of the work which will be done in this room has to do with looking ahead. Therefore the third wall of displays represents a capability to call up information (in the same form as on the second wall) relating to the future. Here we want the best prognoses which statistical technique and the insight of properly trained OR teams can provide. There is surely nothing else, now, that managers can ask for. Everything seems to be up to them.

But the very first question that a sensible management team would ask itself in these circumstances is: what are our alternatives? The people present will have ideas about that. It is also possible, particularly in stereotyped situations, to obtain a set of major alternative courses from the computer. What we want to do next is try them out. Here is the biggest break of all with managerial traditions. In orthodoxy, the people who experiment are scientists; managers, it is reckoned, cannot afford to experiment — they are playing with human lives, shareholders' money, and the future of the business. Their decisions may be mistaken, and they may make mistakes; wise managers regard such mishaps, which cannot after all be recalled, as experiments *faute de mieux* — and seek to learn everything possible from them. But deliberate, cold-blooded experimental intentions have never before been management currency.

Today, thanks to the techniques of fast-time simulation, all manner of experimental situations can be set up in the control centre and worked through by the management team. There is no claim in this that our methods can predict outcomes exactly. Science is not a matter of crystal-ball gazing. The objective, on the other hand, is valid and valuable. It is to explore the responses of the system to various alternative actions, in order to see which areas of a problem are more sensitive than others to the assumptions which management is making. And this is done in order to test which policies are more vulnerable than others to a range of likely events.

For example, consult the model depicted in Figure 38. We know that such a model can be operated on a digital computer, that questions posed by management can be taken away, processed and eventually answered. But it is wholly critical to the arguments of this chapter that this sort of remote batch-processing is *not* the kind of input which a management team requires. First of all, it needs to operate in real-time, using its computer capability as an extra lobe of its own brain, probing the nature of the thing it examines, and getting the feel of the situation. Now this is perfectly possible even with existing facilities, and the package of a real-time interrogative corporate model is commercially available. Even so, it is *used* by System Four and *reported* to System Five. The facility could certainly be made directly available to the board, if one were prepared to equip a control centre — the 'war room' — with telex machines and· keyboards. To my mind, this is unthinkable. A keyboard interface between a senior manager and his computation facilities is sheer nonsense — because he is not a typist. Therefore it becomes necessary to find a better interface; and in order to achieve this I think that a combination of digital and analogue techniques is essential.

What was said a few paragraphs ago about pattern recognition is pro-analogue and contra-digital. Moreover, analogue computation is unbelievably economical, compared with modern digital operations. It is very fast indeed and, above all, it is entirely direct — because the physical layout of the computing elements and their controls can be made to correspond to the sort of animated electrical diagram already envisaged. Although analogue machines have been very much exploited in certain fields of engineering, they have hardly been used in the context of management at all, because managers and scientists alike have acquiesced in the digital convention. Moreover, at the time when most people were taking decisions about what sorts of machines to use we had no solid-state circuitry. The development of this circuitry, which has made the third generation of digital computers possible, has also made huge advances available in the analogue field. Analogue elements are now more stable, more convenient and cheaper than they were and furthermore (because of the commodity of solid-state physics) hybrid analogue-digital interfaces are more readily provided. Given parallel logics, the hybrid machine is a tremendous but largely unrealized answer to the problems raised here.

What does this mean? It means that a large schematic diagram, fully automated, on the lines of Figure 38, would provide the fourth wall of the control centre. Wherever the diagram indicates a variable, there would be a knob and an indicator. Therefore the management group could turn the knobs and set the indicators. In particular, they would manipulate those five critical control parameters A, B, C, X and Y. That would mean that they could decide between various amounts of investment going into the system for every purpose, and distinguishing between the major divisions of the business. Then they would demand to see, on a TV screen, a graphic prognosis for the next ten years of the effect of their decisions on any aspect of the business they cared to plug in. A scheme of this kind is wholly realizable for an expenditure on hardware of the order of £10,000 — which is three orders of magnitude more economical than many of the schemes one sees proposed under the heading of 'Management Information Systems'.

Notes on the Development of System Four

There are two ways in which this chapter could be elaborated into a book. Firstly, one might continue to specify details of models available to System Four. I myself could provide perhaps ten such models which have been developed and tested in practice over the years.[1] But any such book would also have to include an account of the *Dynamo* programme, and its consequent programmes, invented by Jay W. Forrester, and many other models of the firm.[2] The temptation to elaborate on these lines must therefore be resisted, but the reader should be left in no doubt that anything missing from this present account is available, whether one wishes to attend especially to finance, production, labour, marketing or logistics. It is not the operational

[1]Some generalizations about them appear in Chapters 15 and 16 of *Decision and Control*.
[2]*Industrial Dynamics*. See Bibliography.

research technology or experience that is lacking to produce the first System Four control centre. It is the managerial acceptance of the idea, plus the will to see it realized.

The second basis for a book on System Four technology would be the detailed explanation of the electronic analogue system which could be built to implement Figure 38. But this too would be out of place here. Suffice it to say that simple circuits are available to undertake all the basic operations of arithmetic by electrical means. In these circuits the real-world variable is represented by the magnitude of a voltage, and they depend on the use of the high-gain D.C. amplifier which usually operates at more than a million times the original variation. Then we may multiply by invoking Ohm's Law, obtain the additive effect of several variables, integrate our results, and above all study the effect of time-lags in the system. It is on these effects that ultimate stability fundamentally depends in real management systems, and analogue computing readily introduces lags by adding a resistance across a capacitance to leak away the charge at a calculable rate.

These devices are sufficient to quantify the System Four model in a dynamic fashion, and thereby to evaluate outcomes over a period of time for any selection of inputs. Management, as the user of System Four, will experiment with this model in its 'war room', and its task is essentially that of *tracking* a target. The entire servomechanics of such tracking systems are also well understood, therefore it is worth repeating that the only missing link in the realization of a project of this kind is the managerial intention itself.

But in any case, and as was said before, any enterprise already has a System Four. It is usually disseminated, not clearly acknowledged, not institutionalized, not — therefore — terribly effective. If we use a rigorous model, however developed, and a fast convenient transducer of that model which encourages the symbiosis of man and machine, we can — should — must — improve our performance at the senior management level by at least one order of magnitude.

Here is a final, if not original word. The service (System Four) provided to the highest echelons of management (including government) today is concerned almost entirely with stating what has happened in the past — in the hope that this knowledge will somehow illuminate the darkness of an unknown future. Most attempts to look ahead, then, are concerned with the extrapolation of historic trends. The System Four manifestation envisaged here uses all this experience in creating a model which has then to be used as a tool for *inventing* the future (in Gabor's phrase), rather than fearfully predicting what it may hold. We use our brains to do this — we should use our managerial system to the same end.

Look straight ahead down the motorway while you are driving flat out. Most enterprises are directed with the driver's eyes fixed on the rear-view mirror.

Note in the Second Edition

This chapter has been left in its original form for strong historical reasons, which will become manifest in Part IV.

CHAPTER FOURTEEN

The multinode—system five

The direction of the enterprise, with its concentration on where we are going rather than where we have come from, with its *foresight* that is to say, is the thinking part of the whole organization. This, for the body, is the cortex itself — and for the firm it is the senior management. We may ask how System Five is organized to deliberate policies and to take decisions.

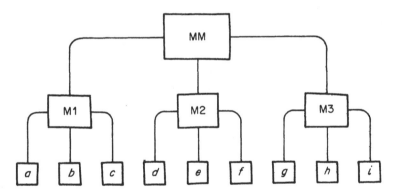

Figure 39. Orthodox view of organization — competent to apportion blame

In Figure 39 is depicted the highest managerial echelon of the firm as it might be seen on a typical organization chart. There is MM — the manager of the whole enterprise, called the Chief Executive, and he has three main subordinates, M1, M2 and M3 who are directors or vice-presidents. Each of these (this is simply a convenience) also has three subordinates, so there are thirteen people considered in the illustration. Experienced businessmen would recognize that this picture is intended to show how the chain of command is organized — that is to say, how accountability is distributed. No one of experience would expect this chart to show how the senior echelon actually *operates*. And yet it is true that some businesses really do operate according to the chart, and the behaviour of most businesses is, more or less, off and on, influenced by it. Let us consider a very serious decision, requiring a yes or no answer from the boss, and work out how the chart seems to imply 'correct' behaviour.

MM sends for M1, M2, and M3 and explains to them the situation. He tells them that each should come and see him independently, so that he can concert their views himself. That seems reasonable, because if they deliberate together outside and come back with an agreed solution, what is the boss for? He will hardly contradict their combined view. M1 goes away and summons *a, b,* and *c.* These are of course his divisional heads — and he repeats to them, his subordinates, exactly what the boss, MM, has already said to him. And, for the same reason, M1 asks his subordinates not to 'gang up on him'; he would rather hear each of them speak independently and then weigh the evidence. Eventually *a* comes back with his view to M1, and so on ... The protocol is followed throughout. It all sounds both reasonable and stately. One might be tempted to say that this is a well-ordered company, not prone to the normal gossip-mongering and squabbling which (even at the most senior levels) appear to influence many major decisions of many enterprises.

All this clear cut, formal behaviour looks as though it might work for one major reason. It assumes that everything goes like clockwork in a properly conducted organization, and completely ignores the fact that all men are fallible. Consider *a.* I am sure he is doing his best to give correct advice, and that he has consulted his subordinates — and they theirs in turn. But after all *a* (although only two steps removed from running the company) strictly speaking knows just one ninth of the total picture. Moreover, his subordinates are a motley crew. Some of them are hard-working, honourable people, but at least a couple are incompetent — and *a* does not really appreciate the fact. Another, and he is most aggressive and convincing, is primarily concerned with his own ambition to unseat *a* and take his job. Furthermore, *all* of *a's* subordinates are fallible, even when being totally honest, thoughtful and responsible in their advice. That is because *their* subordinates, like themselves, have trouble with subordinates. So what is *a's* advice, when he gives it to M1, going to be worth — and how shall we measure that?

Certainly *a's* advice will not be worth full marks, although the organization chart somehow manages to imply that it will. We might measure its worth over a large sample of incidents by asking how often the advice *a* gives turns out to be satisfactory (which means accurate, sober, well judged, in perspective, mindful of implications, careful of staff ... and so on). Some readers might feel, contemplating these criteria, that they *never* receive satisfactory advice. But we must not be too hard on our subordinates, and I shall propose that the advice received — especially at the senior level — is right much more often than not. For instance, we might say that *a* delivers the goods seven times out of ten. That would be, surely, a very high score. But of course the same considerations apply to M1 himself. However, we shall again be kind. Because he is more senior I shall take it that he is right, and offers good advice to MM eight times out of ten. MM himself, although the boss, really must not be thought infallible. But he did get to the top, so let us judge him right nine times out of ten. All of this, you might think, is most charitable.

Now we shall work out the implications of this whole scenario, taking a particular example. The answer (we know with hindsight) that the boss has to produce is 'yes'. This is the 'right' answer in this case. If a is right seven times out of ten it means that he has a 0.7 probability of being right on this occasion. So has b and so has c. Because they have been forbidden by M1 to compare notes, their advice is independent. Now M1 is a cautious man, and I propose that on this occasion the matter is so serious that he has made a private deal with himself. He has decided that he will not say 'yes' to the decision problem unless each of a, b, and c says 'yes'. This decision criterion, secretly decided upon by M1, requires that the three subordinates each be independently right at the same time. The probability that this will happen is multiplicative: that is to say, $0.7 \times 0.7 \times 0.7$. Because of the setup, and because of his private decision, M1 has a chance of 0.343 of receiving correct advice. For instance, b may not be saying what he really means — and M1 is supposed to detect this. We know that M1's judgements are right only 80 per cent of the time. So if M1 is to pass right advice to MM, his chance of doing so this time is 0.8×0.343 — which is no more than 0.2744. (This is where protocol and prudence get you!)

Now M2 and M3 have each done the same thing, with the same probability of success. So, from the point of view of the boss MM, when he privately sees each of his three deputies, the situation (which he is also playing 'correctly' and prudently) is already rather loaded. Believe it or not, he also has decided not to approve the plan unless M1, M2 and M3 *all* approve it. The possibility that these three men will all be independently right is no more than the cube of the previous probability — which is just 0.02. And of course, although he is the boss, he himself is prone to misjudge the advice he receives 10 per cent of the time. The final reliability of his decision, therefore, may be calculated as the multiplicative probability that M1, M2 and M3 will be right together, adjusted by his own success factor of 0.9. This works at 0.018 — the probability that MM will finally be right. So the outcome for the firm of this apparently splendid and sedate setup is that the boss will make less than two correct decisions out of every hundred.

It is true that I have biased the example by 'knowing in advance' that *yes* is the right answer. If we did not know this, we could say that MM will not be pushed into backing a wild scheme very easily — which sounds much more sensible. Even so, prudence on such a scale is stultifying. Evidently enterprises which actually worked like this would not succeed. Evidently, also, firms cannot really be organized to operate like this, however the organization chart looks. Then let us turn for advice to the brain, to the cortex, where the body's policy-making and decision-taking go on. We have met the neurons before — they are the individual decision-takers of the brain in so far as they receive the variety of inputs, and have to 'take a decision' which says either yes or no (their axons must fire or not fire). If we look at a piece of cortex under the microscope, we shall find that the manager neuron is far, far less reliable than we have assumed the human manager to be.

In the first place, many of the dendrites (the nerve processes which attach themselves as input channels to the neuron) peter out in mid-cortex. That is, they do not reach the neuron to which they look as if they were going at all. Secondly, since the input that actually does arrive at a given neuron is the output of other neurons (each unreliable) the neuron under consideration is bound to be pretty unreliable — in terms of its input. Next, as we saw earlier, the neuron firing threshold is critical, and we know that this changes as a result of all sorts of biochemical activity. For example, quite a modest amount of alcohol will totally change the threshold of millions of neurons distributed throughout the cortex — and in an unknown way. It has indeed been proposed that the transfer function of a neuron is an eighth-order non-linear differential equation, in which all the variables are subject to subtle changes on the microsecond scale. Next (and without wishing to cause any sort of alarm) it has been estimated that some 100,000 neurons in our brains go phut every day. They just fuse themselves, and cease to exist. Moreover, they cannot be

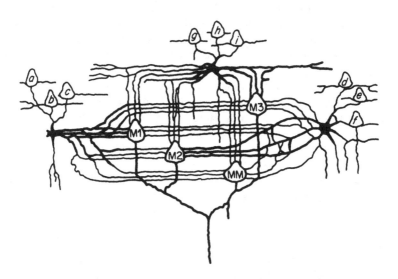

Figure 40. How organizations really work (compare Figure 39, which includes the same elements). Save for the letters, this chart could serve to illustrate the neuroanatomy of the brain's cortex

replaced — this kind of tissue being (unusually for the human body) non-regenerative. So the brain is very very much worse off in the calibre of its executive neurons than is the firm. But the brain works. Although people imbibe large quantities of alcohol they do not really lose their ability to behave roughly as human beings. Though an old man may retain no more than two-thirds of his original complement of neurons, he usually remains a fully paid-up human being until the end (but note some signs of senility that are likely to be attributable to this cause).

The fact is that the brain handles these problems *exactly* as does the firm. Neurons do *not* work independently but reinforce each other. Managers, too, are *not* as a matter of fact often isolated in the way the chart seems to entail. In short: System Five is not the collection of nodes, logically organized to be precise and well mannered, that our first model suggested. It is instead, whether made of neurons or managers, an elaborately interactive assemblage of elements. I call it 'the multinode'.

Then let us by all means try to draw a better organization chart than we had in Figure 39. An attempt to do so appears in Figure 40 — and it will at once be noted, by anyone who has ever looked at a book about the brain, that this diagram (save for the letters) looks extremely like a chunk of cortex. In fact we are now resolving our model of the nervous system to a level of detail much finer than before, and we pass here from the consideration of neurophysiology to that of neurocytology (cytology is the science dealing with cells themselves).

This new organization is still concerned with the interaction between thirteen top managers, who look exactly as they did before — in real life. But it is now conceded that *a, b* and *c* are in a communication with each other, and are capable of formulating a view. What is *not* conceded is that a single transmission of this view to M1 will necessarily convey their considered opinion. *Three* transmission lines have appeared between the concerted outlook of these subordinates and their chief. This accords with cortical architecture; it also accords with behaviour in a real enterprise. On any serious topic, neither the boss nor his subordinate is likely to be content with one excursion into the problem which has to be resolved — given that the problem is at all difficult. My example assumes that there will be three efforts to 'get across what we think to the boss', so say the subordinates. The boss may view this operation as three attempts on his part to find out 'what the hell they are really thinking'.

Secondly, the picture given in Figure 40 does not conceal the undoubted fact that *a, b* and *c talk* to other seniors than M1, even though they are not *responsible* to them. Of course they do. And the other seniors want it that way. After all, in any given case, M1 may be making one of his two gross errors of misjudgement out of every ten. Besides, all concerned know that there are many ways of illuminating problems, and their discussion is a growth process. It is not really a question of counting the heads, pro and con. So this model, based on neurocytology, allows that each of the three inputs to M1, M2, and M3 will not only be repeated three times to each of these seniors, but will be relayed to the other seniors as well. Finally, it is important to pull down MM (although he is the boss) from his pedestal. He does not sit in isolated state — or, if he does, he will not be the boss for long. If he treats his three immediate subordinates with any respect, that is to say as colleagues among whom he is *primus inter pares,* then he will join in the decision-taking process with them. Moreover, he himself is not above receiving messages from the next stage down.

M1, M2 and M3 may (in a protocol-ridden organization) vigorously complain that there are direct channels of communication between their subordinates and their boss. But in any real situation which is at all robust this is exactly what happens — *a* does not entirely trust M1's judgement, perhaps, and besides (this is a real world) *a* wishes to register personally with MM. For his part, MM does not want his life-sources chopped off by M1. Who are these people who advise M1? What are they really like? Are they any good (for this has bearing on the value of M1's advice)? And so on.

Thus we find in Figure 40 an account of a brain-like organization for the top-level decision process. There, as before, are the thirteen executives, but this time they are seen to be organized sensibly. Now let us calculate, on precisely the same presumptions as before, the reliability of the decision which the boss will transmit. Given that all thirteen men are prone to error, it might appear that all their mistakes will now be often repeated — so that the outcome is worse than before. Not so, as we shall see.

There are still three messages coming up each line. But they are not independent. Each message still has a 30 per cent chance of being wrong, but the *joint* chance is 0.3^3. The probability that *a* will now receive a *correct* message from his own staff has therefore become $(1—0.3^3) = 0.973$. But each senior manager is now receiving the message from each of three sources — which gives him a multiplicative probability of being right equal to the cube of the last figure, adjusted by his own probability of making a correct judgement. Now we said that M1, M2 and M3 had a 0.8 probability of making a right judgement whereas the boss, MM, had a 0.9 chance. The model proposed treats the boss as a colleague of his three subordinates — so that there are *four* people equivalently deliberating this problem, as a consortium, each with an average possibility of being right 82.5 per cent of the time. This means that *any one* of the four has a chance of being right which is now:

$$p = [(1—0.3^3)(1—0.3^3)(1—0.3^3) \times 0.825] = 0.76$$

But, because all four of them are deliberating together, the *total* chance of making an error is the fourth power of the chance that any one will make an error:

$$P = [1-p]^4 = 0.0033$$

So the probability that this entire system (Figure 40) will yield the wrong answer turns out to be one third of one per cent. In other words, this management group will (as a whole) hardly ever make a mistake — as long as its members really collaborate.

This is how the brain does the trick, and this is how successful managements already work. It is the way to get reliable results out of unreliable components. All I have tried to do is to provide a cogent explanation for their mutual success. But what surely follows from this is that we ought to retain in our heads a better account of the organization of the enterprise than our orthodox charts supply, and to make various admissions which appear to conflict with the orthodox 'principles of management'. We ought in particular to admit:

1. that any boss is a colleague — *primus inter pares* — of a group which includes his subordinates;
2. that the 'one man, one boss' principle may work in some contexts (there will be only one salary, hopefully), but that protocol must not forbid rich interactions throughout a group, and
3. that there is necessarily more communication between people at the same level in the enterprise — by far — than there is between seniors and juniors.

The first two points, and the third to a lesser extent, emerge from our analysis. More telling evidence for the third point however comes from behavioural science, where many measurements have been made which clearly indicate the truth of the assertion. In the diagram these horizontal pathways have been no more than indicated (because the picture is already complicated enough as it is).

The next question is: how on earth can this kind of system be controlled? Anyone reading this who quickly appreciated that in real life groups of people operate as in Figure 40, rather than as in Figure 39, will have considered that I have been busily discovering the Mediterranean. *Of course* people work like this, he may have thought. The operation of such a system is usually called 'politics'. And success goes to the politically skilled because of the immense complexity of the communication paths. Moreover, the whole ethos of the multinode is political — there are manifest opportunities to manipulate other people to one's own ends, to renegue on one's boss, or one's staff, or one's colleagues.

But there must be a better answer than this. The reason we need a better answer is that the multinode as we know it may actually work, but it takes far too long to work successfully. Its methods were evolved in a more leisurely age, and we investigated in Part I the reasons why more rapid means of adaptation are necessary in a technologically exploding environment. Now the multinode often involves many more people than the small number we have so far considered; people, furthermore, who do not stand in easily demarcated hierarchical positions in relation to each other. The multinode may include colleagues in other countries whose status *vis-à-vis* the people here is fairly obscure, and even pseudo-colleagues (such as senior civil servants in government departments whose views bear on industrial decisions) who have no institutional status at all. Then there are advisers and specialists of many kinds (who may be, for example, in consulting firms or universities) whose views are important to the decision, but who again have no hierarchical rank. All this makes the real problems of real multinodes much more difficult than the problem facing our fabricated sample organization of Figure 39. Fortunately, however, the neurocybernetic model we have proposed fits this more complex reality better still.

We claim we know how the whole thing works. The problem is to make it work more quickly. That must surely mean the introduction of discipline and order, of some sort, into the situation. It also means, however, that no measures may be adopted which would at the same time put the remarkable freedom of action and the wonderful flexibility of the multinode in jeopardy. If people could see how to do this, without putting themselves and their organization into a strait-jacket, there is some chance that they would adopt new techniques. One method, we ought now to agree, must be excluded — although it is the one method most usually attempted in practice, because no one can think of anything else. This is the method of rigorous protocol. The artificial example just denounced was given to make it clear why this approach to the problem does not work. Explicitly: it denatures the system itself — with all its in-built capacity to generate the right answers.

Let us then approach the problem in a scientific way, using what we have learnt from cybernetics, and specifically preserving the characteristics of redundancy and flexibility which make real multinodes so robust in their ability to generate right answers. Here follows a cybernetic plan.

The first difficulty is to know what kind of problem the multinode actually solves. It does not devote itself, its seniority and power, to the determination of trivial outcomes — or it ought not to do so. It is likely to be settling a policy of great importance — and therefore considerable complexity. Thus it is that people think of thinking as a process of synthesizing an integral but elaborate conclusion from a large number of component parts. The decision is seen as a rococo edifice built up clause by legal clause. This is perhaps why there are endless drafting problems facing anyone trying to promulgate an 'agreed' decision.

The cybernetician adopts the contrary position. The output of the thinking process, the decision, has the following form: do *this* (rather than anything else). When the process of thinking originally starts the multinode is faced — not indeed with a number of building bricks in an edifice — but with a seemingly infinite number of possible outcomes between which it must choose. It is the existence of this plethora of possibilities that cries out for decision in the first place. Then, under this model, the process we seek to assist is one of chopping down ambiguities and uncertainties until we may say: do *this*. In short, we would like to measure the variety of the complex decision at the start, measure the reduction of variety brought about by each conclusion reached in the process of thinking things out, and in general monitor the entire operation of the multinode as the variety comes down to a value of one — the decision itself. To do this we shall need two tools: a paradigm of logical search, and an actual metric — a rule and a scale — for measuring uncertainty.

The Paradigm of Logical Search

A paradigm is an exemplar — in this case a basic approach to the general problem outlined which will be serviceable for many kinds of situation. Now there are many ways of conducting a search, and in the case of decision-taking people usually look to *sequence*. What, they ask, is the first thing to decide? What, after that, is the second? On this account, the tools provided so far by management science as aids to the taking of complex decisions rely on the sequencing of logical priorities. The paradigm of this search method is a *decision tree*. ('Do this in the United States, Britain, or France?' Answer: 'France.' 'Do this in Paris, Lyons, or Marseille?' Answer: 'Paris.' And so on.)

Now the understanding of the multinode developed here shows that this paradigm is not what we want. Certainly scientific helpers may try to nominate logically prior decisions, and try to persuade the multinode to settle those first. Usually it will not, cannot, at least does not, do so. The multinode has its own methods. Besides, who is to say what really is the prior issue? This judgement itself is of the sort we just defined as 'political'. No; we must hang on to our insights about the multinode — its redundancy, flexibility, and *freedom*. Our search paradigm must be priority-free. Otherwise we shall be telling the multinode how to do its job in an unacceptable way.

A simple example of a search procedure arises when we want to find a particular place on a map. Maps are divided into grid squares, and we may assume that the scale and grid are of appropriate sizes — that is, if we can get into the grid square we shall find the correct place. Consider then a map divided by equal amounts on each axis, so that there are 1,000 squares each way. That must mean that the map itself is divided into 1,000,000 grid squares. There are two basic paradigms available for the search procedure. The first involves numbering all the squares — from 1 to 1,000,000. When this lengthy task has been completed, it will clearly be possible to say: 'the place we are looking for is in grid square number 342,756.' This method will actually work; indeed, it obeys the law of requisite variety. We have defined our problems in terms of variety 1,000,000, and now we propose to match that variety in terms of our million-variety search. But every schoolboy knows that there is a better paradigm than this. It involves numbering the squares on the horizontal and vertical axes and quoting a grid square by means of these co-ordinates.

This second paradigm specifies a variety generator. So long as we can record 1,000 + 1,000 = 2,000, we shall be in a position to generate their product — 1,000,000 — as total variety. The storage and retrieval problem has been reduced from a variety of 1,000,000 to a variety of 2,000. That is because we have identified a two-dimensional logical space.

As to the search itself, we do not know how many grid squares we shall have to examine before we find the one that we want. Using the first paradigm, with its variety of one million, we *might* hit our target in the very first square; on the other hand, we might have to go on until the very last. So, in general, we say that the average length of search is half a million squares. In the case of the second paradigm, we first identify the row and then the column; this process will take on average $500 + 500$ examinations, making a total of 1,000. Mathematically speaking, the first search takes a number of steps equivalent to half the total variety (500,000) while the second search takes a number of steps equivalent to half of twice the square root of the total variety $-\frac{1}{2}2\sqrt{V} = V^{1/2}$.

The second paradigm is very powerful, just because it is a variety generator. This is the approach we shall use. In the kind of problem facing us, we are not dealing with a two-dimensional map. We are dealing with a decision posed in a large number of logical dimensions. That is to say, the dimensions of the decisions are not just 'north/south, east/west', they are as many major logical variables as the problem may happen to have. Any major industrial decision tends to be concerned with such topics as production, marketing, finance, personnel, research.... These are indeed the dimensions of the problem, since a dimension is defined as a condition of existence. For any problem worthy of the multinode, then, we may say that there are in general n dimensions to that problem (and we may notice in passing that n is likely to be a number not less than five and not more than say, twenty).

For any n that is greater than two the second paradigm will become much more powerful than we have yet envisaged. Remember that total variety is measured by the dimensional varieties multiplied together. Thus, in the case of the map, we had a variety of one thousand in each of two dimensions, making a total variety of one million. If this were extended to three dimensions the total variety would be one thousand million. In general, for our decision-taking problem, total variety is equal to the variety of one typical dimension raised to the power of the number of dimensions, and the average length of search, according to the first paradigm, will be this number divided by two. It is bound to be gigantic. In the case of the paradigm we have selected, however, the average search will be half the number of dimensions multiplied by the nth root of the total variety. This is simply the generalization of the 'map' illustration for n dimensions. Written mathematically, the expected length of search is just:

$$\tfrac{1}{2} n V^{\frac{1}{n}}$$

The discovery made here is of immense significance. After all, in the case of the map which is really two-dimensional, the calculations reveal that instead of taking half a million steps (paradigm one) we need to take only a thousand steps (paradigm two) on average to find our goal. This represents an enormous increase in decision efficiency, because the effort we now have to make is only a fifth of one per cent of the effort originally made. When the number of dimensions considered in the problem rises from two to n, the added efficiency is astronomical.

The model that ought to be made of any complex decision, therefore, should first identify n logical dimensions, and identify also the relationships between them. It should *not* implicitly identify decision sequences, which will be settled by the multinode itself — however much advice we might give it. The point is that when the multinode acts, by reaching some preliminary conclusions — however 'unimportant' — it will be decimating variety at large. This is because the identification of a point in any one dimension severely delimits its possible location in other dimensions too. If this is not intuitively apparent think once more of the map. We are looking for a town, and in one dimension we determine that it lies on a particular latitude. When we look at the map, we find that (perhaps) half of the length of the line depicting that latitude runs through the sea. This fact limits our search on the scale of longitude. How this fact, dramatically enhanced by the n-dimensionality of a real-life decision problem, fits our model of the multinode will become quite clear shortly when we undertake a sample exercise.

The Metric of Uncertainty

The very idea that we need to measure the uncertainty attaching to a decision must have seemed daunting to most people. The fact is, however, that science already has an appropriate measure, which is useful in many areas of scientific application. It is called 'entropy'. Unfortunately, the concept of entropy is itself daunting to many people, and therefore I shall not go into it here. The use of the concept for managerial contexts is carefully defined and demonstrated in *Decision and Control* for anyone who wishes to investigate the detail of this topic further. For present purposes we can manage quite well with a perfectly simple explanation of a perfectly useful tool without involving ourselves in any sophisticated mathematics or physics. (All this, however, has to be mentioned — otherwise knowledgeable readers might accuse me of claiming to have discovered the wheel.)

Uncertainty, as we have seen, is a function of variety. Variety is a measure of the number of possible states of the system. A decision is the *selection* of one possible state from all the others. Then take the case of the map. We have to select one out of a million states (the grid squares). Obviously the measure of uncertainty involved in this 'decision' starts at a million and reduces to one. Now consider a managerial decision, and let us keep both the dimensions and the numbers very small. We have eight products and we have eight machines. Each product can be made on any machine. Then a 'decision' might be defined as determining which of the eight products should be made on which of the machines *now*. This is a two-dimensional problem, carrying a variety of eight in each dimension. There is no difficulty in seeing that there are sixty-four alternatives — and we shall have to select one of them. So this problem involves a variety reduction from sixty-four to one.

Next, we might add another dimension. Suppose there are eight versions of each product — a red, blue, green and so on version. Then the decision we are trying to take is a matter of selecting one answer from $8 \times 8 \times 8 = 512$ alternatives. Now if these numbers were much larger, and there were many more dimensions, the numbers involved in calculating variety would be astronomical. Note the reason for this: they all have to be *multiplied* together. This circumstance at once suggests to anyone who has done schoolboy mathematics the possible use of logarithms. If we use the *logarithm* of dimensional variety in every case, we shall simply have to *add* these numbers together in order to measure total variety. But now there comes a slight snag — the logarithms most people remember using are calculated to the base ten.

The cybernetician uses logarithms calculated to the base two. The reason for this is that the raw material of decision is the distinction between 'yes' and 'no'. This binary distinction (remember Part I) is called a 'bit'. Moreover, we may distinguish between four things by using two bits of information — a father and mother and their son and daughter may be severally identified by 'deciding' whether each is (first) male or female, (second) first or second generation. We need three binary decisions to distinguish between a variety of eight states; four bits will distinguish between sixteen states; five bits will account for thirty-two states, and so on. That is all that is meant by 'using logarithms to the base two'. With ten binary decisions, we may distinguish between 1024 states. And if that does not sound sufficiently impressive, we should note how the numbers exponentially increase. Forty bits will identify one member of a population greater than a million million.

All we are doing now is to devise a useful arithmetical tool for handling calculations about uncertainty. The eight varieties of eight products to be manufactured on eight machines yielded 512 alternatives. This is a measure of indecision — until some conclusions are reached about which variety, or which product, or which machine, is going to count. Now let us use our logarithmic tool. The variety of eight alternatives in each dimension can be replaced by the number of bits (namely the logarithm to the base two) required to specify it. For variety eight, the answer is three bits (these three: $8/2 = 4$, $4/2 = 2$, $2/2 = 1$). The total variety, instead of the $8 \times 8 \times 8 = 512$ *alternatives,* is now $3 + 3 + 3 = 9$ *bits.* Needless to say, these two versions of the metric are equivalent, since nine bits equals 2^9 variety $= 512$.

The essence of the technique offered here is that we should make a model of the decision to be taken, a model not based on sequential priorities, and that we should measure the total variety of the decision. Then any conclusion reached by the multinode will chop away variety from the total uncertainty. Moreover, the variety eliminated will be not simply the variety appertaining to the alternatives directly eliminated, but chunks of variety appertaining to other dimensions of the problem now found to be irrelevant as a consequence of the primary decision. Remember: the town we seek is not only on one particular latitude, but also it cannot be in the sea — and that limits the longitude.

When the multinode begins to take decisions, which it does by cutting back variety in a particular logical dimension, it implicitly amplifies the variety reduction. To go back to the example of the eight varieties of eight products produced on eight machines: suppose we rule out four machines. The variety is now $8 \times 8 \times 4 = 256$. Or, as we should much prefer to say when we have got used to the idea, we had $3 + 3 + 3 = 9$ bits, and these are now reduced to $3 + 3 + 2 = 8$ bits $(= 256)$. But here is the crucial point. We *think* that we have reduced our variety by one bit. In fact, because of the multi-dimensionality of the problem, this is an underestimate. In eliminating four of the eight machines, we have (as a matter of fact) made it impossible to produce more than two products. The other six require the use of the eliminated four machines. So the possible products themselves now represent a variety of only one bit — as a consequence of our first decision. But, in turn, these particular two products could only be made in eight colours by the use of the very four machines we have now abolished. The remaining machines *on their own* can produce only one colour. So, although we are left with four machines we have only two products to make — and colour is no longer an issue. Thus we can now decide what to do on the strength of a mere three bits of information — only $2^3 = 8$ alternatives remain.

What we have been doing here is to investigate the power of our second search paradigm operating in n dimensions (although n was no more than three in this case). The mechanisms by which this power is deployed are the *clumping* together of logical variables, and the *nesting* of these variables in different dimensions. Thus, although the multinode may not sequence its decisions in a reasonable order of priority, any decision taken is likely to reverberate throughout the decision system — thereby axing variety at an alarming rate. There are two points to be made about this fact.

The first is that the apparently appalling uncertainty surrounding any real-life decision at the beginning very rapidly decreases — until there is only a little bit of decision left to take. Indeed, there are mathematical reasons for believing that variety decreases exponentially with the number of subdecisions taken. The second point is more interesting from the standpoint of managerial psychology. It is not at all clear (speaking from observation) that managers belonging to the multinode realize the extent of the reverberations which apparently minor sub-decisions cause. Therefore they under-rate the importance of reaching a logical sequence of decision. Perhaps a major dividend paid by the procedure described here when it is used for monitoring actual decisions is that, without pre-empting the freedom of the multinode, it is able to point out (even in quantitative terms) the impact of what at first sight might look like minor decisions on the total decision's structure.

With a search paradigm and an entropy metric the multinode has all it needs in the way of scientific aids for the purposes under review. But experience has shown that people find it difficult to understand exactly how this technique works in practice. Therefore this chapter concludes with an example. It would be pleasant to provide an actual example of the use of the technique in practice (for indeed it has proved most powerful), but, unfortunately, this is not possible — actual studies are enormously complicated. They require more background information for their understanding than could possibly be provided here, and more algebra than an illustration warrants. Secondly, they are highly confidential. It is not worth using this technique unless the problem is really very serious indeed, and an example might be traced to its source.

Moreover, the strength of this technique is precisely its potent display of any managerial weakness which might exist. That is because when the multinode takes a wrong decision, or takes decisions in a logically inappropriate order, the fact is dramatically displayed. The gradually eliminating variety — which we said ought to follow the curve of exponential decay — suddenly (in every single real-life example so far encountered) *rises* in the course of the multinode's deliberations. This should not be. It is of course due either to the rescinding of earlier decisions inappropriately taken, or to the re-definition of the problem itself. In both cases, the fact that this technique is being used offers enormous help to the managers concerned, but there is no doubt that a recital of the circumstances would make them look stupid in public. The chapter therefore ends with a fabricated example of the use of this approach.

An Example

We are considering the inauguration of a new product. The factors we shall take into account are not exhaustive, but they are typical of the factors which managers must consider. In defining them we shall find ourselves nominating six dimensions of a logical decision-space. Next, the number of alternative values attached to each logical variable are chosen arbitrarily, but again they have some verisimilitude. The problem is (as it were) to decide on a new product, but the multinode at once recognizes that it is not just a matter of saying: 'we shall make eggs out of wire netting.' 'Deciding on a new product' means specifying all manner of features of the product — including the whole concept of its development, manufacture and sale. That is why the decision comes to be regarded as something elaborate. But we shall adhere to the view that it is really something simple carved out of elaboration, an initial uncertainty reducing to the statement: do *this*. Let us follow the process through, inventing plausible variables, and attributing plausible variety to each.

The Decision Algebra

Variable		Variety No.	Log_2
P = production	— plant strategies	— 4	2 bits
M = marketing	— marketing strategies	— 8	3 bits
F = finance	— cash flow plans	— 8	3 bits
S = staffing	— personnel policies	— 4	2 bits
R = research and development	— development routes	— 16	4 bits
D = distribution	— selling plans	— 8	3 bits
		131,072	17 bits
		(multiplicative)	*(additive)*

Having listed the relevant logical variables and measured their variety we discover that the total uncertainty to be resolved is seventeen bits. This means that we shall need to take seventeen binary decisions at least, in order to reduce the possible alternatives of 131,072 outcomes to one alone. It is this multiple and sequential decision-taking process that we seek to monitor.

The next step is to determine which variables bear on which other variables. Any decision about plant strategy must affect the cash flow plan; it certainly affects the personnel policy (we may have to close a factory); it affects the development route (certain machines we own may not now be available). We may however decide that what we do about plant will not affect either the marketing strategy or the selling plans — we might, for instance, collect our manufactures into warehouses wherever they are made. Then we should consider the effect on F, S and R of any likely decision about P. Having made this analysis for each of the logical variables, we shall be able to write out a full list of logical dependences, where the asterisk means 'any decision about the antecedent bears on the consequent'. It might look like this:

Statement of Basic Dependence — (A)

P *FSR
M*FSDR
F *PMRD
S *PFD
R *PFSM
D *FSP

It should be noted that logical dependences are not necessarily reflexive. In this example, any decision about the personnel policy may have a bearing on cash flow — redundancy payments might possibly have to be made — but decisions about finance are judged not to affect the staffing policy. (This could be otherwise, of course; this is a fabricated but plausible example.)

The next step is to *derive* from Statement (A) a preliminary logical 'clumping' of the variables. After all, *either* P *or* M affects F *and* S *and* R. If we happen to be adept in the use of logical algebra and its notation, we shall start at this point to write down formal propositions in symbolic logic. But there is no need for this, and the following table, which follows directly from Statement (A), will be a help.

Statement of Basic Dependence — (B)

	P	M	F	S	R	D
P			*	*	*	
M			*	*	*	*
F	*	*			*	*
S	*		*			*
R	*	*	*	*		
D	*		*	*		

With the intention of getting what we know of this decision system into logical clumps, we shall now start writing propositions which draw the variables together — starting from the visual inspection of the table.

Restatement by Logical Clumps — (C)

$$PM*FSR \quad ... (1)$$
$$FR*PM \quad ... (2)$$
$$RD*PFS \quad ... (3)$$
$$MF*RD \quad ... (4)$$
$$SD*PF \quad ... (5)$$
$$S*D \quad ... (6)$$

Now check, from Statement (A), that every dependence has been included. Notice, too, that already we have stopped thinking in terms of what the letters mean. This is the strength of a manipulative algebra: it makes thinking both easier and more rigorous.

The final aim of our exercise is to be able to write down the whole decision system as a single proposition which incorporates all logical dependences. Thus the next stage in the clumping process involves the merging of the six propositions at (C). Examine how that is done by taking a first step in this direction. Proposition (6) is boring — it involves only two variables. We shall dispose of it by incorporating D's dependence on S wherever S occurs. To do this a new symbol is needed: an ordinary full stop, meaning 'and'. In proposition (1) consideration of either P or M calls for the consideration of F *and* S *and* R; we now know that consideration of S also entails consideration of D, but this is not true of F or R. Rewriting, then, (1) and (6) together become:

$$PM*(FR.S*D)$$

This statement should be examined very carefully, because we here add to the notion of *clumps* the notion of *nests*. PM and FR and clumps; but everything inside the bracket is a logical nest — because the whole thing is predicated on PM. Notice that without the brackets the statement might have been taken to mean: PM*FR *and* S*D. This would be a wrong nesting. It is true but inadequate.

Now follow the process through for propositions (3) and (5), and we are left with five propositions — those amended being marked with an *a*.

First Nesting Statement — (D)

PM*(FR.S*D)	... (1)*a*
FR*PM	... (2)
RD*(PF.S*D)	... (3)*a*
MF*RD	... (4)
S*D*PF	... (5)*a*

What happened here to proposition (5) is quite interesting. Immediate substitution gives: (S*D.D)*PF. Both the extra D and the brackets are redundant. Thus (5)*a* can be read as either (S*D)*PF or S*(D*PF) — both of which statements are true.

It is immediately obvious now that we can dispose of proposition (5)*a*, because it has taken on a familiar form— PF is predicated on S*D, a statement which already occurs twice. Then:

Second Nesting Statement — (E)

PM*(FR.S*D*PF)	... (1)*b*
FR*PM	... (2)
RD* (PF.S*D*PF)	... (3)*b*
MF*RD	... (4)

Inspection of Statement (E) now suggests the amalgamation of (1)*b* and (3)*b*, since the right-hand sides are nearly equivalent. To make them so, we shall have to remove R from the first and P from the second, and incorporate these two variables on the left-hand side of the implication, thus:

$$[(PM*R)(RD*P)]*(F.S*D*PF) ... (1)c$$

In making this step we have re-clumped as well as re-nested. This is because there is no unique formulation of a composite logical problem, any more than there is a unique formulation of a set of equations in mathematics. Algebras are means for manipulation, and the criterion of success is appropriateness. $a^2 - b^2$ may be an appropriate way of expressing the difference between two squares for some purposes, while $(a + b)(a - b)$ may be more useful on another occasion. Both expressions are 'right'.

The present exercise is going well, because we have disposed of half the original statements. We have one complete statement left, showing dependences in clumped and nested form, plus two of the original clumped propositions left over from Statement (C) — namely (2) and (4). Let us turn our attention to them:

$$FR*PM \quad \dots (2)$$
$$MF*RD \quad \dots (4)$$

Since these dependences have an antecedent F in common, it would probably be best to rewrite this expression in terms of it: F*PMRD (check with Statement (A), after all!):

$$F*PD (M*RD) (R*PM) \dots (2)a$$

which can be rewritten:

$$F* [PD.M* (D.R*PM)] \dots (2)b$$

This may be inserted where F occurs on the right-hand side of expression (1)c, but we cannot ignore the residual statements from propositions (2) and (4) that M*RD and R*PM, since these antecedents occur on the left-hand side of (1)c. There are several ways of incorporating these, but the most convenient seems to be:

rewrite   (PM*R) as (PM*R) (M*D) because M*RD
and   (RD*P) as (R*PM) (D*P) because R*PM

Then the left-hand side of (1)c reduces to:

$$[(PM*RPM) (M*D*P)]$$

Following this manoeuvre, the entire expression becomes:

Final Statement — (F)
$$[(PM*R*PM)(M*D*P)]* [F*[PD.M*(D.R*PM)] S*D*PF]$$

The final F is printed in heavy type. This convention is used to indicate that the full statement of its consequences has been omitted. The logic is of course fed back to the preceding F.

As remarked before, there are many logically equivalent ways of writing this complete expression. What has been gained by setting out one of them in so complex a form? The question is particularly relevant, given that the total proposition could (in terms of logic) be much compressed. The answer is that we are seeking to understand the logical decision system, and to provide ourselves with many inlets to it — since the multinode may select any entrance it likes.

Suppose that a decision is about to be taken affecting the selling plans. One of the eight plans contemplated is beginning to look unattractive, and has been eliminated. Then we enter Statement (F) — from the left — looking for D. The first guidance is that we must consider its influence on P. Next we observe that F is affected, and that consideration must be extended to M (P having been considered, and D being redundant). Considering M involves effects on R, which turn back to affect both P and M. Next, F also means thinking about S, which directly affects the D we are talking about — which affects P and F as we know already. That is an interpretation of the system starting with D. Try to reach a sensible rule for examining impacts of the D decision from the original table, Statement (A). The re-entrant variables quickly tie one's thinking up in knots. Try to draw a diagram: it looks like some knitting which the cat has been investigating. We are in thrall to proliferating variety, once again.

We already have useful guidance from the decision algebra, but the real goal is the creation of a useful metric — the measure of decision. Now for this purpose we ought to write our Statement (F) in full, that is to say we should indicate alternatives. P has four forms: the possible plant strategies. Then where P appears in Statement (F) we should write:

$$P(p_1, p_2, p_3, p_4)$$

and so on.

Then let us return to the consideration of D — or, as we should now say, $D(d_1, d_2, d_3, d_4, d_5, d_6, d_7, d_8)$. According to the illustration, one of these plans is eliminated: that is a decision. The first conclusion is that we have reduced the variety of D from 8 to 7 — a reduction from 3.0 to 2.8 bits. That is a reduction in *total* uncertainty of 0.2 bits. Call this the *ostensible* amount of decision taken. But we know there is more to the matter than this, and we have the rules by which to work out the consequent effects. What about those four plant strategies for instance? Plan 2 and plan 4, we realize, are inoperative, for although we long ago declared that the plant strategy has no bearing on the selling plan (because of the warehouses), the reverse is not the case. Let us say that the d_8 possibility, now eliminated, was the only selling plan involving distribution in remote areas of the country. Sales in these areas were precisely what made plant strategies 2 and 4 viable, because they were to use remote factories. Had these plant strategies been eliminated first, however, plan d_8 could still have been implemented by the use of direct mail.

Thus it is that in the process of eliminating a mere 0.2 bits from the total uncertainty of 17 bits in the abolition of alternative d_8, we have also eliminated one whole bit of uncertainty originally attaching to P. But we showed that all this affects F. Indeed, yes: cash flow plans, f_1, f_2, f_6, and f_7 all hinged (it turns out) upon the use of plant strategies 2 and 4. The F variable variety goes down from 8 (3 bits) to 4 (2 bits) — another one-bit reduction of uncertainty. The logic then tells us to consider the effect on M. Now if we can no longer distribute (d_8) to remote areas, then our marketing strategies are undeniably influenced. Surely, indeed, we should have thought of that *first*? If so, how did the d_8 decision come to be taken — before M-type considerations were debated? Who did this, and were they right? These are just the sorts of question that our monitoring technique prompts us to ask, and ask fast and directly.

Still, it is possible that the d_8 decision is, after all, absolutely dominant. Then most of the marketing strategies, which devoted so much attention to the problems of remote areas, may be irrelevant. Suppose that five of them are now abolished. That leaves three — just 1.58 bits of uncertainty. We are led straight to R at this point. For this variable, oddly enough, nothing is changed. The implications of this particular scenario do not turn out to affect the nature of the product at all. So R's effect on P and M does not, on this occasion, cause reverberations. However the route (D*P)*F*S is still before us. Now s_1 and s_2 were both staffing policies dependent on this chain — and out they now go as not needed (it is just too easy to invent the reasons for that). Another one-bit reduction of uncertainty is effected. But this affects D.

On the face of things, we have come full circle. We started from D, surely. True, but in particular we started by eliminating d_8. How about d_2, d_4 and d_7? It turns out (we shall now plausibly declare) that the consequential elimination of five marketing strategies and two staffing policies — as a result of the d_8 elimination — react on D to eliminate these three further selling plans. That, we know, logically affects P and F. Fortunately for this exposition (we shall self-indulgently say) the plant strategies are not further affected — although, heaven help us, they might in principle have been affected. But F *is* affected. Elimination of consequential variety from F was originally due to the elimination of two plant strategies. But now three more selling plans have gone out, making nonsense of f_5 — which was devoted to their needs. Now look at that re-entrant **F**, the one in heavy type. We shall have to go through the whole argument again from the first appearance of F, since it has by now been reduced to a variety of three (1.58 bits)...

Someone said d_8 was out, and that was agreed. The uncertainty of the whole decision underwent a reduction, the ostensible reduction, of 0.2 bits. Now we shall review the battlefield, and determine the real strength of that decision.

D   originally 3.0 bits reduced to 2.8 bits (ostensibly)
P   originally 2.0 bits reduced to 1.0 bit (consequentially)
F   originally 3.0 bits reduced to 2.0 bits (consequentially)
M   originally 3.0 bits reduced to 1.58 bits (consequentially)

S   originally 2.0 bits reduced to 1.0 bit (consequentially)
D   latterly 2.8 bits reduced to 2.0 bits (reflexively)
F   latterly 2.0 bits reduced to 1.58 bits (reflexively)

Here then is the consequential outcome of the very first decision — to eliminate d_8.

Variable	Original Variety	Resulting Variety
P	2 bits	1.0 bit
M	3 bits	1.58 bits
F	3 bits	1.58 bits
S	2 bits	1.0 bit
R	4 bits	4.0 bits
D	3 bits	2.0 bits
Total variety	17 bits	is now 11.16 bits

By one small decision, ostensible score 0.2 bits of uncertainty eliminated, we have in fact reduced uncertainty in a single stroke by 5.84 bits. The possible alternatives have been reduced from over 130,000 to a little over 2,000.

This is the power of the multinode and its multidimensional search paradigm. It is a power which the multinode itself already has, but of which it is not quite self-conscious. That is why it needs a monitoring technique. We are trying here to explain the strength of group decision-taking (not to invent it), and to provide a means of facilitating and expediting outcomes (not of usurping them). Lengthy comments could be written about my experiences with this tool, but I will be content to reinforce the explanation given earlier as to the alternative reasons why selection entropy may actually rise in the course of a lengthy decision process.

Suppose that the blobs on Figure 41 mark sub-decisions, taken at the times shown (the falling uncertainty being calculated by this technique). Then, strictly, we should draw the chart as a histogram, in which the uncertainty reduces only at the moment of agreement on a sub-decision. Here is a curve instead — it gives a better indication of the flow of events, and is a least partly justified by the thought that the multinode *converges* on a conclusion.

It is evident that things were going well until the fourth sub-decision, taken at time-interval 7. But at time-interval 8 half the uncertainty so far eliminated was suddenly pumped back into the decision system. Whoever is manipulating this technique will certainly know *what* has happened; he is doing the recording and measuring, and he knows perfectly well which constraints have been released. But, strangely enough, he may not find it easy to understand *why*. The alternatives are: 1. that a decision has been unmade, and 2. that the problem being resolved has changed.

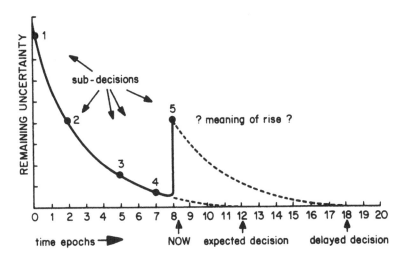

Figure 41

How could anyone fail to see the correct interpretation? If a decision has been dramatically, deliberately, consciously unmade ('we made a mistake'), or if the problem has been formally re-defined ('there are completely new factors now'), there is no problem. But in real life the multinode — comprising a lot of people — may not be at all sure what has happened. The only agreement is that whereas there used to be a consensus about sub-decisions 2, 3 and 4, there is no consensus any longer. If the monitoring technique can successfully demonstrate what has really happened, it has performed a valuable service indeed (although this will itself take some 'selling', because motives within the multinode are complex and conflicting).

Be pragmatic instead. What is important about the situation at time-interval 8? Simply that the final decision (do *this*), which we confidently expected at time-interval 12, is going to be very much delayed. At this point the leader of the multinode, the chief executive, must fight hard to regain what appeared to be the consensus, or he must accept the inevitable delay, or he can *subdivide the problem*. This third alternative is most interesting in practice. It turns out that much procrastination in major policy-making is due, not so much to 'changing' the problem, as to illuminating it (optimism) or befuddling it (pessimism) so that uncertainty surreptitiously increases.

Unfortunately, the chief executive has a fourth course open. It is to do nothing. The decision may then drag on for ever; every time we approach the one-bit answer 'do *this*', uncertainty is pumped back. I have one chart with six peaks — the final one containing exactly as much uncertainty (after several years) as the very first. This can mean only that the multinode as constituted is unable to rise to the complexity of the problem it faces.

CHAPTER FIFTEEN

The higher management

With System Five we have come to the end of the hierarchy of systems we undertook to consider. Why should this be 'the end'? After all, we have become used to the idea that every system is embedded in a higher-order metasystem, which alone is competent to handle the structure of the lower-order system. We know from considerations of mathematical logic (or meta-mathematics) that the formal language in which we define any system is likely to be incomplete: it will result in undecidable propositions which can be answered only in the metalanguage appropriate to a higher-order system. Then we seem in logic to be committed to an infinite regression of languages and systems, whereas in both physiology and management we come to a necessary stop.

This is not because the theories of logic are after all defective, but because all physiology is limited by a finite anatomy. Once a system has been defined according to a particular taxonomy, it must reach *terminal* boundaries prescribed by that definition. For example, if the brain is defined as that mass of tissues held within the head, then the terminal boundary is necessarily the skull. Had we chosen to use the taxonomy of atomic physics to describe the brain, however, we should have found that the electron in the brain is not bounded by the skull at all: the probability that defines that electron may manifest itself somewhere else in the universe at any moment. The terminal boundaries, then, are functions of the taxonomy employed, rather than of 'reality'; that is precisely why they are always logically unsatisfactory. The brain and the firm must therefore *expect* to be confronted by undecidable propositions at the point where they run out of metalanguages in which to understand them. Man's problem and preoccupation with the nature of his own existence in the universe is surely of this kind, and the firm's policies will always in the end be short of metasystemic guidance. In neither case does this simply mean that we cannot acquire enough contextual information. It means that we are bereft of the tools for comprehension.

Despite all this, the problem remains: although we are constrained by anatomical boundaries to stop somewhere, why stop *here*? The answer was given in Chapter 4 during the discussion of heuristics when (Point 11) it was said that the ultimate criterion of viability must indeed be the capability to survive. This is both a physiological and ecological criterion — and certainly not a logical one.

This book has been wholly about the *viable system*. There must be criteria of 'independent' viability, even though any system turns out to be embedded in a larger system and is never completely isolated, completely autonomous or completely free. For just as we recognize the separate identity of even inanimate objects such as stones, so we recognize the viable system as having such an identity, and distinguish it from the systems which abut and enclose it precisely in terms of life and death. The criteria used here are therefore neurocybernetic criteria; a set of logical criteria is developed in the companion volume, *The Heart of Enterprise*.

When the viable system dies, it continues a physical existence and an observable interaction with contiguous systems. But it has lost its identity — precisely in terms of its coherence as a viable entity. We should say this of a firm as we do of man. When a firm is first taken over by a larger enterprise, shareholders and employees are likely to be assured that the identity of their firm will be preserved. Its name will continue — after all it is worth money in terms of goodwill. The board will continue to exercise complete control. The realities are otherwise. The goodwill of the larger corporation is worth more than that of the smaller, so the firm's original name is increasingly subsumed within the corporate name, and is often lost altogether after a few years. As to the board, it soon learns that its freedom of action is heavily constrained. It must stop being a directorate and become a management group. In short: the firm has become one of the units of the new whole — a System One.

Despite this, that firm — just like the other units of the corporation — must itself remain viable. And the industry of which the corporation is a unit must remain viable too. Thus to set the cut-off point on the infinite logical regression of metasystems at the ecological condition of viability solves the problem of identity, although it does not solve the problem of the undecidable.

We may not enrich the organization of the system we have studied, whether the brain or the firm, by adding new levels of metasystem. They are not required to explain viability. Hence elaboration of the model results in the identification of subsystems and even of trans-systems (as we might call systems that partake of the character of more than one system at a time). It does not result in the identification of a new metasystem, a System Six. Then it looks as though all viable organisms are singularly vulnerable at the cut-off point where the logic runs out.

They are. But because we humans are self-conscious beings there is one trick left. We may try to stand outside ourselves, outside our brains and our firms, and to survey the thing that we are. This operation, for a man, is often called an examination of conscience. And indeed I have heard a particular official in various companies referred to as 'the conscience of the firm'. But I prefer to talk about this faculty as *the higher management*.

This term was introduced in Chapter 1, by analogy with the subject known as 'the higher arithmetic'. It does not at all refer to seniority (compare the phrase 'top management'), which makes it a rather poor term, because it sounds as though it does. However, there is no accepted or readily coined term for this concept, which is indeed sufficiently subtle that any term will be misunderstood by those who are not following the argument. We may not say 'meta-management', because we are bound to include everything we know and understand about the control of the viable system in System Five. This is not then a metasystemic activity, but almost *extra*systemic. If we are not careful it will sound as though we lay claim to mystical insights, as indeed do those who talk about conscience in the human condition.

The higher management is about a policy calculus, above all about the nature of the viable system. For if, as we have been arguing, viability is the criterion of identity and of organizational structure, then it is vital that our whole notion of managing does not do violence to it. The beginning of wisdom here seems to me this very recognition of identity. This ideas recurs in all branches of modern management thinking, but I do not reckon that managers recognize the underlying unity here. Let us take some examples.

The integrity and dignity of the single human being has been reasserted by behavioural scientists who have studied organizations in recent years. Management has in consequence been led to a new perception of the need for participation in affairs by people who used to be regarded simply as servants or at best as cogs in the machine. The human being has identity. The human being is a viable system. Secondly, consider the way in which management has been led to develop the organizational handling of cost centres and profit centres, headed by their own managers — who are held accountable. That notion of accountability is the cut-off point; these centres are viable systems. Thirdly, there is an undoubted emphasis these days on decentralization within the very large enterprise. The major unit of the enterprise is a viable system. Fourthly, we should note how, as enterprises have grown larger and more complicated, and have turned themselves into corporations and conglomerates, they have begun to lose their sense of identity. This is why there is a contemporary emphasis on determining written objectives, on reorganization at the top, on experimental high-level managerial units (such as the 'president's office') and on *corporate* planning (my italics). These activities have all emerged as a response to the need to reassert coherence and identity in the firm, because the firm is a viable system too.

If we wish to test the generality of this emergent generalization we may look at other organizations altogether. A trade union sees itself as a viable system, because it wishes to survive. There are many threats to its identity, most of which are associated with changes in technology which render the original objects of the union obsolete. Unfortunately, the union response is, on the whole, to reassert its identity within the obsolete framework — thereby sizeably increasing the threat. That however is an accusation of mistaken strategy; the legitimate aim of survival is the same as before. New nations (it seems to me) make similar mistakes, but again there is no mistaking the evidence of a need to assert identity as the prerequisite of survival. That leads to what I call the 'airline syndrome' — whereby a young country must have its own national airline, whether doing so makes economic sense or not. The same phenomenon, in another guise, may be observed in mature nations which feel threatened. We follow our technological noses into any project, however expensive and irrelevant, which reasserts identity and thereby offers evidence that we have indeed survived. Examples of this are the moon landing by the United States, and the Concorde project of Britain and France.

To recapitulate: there is an ecological answer, given in nature, to the abstract logical problem presented by an infinite regress of metasystems. It is the identification of the viable system, its determination to be itself and to survive. Then we must expect that an organization of viable systems into some large viable whole will be organizationally recursive. This is the general statement of the point argued *ad hoc* before. After all, we reproduced Figure 27 within the units of Figure 27. Hence:

Recursive System Theorem

> If a viable system contains a viable system, then the
> organizational structure must be recursive.

This theorem finally validates the five-tier hierarchic model we have been using all along. If the viable firm is organized like this, so is its major viable unit. If the unit is organized like this, so is its viable sub-unit — the individual factory, for example. If the factory is organized like this, so is the individual viable shop of which the basic unit is the section of which the basic unit is the man. The shop, the section and the man then are each organized like this, and we know that the man is so organized, since that is where the model came from in the first place.

The theory of numbers, called the higher arithmetic, deals with the properties of natural numbers rather than with the numbers themselves. A famous exponent, the late Professor Davenport, notes that 'a peculiarity of the higher arithmetic is the great difficulty which has often been experienced in proving simple general theorems which had been suggested quite naturally by numerical evidence'.*

The higher management has the same problem in recognizing its own general theorems, of which I have just proposed one. That is, I think, because people look in the wrong place for the threads which unite organizational theory. The major thread unravelled by management cybernetics is the thread of variety — its generation and proliferation, its reduction and amplification, its filtering and control. For variety is the very stuff and substance of modern management in a newly complicated milieu, just as physical matter was the stuff and substance with which our forefathers had to wrestle.

When we make our models and classify our insights in terms of variety, we perceive what management is really about — whatever the variety sources may be. At all times the management process seeks to procure requisite variety in stabilizing the enterprise towards survival. This it does either by devising methods for reducing the variety with which it is presented, or by seeking to increase its own variety, or (more usually) by doing both at once. In the foregoing table many of the most familiar devices which management adopts are listed. They would not normally be seen as having much in common with each other; some are related to personnel policy, some to methods of accounting, and so on, but we detect in them all a common endeavour: it is the need to attain requisite variety.

As has been hinted before, every variety reduction *ipso facto* reduces information, and is therefore dangerous. But it must be done. Every variety amplification increases information, and leads *ipso facto* to instability. That risk must also be run. We shall better know what to do, and how to undertake variety-engineering, if we see all these devices for what they are, keep in mind the associated risks, and above all realize that it is possible to trade one kind of instrument for another. For example: if it is expedient to relax constraints hitherto applied to employees in the interests of an enlightened personnel policy, variety will increase; it may then be possible to avoid overloading in System Five by reducing variety somewhere else.

It is against this background that we should return to algedonics, and especially to all those mechanisms discussed (in Chapter 10) in terms of the model drawn from the ascending reticular formation of the brain stem. So far we have seen in this mechanism what is really a variety *generator*. If, we said, many filters are operating to reduce variety within the organization, System Five may easily be lulled into a sense of false security. Special filters would be needed, working on collateral information channels, to reinstate requisite variety regarding threats to survival. But now we must look to this strange structure (the core of the brain stem, the 'climate' of management) as a variety *reducer*. In both the brain and firm, it appears to be the most massive variety reducer of them all.

Some organizational reducers of world variety ◄——————— Requisite variety			
Class	Name	Meaning	Danger
Structural	divisionalization	by factories or products	loss of corporate synergy?
	specialization	by market segments	loss of market synergy?
	functionalization	by profession or service	loss of collaborators' surplus?
	massive delegation	top men free to think	withdrawal symptoms?
	utter involvement	immediate problem-solving	loss of wider opportunities?
Planning	short-term horizon	ignore distant future	lack of continuity/investment?
	long-term horizon	let immediate problems solve themselves	'in the long run we are all dead'
	settling priorities	sequential attention	destroy systemic interaction?
	very detailed planning	well-oiled machinery	obsession with trivia?
	management by objectives	decide where we are going	loss of adaptability?
Operational	management by exception	ignore routine chance results	using wrong model?
	close administration	cut down argument and anomalies	curbs freedom to react?
	averaging/aggregating	taking one year with another, etc.	unassailable optimism?
	sacking innovators	prevent rocking the boat	creeping paralysis?
	management auditing	keep a continuous check	stifling initiative?

*The Higher Arithmetic. See Bibliography.

The first hint of this role was carried in the closing paragraphs of Chapter 10. Because the reticular formation transmits algedonic information — that relating to threats, to pain and pleasure, in the extreme case to crisis — the best orientation of managerial structures is towards deciding what at any moment is the right form of variety reduction for the organism as a whole. So despite all our variety engineering, all our plans for what we ourselves should do as creatures with a brain, or for what the firm should do since we are its management, the most massive of the variety inhibitors is essentially *self-organizing*. The mechanics of this device were laid bare by the late Warren McCulloch and his collaborators (see Bibliography).

Trade-Off ──────► Some organizational amplifiers of management variety			
Class	Name	Meaning	Danger
Structural	integrated teamwork	share knowledge and experience	loss of accountability?
	work through henchmen	amplifiers of the boss	transmit his faults?
	diversification acquisition	generate } new acquire } areas of business	overstretch managerial ability? reverse takeovers?
	reorganization	broadening everyone's experience	hopeless confusion?
Augmentation	recruit managers	add to } existing managerial	face does not fit?
	recruit experts	enhance } capability	wrong advice? political involvement?
	consultants to advise	gain from best practice	slanted? irresponsible?
	consultants to implement	increase power to hatchet	hatchet wrong people?
	consultants to absorb variety itself	inhibit action while *sub judice*	illusion that problems solved?
Informational	conferences	encourage participation	open flood-gates of criticism?
	improve management information systems	enrich specific knowledge	inundation by data?
	training	enrich general knowledge	unrequited ambitions?
	management development by T-Groups	enrich self-knowledge	disintegrate personality?
	open door arrangement	employees come first	collapse of authority?

Readers are by now alert to the existence of redundancy as a powerful protective mechanism in circumstances where the organization is computing with unreliable components (see Chapter 14). Organizations are collections of decision elements and the channels by which they are connected — the neurons and their processes in the brain, men and their communications in the firm. In the last chapter it was shown how the constructive employment of apparently superfluous numbers of nodes and channels provides immense protection against error, when everything about the system (the nodes and channels themselves, as well as the information in process) stands a finite chance of being wrong. If these nodes and channels are the only components of the system, and if they are already redundant, what other form of redundancy could there possibly be? McCulloch discovered it. His name for what is not a physical but an organizational entity was 'the redundancy of potential command'.

Think of the anastomotic reticulum, that (apparently) undifferentiated network connecting a sensorium to a motor plate. Think also of an intricate managerial process, of which that is a model. Where in all of this is the centre or focus of command? There is no simple answer. At this level of intricacy and subtlety brainlike systems are not organized into a pyramidal command structure looking like a family tree. No; the command centre changes from time to time. Its location is a function of the information available to a given concatenation of cells. It is the information flow that determines which concatenation matters, and that therefore delineates the command centre. This is why we call the system self-organizing.

Who, for example, really decides to buy a quarter of a million pounds' worth of highly expensive machinery in the firm? It is not the senior manager who alone is authorized to undertake expenditure on this scale. It is the little group of employees, possibly very junior, which understands the need for this equipment, which has created its appropriate specification, and which has made the unassailable case for its purchase. Admittedly, the case could be vetoed by a more senior group, either on the grounds that the money would not be forthcoming, or because some other expenditure has higher priority. But we are not talking about the right of veto, we are discussing intelligent decisions. This decision was really taken at a junior level by a self-organizing group.

Now we come to McCulloch's concept. If command centres within the reticulum are of this kind, then *any* concatenation of cells might become a centre of decision — depending on the information flow. Call such a (as yet unidentified) concatenation a 'centre of potential command'. The redundancy of such centres is a further massive protection to the organization. That assertion can be examined by looking at the situation in which there is no redundancy of potential command.

If the firm has used divisionalization as a major variety-reducing device, and has in fact erected a wholly and rigorously pyramidal structure, it will have a fixed and countable number of possible command centres. If each of these has a set of objectives (a further variety reduction) there can be no redundancy of potential command, for if the organizationally 'wrong' unit acquires all the information really needed to take a decision, it will be unable to do so. Its only recourse is to speak to the appropriate group — who, in an organization of this type, will most probably flatly repudiate that approach as 'none of your business'. The variety engineering has been done in the wrong way. I am able to say that quite flatly because the organization described is designed to be totally non-adaptive.

Suppose instead that we ensure the redundancy of potential command. This organizational design will constitute a variety amplifier of high order. Then the organization will take a lot of controlling. The device, on the face of things, is likely to run amuck. We might then well ask, as we have learned to ask, why the brain employs such a mechanism — and why the cortex is not hopelessly overloaded by the proliferating variety so engendered. The answer is that the redundancy of potential command turns out to be the prerequisite capability of any self-organizing system, and that given this prerequisite the system will indeed organize itself.

Thus it comes about that the algedonic controller, for both the brain and the firm, is the biggest variety reducer of them all. It determines the *mode* of behaviour. In animals, including man, there are relatively few and mutually incompatible modes of behaviour. McCulloch and his collaborators identified some fifteen behavioural modes of vertebrate activity — this, please note, for organisms that are ostensibly capable of enormous variety proliferation. Examples of the major modes are: sleeping, eating, drinking, fighting, fleeing, hunting, searching, urinating, defecating, mating. The behavioural mode is selected by the reticular formation according to the redundancy of potential command, and it proceeds to *dominate* the behaviour of the viable system. As I said, the modes are mutually exclusive, and the fact that an animal busily fleeing may urinate as well does not mean that it is in the urination mode. If there are about fifteen modes, and if they have the same kind of 'weighting' in the brain, then the selection of one mode by the reticular formation reduces the whole system's variety capability by fourteen-fifteenths — which is a lot.

Now let us apply the lesson to the firm, for indeed it offers what is in many ways the most valuable insight of all. A firm which is well organized on the lines of modern management thinking, a firm which is not, that is to say, cripplingly authoritarian, will have to some degree the capability of potential command redundancy. This operates, as hinted earlier, to create a pervasive climate in the human society which consitutes the firm. That in turn settles the mode of operation for another epoch of time, and that mode excludes all other possible modes — except (as it were) accidentally, on the side. This revelation has explained a very great deal to me personally. It conforms exactly to observed behaviour, as far as I know it. And yet (until I had the model) the idea was seemingly so implausible that it never crossed my mind.

A large number of human beings 'should' between them surely maintain an equilibrial outlook. We think of a social group as establishing a *via media* — and indeed criticize it for the very mediocrity of its decisions. It does do this, and we do well to criticize. But I now see that this performance is undertaken in terms of conscious and intellectual decisions which belong to System Five activity. But System Five is preconditioned by System Four, and in particular the reticular structure which settles the behavioural mode. People are near to the true point when they talk about states of morale. You cannot expect (one instinctively feels) aggressive commanding action by a firm threatened by takeover, beset by strikes, and otherwise in a state of near despair. But the concept of behavioural modes, as revealed by the model, is richer than this. We are not after all talking about emotional states, but about survival patterns created by algedonic controls.

The first three modes in which a company may be trapped to the exclusion of other modes seem clear enough. The first is the mode of sustained activity; it is the normal state of affairs in very large organizations (simply because their filtering systems are unable to distinguish other modes) and it is relatively rare in smaller companies for whom the recognized failure to advance constitutes regression. That remark gives us the clue to the next two modes — growth and retrenchment. These three behavioural modes exist on the same scale, so there is no difficulty in realizing their exclusivity. But I will suggest that the next easily recognizable mode of behaviour is the crisis mode. This might readily derive from either of the last two, and might well appear to be simultaneous with either of them.

The reticular formation teaches us otherwise, and I for one respect its advice. For the crisis mode is certainly dominant when it occurs — so much so that everyone tends to forget which of the three scalar modes was operating before crisis supervened. Some firms, even large ones, exist habitually in the crisis mode, so that either growth or retrenchment considered as a basic strategy becomes a behavioural accident. That is to say that crisis as dominant may lead either to a panic retrenchment, where many activities are closed down in an effort to reduce costs in the short term, or it may result in acquisitions and mergers. The arbitrariness of this accompanying state has something to tell us. It is that the dominant emotion which accompanies the crisis mode is quite simply a feeling that we must get out of it. Any route, in any direction, seems acceptable — as long as the crisis mode is supplanted. This is the heyday of arational (not irrational) management. Now obviously crisis is a dangerous state to a survival-seeking organism, and this doubtless accounts for the arationality of the outcome. At any rate, this theory of the exclusivity of behavioural modes offers the only explanation of which I am aware for the unpredictability of 'the way the cat will jump' in these circumstances. It should also be noted that it is characteristic of the crisis mode that attempts to escape from this way of life characteristically involve re-entry rather than escape. Most of the things one tries to do by way of escape drive one back into crisis. So there is a positive feedback mechanism — the desire to escape becomes ever stronger as the attempts to escape increasingly fail.

A fifth characteristic mode, different from the three scalar modes and the crisis mode, seems recognizable. It is the *moribund,* a behavioural state which *looks* like sustained activity, but which is in fact a steady decline towards death. Many firms experience this mode with equanimity. They consider themselves to be in an epoch of sustained activity, which appeals to the intellectual, *via media,* strategy maker. The facts are however that all the markets are quietly declining. The impact of such facts can be offset by claiming to recognize the decline as a function of temporarily adverse conditions. These may indeed be offset by various devices, such as small price increases that are claimed to be the inevitable outcome of rising costs. The firm which is self-engrossed, which does not think in terms of 'the higher management', may continue this self-deception for a very long time. The well-nigh inevitable outcome for such a firm is the receipt of a takeover bid, for other firms — competitors, suppliers, consumers — have no motive for self-deception where the affairs of our firm are concerned. That is why they see the truth sooner than we do — and move in.

The next mode which I seem to recognize has few, if any, parallels in the animal kingdom, apart from man himself. It is a mode of self-destruction — the so-called death wish. This presumably derives from a sense of inadequacy, and may lead to a pathologically masochistic frame of mind — or (in the case of the firm) climate of opinion. I have known several firms reduced to inanition as a result of a failure to metabolize creative talent already available within the organization. Such a firm may exist for a long time in the crisis mode, and imperceptibly but definitely switch into the self-destructive mode as its sense of inadequacy overwhelms it.

There is certainly positive feedback available to this transition too, in that the market quickly recognizes such symptoms. By its reactions, formal and informal, and by the consequences for the share value, the firm's masochistic tendencies may soon be reinforced. The typical outlook here is a reverse takeover. But let us remember that the behavioural mode is exclusive of other modes. While this is happening there may be appearances of (for example) growth-dominant behaviour. They are illusory. A firm in this mode may exhibit crisis behaviour and also declare itself to be a growth concern. Learn from the model. It is the dysfunction of the adaptive mechanism which is at fault, and the firm is *actually* in the retrenchment mode. The appearance of crisis is due to the lack of policy — even about retrenchment — which generates panic among the bulk of the employees who do not understand what is going on. The illusory appearance of a growth mode is due to the refusal of senior management to believe that they cannot cope with the situation, so that they declare unrealizable targets in which they may in all honesty believe. Despite these confusing appearances, the real mode of behaviour is not survival-worthy; it is decline. The firm is like an animal intent upon fleeing which nevertheless urinates and defecates — irrelevantly — at the same time.

The sixth mode seems to be one of unfeigned aggression. It is distinguished from the growth mode by the fact that there is no objective basis for growth. In nature, the aggressive mode which is not based on discernible needs and opportunities is usually disastrous. This is not so in business, for reasons we shall uncover in a moment. Whether in nature or in commerce, aggression is read by others as significantly based in the first instance. Viable systems are not supposed to become aggressive without cause, or — more particularly — without soundly based expectations of success. In both cases, aggression is in the long run met by 'calling the bluff'. This happens less often in business than in nature, because businesses are supposed to be run by managements of high judgement. This fact loads the dice in favour of the pathological aggressor. Moreover, even though his bluff be called, he may often escape behind a high-variety smokescreen which effectively disguises the bald truth. In getting out he may make a lot of money, which fact (by positive feedback) increases rather than diminishes his chances next time round.

These considerations lay bare another truth. The time-lags in the managerial context are too long. The firm remains locked in one mode because it believes that it cannot readily change course — and therefore it disregards its opportunities of doing so. Perhaps this is partly due to systems of annual budgeting. In nature the viable system does not make this mistake; it is conditioned by evolution to be 'quick on the draw' where a change of mode is concerned. Introspection will reveal how little inertia has the reticular formation. In management, the inertia is very high. When it comes to government, the inertia is so high as almost to deny the mechanisms for adaptation enjoyed as of right by any viable system. The reason for this in large-scale enterprise is the belief of all concerned in inertia itself. Opportunism is a dirty word, it betokens irresponsible action. The viable system in nature seizes its opportunities, so that a man making love will switch to a fleeing mode when he hears the husband's footsteps on the stairs, but may equally stop fleeing if the opportunity to make love suddenly presents itself again. Companies and nations have failed in this rapid reticular switching, and (I repeat) excuse themselves with cliché-ridden talk about 'the responsible conduct of affairs'. So we return to a long-standing issue in this book: artificially contrived viable systems do not pay sufficient attention to the immediacy of response, nor in general to the instabilities or (worse) the rock-hard over-stabilities engendered by differential time-lags inside the informational circuit.

There may be other behavioural modes than these six which I have been unable to isolate. But beware. We incorrectly identify modes if they are not mutually exclusive except by accident. Many of the apparently more complicated behaviours which companies exhibit seem fundamentally to belong to one or other of these basic six. The whole of this matter requires further research. In the meantime, let us note well the existence and large-scale efficacy of this variety-reducing technique of immense potency. The other trouble is that we have so far failed to institutionalize so important a mechanism. It usually seems to operate without anyone at all becoming aware of the fact, still less of the mechanism involved.

What might this mechanism be, and what 'further research' might be productive? Neurocybernetically speaking, we have the model of the reticular formation of the brain stem, already mentioned, which fortunately lends itself to mathematical description (see References, under A4). Managerially speaking, we have as a start the observations discussed in the last few pages, which have been greatly reinforced by experience since I first recorded them (see, especially, Part IV of this edition). At the time of the publication of the first edition, I knew of no mathematical approach which offered any prospect of handling the sudden switches in behavioural modes that I was describing. In fact, Réné Thom's seminal work (*Stabilité Structurelle et Morphogénèse,* W.A. Benjamin, 1972) appeared in that same year, and gave rise to a whole new area of mathematical analysis now known as 'catastrophe theory'. What is 'catastrophic' is the sudden switch of mode (that is, the catastrophe is not necessarily disastrous, as in the ordinary English usage). The mathematics, which remain a highly contentious topic among mathematicians, *fold* an infinitely differentiable plane surface in a three-dimensional space. The result is that changes do not necessarily occur gradually, as they must (however swiftly) in a plane space. Changes may occur *instantaneously,* because a trajectory simply 'falls off' one fold, to reappear on the next fold. Putting all these notions together, it should be possible to devise a powerful and testable — and moreover, a predictive — theory about corporate behavioural modalities. A start was made (see joint paper with John Casti cited in References D of the Appendix), but there has not been time to pursue it. The main difficulty is to propose an acceptable metric for any empirical verification of the theory.

The next remark which ought to be made about the reticular formation, that algedonic controller, is that it is indeed a trans-system. Essentially, it connects System Three with System Four, but in so doing it creates a new dimension of decision, geared to survival. There was emphasis earlier on the arbitrariness of all organizational divisions, and on the need to re-connect across any boundaries which were created. We have found in System Three the immediate response mechanism for dealing with internal and current affairs; it has been contrasted with System Four, dealing with external and future affairs. That distinction looked biologically valid. The very fact that the distinction is so profound in terms of survival capability, as compared with the arbitrary distinctions which managers have invented to distinguish between production, sales, finance and the rest, leads to a very special risk of polarization in the firm's affairs. So it is in the brain also, where a failure to bridge this mighty gap would lead to instant death.

Once again, it is the reticular formation — the algedonic controller — which guarantees survival. We saw in Chapter 10 that the reticular formation spans the two structures of Three and Four morphologically. So it must be in the managerial context too. The behavioural mode of the organism is fixed *across* Three and Four — if it were not so either one or the other would be ill-served, leading to the death of the organism. As it is, and the mode having been fixed, System Five can act (albeit in a most superior capacity) only within the context of this conclusion. Try introspection once again. If you *know* yourself to be in a crisis mode, which you may be wholly unable to analyse, one thing is certain: you will not sit down to play a game of chess. There are other things to do. Moreover, if you attempt to analyse the mode of behaviour which is set in this way, you may expect to become distraught once the redundant potential commanders have operated. *The senior controllers inevitably work within the framework set by their juniors.*

Ultimately, neither the brain nor the firm is an analyser, but a recognizer. That is why speed of recognition is so important, while analytic power is relatively unimportant. We must recognize and then react. Otherwise analysis may consume too many precious weeks, and a viable response to a threat will be (as the lawyers say) 'out of time'. A great deal of serious analytical work in management is wasted for this reason. It becomes an intellectual game that is played concomitantly with, but not affecting, the progress of real events.

The model as we now see it exists to be used. It has taken nearly thirty years to develop to this form, the first twenty mainly in the context of the firm. But it is not some kind of strait-jacket. Think of it instead as a well-structured language for discussing viable systems.

In the years since this book received its title, which could hardly be changed without impropriety, the model has been applied to all kinds of organization, and not only to firms. From a learned society to a university faculty, from schools to hospitals, from one branch of social service to another, from government agency to department of state, from province to federation, and eventually (as will be seen in Part IV) in a multiple application to the socio-industrial economy of a whole nation, the diagnostic power of the tool has proven worthy. Hence a final reminder of the fundamental cybernetic thesis may well be in order: if there are natural laws governing viable systems, then all viable systems will be found to obey them.

I end with this reminder for a particular reason. A body of distinguished opinion in the circles of management science has developed a classification of large systems which appears to me disastrously unhelpful. It says that some systems exist in which the whole is there to serve the parts, while others exist in which the parts are there to serve the whole. These are sometimes referred to as heterogeneous and homogeneous systems respectively. Anyone who has mastered the nature of the cybernetic model offered here will understand why I regard this classification as meaningless. It is analogous to the *canard* that firms are either decentralized or centralized. We could not make physiological sense of that old contention; I do not think we can make either physiological or ecological sense of the new one.

The viable system is a system that survives. It coheres; it is integral. It is homeostatically balanced both internally and externally, but it has none the less mechanisms and opportunities to grow and to learn, to evolve and to adapt — to become more and more potent in its environment.

In all of this the viable system may succeed sensationally, spectacularly fail or it may muddle along.

The amoeba succeeded, the dinosaur failed, the coelacanth muddles along.

You and I have our own problems of survival. As to the firm, as to government, as to society, as to the future of mankind — all viable systems — we shall see. Structural change is so potent a business, and so traumatic to undergo, that people prefer to pretend they cannot see what their own eyes insistently report, rather than commit themselves to the re-shaping which is necessary. Even in the cases quoted above as applications of this work, my guess would be that organizaitons cannot face up to more than a quarter of the reshaping that their long-term viability demands. This is of course the reason why so many enterprises are in a state of *continuous,* never mind continual, reorganization. People pretend that the great upheaval is almost complete: it never is, and the viable system becomes increasingly unstable as a result. This in turn makes every enterprise vulnerable to attack. When the management or the government has fallen, when its policies are in disarray and its people in despair, we can pretend no longer.

In another era of manifest instability, the 1930s, Louis MacNeice noticed this same pretence — and its consequences:

> The glass is falling hour by hour
>   the glass will fall for ever,
> But if you break the bloody glass
>   you won't hold up the weather.

PART FOUR

THE COURSE OF HISTORY

To Fernando
for our friendship

costó pero salió

Estáfor

Summary of Part Four

Each of the summaries has incorporated the advice to re-read the earlier summaries. The last summary, which introduced Part III, ended the 'old book' by saying that Chapter 15 was 'very much a final chapter', and that it sounded 'a bit metaphysical'.

As if in answer to these two allegations came the work in Chile, which was founded — as to its cybernetics — on the original manuscript of this then-unpublished book. Hence Chapter 20, and not Chapter 15, is now 'the final' chapter. As to the 'metaphysics' ... nothing could have been founded in a more profound reality than 'the Chilean process'.

The first four of the following five chapters tell a story which is organized according to its basic chronology. A project began in Chile late in 1971, under the aegis of President Allende, and Chapter 16 accounts for its inauguration. Chapters 17 and 18 develop the story, and continue up to the extraordinry events of October 1972, which (with hindsight) appeared to mark a watershed. In Chapter 19, that story is concluded. There seems little point in offering further analysis here, in summary, of a chronicle which steadily unfolds itself in the text.

The final chapter proffers a prospectus for the future of applications in managerial cybernetics. It does not contain any prescriptions, simply because it does not make any predictions. Instead, Chapter 20 prepares two models which — it argues — are basic to the innovatory management of any such future. Firstly, it ought to be expected that the impetus to radical change derives from a **critical** *situation. If so, it is necessary to comprehend the nature of crisis itself in the kind of society by which the last part of the twentieth century is characterized. Secondly, and because of these very societary trends, it is of the utmost importance to determine what the 'progress' to which all aspire actually means. The model put forward for this is based on the Aristotelian concept of* **entelechy** *rather than (for instance) per capita income or life expectancy.*

Thus the book ends with consideration for the perilous future of a planet already torn by almost unimaginable dissensions and cruelties, which are perhaps more a function of gross mismanagement than of brutish greed. Surely the destruction of the Chilean democracy on which this Part is based, is an example of the working out of counter-productive policies by which (maybe well intentioned) super-powers conspicuously mishandle their power — and snuff out **the viable system.**

CHAPTER SIXTEEN

A flying start

The story of the use made of managerial cybernetics in Chile is a complex one. My own involvement in it was total. It seems to me that the posture of a 'neutral scientific advisor' became untenable after the experiences of World War II, and especially since the full circumstances surrounding the holocaust in Japan 1945 became known. This book has already tried to demonstrate that the role of System Four is in cybernetic principle part of the command axis; and if it is not, then in political practice nothing will happen. Thus I do not understand the outlook of the scientific overlords, in Britain for instance, who happily survive in government for a professional lifetime, while parliaments of opposite tendency come and go.

This is said for two reasons. Firstly, I think that the acceptance by both ministers and their scientists that scientific neutrality (which I take to be bogus) is possible, largely accounts for the confusion in Britain over such issues as the choice of energy sources, defence systems, transportation systems, and the like; and also it accounts for the almost total failure to make good use of science in structuring the managerial process itself. Prime Ministers of both parties, when determined to 'do something' about swelling and inefficient bureaucracy, have promptly co-opted successful businessmen on a part-time basis to this obscure end. But the objectives of private profit and the public good are completely different; businessmen do not understand the nature of a viable *system*, but only the notion of economic viability; and the problem is not a part-time affair. If only it were: surely we see in all this the abysmal failure of ministers even to perceive the magnitude of the problems they face, never mind to address them with competence.

The second reason for the opening declaration is this. I am a cybernetician and also (as C. West Churchman calls himself) a 'research philosopher'; but I am certainly not an historian. Moreover, historians appear to be no less subjective than scientists, when it comes to their dissensions. But it is better to rejoice in the human condition than to pretend to exist outside it, while yet in the corporeal substance. It follows that I can tell this story only in the first person, and in an autobiographical vein. Indeed, people who ask about the work always ask for details as to just how such an extraordinary undertaking came about, and how it continued. This book is, however, about managerial cybernetics; therefore I have ruthlessly expunged from the story mere gossip and my own opinions, and have stuck to the facts as I knew them. But I have not dressed up those perceptions to a pretence of objective omniscience. Moreover, I consider that 'case studies' should reveal far more of the stresses under which the dramatis persona — who include the management scientists — operate than they customarily do. There was plenty of stress in Chile. Thus, to complete the opening paragraph, I declare that I could have pulled out of Chile at any time, and often considered doing so; but I did not, and therefore I hold myself accountable for the part that I played.

It began in the summer of 1971. The manuscript of the first edition of the book you have so far been reading had gone to the publishers. I had also completed most of a book called *Platform for Change*, which is an account of my efforts to project managerial cybernetics internationally during 1970, and to which part of this story eventually became a suffix. I myself was proceeding with many affairs, when a letter arrived from Chile. It is true that I had had vicarious dealings with Chile before, since my (then) consulting firm SIGMA (Science in General Management) had undertaken work for the steel industry and for the railways there in the early sixties. But although I had been concerned with that work, I had never been to Chile: teams of SIGMA people had been there for several years, but as Managing Director I did not then conceive that I had the time to go. So what now, dated 13th July 1971, was this letter from Chile?

Like most Englishmen, I was aware that Dr Salvador Allende had become president of Chile the previous autumn (1970). The fact was remarkable, because this was the first Marxist president to be democratically elected anywhere in the world, and at the time his new government was a focus of international attention. Moreover, it was a minority government, carrying 37% of the electorate; therefore it had a battle on its hands in both the congress and the senate. Nothing daunted, the president had embarked on the massive nationalization of the banks, and of the major companies working in Chile: naturally, for a Marxist, a programme of nationalization of the means of production, distribution, and exchange was fundamental to his programme. This I knew; but I did not know the means whereby this wholesale nationalization of the economy was being achieved. It was done through state agencies, and in particular through an institution called CORFO (Corporación de Fomento de la Producción).

This organization, it turned out, had been set up in the thirties as a kind of national merchant bank — to assist industry. The government was now using it as a vehicle for the nationalization programme in which it was engaged, so that many foreign firms per week (having been paid due and negotiated compensation for the most part) and the banks (whose shares were being bought by CORFO) were arriving as entities within that corporation. Thus the role of this institution bears comparison with that of (what was later to become in Britain) the National Enterprise Board. And the letter that I received come from there, under the signature of the Technical General Manager, by name Fernando Flores. He introduced himself also as the President of INTEC (Instituto Technológico de Chile), which bears organizational comparison with the National Physical Laboratory in Britain — although it is of course much smaller.

This letter spoke of 'the complete reorganization of the public sector of the economy', for which it appeared its author would be primarily responsible. He had read my books, and had even worked with a SIGMA team ten years before. He went on to say that he was now 'in a position from which it is possible to implement, on a national scale — at which cybernetic thinking becomes a necessity — scientific views on management and organization'. He hoped that I would be interested. I was.

We met in London the following month. Fernando Flores filled out the details, and I became enthused with the plans that the government was making. Flores himself had been teaching cybernetics in Santiago — he was a professor of management science and a vice-rector of the university — for several years. But he had also been a founding father of the MAPU party, which — although small — was an influential member of the Unidad Popular coalition that had brought the President to power. And, of course, this is why he had been enticed from the university to his new position at CORFO. What he told me in London was that he had collected together a group of his closest friends, associates, and former students, as a government team within CORFO — and he wanted me to come over to Chile to take charge, in some as yet undefined sense, of the deliberations of this group. I was excited by this invitation, but somewhat cautious. We made a deal that I would visit Chile in November 1971, when we would all get some new perspectives on what was happening and what could possibly be done.

Thus it was that I cancelled many engagements, and spent a long time studying the Chilean problem — the history of the country, and its current political scene. The more I learned the more I came to understand what was already being called 'the Chilean process'. Eventually I arrived in Santiago on 4th November 1971, just as the first anniversary celebrations of the election of President Allende were in full swing. Fernando Flores was there to meet me, and we immediately went into session. That night, I met five more of the people who were to be so influential in the project that was soon to be devised.

It has always seemed to me that organizations, and particularly government organizations, take far too long in the bureaucratic process of merely contemplating change. Events overtake affairs before anything significant can possibly happen. It was not so in Chile. The group of us worked to exhaustion every day for eight days. During this time, I was able to meet with various influential people in the country, inlcuding the directors of major national programmes, and the then Minister of Economics. By the 12th November, 1971, we had all agreed on a plan for the cybernetic regulation of the social economy of Chile. It seems astonishing, looking back, that so much was done in that short time; but I was prepared, my new colleagues were prepared for the approach that they knew I would in principle offer, and in that period they all read the draft manuscript of the first edition of this very book.

The primary point of which I had to convince my friends was that we should firmly take the wholly innovatory step of seeking to regulate the social economy in real time. Even the most advanced countries in the world suffer from a vast lag in the receipt of economic data, and they suffer too from the bureaucratic time it takes to process these data towards any kind of conclusion. I had taken the posture that all of this, given the current state of telecommunications and the computing art, was totally unnecessary. In the world's most advanced countries, economic data arrive very late, perhaps the average delay is nine months, before the total picture is seen. This means that most economic decisions are taken out of phase with economic reality. Knowing that this is so, the advanced countries spend a great deal of money in trying to offset the errors thereby induced: they engage in econometric studies aimed at projecting data — not indeed into the future — but only into the present.

Notoriously, the answers come out wrong. Why do this? It is perfectly possible, these days, to capture data at source in real time, and to process them instantly. But we do not have the machinery for such instant data capture, nor do we have the sophisticated computer programs that would know what to do with such a plethora of information if we had it. Yet all of this is well within the compass of current technology.

The Chilean team took that point with ease. They were moreover pleased with the idea that Chile should seize a world lead in the practice of economic regulation: it was wholly consistent with their belief that Chile could show the world the 'peaceful road to Socialism' — which would necessarily involve innovations of a major kind. Even so, they were lugubrious. The country's electronic technology was antiquated: there was no foreign exchange to buy a lot of computers, teleprocessing equipment, video units, and so on, even though their scientists well knew how to use them. How could we develop a system that would be twenty years ahead of its time, using equipment that was already out of date? The answer to that was that the rich world had never understood the *managerial cybernetics* of electronic technology, and had therefore absurdly misused it. (From the time when computers were still experimental, I had been demonstrating this fact in a constant stream of writings, which the team had mostly read.) I outlined a plan to do the job, using the equipment they already had. They took the plunge.

Thus it was that during these strenous days, I prepared two papers, dealing with the regulation of the social economy. Before stating their contents, I recapitulate two points. Firstly, we had a shorthand. The general terminology of cybernetics was perfectly familiar to the team, and the specific terminology of this book was our *lingua franca*. There was no need for long-winded explanations. In particular, we had explored the notion of **recursions** of the viable system in lengthy discussions. Secondly, the target of real-time regulation had been conceded. There was a third point. I was being updated rapidly on the political context of these affairs, and Fernando Flores was making it very clear that he had wider plans (as his first letter had implicitly indicated) for cybernetic thinking in government than 'merely' to succeed in the present task. It was for this third reason that my first paper in Chile had a resounding title:

Cybernetic Notes on The Effective Organization of the State with Particular Reference to Industrial Control

Recursively speaking, the Chilean nation is embedded in the world of nations, and the government is embedded in the nation. This was understood; all these are supposedly viable systems.

The government should be concieved as a viable system (System Five being the President of the Republic) in which System One consists of the Headquarters of each major function — health, education, finance, industry . . . .

Picking out industry as a viable system embedded in this (System Five being the Minister of Economics), we find a set of industrial sectors constituting System One. These include such elements as food, textiles, automotive . . .

Each sector (System Five being the Undersecretary for Economics with his appropriate committee) contains, as System One, a set of enterprises, or firms.

Embedded in the enterprise is the plant; within that the department; within that the social unit of a working group; and within that the individual worker — viable systems all.

The paper with the above heading concentrated on the organization of the enterprise, of the sectors, of industry itself, and of the state *insofar* as its relationship with the social economy was concerned.

Note: in terms of variety engineering, there seemed to be too many sectors to be contained, as constituting System One, in total industry — conceived as a viable system. It is noteworthy then, that there were soon to emerge four 'ramas' (branches), constituting heavy industry, light industry, consumer industry, and material supplies industry. This inserted an extra level of recursion. It was probably a political decision, but it was also sound cybernetics.

The paper proceeded to draw very preliminary mappings of the (generalized) enterprise, the (generalized) sector, the industrial headquarters, and the government itself, in terms of the viable system model. This was a swift attempt at a preliminary diagnosis of weakness, as spotlighted by the model.

There followed a section on planning, as a continuous and adaptive process. (The principles then briefly advocated later developed into the planning theory which may be consulted in Chapter 13 of *The Heart of Enterprise*.) This section was intended to highlight the differences between our cybernetic approach, and the approach whereby a 'national plan' based on time horizons and the usual estimating procedures, had already been created by an orthodox government agency. There were ample reasons why, contrary to expectation, the work discussed here was not related to that effort. The cybernetic reasons were paramount in my mind; but the political reasons were also clear enough.

The paper was completed with a section on information flow in this embedded set of viable systems. It pressed the uniform use of the model at all levels of recursion as constituting a powerful variety reducer. It stressed the value of indices, formulated as in Chapter 11 of this book, as homogeneous units of measurement. Thirdly, it marked the issue that by putting great effort into a highly sophisticated computer program, capable of assessing the data that we proposed to collect and process in real time, we could supply a tool to management at **every** level of recursion **regardless** of its managerial content — because of the uniform model and the indexical homogeneity.

The team accepted this paper almost without comment, because it was effectively a summary of our vigorous discussions on what should indeed be the general framework of the approach.

The second paper, however, left me to propose the project that would start this work moving, and gear it to achieve something in a very short space of time. It had been explained to me with vigour by the Economic Undersecretary, Oscar Garretón, just what economic pressures the government were feeling. The workers had received wage increases of forty per cent, as part of a deliberate redistribution of wealth, and peasants (who had often had no actual 'wage' at all, but only benefits in kind) were also entitled to a similar basic wage. Copper prices had dropped; and copper was almost the whole of Chile's foreign earning capacity (at least eighty per cent). Therefore the large balance of payments deficit was becoming larger. The gross national product and industrial production were rising (probably by about seven per cent); and in the municipal elections the Government's poll had risen to fifty per cent. So far, so good; but there was an artificial euphoria in the air. Thus the lower-paid were spending, the higher-paid were not investing, and foreign credit and technical support were non-existent. This was a clear recipe for inflation, consumer shortages, and every kind of trouble. It was generally thought, internationally, that thirty-five per cent inflation had brought down the previous government of the Christian Democrats. Unidad Popular had reduced this very substantially. But within a year, in all circumstances, the foreign reserves would run out . . . .

Now I had always propounded the view (see especially *Decision and Control*) that the **time-scale** of managerial problems is one of the most vital parameters involved. There is no point in telling a manager who has to give a verdict by the end of the month that a properly conducted scientific study will take a year. The management scientist has either to cut corners, or to bow out. That statement, in invoking personal responsiblity, refers back to the opening paragraphs of this chapter. But it says something more — in fact, a great deal more. If the managerial time-scale is a basic parameter of the problem, then a management science that ignores the fact is not a science at all. This is clear in neurocybernetics. 'Shall I, or shall I not, run for that bus?' 'Shall I hit this man who threatens me, or run for it?' The brain that replies: 'This is all very dificult; heart and lungs must be consulted; adrenalin checks must be made; then there are statistical extrapolations . . . I'll tell you in half an hour', is *no good*.

The second paper that I wrote tried to take into account all that I had learned from Garretón, and certainly checked out with Flores. It left some of the younger scientists in the team gasping for air. The first title of the project was later superseded; it became:

Project Cybersyn

OBJECTIVE:
To install a preliminary system
of information and regulation
for the industrial economy

that will demonstrate
the main features
of cybernetic management

and begin to help in the task
of actual decision-making
by 1st March 1972.

It was already the middle of November 1971; but it was my judgment that we needed such a crash programme — because of the rate at which the economic situation was deteriorating.

The code-name Cybersyn is an abbreviation of 'cybernetic synergy'. The paper proposed a **plan of action** whereby, in four and a half months, the above objective would be achieved. On 1st March 1972, it declared, we should be ready to start the regulatory operation and to produce results — for a sample of enterprises in a sample of sectors.

If we were going to work in real time, we should need a communications network extending down the three thousand miles of Chile. This was nicknamed Cybernet.

Cybernet was a system whereby every single factory in the country, contained within the nationalized social economy, could be in communication with a computer. Now ideally, this computer would have been a small machine, local to the factory, and at best within it, which would process whatever information turned out to be vital for that factory's management. But such computers did not exist in Chile, nor could the country afford to buy them. Therefore it was necessary to use the computer power available in Santiago: it consisted of an IBM 360/50 machine and a Burroughs 3500 machine. There was no intention to centralize the economy, as any reader of this book will surely know; but if computer power were to be made available to the workers' committees running individual plants in the country, then it would be essential to provide the links of communication necessary to that end. Again, this presents no technical problem in an age of teleprocessing; but the fact was that Chile could not afford teleprocessing equipment either. And so we resolved the problem by the only means available, namely the telex network already instituted in the country, linked together by microwave communication that had already been established for other purposes (namely the tracking of satellites). These microwave linkages existed from Arica in the far north of Chile down to Santiago, and beyond to Puerto Montt. And there were in addition radio links that could complete the network down to the world's most southerly city, Punto Arenas. The plan for Cybernet, therefore, called for the requisitioning of telexes, and the use of the communications links to put everyone in touch with everyone else — and with the computer system in Santiago. The plan allowed just four months for this to be accomplished (and it was).

Now the intention of Cybernet was to make computer power available to the workers' committees in every factory. How could this be done? The basic idea was that crucial indices of performance in every plant should be transmitted daily to the computers, where they would be processed and examined for any kind of important signal that they contained. If there were any sort of warning implied by these data, then an alerting signal would be sent back to the managers of the plant concerned. The next problem was: how to come by these crucial indices . . . .

Readers of this book by now understand the concept of the triple index, which measures productivity, latency, and their product — the overall measure of performance. But the problem remained: to which activities in factories ought these measures to be applied? Accordingly, under the direction of Raúl Espejo, the Senior Project Manager in Chile, and Jorge Barrientos, another senior member of the directing group, operational reasearch teams were formed to make analyses of every sector of the social economy, down to plant level. Their primary job was to construct a **quantitative flow chart** of activities within each factory that would highlight all important activities.

For example, we certainly needed to measure the state of input stocks of raw material, and of output stocks of finished material. We needed to measure any process that might prove to be a bottleneck in the system. And there were other standard measures too: for example, it has always been my ambition to find a measure of social unease. The best approximation to such a measure that I could envisage at this time was the ratio of employees on the payroll to those present on any given day. In short, absenteeism is some kind of measure of morale, as I had learnt from work dating back into the 1950s by Professor R.W. Revans. Thus the OR teams would be charged with making models of every factory that would bring out these, and similar crucial measurement points. And they would agree with the management (in most cases by now a workers' committee) on the values to be attributed to 'capability' and 'potentiality' — as defined in this book. Then, given that these two figures, for any index, could be stored within the computer, and given, thanks to Cybernet, that a daily 'actual' figure could be transmitted, the computer would be capable of computing the triple index for every indicator for every factory. (In practice, it turned out that some ten or a dozen indices were adequate to monitor the performance of every plant; and so by then we knew the scale of the computer operation involved.) The teams were also to be instructed to make it clear that, as time went on, each participating factory would be free to add any index that it liked — without, if it wished, declaring what that index measured — and the system would monitor it for that management.

But before reaching the computer problem itself, we have to understand the human predicament of the people running these factories. For instance, some of the managers supplied by the hitherto owners were foreigners, who had engaged in very little training of their Chilean counterparts. And when the government of the Unidad Popular took over, most of the foreign managers immediately left the country — in many cases taking all their records (sometimes even their order books, for subsequent discharge elsewhere) with them. Chilean managers themselves at first took a rather passive role in the development of 'workers' control', but this noticeably evolved into an aggressive and negative attitude. So the workers' committees left in charge, headed as they often were by an *interventor* (a man of knowledge, often an academic, selected to help the workers' committees unravel their problems), needed tools which they personally could understand.

The quantified flow charts created by the OR teams were meant to portray the operations of the plant in iconic form. But it seemed to us that if every plant in the country were depicted, albeit iconically, in a different format, then it would be very difficult for everyone involved to understand what was happening. Accordingly, a design team was set up under a Chilean industrial designer of world stature, Gui Bonsiepe, to establish the rules whereby the quantified flow charts would be set down on paper and on film. It was understood that *processes* would be shown as boxes whose size was proportionate to the amounts of materials or other measures that they depicted; it was understood that *flowlines* would be shown, not merely as arrows, but as lines whose thickness depended upon the relative flow involved. And nonetheless, if quantified flow charts were to be the common language of the whole system, they needed iconic conventions in common themselves — extending even to the question as to the radius of the curvature of a rectilinear movement in the flowline, the radius of the curvature involved in depicting a box without square corners, colour schemes, and so on. All this was nominated for sound ergonomic reasons: the brain can accept only so much variety, and these flowcharts were intended to replace orthodox representations in which such conventions as balance sheets also reduce input variety to the bewildered brain.

Finally, the further ergonomics of the 'operations room' as a proper 'environment for decision' were accepted, entirely (at this time) on the basis of Chapter 13. The plan demanded the creation of such a room, as a centre from which to conduct these affairs, but also as a **prototype** of the new decision environment that would replace the traditional 'boardroom' style of management. We had discussed this in experimental terms; we had envisaged building a factory to turn out operations rooms. For, if our mission were successful, they would be required in every plant, every enterprise, every rama, as well as in total industry and the running of the state itself.

All of these matters were contemplated in the original plan which was completed in eight days, within the context of the first paper. Teams should now be formed inside Chile said the plan, and be given four and a half months to establish the network called Cybernet, to break the back of the operational research enquiries into a large sample of the major plants in the country, to

255

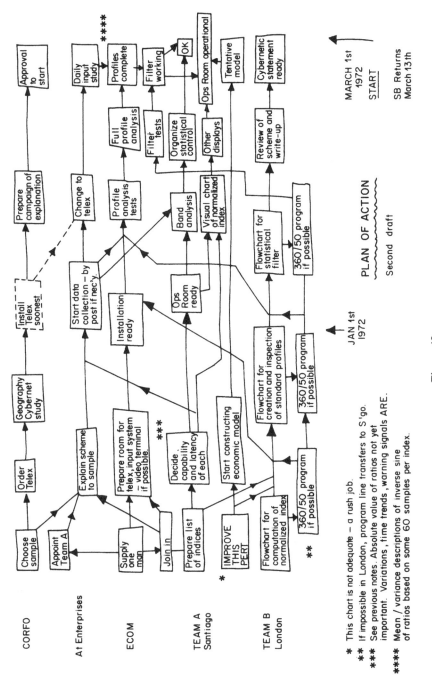

Figure 42

design the iconic system of representation which would support the indexical measures that were being elaborated, and to construct a preliminary operations room. My own task during this period, according to the plan, was to return to England. Somehow, I had to originate a computer program capable of studying tens of thousands of indices every day, and of evaluating them for the importance of any crucial information which their movements implied, so that alerting messages could be sent back to the managers in the plants. I asked for the commission to sub-contract the work required for this program, since I had done this kind of system building many times before (as my Chilean colleagues well understood), and since the computer people in Chile — brilliant though these scientists were — had many other duties to perform. Secondly, I should need to investigate prospects for a simulation system in the operations room that could accept the input of real-time data. This would be a completely novel development in operational research technique.

The PERT chart appended to the original plan is given in Figure 42, just as it was. It is clear what was meant earlier by the reference to 'cutting corners': a first action (see footnote*) commands: 'improve this PERT'. It shows the actions needed to be taken by CORFO in respect of Cybernet. It shows (although there was much more oral explanation) what Team A should be doing, first in the enterprises, and then back at base. It shows the role of ECOM, the national computing centre, where Isaquino Benadof was to become informational project manager for Cybersyn. It shows what Team B ought to do back in Britain to initiate the statistical filtration program.

Also included in the plan was a specification for an interdisciplinary team itself. It included the words: 'beware of people who have carved out a piece of the field and who want to grow flowers on it'. Of economics, that most relevant subject to this work, it said: 'no econometric models have yet proven adequate. We have to *invent* econometrics'. Having listed all the specialities required, it said:

Important Qualification for All — it limits the search — none of these professionals is to despise the professional area of any other.

The plan ended: 'I return in March'.

The presentation of this plan to the team, as mentioned earlier, was an exercise in the suspension of disbelief. Could it possibly be achieved? Perhaps it was not my *contention* that it could, but that I had said: 'I return in March', that won the day. At any rate, agreement was unanimous. Plans were made to facilitate that future, and for my return; and a communications system was determined whereby there could be constant Telex interaction between Teams A and B, in Santiago and London respectively. All that remained was for Flores to obtain permission to advance all this from the highest level.

We may well reflect, these years later, on this episode. It shows just how much proper preparation on all sides, the recognition of realities, monstrously hard work by all concerned, and burgeoning friendship, can do. Such things have happened before; it is to be hoped that they will continue to happen — in place of the deathly prescriptions of bureaucracy.

On the evening of November 12th, Fernando Flores arranged a dinner for all concerned in a very relaxed location. Beforehand, I was to go to the Ministry of Economics. There I reviewed matters with the Undersecretary. We went together to La Moneda, the presidential palace. Obviously, Flores had prepared the whole event. Nontheless, he did not come himself. A cynic could declare that I was left to sink or swim. In fact, I received this arrangement as one of the greatest gestures of confidence that I ever received; because it was open to me to say anything at all. I remembered it, many times, later — when in near despair.

The atmosphere, when I finally reached the rendezvous where the whole group was waiting, was understandably electric. 'The President says: Go ahead — fast.' It was an evening of great excitement and high expectations.

Dr. Allende had been forthright on this occasion, as he always remained. He particularly wished to be satisfied that the plans were decentralizing, worker-participative, and anti-bureaucratic. Since these very intentions had been fundamental to our work, there had been no difficulty at all in convincing him. It is also noteworthy that he exhibited an intellectual serenity in the process of grasping a vast new concept in a very short time that I found amazing. It was contrary to all previous (and subsequent) experience. Of course, he had been prepared; but other top men have also had their briefs. Of course, he might not *really* have understood; but a consultant learns to judge that by the questions. He did not waste a single one.

The 'real-time economy' hurdle was rather difficult. If it were at all possible, why had not the First World done it? Because they did not understand managerial cybernetics. The Third World could leapfrog over their backs — given such understanding. This argument was clearly difficult for the President to take, just as it is difficult for the Chairman of a little English company to believe that whole new vistas of managerial acumen are open to him — when ICI and Unilever, and the nationalized industries, 'have not done it'. The President said that Chile might very well do it; the idea had his blessing; but how could a small socialist state continue to exist in a capitalist milieu? The notion of cybernetic recursions was thereby invoked ... I still cannot answer that question.

I took half an hour to rough out, on a piece of blank paper on the table between us, the model of any viable system — and its recursions. This was the substance of the two papers that I had just written — but it included the cybernetic theory of this whole book. It is not possible to know how far he was prepared; but certainly it was known to me that the President had medical qualifications. Dr Allende had been a pathologist. Without hesitation, I embarked on an account of the viable system in neurophysiological terms. Again, his questions were probing, but he had no difficulty in accommodating to the model that is called *Brain of the Firm*. Gradually, I built up, on that piece of paper between us, Systems One, Two, Three, and Four. I explained the need for a System Five.

Much earlier in this Chapter, in relation to my first Chilean report, the remark came: 'The government should be conceived as a viable system (System Five being the President of the Republic)'. I drew the square on the piece of paper, labelled Five. He threw himself back in his chair: 'at last', he said, *'el pueblo'*.

This remark, as I have previously attested, had a profound effect on me. If the Compañero Presidente had a weakness, and which of us has not, it was a certain pride in his office. He liked to dress up, he liked to wear his sash, he liked to sit on his throne-like chair in La Moneda. But, when it came down to cybernetic science, he — System Five — was 'the people'. He was eventually to die in that exact posture.

This meeting, and that abandoned meal, being over, I returned to London on the 13th November, 1971, with all the plans in hand.

Ten days.

CHAPTER SEVENTEEN

Into its stride

During the twenty-four hour flight back from Santiago to London, I drew up a tentative flow diagram of a statistical program suite, intended to monitor thousands of indices on a daily basis . . . .

However: if it took a chapter to account for the first ten days of this activity, and the time-base of the story were now reduced to one day, this book would never be concluded. In fact, though with hindsight, the story of management cybernetics in Allende's Chile falls into four distinct epochs. The opening epoch was recounted in Chapter 16. The second epoch, which must be covered in this chapter, takes the story up to a crucial date: October 1972 and its aftermath. The treatment now will be to discuss activity by topics, rather than as a diary; so that the dates mentioned are in temporal order for each topic, but cross-referencing between them is left to the reader's integrative perception. Because the account of each topic is intended to be self-sufficient, there is a slight overlap sometimes with the introductory story of the first ten days.

From the start, as witness the quotation from the first letter from Fernando Flores, it had been the intention of his 'core' group (in which I was immediately happy to count myself) to use cybernetics as 'the science of effective organization', in all managerial affairs that could be influenced by that group and its supporting teams, on a national scale — *'at which cybernetic thinking becomes a necessity'*, the first letter had said. Thus, also from the start, we were discussing wider issues than the regulation of the social economy. Flores himself moved, as was fairly predictable, into the government: first as Undersecretary of State for Economics, then as Minister of Economics, later as Minister of Finance, and finally as Secretary of the Cabinet. Meanwhile, the country was increasingly under threat, both from foreign opponents, and from internal dissentions. These included not only the left-right politics of Chile as a nation, but also internal squabbles within the Unidad Popular coalition itself. Thus, over the whole period of my two-year involvement, the exigencies of practical management changed the emphasis of what I personally was doing, and the tasks allocated to the growing number of teams depending from the core. Surely that is a *proper* use of management science. It should not develop its own ideology; but it should attest to one. If not, what is it doing there? Popular accounts have concentrated on the technological aspect — the socio-economic regulation adumbrated in Chapter 16; but they give a lopsided view of the affair, and make it vulnerable to charges of 'technocracy' (as shall be seen later). The reality was that I have no record, nor recollection, of any core group discussion which was not focussed upon the needs of the people, or the intellectual and perceptual development of themselves and their leaders. The potency of science, and skills of technology, were to be aligned in their service.

Meanwhile, however, it is a fact that we launched the very definite plan of action at the end of the first ten days which was depicted in the last chapter. It is also a fact that this plan was accomplished by March 1972 as intended. The ostensible exception to this was the creation of the 'operations room'. What was achieved by the first plan was not the eventual result — see later — but simply a kind of informational headquarters; specifications for the room that was intended to create the 'environment for decision' of Chapter 13, and to become the prototype physical basis of Chapter 16 for a new style of management, were not even drawn up until the 'start' (as the Chapter 16 PERT chart calls it) in March 1972.

During that month, indeed, while I was in Chile, cybernetic deliberations were advanced by the core group on many fronts, and in particular the People Project (see later) was launched. But Project Cybersyn received a new boost; because, following the success of the first plan, we could now think in terms of putting together the basic tools thereby created in the cause of cybernetic synergy. Of course, they had been devised to this precise end, and all needed much development, but it was enough to gain approval for 'the start'.

The final section of the March report, which will be alluded to under each topic, was about programming. It included a personal statement: 'The month following is a bad one for me: Rome, Georgia, Washington, Philadelphia, Zurich, St. Gallen, Vienna'. Despite my sense of commitment to Chile, I was still working as a general consultant. The reaction to this was to be decisive for the next eighteen months, if not for ever in spirit; and perhaps those whom I let down at the time will at this late date accept the slight that was implied but not intended. President Allende wrote to me on 28th April, 1972, saying that he considered it 'of prime importance to count on your presence in Chile in a more permanent way and in a more executive role'. In May 1972 I was confirmed as Scientific Director of the work of which Fernando Flores was Political Director. It seems necessary to record this; for had it not been so, the momentum of the work at large could not have been sustained. There is a limit to what anyone can do in an *advisory* capacity, unless he accepts *responsibility* too. This sentence, in my opinion, should be taken as the cynosure of System Four.

The Cyberstride Program Suite

The purpose of this suite was to monitor information flows (as depicted in Figure 27) at all levels of recursion; to provide alerting signals to Systems 3-2-1 of any *incipient* change (so that action could be taken to avert trouble *before* it occurred); and to provide the 'arousal filter' to Systems Four and Five (as depicted in Figure 32). This purpose is founded in the notion that the data informing all regulatory systems should be prospective and anticipatory, rather than retrospective and a matter of historical record.

By using only two-digit ratios as input to the suite, as specified in Chapter 11, a massive reduction in regulatory variety is attained; and it becomes worthwhile to invest heavily in a single program (this being contrary to EDP practice, in which ad hoc programs are usually written for each application).

The statistical thinking behind the approach is rooted in the quality control practices that have been commonly used on the shop-floor for thirty years. But since there has been no general movement towards their application in managerial contexts, it might seem strange to have based the regulation of an entire social economy on their use. Therefore I record references to the genesis and development of such application at the end of this section.

The program is first of all required to examine an arriving Actual figure, and to test it for acceptability as a legitimate member of its own statistical distribution. These, the so-called 'taxonomic' distributions, were the initial samples drawn according to the PERT of Figure 42, with some sixty sampled values; and there are simple statistical tests for assessing the probability of legitimate membership. Next, by looking up the appropriate values for Capability and Potentiality, in the program suite's lexicon, the three indices are created. These are statistically 'normalized' by a trigonometrical transformation, since distributions of ratios, which have a limiting value of unity, are notoriously skewed to the right. (The original intention was to transform to the inverse sine, but methods were later found to choose the appropriate transform for each time series.) Then comes the statistical filtration which detects incipient change. The techniques I had used in the past were clearly out of date, but my own PERT chart called for this program by March 1972 — and it was already late November. The scientists and programmers at ECOM (the National Computing Centre in Chile) were overloaded . . . .

Accordingly, it was decided to subcontract this work to London, if a contractor could be found to undertake such difficult research-cum-programming in so short a time. Moreover, we needed a group who also understood the operational research features of the Cybersyn project: the nature of the modelling processes and techniques of data capture that were being developed in Chile. As a Briton, I knew whom I wanted — they were a group of consultants within the London branch of the international firm of Arthur Andersen and Co. The arrangements were made, with an old friend David Kaye directing and with Alan Dunsmuir managing the job from day to day. It is relevant to record how the apparently absurd time constraint was handled. This comes from a report to Chile in January 1972 (work began on the 10th):

'The investigation established that if work on the suite began immediately, it would not be completed until the 19th June 1972. The reason for this was all too clear. A fully developed, watertight version of the suite, tested and documented for use many thousands of miles away, must be expected to take a lot of programming. Meanwhile, I was insisting that something be ready for (at the least) experimental use at the planned date — namely by 13th March .... It seemed to me that a version of the suite should be prepared for March, and that the 'debugging' of these programs could then continue into June to produce the polished job. However the contractors convinced me that this plan would not be practicable. An experimental program (henceforth known as the 'temporary suite') could indeed be installed by March. But it would have to accept input restrictions, and corners would have to be cut in the development of the logic. Therefore it would not be possible to create the final version (henceforth called the 'permanent suite') simply by 'cleaning up' the temporary suite. The two projects were separate. However: if the two suites were developed in parallel, much would be learned by the interaction of the two programming teams, and therefore the extra money spent would not be entirely wasted.'

This is what happened; the consultants started the work in London. And almost immediately, I was confronted with an extraordinary decision.

No sooner had we reached a conclusion on the precise mathematical techniques to be used in generating the statistical filter itself, than I received a phone call late at night from Alan Dunsmuir. Had I read the *Operational Research Quarterly* for December 1971 (see Reference 1), and in particular a paper by Harrison and Stevens called 'A Bayesian Approach to Short Term Forecasting'? Hardly so, given all that was happening. I stayed up all night with this paper, and next day we determined to scrap the agreed mathematical approach in favour of theirs. It was a bold step. This comes from the previously quoted report of January 1972:

> 'Briefly, the method uses Bayesian probability theory to quantify a multi-state data-generating process. The filter can automatically recognize changes in the stream of input indices, and determine whether they represent transient errors, step functions, or changes in time trend and slope. The especially attractive cybernetic feature of the system is that the filter responds to the increasing uncertainty which surrounds change by increasing its own sensitivity whenever change is signalled. Forecasts are produced in terms of a joint parameter distribution, which is more robust than a single figure forecast.
>
> The expectation is that this 3 - 2 - 1 regulator will discard all input data that indicate performance as continuing within chance variation around the standard indexical distribution, and that it will use significant data to produce forecasts of imminent change that will be made available immediately to the managers of the economy. These people will now be in a position to forestall events — if they wish to, and if they know what action to take (see later). At any rate, there is nothing retrospective or historical about the data collection system, which is wholly oriented to prediction.
>
> It is a primary aim to avoid creating a vast bureaucratic machine, and the true intention of the 3 - 2 - 1 regulator is simply to discard all the data once they have been wrung dry by this powerful on-line system. However, arrangements are being made for the time being, to store data so that comparisons can be made with the data generator of the Operative Plan.'

(The Operative Plan will be mentioned later under Project Checo.)

The project manager for Cyberstride in Santiago was, as previously mentioned, Isaquino Benadof at ECOM. He later took over the whole data management programme, which was originally directed by a distinguished Chilean professor — Hernán Santa Mariá. In March 1972, Alan Dunsmuir was at ECOM. The temporary suite was duly working, and therefore Project Cybersyn could proceed on course. The first printout from the permanent suite, which was brought out in its first form a little later by John Brister, is dated 11th November 1972, although it had been due by the end of August, and therefore 'belongs' to the epoch of this chapter.

Computer people will sympathize with those named in this story. The challenge was very great. Moreover, nothing was known about the performance of the Harrison-Stevens techniques in advance. It was found that each time series had to be specifically 'tuned', and in May it was taking a week to deal with eight series — because of the shortage of available computer time. Eventually programs were written that could cope with the tuning issue. By July, the temporary suite was running without problems, and thirty indices were routinely being processed. In the meantime, the permanent suite was taking shape. The 'corner-cutting' in the temporary suite caused many problems; but as Dunsmuir had argued at the start, its direction was being shaped by experiences with the temporary suite. In particular, changes were made to deal with the need to generate algedonic signals (see Project Cybersyn). The problem of adequate computer time was solved by switching the work from the IBM 360/50 to the new Burroughs 3500, which was practically empty. By the end of this epoch, something like seventy percent of the socio-industrial economy was operating this system, involving about four hundred enterprises, through Cybernet: and these were major components of Project Cybersyn — especially as far as Systems 3 - 2 - 1 were concerned at all levels of recursion.

Note on genesis and development (Reference 2):

The fundamental technique that lies behind Cyberstride for the control of Systems 1 - 2 - 3 was first developed in the years 1949 - 53 for the control of steelworks production. This application was prior to the availability of electronic computers, and the whole system was operated by hand using nomographs to compute standards, desk calculating machines to compute indices, and visual control charts to provide the probability filters. A paper explaining how the system worked was presented to the Royal Statistical Society in 1953, entitled 'The Productivity Index in Active Service' (published in *Applied Statistics*, Vol.IV, No.1), while an earlier paper (Vol.II, No.3) entitled 'A Technique for Standardizing Massed Batteries of Control Charts', showed how visual statistical control procedures were standardized to facilitate filtering. In subsequent years the approach was generalized, following other applications — incorporating the use of computers. It was discussed in one form as the 'Sketch for a Cybernetic Factory', Chapter XVI of *Cybernetics and Management* in 1959, and in another form Chapter 13 and 15 of *Decision and Control* in 1966. By the publication (March 1972) of the first edition of this book, the role of what became the Cyberstride Suite in a cybernetic management structure seemed evident. It is updated in terms of microcomputers in *The Heart of Enterprise*.

The Checo Programs

The basic tools for handling Systems 3-2-1 information have been discussed: Cybernet and Cyberstride. Information about the *internal* operations of any viable system will, in certain circumstances that were examined in Part III, be transmitted to Systems 3-4-5. But System Four is charged with the task of providing plans to steer the whole organization — which is not merely the sum of Systems One in their particular environments. In the case of a national economy, the environment is firstly the whole of the nation (and not some sector of it), embedded secondly in the environment of the community of all nations.

In Chile, there was an institution known as ODEPLAN (an acronym for the National Planning Office), which in theory reported to the President through a Director holding ministerial status. It had little influence in practice. Its methodology was based on that favoured by national planners in many parts of the world, and particularly by the Eastern bloc: input-output analysis. Its work was published, and very polished within these terms. But, as one of the core group wrote: 'in point of fact it has become an institution dedicated to preparing the National Accounts and developing statistical reports'. Odeplan was not poised to create a true System Four function, any more than the National Office of Statistics and Census could have performed the System Three function that Cyberstride would fulfil. One can find comparable institutions in most countries; and it seems ironic that although they are usually *defined* — as in Chile — in terms of the Four-Three functions of a viable system, they nowhere embrace a methodology that could conceivably *discharge* those functions of a viable system. ('Nowhere' means 'nowhere as far as I know'. But I can certainly list some countries other than Chile of which the statement has at some time been true, to my personal knowledge and indeed distress: Britain, Canada, India, Italy, Denmark, and Jamaica.) In fact, the Chilean 'Operative Plan' mentioned in the last section was under the control of the Budget Office in the Ministry of Finance, which is exactly where one would expect to find the real power.

Chapter 13 indicates the route, taken via systems models and their simulation, that I had successfully argued we should take during the first meeting in Chile — witness the activity of economic modelling shown in the PERT chart of Chapter 16. Let the January 1972 report from London, which restated the case, again take over the story.

'It is certainly possible to contemplate the use of large input-output analyses as a means of balancing the Chilean economy, but there are three major problems about this approach:

(i)   matrix models are very poor in *structure*, since structure can be depicted only by listing constraints on the equations which the rows represent. This is a shortcoming even when the structure is known and accepted. But if (as I take it) an objective is actually to *re*structure the Chilean economy, this is a poor tool indeed.

(ii) it is very difficult to introduce stochastic elements into input-output models — yet economic life *is* a stochastic process.

(iii)   Chile is plunged into an epoch of rapid change, and therefore the most important feature of any System Four representation of the economy should be the adequate reflection of its *dynamics*. Input-output is deplorably static.

I therefore recommend a wholly different approach. We need a simulation model of the industrial sectors and their interaction embedded in an environment that takes account of investment capability in terms of both foreign exchange and domestic savings. The emphasis will be on structure (which can be changed — by inserting new feedback loops for example) and on the dynamic interplay of the factors modelled (which produces 'multiplier' effects of crucial importance). This model would be used to mediate between the detail of current performance (arising from the 3-2-1 monitoring system) and the current structural situation (as reflected by the Operative Plan) on the one hand, and the formulation of strategy on the other. System Four, in short, is a mediator between Systems Three and Five.

With a simulator of this kind, we can investigate the nature of the *trapped states* in which the economy is currently enmeshed, and which appear to be functions of a metasystem that extends beyond the national boundaries. For example: if foreign exchange earnings have been used to support a service sector supporting in turn the high-consumption low-saving pattern of the élite groups to whom they flow, then this would count as a trapped state. When these systems are demonstrated, the effect of single measures (land reform, copper nationalization) will (predictably) be seen as sufficient in themselves to break out of the traps. Cybernetic considerations certainly suggest that new structure, involving new information pathways and the harnessing of motivational factors, will be needed to achieve Chile's radical political goals. The simulator will be the government's experimental laboratory.

Can this be done? The first PERT chart called for a *tentative* model of this kind by the March deadline. On this time-scale, there is only one way into the problem, and that is to make use of the immediately available DYNAMO compiler that has been extensively developed over many years by J.W. Forrester of MIT. I have directed three projects in the past using this compiler, and have found it a powerful and flexible tool.

Accordingly, I sought out R.H. Anderton, a systems engineer brought up in the aerospace industry who switched to OR and the human sciences, and whose work is referred to in Chapter 13 of

Brain. He managed one of the three projects just mentioned, and is in my opinion (*exponential deleted*). He holds a senior job in industry, but is thinking of switching to academic life. We also involved K.A. Gilligan, a mathematical physicist and statistician who went into OR and has been involved in real-time corporate modelling.'

In this way the Checo (CHilean ECOnomy) research was born. It was under the direction in Chile of Mario Grandi. Another Chilean, Hernán Aviles, came to London for training. Obviously this was a mammoth undertaking. But the first runs of a tentative internal model were being made in June 1972 (against the target date of March), and by September there was an experimental model of the economy, at the macroeconomic level, which included sub-models of the generation of national income, inflation, and foreign exchange. The Light Industry *Rama*, and the Automotive *Industry*, had been chosen at two different microeconomic levels of recursion. Simulations were run for years ahead; they were thought provoking; but the team saw itself as 'learning the trade', and no-one was anxious to place reliance on the results. Communications with Ron Anderton, by this time at Lancaster University and having other commitments, were not easy. The development came to a virtual halt after the third epoch (next chapter); therefore it does not seem worthwhile to give elaborate details — although these are still preserved.

But while the Checo team was undertaking these experiments in the spirit of a prolegomenon to a full-bodied System Four, I had certain drives of my own to discuss with Mario Grandi, and often his team, on a short-term basis.

In the first place, study was required of the dissemination of results (when they were obtained) of any national model to the sectors, of any sectorial model to the enterprises, and so on — down to the workers' committees. The problem of recursivity in the viable system had not been solved for System Four, although it had been for System Three (see Project Cybersyn later). The Checo team set out to study these issues, and with some success: there was nothing to block their progress, and they were a well-balanced interdisciplinary team — which included a psychologist (and which other national planning group could boast such an active member?). Had the work gone on, much would have come of this initiative, as the perusal of later sections will imply.

Secondly: the real reason for lack of confidence in the results of the simulations that were coming out, was (not that the team was inexperienced, as their humility declared, but) that the data were untrustworthy. As is usual with national figures, they were out of date; and, also as usual, they were differentially lagged. Too little attention has ever been paid to these, and associated, dangers in the origins and development of *Dynamo* simulations that have achieved world-wide attention, and continue to do so. Obviously, my own plan was not to rely on such 'national statistics' any more. I wanted to inject information *in real time* into the Checo programs *via* Cyberstride. Thus any model of the economy, whether macro or micro, would find its base, and make its basic predictions, in terms of aggregations of low-level data — as has often been done. But Checo would be updated every day by the output from Systems 1-2-3, and would promptly re-run a ten-year simulation; and this has never been done. This was one of my fundamental solutions to the creation of an effective Three-Four homestat; it remains so, but it remains a dream unfulfilled.

Thirdly, and despite the professionally admonitory warnings of the Checo team, I needed any indications that I could get in addressing the problems discussed under the later topic heading 'Externalities'. I did get such indications. Time did not permit the fructification of the plans made under this heading, but I have no reason to think — with hindsight — that the indications of the Checo simulations were misleading.

The Operations Room

In Chapter 13 a basic design was given for an operations room: we built it in Santiago, according to that specification — with the exception of the use of a hybrid computer there advocated for economic simulation. As previously explained, we used the digital program *Dynamo* to begin the Checo investigations, because it already existed and we were in a hurry; but a sub-contract was initiated in Britain (because the analogue hardware could not be found in Chile) to pursue the 'hybrid' idea. It did not come to fruition: basically the reason was that the research group were waiting for the Checo team to reach conclusions about the models they were constructing before they themselves could do very much.

The room itself took a long time to find, because no government office was big enough to hold it. The detailed design, by Gui Bonsiepe and his team at INTEC, called for a hexagonal room ten metres across-flats. There was to be no obstruction in that arena; and furthermore there had to be annular space around the room in which to house the equipment working the screens. It is ironic that we finally took over the lease of the building which had earlier housed *Readers Digest*. Roberto Cañete was in command of the Operations Room construction, and naturally also ran the communications centre of Cybernet. The layout follows.

First came the animated Figure 27, two metres high, and built by Technomation Ltd in Britain. This was in reality a cupboard, housing the spinning polaroid discs that produced the effect of movement, the screen itself being the cupboard door. Thus, the squares and circles of the model could be marked from inside to show that mapping of the model for which any meeting had been called: elements could be named, and basic levels of performance could be indicated in terms of the three indices. Alegdonic signals were (as proposed in the Chapter 13 description) indicated with 'flashing red lights', but we dispensed with 'the ringing of bells'.

Next came two screens, one displaying alerting signals for Systems 3-4-5 for *this* enterprise, and the other algedonic signals from contained (subsidiary) enterprises that had now reached *this* level of recursion (more on this later). These screens were designed and made in Chile *via* INTEC. The ergonomics was advanced — but they had to be worked by hand! As usual, there was no money for the proper interfaces. Had there been a teleprocessing facility, however, I should personally have opposed the use of video units in this room, and preferred to have some kind of electro-magnetic switching instead. The symbols to be manipulated were bold and clear: they had been properly designed, and all could read them. Video units would not be large enough to be seen on the wall, and each member of the meeting would find himself peering at his own shimmering box. The issue is exemplified at airports, where both systems are in use.

Similar arguments apply to the machinery installed for calling up the information that the meeting would need, having read any warning signals about incipient change. There is no need to repeat the arguments of Chapter 13 about the iconic representation of data; and it is *possible* to use iconic charts with colour TV. But the loss of clarity, and even (in my own perception, at least) serenity, induced by 'flicker' made me personally satisfied with the optical system that we used. The equipment was called Datafeed, and it was made by Electrosonic Ltd. in London. It had three information screens, that could be in use simultaneously, each being the target screen for five back projectors. Thus the iconic-picture-carrying capacity of the set was $3 \times 5 \times 80 = 1200$. These screens were surmounted by a large lexical screen, fed by a sixteenth back-projector. In order to call up a picture advertized in the lexicon, each member of the meeting — using buttons in the arm of his chair — could firstly command control of the equipment, next select one of the three screens, and thirdly select one of the iconic pictures to show on that screen. Of course, he could place three representations side by side, and make comparisons.

It is clear that it is not feasible to display 1200 titles on one screen simultaneously: a lexical list of thirty titles was the maximum that the ergonomists found effective. Hence the total lexicon was split into classes of classes. 'Here is the list of consumer industries. You want to know about textiles! Here is the list of textile companies' . . . . and so on, until the detailed information available on a specific problem could be called onto a display screen. There was another ergonomic aspect to the design, with was drawn up in April 1972. The selection of one out of thirty is a five-bit decision: five control knobs, each either pressed or not pressed, can select between thirty-two items. In conformity with the ergonomic considerations advanced in Chapter 13 and in this chapter, I determined to use the system of five knobs — rather than any numbering system, with 'big-hand' controls — large knobs, with strong springs, that could be **thumped**. Once more: this room was a prototype room for use by workers' committees, and not a *sanctum sanctorum* for a governmental élite.

The final pair of screens were for Checo simulations. An animated chart of the economic model, using flexible lines so that the meeting could make alterations, add feedbacks, postulate new relationships, covered one wall. The flow lines on the animated Dynamo representation moved by the reflection of polarized light this time — an interesting and effective ergonomic innovation. Beside this screen was a primitive back-projection screen on which the results of simulation could be shown. (This would eventually have been the place for the hybrid computer, tracing out projections with a multiple pen-head on moving paper, which would then be magnified onto the screen as they were being drawn.)

Five walls were used, and the sixth was blank: we shall see why later. Everything about this room had to be specially designed, made and built. The Gui Bonsiepe team and two British subcontractors had to be kept in touch. Specifications were changed as the rest of the work progressed. And, as mentioned, no-one could for some time find a suitable physical site. No doubt the original date of 9th October fixed for completion was extremely optimistic. We were exactly three months late. The building was taken over on 1st December 1972; everything was finished and in experimental working order on 10th January 1973. Photographs of the room appear on the *inside* of the dust jacket of my book *Platform for Change,* and full details of the ergonomics involved appear in Bonsiepe's book (Reference 3).

Project Cybersyn

We saw in the last chapter how this project came to exist and what its intentions were. By now we have seen how the four main tools were created: *Cybernet,* yielding a national network of industrial communications to a centre in Santiago, through which anyone could consult anyone else, or gain access to decision-takers in other locations; *Cyberstride,* the suite of computer programs needed to provide statistical filtration for all homeostatic loops at all levels of recursion; *Checo,* the model of the Chilean economy, with simulation capacity; and the *Opsroom,* a new environment for decision, and dependent for its existence on the existence of the other three. But tools are useless in the hands of people who do not know how to use them, and a programme for the disemination of information had to begin as from the March 'Start'. Next, tools are useless until they are activated: how were data to be presented to the system?

All of this involved a massive and continuing exercise in (what I should call, in the original World War II sense) operational research. That is exactly what it was: *research,* by highly qualified interdisciplinary teams, into *operations,* namely production companies, with the prospect of discovering *models* and sets of *measures.*

By July 1972 there were many of these teams organized by ramas. Raúl Espejo himself was controlling the work in the Light Rama (covering the automotive industry, and manufacturing firms in rubber, plastic, electrics, electronics, copper), and the light mechanical industries (refrigerators, washing machines, and so on). Jorge Barrientos was dealing with the Consumer Rama (agro-industrial, textiles, fishing, pharmaceuticals, and food). In the Construction Rama (involving forestry, with its products of wood, furniture, pulp, chemicals, chipboards; and building materials — cement, prefabricated concrete, plaster, house construction units) the work was directed by Humberto Gabella. In the Heavy Rama, we confronted a different situation. All the energy industries, iron and steel, and petrochemicals had been state owned for a long time. We were not dealing with workers' committees and *interventors,* as in the three hundred newly nationalized companies, but with established and very senior Chilean managements. What is more, there were in-house OR groups serving these managers. As to the copper industry, newly nationalized amid an international furore, new moves of whatever kind might aggravate existing difficulties. It can readily be understood that the Heavy Rama presented these innovatory initiatives with a highly-charged situation, politically fraught. Thus, rather than appoint a senior Corfo man to this rama, we sought the cooperation of each management separately and, on the whole, we got it — with the OR people concerned either 'in touch with' or 'reporting to' me directly (two cases of each nuance).

The teams selected and trained for these urgent and important assignments in the three ramas were picked for their professional merit, and without regard to their political stance. Not surprisingly, a typical Chilean professional would be inclined to treat a worker with some condescension — unless he had strong political convictions towards the left. There were several incidents, and at other times attitudes were taken, where this tendency disquieted me. Especially, the teams were briefed to *explain* the quantified flowchart model in a plant, then to *enlist help* in creating it from those who worked there, and then to *obtain agreement* on the performance measures to be used. It was clear that this was not always being done in the intended spirit; and it seemed likely that this fact aided detractors who later wished to call Cybersyn 'technocratic'. It is again a reflection on the complicated nature of the Five-Four relationship that the political director (Flores) and the scientific director (Beer) held opposing views about this matter — each taking the position that the unthoughtful might well attribute to the other. At first sight, that is to say, the politician would be expected to demand political loyalty in professional staff engaged in work of such potency, while the scientist would be concerned to see that the best staff were chosen on professional merit. What happened was the politician could not afford accusations of partiality, while the scientist looked for the hard work engendered by total commitment.

Assuming that it is clear how to set about modelling a plant as a quantified flow chart, as in Figure 43, let us turn to the problems of modelling the higher levels of recursion in which are embedded the lower, like a series of Chinese Boxes or Russian Dolls — and viable systems all. Suppose that the firm's operations are a series of plants, and that the firm is one of several operations constituting System One of a corporation. All three configurations can be mapped on to the viable system of Figure 27. Now the wavy lines connecting the operations of the *plant* have to do with whether one process feeds another, and by what ratios the outputs of these individual machines are broken down between other processes. By the same token, the flowchart for the firm specifies whether, and if so how, those wavy lines connect plants together, and by what ratios, and so on. By the time the corporation is reached there may be *no* connexions on the wavy lines between operations — beyond the effects on each other of the competition for finite capital. The point is that the *flow pattern* of all this is different for each level of recursion, although the structural model is the same. By a similar argument, the flow pattern on the horizontal homeostats linking operations with environments will be different for each level of recursion, because the environmental domains are quite different. This paragraph, then, explains that by using a universal model of viability as a sourcebook or guide to any viable system, then empirical research may be designed at each level of recursion, the result being a set of flowcharts, each unique in pattern. It follows that the quantification at each level must also be unique (because it has to apply to *this* flowchart and no other). Thus, the proposition is demonstrated:

- information must be tailor-made to suit the appropriate level of recursion.
  Reductio-ad-absurdum: do not send the day's output figures for a limestone crusher in Arica to the Minister for Economics.

However, there is a difficulty about this in practice. Where can one *find the figures* for the flow-charts of the higher levels of recursion?

- there *is* no empirical production information about any level of recursion higher than the plant.

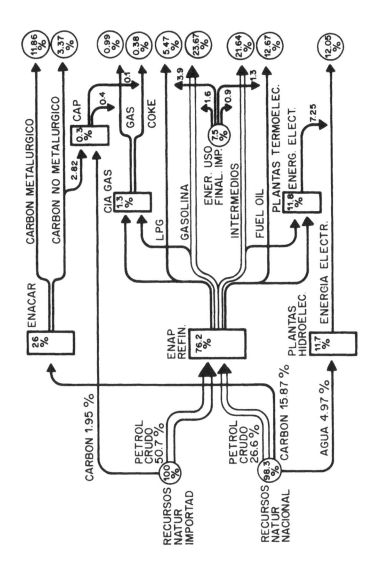

Figure 43. ENAP slide

> *Reductio-ad-absurdum*: when you were a plant foreman,
> you could observe Charlie being lazy; now you are
> president of the corporation looking out of your
> skyscraper window — and you see only clouds.

There is a genuine paradox here which caused us trouble all through. To grasp its menace, it is necessary to see clearly that there is only one collection of valid data throughout the whole series of recursions — and that is at the ground level of action. As to production, there is *no* production except in plants. As to sales, there may be expensive work done at corporate level: but that *is* the 'ground level of action' for corporate affairs. These facts are entirely paralleled in the neurocybernetics of the viable system. We are almost wholly dependent on sensory data, even at the limits of imagination and illumination. (If there are invisible rays projected through outer space at the pineal gland, that would explain a lot; but such an input would still be a senory datum.) And the reason for saying that we are so dependent, is that we *learn how to perceive*. (See especially Reference 4.)

In management the form of the paradox is the same. We learn how to perceive lower levels of recursion, so that the flowchart of our own level may be quantified — using the only variety reduction techniques that management accounting understands: essentially totals and averages. If the problem were simply that massive averaging may suppress whatever is really interesting, which is often the case, no matter: given Cyberstride.

This at least has the advantage over standard costing techniques that it assesses the importance of incipient change (via both the probability *and* the site on the flowchart model to which it is applied) rather than to report a (probably percentage) variance that has already occurred. But that is only part of the problem. We should be concerned that the paradox reported on may *distort* all quantified flowcharts but one's own. In Chile, we referred to shop-floor indices at the level of the enterprise as atomic, and then noted s-molecules at the sector recursion and r-molecules at the rama recursion. Problems of agglomeration were solved in a rather rough-and-ready fashion, and much more remained to be done. But the problem is surely clear: how does one quantify two different molecules made up of the same set of atoms? Juan Bulnes produced the basis of a neat theoretical solution in which the dendritic structure of the FORTRAN compiler itself was used as the mapping for the molecular structure. But our molecules may not be dendritic .... Perhaps a topological device is missing in order to facilitate this mapping — a device analogous to the benzine ring, or the DNA double-helix.

So far we have been talking about connexions between the recursions in terms of structural modelling and the specification of measures — that are atomic, but must needs emerge as molecular too. But all this is the initial and static framework for an interconnectivity between recursions that is most emphatically operational and dynamic. Action happens; homeostats circle; information flows. Then who gets to look in on all of this activity? The answer is Systems Five, Four, Three, Two and One of the viable system concerned, which is a firm (we may call it Beta) — first of all. Next, we recall that Beta constitutes a System One in Alpha. Then Systems Five, Four, and Three in Alpha have, as its metasystem, the authority to delimit the autonomy of any Alpha System One — which, in this example, is the whole of Beta. But it should do so according to the cybernetic rules, which we have studied, and which are intended to preserve the maximum autonomy for Alpha System One consistent with preserving the coherence of Alpha as a viable system itself (and it is certainly convenient to Beta that it should).

Suppose then, this being the scenario, that we supply Beta with the whole *Cybersyn* package: the four tools, and a computer. Beta proceeds to create the atomic indices, and to act on notices of incipient change from its computer. Its autonomy preserves it from nosey-parkerdom in Alpha System Three. But Beta is an Alpha System One as well. Therefore Beta makes up, out of its total atomic data, some kinds of aggregated package to send to Alpha Three. These packages *could* be molecules (in the sense defined). But it is likely that the molecules Alpha Three needs contain packages from *all* Alpha's Betas, and not just from the one we are considering. So probably these packages, which we hope are not just lists of totals, will be some sets of indices produced as weighted mathematical functions of atomic components. At any rate, this has to be agreed; and when it is, Alpha respects the autonomy of Beta in other respects.

With its *molecular* indices, Alpha is in a position to quantify its *own* quantified flowchart, and to submit its *own* managerial indices for filtration by Cyberstride. And so on, up the scale of recursion. This arrangement resolves the paradox with which we started; since each level of management has its uniquely appropriate molecular data system, even though atomic data are the same, with which to quantify its unique flowchart. Moreover, the schema represents maximum decentralization, since any given level of recursion receives directly only its own Cyberstride reports.

'Receives directly' only its own: there are then indirect reports from lower levels of recursion in the special circumstance of algedonic signals needed to operate the Arousal Filter of Figure 32. The essence of the matter is that if an Alpha System One is in trouble, it will try to get itself out; it is after all also Beta, a viable system. If it cannot do that in a reasonable time, it recalls that it is after all an Alpha System One, and sends an algedonic signal for help.

How shall it do so? And what happens if it is too cocksure, or too lazy, or too corrupt to mention its problem in Gamma to Alpha? (Gamma is of course a

System One of Beta, and something about which Alpha would normally know nothing — this being Beta's job.) The solution to both problems is that the alerting signal of incipient change, which should stay with the autonomous Beta, will *automatically* convert into an algedonic signal from Beta qua Alpha One to the Alpha metasystem, *unless* Beta succeeds in overcoming the problem — which is its job. This procedure, which is logically faultless, contains an operational problem. This is not the problem: 'what counts as action?' since that is a matter for Beta management; all that interests Alpha is that Beta homeostats are operating within physiological limits. No, the problem is to know **how long Beta should take to restore homeostasis,** before the Beta-alert converts to an Alpha-algedonic signal. The system at this point could become oppressive; and therefore the operational research teams, in addition to creating quantified flowchart models with the *help* and the *agreement* of workers' committees, were expected to nominate the physiological recovery times for each index on the same terms: that is, with help and agreement. It is not difficult to persuade people that their best interest is served by automatic notification of their difficulties — provided that they themselves have control of the parameters of the system under which this will be done.

We have seen the appearance and meaning of an algedonic signal lifting itself by a level of recursion from Beta to Alpha. But Beta qua Alpha System One is submitting data for the Alpha Cyberstride in any case. Yes: but it is submitting *functions* of atomic indices in that capacity, and not atomic indices themselves. This is the precise difference between the incipient change alert and the algedonic arousal — that the latter moves to the next higher level of recursion. Here, of course, adequately prompt help may again be unforthcoming: in which case, the algedonic signal will rise *another* level of recursion. In principle, then, it is possible for an algedonic signal originating at plant level to reach the Minister himself. If that were ever to happen, it would be a disgrace: the management at plant, enterprise, sector, and rama levels of recursion would all have failed. This is why the principle is precious: it is clearly an instrument of *cohesiveness* in the nest of viable systems. But, again, it offers the maximum decentralization that is consistent with cohesion — since, if all concerned do their agreed jobs properly, algedonic signals will rarely be fired.

Details for implementing all this were worked out during the second epoch. The PERT chart (Figure 44) dated 20th July 1972 shows, in the middle section, the development of the tools Checo and Cyberstride, as already discussed. In the lower part of the picture is the plan for bringing the daily data inputs generated by the quantified flowchart analyses on-stream in Cyberstride. The four ramas are listed, and the government-owned corporations are phased into the plan at weekly intervals. It will be realized that the corporations cover, under their general titles, multiple enterprises that in turn include multiple plants; for example, 'CAP' is the acronymous name for the entire iron and

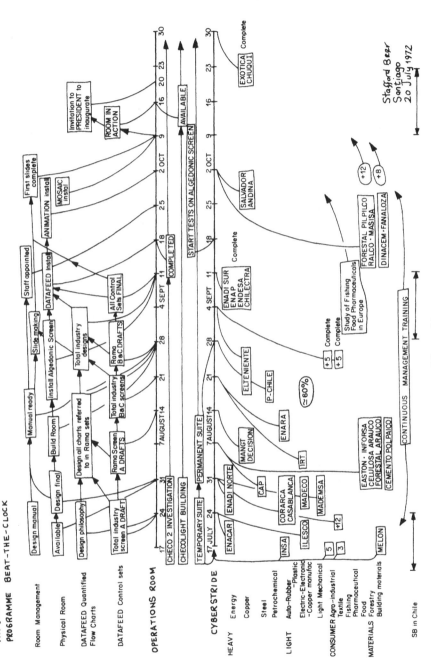

Figure 44

steel industry. In the top part of the chart appear the activities that mesh together to put into physical effect the modus operandi of the Opsroom. Not shown there is the integrative study that later proved necessary to provide a taxonomic system for the display and storage of data in terms of the atomic/molecular recursive logic discussed in the last few paragraphs. This piece of work emerged as a paper called Models for Action, and it occupied much of my time during September 1972 (when it was issued). It seems that the designer of a total system must attend to any inadequacies that appear in the underlying logic of his own vision himself — otherwise he loses control of his own understanding of the project's development. In such cases, he has to resist accusations as to a neurotic preoccupation with detail, and ensure that the structural foundations are indeed secure.

Getting such balances 'right' in terms of the exigencies of the national situation was difficult: balances between policies and details in the project work, between meticulous research and adequate explanation, between precise and approximate measurement ... very real decisions in project direction in such dimensions as these must be taken if the time parameter of the managerial problem is to be accepted as central to that problem. A coup d'état had aborted in March, and its leaders had been captured; as the year wore on, economic pressures steadily increased; it was evident to us all that we were engaged in a race against time. Hence the title of the chart (Figure 44) as given in July: Programme Beat-the-Clock.

The People Project

It may be recalled from Chapter 16 that the first of the cybernetic papers written in Chile (November 1971) was called *The Effective Organization of the State*. By March 1972, Project Cybersyn (also known as Synco in Chile, because of more felicitous assonance in Spanish) was formulated as an approach to the regulation of the social economy; and we have just been reviewing its progress in the second epoch. Also in March 1972, however, we addressed the basic issue of the organization of the state that is not economic, but societary. Parallel to the paper on Cybersyn, therefore, I wrote a second about a project to examine:

> 'the systems dynamics
> of the interaction
> between government and people
>
> in the light of newly available technology
> such as TV
>
> and discoveries in the realm
> of psycho-cybernetics.'

Just as it was necessary to speak briefly about the economic situation in approaching Cybersyn, so it is necessary to speak briefly about the government-people arrangements that were at issue at that time. Strangely enough, the arrangements were basically the same, and also the criticisms of those arrangements, as are familiar enough in Britain — and many other countries with a long-established democratic tradition. There was a bi-cameral legislature; critics doubted the efficacy of the upper chamber. There was an independent judiciary; critics wondered whether its interpretation of the law was in touch with public mores, and whether its ponderous administration was not completely out-of-date. There was a very large bureaucracy for the country's size; critics thought it should be streamlined at the least, and perhaps the executive arm of government should be put on a different footing altogether.

The novelty in Chile seemed to be, not that the three arms of government exhibited these familiar features and attracted these usual criticisms, but that there was a real possibility that the government might actually do something radical about them. International commentators were fond of reporting that the president was under strong pressure from his own left wing to take drastic action. The more perceptive of them recognized the resolute constitutionalist in Allende — and therefore concluded that he was in a dilemma. My own reading does not invoke any such dilemma — because the president's personal views on all these points determined on radical change, and determined also on the use of constitutional methods to bring it about.

The situation can be summed up in reference to the so-called 'People's Assembly'. Suppose that the bi-cameral congress were replaced by such an invention, and that this change were made through a referendum held under the constitution, then there would be potent consequences for the other two arms of government as well .... Such matters were under debate within the parties. But what would actually constitute a 'people's assembly'; what would it do, in cybernetic terms, as a variety regulator; how could modern technology be used to enhance its value and effectiveness? The March 1972 paper, paralleling the launch of Cybersyn, was addressed to these preliminary questions: here is the gist of it (but not verbatim).

The Management of Variety in the Political Context

People generate massive variety, which has somehow to be greatly attenuated if a government is not to be overwhelmed by it.

Typical methods of variety attenuation in a democracy include:

- formation of parties, to represent large blocs of variety across the country,

- election of representatives, to represent blocs of variety by locale,

- division of time into
  - period of presidential office
  - period between elections

  which introduce artificial epochs of relative stability.

The decisions of the government have low variety compared with their needed application to the case of the individual citizen.

They have to be amplified, and in the past this has been the role of bureaucracy.

Time cycles in the past have been very extended. It takes a long time to change one's parliamentary representative; it takes a long time for the bureaucracy machine to grind out an answer.

But the system met the Law of Requisite Variety, and its homeostats (though sluggish) worked.

Inject into this situation two NEW effects:

(i)   the explosive rate of change due to the growth of technology, the rise of political aspirations, and the outside-world condition;

(ii)   the availability of mass media of communication — especially TV.

Government now communicates directly with the undifferentiated mass of the people, as if it were speaking to the individual, and creating the illusion in the home that it is. The context of this false dialogue is that the individual is also supplied by the new media with a proliferation of information and misinformation about things — as soon as they happen.

Looking at the outside loop in the diagram at Figure 45, we see this effect as

- massive amplification of variety, insofar as single-sentence utterances may be developed into hour-long simulations of imagined consequences,

- massive change in dynamic periodicity: the government is reporting to the nation daily, instead of accounting for itself at election times.

But the return loop does not change. The variety that the people generate is attenuated as before.

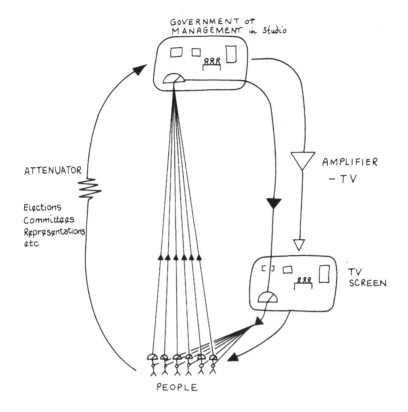

Figure 45

This situation attempts to disobey the Law of Requisite Variety, and disbalances the homeostatic equilibrium in both richness and in period.

Then it is predictable that the people, thus affected, will build up pressures in the system that can no longer be released — because the filtering capacity cannot contain the flow.

This is bound to lead to unrest: demonstrations, agitation, perhaps violence, possibly revolt.

It follows that the people should be provided with new means of communication with the government which

- match the amplification of government variety with less attenuation of their variety (re-establishing peaceful conditions for the operation of Ashby's Law)

- operate on the same time scale — that is immediately

- use technology to serve the people as well as the government.

The Notion of the Algedonic Loop

In the diagram the *inner* loop represents such a scheme. People watching TV are seen communicating directly with the government.

The main methods for doing this elsewhere have been

- plebescites
- public opinion polls
- the installation of a computer in the inner loop to receive public reactions on a large scale, process them, and present them publicly on the screen.

Only the third operates in real time.

Besides, there is the same objection to each one. Each pre-empts issues by structuring the questions. Thereby

- people find themselves answering questions they wish had not been asked (or not asked in this form) thereby appearing to support policies they do not actually approve,

- people cannot comment on issues not explicitly laid before them,

- people may not be sufficiently analytic or articulate to cope with this kind of process,

- people may not answer truthfully because they fear identification and possible victimization,

- the whole system *could* be used as a giant teaching machine to condition the public (some authors in the United States actually advocate this). Advantages — such as changing eating habits to suit the food supply — could easily be outweighed by loss of freedom ...

It is a formidable list of objections.

An algedonic loop works on a non-analytic, non-articulated scale of 'pleasure and pain'. It uses the brain as its computer, structured and programmed by individuality and life experience, to produce an output indicating a degree of satisfaction that does not have to be 'rationalized'.

This is at last an attempt to provide a metric for Aristotle's eudemony, or 'state of general well being'. The algedonic meter (pictured in Figure 45) is a simple analogue device, with interleaved segments in different colours. Thus to turn the central knob changes the proportion of the 'happy/unhappy' display — and also the electrical input to the circle of which this meter is a member.

Someone holding an algedonic meter sets the display by moving the pointer anywhere on a continuous scale between total disquiet and total satisfaction. She/he does not have to explain anything — only to respond algedonically, which people may be observed to do all the time.

There could be an official locale, housing a television set and a properly constituted sample of people, having one meter between (say) three. The meters drive a simple electrical system, which sums the voltage for this locale. The rest of the proposed structure for a People's Assembly is shown in Figure 45.

Now: when a broadcast is taking place, the people's eudemony is indicated on a meter in the TV studio — which everyone (those in the studio and the public) can see. The studio meter is driven by the sum of the people's meters.

This closes the algedonic loop. It is a system that appears to respond to all the criteria previously noted. It is practicable and it is inexpensive.

It is noteworthy that this system, shorn of its technology and therefore of its formal existence, already tries to be. It is experienced as clamour of various kinds.

'It is proposed to create a new public response system, in order to provide convenient and legal outlets for pressures that are already making themselves manifest. These pressures constitute political power — in the limit they may overthrow governments.'

This statement ended the second of the papers presented in March 1972.

Algedonic Participation

There was great interest in these tentative ideas. Because they responded to a need which was real in political terms and predicted by the cybernetic analysis of variety balances, everyone from the President down took them seriously. In some advanced countries, there are plans to equip households with attachments to telephones which will enable respondents to 'vote' in response to the programme they are watching on the television set. However, the planned systems are digital rather than analogue, and their *modus operandi* is open to all the objections listed earlier. Moreover, they are conceived in the commercial context as tools of 'instant market research'; and their protagonists do not seem to have considered the inevitable political consequences of introducing such technology — for whatever purpose. Democracy suffers as the result of technical advances installed for adventitious reasons, because of the resulting variety disbalancing; yet there is a deeply reactionary response to any possible reform of the democratic process itself that calls technology in aid.

It was not so in Chile. I was enabled to form a liaison with an institute called CEREN, dedicated to social science, and to develop these concepts with two of the country's leading sociologists. A prototype system of ten algedonic meters, linked by a single wire in a loop through a large summation meter, was built in England by my son Simon Beer (an electronic engineer), and taken to Chile for experimental purposes. Because each station could make an arbitrary move at an arbitrary time, the summation meter had to be very heavily damped; otherwise, there were no technical problems.

In Figure 45, we saw the legend 'Government or Management in Studio'. Now the effective channel (Canal 13) of the public television broadcasting system in Santiago was in the hands of the political opposition, and a channel available to experiments in social democracy was (in my opinion) overdue. It should now be understood why there remained a blank wall in the Operations Room: it was intended to house an algedonic meter. The idea was that the (electrical) People's Assembly, disseminated throughout the nation, would be able to *participate* in arguments broadcast from the room — not by responding to questions hurled at them over the air, for this route leads to logical reductionism and to political demagoguey; but — by the continuous registration of a combined degree of satisfaction with events. It has to be noted that not only would the meter be visible to those present in the room, but also to the public whose meter it is . . .

The practical issue as to how these ideas could best be advanced led to a proposed experiment which was prepared but, alas, not finally undertaken by the time that the government fell. A brief account of it will reveal the cybernetic complexities that always arise when informational loops are closed onto themselves, and also how variety equations come to be resolved without communication 'channels' in the ordinary sense of that word. The experiment was to be concerned with the management of a factory, in which worker participation would be continuously effective via algedonic loops.

Suppose that a small group of us forms a working team running a section in a plant. On the wall is our algedonic meter. With characteristic phlegm, we have set our meter at mid-distance between high and low eudemony. Similar meters exist in every section of the plant; there are large summation meters in the entrances to the works, and also in the boss's office. Grossly irritated by the failure of raw material supplies for our machines, we agree to change our algedonic setting to one of low eudemony. On clocking-off, we observe that the summation meter for the plant is registering high eudemony. Have we been over-hasty, then, and should we conform to the consensus? Or are our workmates blinded by managerial blandishments, and have we a duty to open their eyes and campaign for better arrangements? The meters make explicit the outcome of continuous dialogue among the workers themselves, as to their satisfaction with conditions in general, which would otherwise remain implicit in a host of small encounters never fully articulated.

More important, however, is the fact that the workers have absolute assurance that the boss knows the state of eudemony as registered by the summation meter. The boss knows that the workers know that he knows. The workers know that the boss knows that the workers know that he knows. The expectation is that requisite variety will be mediated by this algedonic closure, using no more than one loop of low-tension wire as the physical 'channel' of the system. If this point is well taken, then it is possible to project the notion into the national government scenario previously painted. Imagine a group exploring a problem in the Operations Room in the presence of television cameras; imagine the algedonic meter sinking as unpopular lines of enquiry were pursued; the viewers know that the meeting knows that they know that the meeting knows .... One would expect positive reinforcing feedback in this kind of participation, which might well facilitate binary decisions fed by analogue inputs — which is just the way that the nervous system works.

There are manifest problems in all this, but they are not technological nor economic. Psychological research was being undertaken to establish the 'rules of the game' if genuine participation were to be effected. Sociological and demographic research was proposed to underwrite either a sampling scheme or a constituency scheme of general franchise. Political questions had to be addressed, especially that of security: but the dangers of rigged ballots and undue pressure are always with us, and a new kind of technology does not necessarily exacerbate them. At any rate, I hope that new experiments on these lines will be facilitated somewhere. A plausible experiment, for example, would be to equip a conference hall with closed algedonic loops: would the speaker become yet more steadily boring and obscure as the summation meter steadily dropped — for all to see?

A preliminary experiment on these lines was undertaken in Chile, with a group of about fifteen people. Remember that the prototype ring had only ten metres, and note that the 'subjects' were all friends within the project. The lecturer commented on the interest and excitement engendered; but his friends rapidly learned how to rig the system. They joined in plots to 'throw' the lecturer by alternating positive and negative responses, for instance. But if coalitions are not permitted in democratic assemblies (compare the arguments about secret ballots in trade union affairs), outcomes may well be sterile. The most positive result of this limited experiment was surely the lecturer's comment, having been at pains to follow the public feedback, that the experience 'suggests that isolated speakers usually keep cool because they don't have the slightest idea as to what the reaction is'. This could well be true.

The over-riding *cybernetic* consideration in any large-scale application such as a People's Assembly is the problem of time lags in the public's ability to recognize the implications of given policies. And let this not be dismissed as an issue belonging to the next century, because the cybernetics of democracy are already in place — regardless of a more advanced technology, which might actually ameliorate rather than exacerbate the problem. It is hard to say whether a trigger-happy response leading to wild oscillation is better or worse than a slovenly response to events already dead. What can be judged is that it is within cybernetic competence to design feedback functions that correctly handle time lags, but that these designs would be very difficult to implement in conditions of free-range comment via the mass media — which are conditions rightly prized. There is huge scope for research in these social cybernetics; huge need as well, since the existing checks and balances (such as they are) are now in process of dislocation through a new generation of electronic intervention in societary communications. Meanwhile, reflect on the words of the late R.H.S. Crossman, who said to me just after leaving office following the defeat of his government: 'I took the blame for my predecessor's foolish decisions, and now my successor will get the credit for my wise ones'. Note not only the reasonableness of this complaint, but the ease with which opinion (just like the economic policies criticized earlier) can become locked-on to a response that is exactly out of phase.

Vox Populi...

The people have their voice. However, the channels open for its direct expression are, as we have seen, heavily attenuated; and the scheme just described was intended to restore variety and also immediacy to the people's voice. But there are other amplifiers.

First of all, the role of the artist, the poet, and the musician in the expression of every kind of popular aspiration is generally accepted as powerful in all politically self-conscious nations. In Chile, I spent every spare minute with such people — mainly out of sheer exuberance. Even so, no-one doubted (least of all they themselves) that they played a major role in the political struggle. Once again, a closed loop amplifier is detectable in cybernetic terms. A piece of art — picture or cartoon, sculpture, or wall-painting, marching-song or folk lament — focuses emotion by selecting a set of states from a plethora of variety that is in total too gigantic to be apprehended, except perhaps as a great sigh. If the selection is well-made, then individuals will identify with this art-work, reinforcing its effect by their popular acclaim. This is particularly obvious in the case of music, since all may participate in the act of its live performance.

Once more, we see huge systemic effects (in this case, the negentropy of political awareness rising rapidly) in the absence of iterative 'channels' linking the artist and the public. Even the initial 'message' may not be overly political, as it is in a protest song: simply to be evocative of fond emotions may be sufficient. But if the artist can focus the voice of the people to their satisfaction, he may also put words into the people's mouth — and always has done. In this the artist accepts, and knowingly accepts, a responsibility. But because science has indeed been largely sequestrated by the rich and powerful elements of society, science becomes an integral part of the target of protest for the artist. Each makes his own *Guernica*. My own view, which I set about propagating in these circles, is that science, like art, is part of the human heritage. Hence if science has been sequestrated, it must be wrenched back and used by the people whose heritage it is, not simply surrendered to oppressors who blatantly use it to fabricate tools of further oppression (whether bellicose or economic).

Secondly, the voice of the people can (by the use of elementary modern technology) be made to resound in the people's own ears. It is commonplace, all over the world, to see those who live in economically depressed areas despondent, and robbed of all will to improve their lot. They sit in doorways, telling each other that nothing can be done, and hope that one day a government programme will rescue them from their penury and despair. In Canada, however, I had had dealings with a project known as *Challenge for Change*, whereby teams of young sociologists and film makers had set out to gain the participation of the people on the Eastern seaboard of Canada in their own self-improvement programmes. This project, fathered by the Ministry of State and mothered by the National Film Board, used mobile hand-held television equipment as its primary tool. Edited video-tape of members of the dispersed community all saying 'nothing can be done, no-one is interested', when shown in the community hall to themselves, clearly demonstrated that everyone *was* interested, and that therefore something *could* be done . . .

These remarks oversimplify, and do not pretend to be a proper account of the Canadian work. However, the approach had something to offer Chile, as we studied the role of communications in society, and I set about recruiting a team of Canadian social scientists willing to pilot experiments. There was an enthusiastic response. But, over a period of months, I was unable to obtain appropriate equipment — little of it as was needed. We did indeed face the rigours of technological as well as economic blockade.

'The Manual'

The last of the components of the People Project that was being advanced throughout the second epoch of the work, and running *pari passu* with Project Cybersyn, was known to us as 'The Manual'. The idea emerged in debate between Fernando Flores and myself. If we thought that we were beginning to understand the cybernetics of government, and if we wanted to redesign the governmental process, then there ought to be 'a manual' in which some key principles were set down — in such a way that all could understand them.

Mulling over this requirement, I thought that seven principles, plus or minus two, would be their number — since this figure so often appears as delimiting the discriminatory ability of the human brain. To err on the safe side, perhaps something useful could be said by five principles ... Ah: there are five subsystems in the viable system. By this route, I set out to analyse what was most important about each of the subsystems One to Five from the standpoint of the ordinary citizen: what was most notably wrong in each case, and how could it be put right. I wrote five essays to myself, and refined them; I discussed the issues with everyone I could think of, and most notably a workers' leader of no learning and profound wisdom. In the end, I had five principles, each expressed in a single cybernetic sentence, and each relating to one subsystem — although out of numerical order (the order being: 5,2,1,3,4). Here are the five cybernetic statements:

First Principle
System Five within a people's government cannot be an élite ruling class: it is somehow the embodiment of the mass of the people themselves.

Second Principle
The speed of response in an essentially lagged servomechanism is critical: note especially the anti-oscillatory Systems Two.

Third Principle
Variety engineering enables us to design homeostatic subsystems that obey the Law of Requisite Variety, and determine a recursion of metasystems: this preserves System One autonomy.

Fourth Principle

Command is neither a matter of wielding authority nor of overloading the central axis with variety-attenuating regulations: System Three delegates authority and accountability to the elemental level, and looks for synergistic advantage in taking a synoptic view of Systems One.

Fifth Principle

Special attention is necessary to System Four: otherwise System Five identifies with System Three, and the whole cerebral metastructure collapses; instead of adaptation and self-determination, we are left with crisis management.

This was to be the cybernetic substance of 'the manual'; but now it needed translating into simple statements that could be distributed to the people through booklets, leaflets, posters, and (I hoped) songs. After many attempts at this translation, I finally produced a booklet entitled 'Five Principles for the People, towards Good Government' in early September 1972. It began with a statement which I hoped that President Allende would sign:

'The revolution of ownership
is two years old.'

'IT IS TIME
for the revolution of government
to begin.'

This statement would be dated from the official inauguration of the Operations Room, so that the whole movement towards bureaucratic change would be totally visible and universal. The five principles were each couched in two forms: STOP the existing practice, START the new one. And each time: 'CHANGE is a state of mind that everyone shares' — a definition evolved for this purpose, but which perhaps has some general merit. There were appropriate drawings to illustrate the five themes, and the booklet is reproduced in an appendix to this section.

Having spoken of 'translation' (namely from the language of cybernetics into the English language and the cultural norms of an Englishman), it is necessary to add that a second translation would be required that I should not attempt — into Spanish, and into terms of the Chilean culture, with sectarian politics intervening. Whether this production would ever have been completed and published as a booklet cannot be judged, for other matters arose ... In the meantime, however, I determined to tackle the question of songs. As already remarked, music was a major amplifier in the cultural system.

The central figure among the musicians with whom I mixed and became friends was the famous folklorist Angel Parra. He was at first quite amazed that I expected him to sing about the scientific inheritance of the people: this is hardly a familiar idiom of the folklore genre. However, he had been following our progress with great interest, and he eventually agreed. In this 'translation' of the manual, the cybernetic finesse of the five subsystems commentary was assimilated into a political appeal for reform — which somehow made all five points through the recounting of then-current events and preoccupations. And the two basic messages of the manual came through strongly in the chorus:

> 'Then let us STOP
> who do not want
> the people to win this fight —
>
> And let us HEAP
> all science together
> before we reach the end of our tether'

or, better, in the original:

> 'Hay que parar al que no quiera
> que el pueblo gana esta pelea
>
> hay que juntar toda la ciencia
> antes que acabe la paciencia'.

Angel Parra called the song: 'Letanía para una computadora y para un niño que va a nacer', which in English says: 'Litany for a Computer and a Baby about to be Born'. It is a proper theme; and, as the impact of microprocessors becomes felt, it is a theme to which people's attention must be increasingly directed. Because computing in all its forms is becoming exceedingly cheap, the mass of the people can in principle be freed from drudgery; because the cybernetics of techno-social change is not understood by either the government or the people, it is likely that in fact the mass of the people will be 'freed' from gainful employment . . . .

5 PRINCIPLES

FOR THE PEOPLE

TOWARDS GOOD GOVERNMENT

" The revolution of ownership
is two years old.

" IT IS TIME
for the revolution of government
to begin. "

~~~~~~~~~~

20th October 1972

First Principle : GOVERNMENT IS THE PEOPLE'S HELP

FINISHED

The view of government
- as incomprehensible
- as the people's burden

STOP THIS ↑ WHENEVER YOU CAN

Never despair

CHANGE is a state of mind
that everyone shares

STARTED

The view of government
  — as the people thinking what to do
  — as acting together to do it

The Compañero Presidente says: "Government is the people."

The wishes of the people will be made known to the Government at all times.

We shall use TECHNOLOGY, which belongs to the people, to do it.

Second Principle: TO HELP MEANS
~~~~~~~~~~~~~~~~~~~~~~~~
HELPING NOW
~~~~~~~~~~~~~~~~~~~~

FINISHED

Red tape + muddle
= endless delay

STOP THIS ↑ WHENEVER YOU CAN

Never despair

CHANGE is a state of mind
that everyone shares

STARTED

Immediate contact + immediate response
= fastest possible action

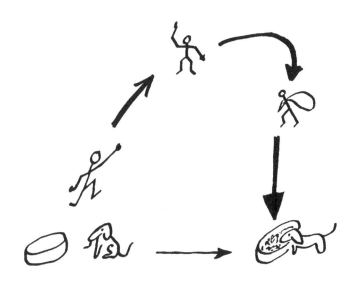

We have already used TECHNOLOGY to
link 60% of the social sector directly
to computers in the nation's capital,
which send back immediate advice to the
enterprises.
We shall extend this kind of service to all
of the people by some means.

Third Principle :   THE ROAD TO HELP

HAS SIGNPOSTS

FINISHED

Bureaucracy
Petty officialdom
Despair
No answers

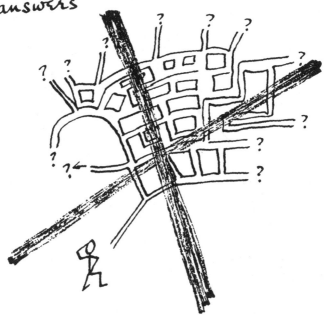

STOP THIS ↑ WHENEVER YOU CAN
Never Despair
CHANGE is a state of mind
that everyone shares

STARTED

One official deals with a few problems
One straight link goes higher up
The links can reach the President himself
Answers

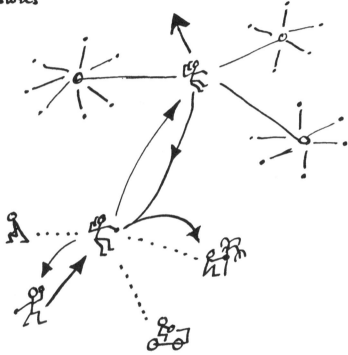

WE shall replace bureaucracy with a precise
and clear network of officials, whose only
job is to help — to give answers.

WE shall keep paperwork to a minimum
—essential records. The people cannot eat
paper.

Fourth principle :   HELP IS A NAME

&s FACE

FINISHED

Blaming faceless people
"It cannot be done"
(and bad luck)

STOP THIS ↑ WHENEVER YOU CAN

Never despair
CHANGE is a state of mind
that everyone shares

STARTED

Direct personal responsibility

" **I** will do it .....

...... or **I** know **WHO** can "

Of course Officials really want to help.
After the Third Principle is obeyed, they
will have the opportunity and the time
to know the people they are proud to
help.

Fifth Principle : THE FUTURE STARTS
                        TODAY

FINISHED

Managing a perpetual crisis
Everyone busy grabbing what they can
——▶ the same old problems later on.

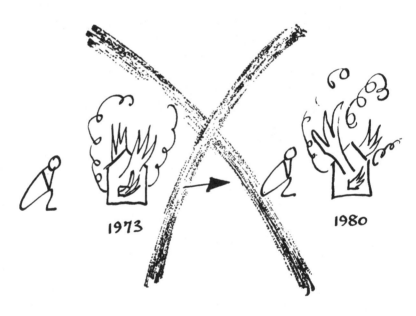

1973   1980

STOP THIS ↑ WHENEVER YOU CAN
Never despair
CHANGE is an attitude of mind
that everyone shares

STARTED

Thinking for the future, which is just beginning
Planning for our children's children
⟶ a better society

1973   1980

The future is not a blank, nor is it inescapably
worsening. For the first time in history, MAN
knows enough to provide the kind of society that
HE wants.
We shall help the people to understand the options.
Then the people must decide.

IF THE GOVERNMENT **IS** THE PEOPLE

THE REVOLUTION OF GOVERNMENT

STARTS WITH **YOU**.

Externalities

As time wore on throughout 1972, Chile developed into a siege economy. How ironic it was that so many eyes were focused with goodwill on the Chilean experiment in all parts of the world, while governments and other agencies, supposedly representing those liberal-minded observers, resisted its maturation with implacable hostility. The nation's life support system was in a stranglehold, from financial credit to vital supplies; its metabolism was frustrated, from the witholding of spare parts to software and expertise; literally and metaphorically, the well-to-do were eating rather than investing their seed-corn — with encouragement from outside. Even more ironic, looking back, is the fact that every advance Allende made, every success in the eyes of the mass of the people (which brought with it more electoral support), made it less likely that the Chilean experiment would be allowed to continue — because it became more threatening to Western ideology.

Central to this economic plight, which (see Chapter 16) had been forecast, was the question of foreign exchange. As mentioned, foreign earnings hinged on copper exports, and we were to see the spectacle of the 'phantom ship' full of copper that traipsed around European ports looking for permission to unload. (It was said that the Chilean government had refused compensation in taking over the copper industry; in reality, it had tabled the totals of foreign capital invested together with the revenues taken out of the country, and had raised the question as to who should be compensating whom.) Whatever the rights and wrongs of this copper problem, however, the intention formed by the 'national plan' to invest most available foreign income in the copper industry appeared absurd. Not only was such a strategy politically vulnerable — as we already knew; it made no economic sense either. This was where the Checo simulations, however 'unreliable', had their impact. What they certainly did convey was the rate at which an economy under such pressure was likely to change, compared with the rate at which investment in the copper industry could conceivably pay off.

Here was a dilemma indeed. From the point of view of responsible Chileans, it would have been outrageous not to invest the maximum of foreign exchange in copper; was not the failure of US ownership cited in exactly these terms? Nationalization had been a recognition, not only of the economic exploitation of the outstanding national resource, but of a decade of neglect in investment that would have a catastrophic effect in the longer term. Selective mining, inadequate maintenance, the failure to reshape the development of the resource, had led to disastrous outcomes already: these were the specifics of the indictment of the foreign ownership. Looking back, a member of the core group immediately reeled off different, explicit examples from five different copper sites — adding the cybernetic point that investment in copper, since it produced the maximum *surplus* in foreign exchange, provided positive feedback (and not simply exchange) to the Chilean economy. Even so, what was said in the last paragraph had its own validity at the time. The story reflects a perfectly general political double-bind. Of what avail is long-term planning, conducted in absolute dispassion and disinterest for the sake of a future generation, if survival in the short-term is thereby surrendered, and that future is consequently barren? Alternatively, of what avail to the future generation is an inheritance of the denial of its interests in favour of the earlier survival that made its very existence posible? Somehow the whole dilemma was summed up in the fact that when Angel Parra wrote a haunting song called *El Barque Phantasmo* about the ghost ship carrying copper which no-one would unload, and when Allende approved it to the extent that he wished to take disc pressings as gifts to the members of the United Nations he was shortly to address, the President was thwarted. The record-pressing company was on strike.

The Checo team had built a preliminary model of inflation, as mentioned; and we wanted to understand, through this, the nature and the risk of hyperinflation. It was argued in text books (remember that the date was 1972) that monetarist policies could hold such a situation. Therefore I made a systems-theoretic model of monetarist economic regulation, checked it through with a leading British economist prominent in support of this approach, and tried to use it in the context of the Checo work. The cybernetics of monetarism seemed totally inimical to the cybernetics of a free society as the Chilean experiment had defined it (or as I would define it anywhere else today), because the regulatory tool embodies a model of what must be regulated that denies variety proliferation in pursuit of adaptation and evolution to any changing economy. Remembering the cybernetic theorem that declares a regulator to be effective only insofar as its model of what is regulated is adequate, we see in monetarism a diminution in variety of the real economic world entailed by a regulatory model that cannot encompass more. *Only variety can absorb variety*: Ashby's Law can be met **either** by expanding regulatory variety to absorb evolutionary variety, **or** by curbing evolutionary learning until variety in the economy matches the regulatory variety disposed by the only regulator — the money supply — that the ideology of the status quo is prepared to acknowledge.

Having come to this conclusion, I intensified the search for novel and evolutionary activity whereby the Chilean economy might *very rapidly* enhance its foreign earnings. Of course, this meant looking for national assets, other than copper; of course, moreover, diversification had been a major concern in Chile for many years. Even so, I identified three possibilities in which there seemed reason to hope. The first was skilled artisan labour. There seemed likely to be an expanding market in the First World, aching under the dull uniformity and plastic gimcrackery of its domestic architecture and design, for handcrafted products — especially those that draw on so rich a heritage of symbolism, texture and colour. The second was wine. Chile produces vast amounts of wine, and drinks most of the best of it — exporting only the cheapest in relatively small quantities. In fact, the best Chilean wine is excellent; there is an advanced oenological institute, and a general belief that Chilean vines (originally from France) were the only vines in the world to escape altogether the phylloxera epidemic of the late nineteenth century. The third natural asset was three thousand miles of coast line, and the fish in those seas — notably anchovies.

With the help of others in the core group, appropriate contacts were made with government people in all three areas. It was difficult to quantify the possibilities for mobilizing artisans; but there were soon hard facts and practical possibilities with which to clothe the other two skeletal ideas. Moreover, it emerged that there was a sizeable mountain of pig iron available for immediate export. I returned to Europe armed with these dossiers, and with the promise that two authorized negotiators for the Minister could be called into the situation at any time.

It so happened that during this period I was a partner, one of five, in a consortium (now disbanded) which had the aim of facilitating major international enterprise. The other four partners listed an international jurist, a physicist and ex-diplomat, a foreign banker, and a well-known professor of economics. All the partners had strong connexions world-wide in their own fields, and the plan (which proved to be very far ahead of its time) was to seek synergistic developments in large-scale projects of all the expert inputs that would be required. It seemed that the fisheries project offered an ideal prospect for the intervention of this partnership. Thus, while I was hawking pig-iron (and discovering that the steel industry cartel across Europe was yet more powerful than when I had left the industry twelve years earlier), and also trying to establish that a wine market existed in Britain for a medium-priced product (there is a sizeable gap in quality and price between Chateau Plonk and the Appellation Controlée, for which a Chilean wine could have been tailored), my partners were considering fish.

The Japanese were already fishing these waters from very powerful vessels, to the chagrin of the Chilean fishermen — who accused the Japanese of poaching inside territorial limits. Our idea was to hire large factory ships, which would produce fish-meal continuously at sea. No delays here: such ships seemed to be available, at a price, and no shore stations would be required. The product would probably be sold to the Chinese Republic. There would be legal and political problems back in Chile, but the two negotiators were confident of handling those.

None of these plans was to mature; and it is impossible to prove exactly what went wrong, because at all times the negotiating space was thick with unreal demands and feeble excuses. My own considered judgement, with hindsight, is that the deployment of a large piece of capitalistic economic machinery in support of an avowedly neo-socialist cause is basically untenable as a proposition to both sides — even though each can provide a rationale for reaching agreement. (Note the expression *neo*-socialist: this analysis would not apply to East-West trade agreements which are basically capitalistic in each direction.) I have already reported President Allende's words to me: 'how can a small socialist state continue to exist in a capitalist milieu?' Of course it cannot — without very powerful support, as Cuba had, and Chile had not. By the end of this epoch, another *coup d'état* was attempted: the President later called it the 'September plot'. There was much unease; There was a sense that irresistible forces from outside the country would use whatever sympathetic internal interests they could find to bring the government down. Even so, the coup was overcome, and the Commander-in-Chief again pledged the loyalty of the armed forces.

CHAPTER EIGHTEEN

The October watershed

This personal story of my involvement in Chile, which began at the end of 1971 and came to an abrupt halt at the end of 1973, had its major turning point just half-way through — at the end of 1972. October of that year saw the beginning of the third epoch, as perceived from my own standpoint. Some of the matters discussed in the last chapter have already overshot that date; but that was simply because it was convenient to trace through continuations of actions taken during the second epoch. This being so, however, it is as well to recapitulate the situation as it was at the start of the new epoch.

As far as Project Cybersyn was concerned, the physical facts were consonant with the development programme, given that the operations room would be late. Cybernet, the telecommunications network linking the socio-industrial economy of Chile, had been working since March, and was gradually being improved. It was controlled from the communications centre that was to serve the operations room, and the rubrics of its behaviour were by now well established. Chilean-built equipment for the room was nearing completion, 300 kilometres south of Santiago; two of the British-built consignments had arrived (and the last came a few days later). All suites of computer programs were working as expected. Roughly 60% of all enterprises constituting the socio-industrial economy were by now included in the Cybersyn system, although many of the indexical time series had not yet been properly calibrated on Cyberstride.

The managerial facts surrounding all this were, however, a different matter. The political situation had begun to deteriorate seriously in September. Fernando Flores was due to leave Corfo, and to become Undersecretary of Economics: he had to bring Cybersyn, at least, into the (political) open. Accordingly, a day-long meeting had been held on September 2nd for a large number of people who were inside the project, or connected to it through the ramas, or who were politically involved. This meeting, held at Los Andes, had instituted a destabilizing change in the control of the project. Both he and I had spoken at length about the political intentions behind the cybernetic science. These were of course the managerial purposes of the work from the beginning; but many of those working on the details saw themselves as politically neutral professionals, and some of these were distressed to be told that all future disclosures about the work must explicitly recognize the political intent. A few days later, I handed over the booklet *Five Principles,* with which Flores was delighted; and it became obvious that there would have to be major changes in the management team that was actually implementing the results of the cybernetics on which we had embarked a year before. We travelled to Europe together, although on separate missions, and discussed these issues all the way.

Thus it was that, back in Chile early in October, with the sense of unease within the project grown to alarming proportions, a new management team was appointed by the new Undersecretary. Raúl Espejo was confirmed as head of the scientific project Cybersyn. Enrique Farné, whom I did not know (but soon would, very well) was to be responsible for all cybernetic implementations; Hermann Schwember was to be responsible for the wider implications, including these of international import. This was a man whom I knew very well indeed: he had always been in the core group, and had remained in close touch throughout. This was, however, the first time that he had been given specific duties within the work. My own role was unchanged; but the managerial team was now a 'troika'. Each of the three horses was very powerful: but would they all pull in the same direction? Before we could find out, the worst crisis of the government to date broke upon the country.

The Gremio Strike

The *gremios* were usually depicted by the English-speaking media as 'trade unions'; but they were nothing of the kind (and the Spanish word for trade union is *sindicato*). Perhaps the term 'craft guild', used in the medieval sense, captures much of the sense of *gremio*. In more modern language, no doubt Engels would have called these people petty-bourgeois. They were, for example, the owners of small fleets of lorries, by which the country's transportation system largely operated. They were also retailers, owners of local shops and small distribution centres for daily requisites. The *gremios* were insistent on the protectionist line; they saw themselves as threatened by the potential nationalization of transportation and distribution under the government of Popular Unity. Indeed, they had the power to paralyse both these systems on a nationwide scale; and they had made half-hearted efforts to do so before. Their problem was that they could not sustain their 'strike' action for long — because they ran out of money.

By the 12th October 1972 a very strong action by the *gremios* was in full swing. It seemed ridiculous, because (surely?) it could not be sustained; my log of that day records this view:

'The small entrepreneurs are merely antagonizing the people they are starving of food, cigarettes, petrol .... Therefore the government can safely act, and have readily moved in the military. The people approve; the army prefers the image of saviour to that of stickman. But of course it means that instability grows.'

Instability continued to grow; the President declared a State of Emergency, and appointed a military governor in Santiago. From the rate at which the crisis escalated, it was evident that this was a serious attempt to pull the government down. Far from being a 'ridiculous' gesture, it was a massive assault, and it was soon obvious that external resources were being made available in its support. Fernando Flores was appointed as Coordinator of Interior Government.

As the begetter of our work, Flores had a mastery of the cybernetics of the problem that faced him. However, he was conscious that the operations room was not ready; the disseminated network for governmental regulation prematurely announced in the Third of the *Five Principles* did not yet exist. On the other hand, the communications centre was in smooth running order — ready to serve an opsroom; moreover Cybernet existed nationwide — although it had not been designed for controlling distribution. He moved fast. An emergency operations centre was set up next to the communications centre, and divided into eight functional commands (transportation, food, and so on). One of our own people was put in charge of each. Similar centres were set up regionally, on the disseminated net model, using Cybernet. Within twenty-four hours messages were flowing, non-stop round the clock, at the rate of two thousand telexes a day. This instantly posed an enormous problem in providing the requisite variety to handle such an inundation. Two of the senior cyberneticians organized a filtration system: some signals were algedonic, requiring instant decisions, while others could be attenuated into elements of the pattern that established the factual situation *in real time*. There are major lessons to be learned from this experience, the first group as illustrating the cybernetic principles of the national system, and the second as teaching much about innovatory praxis.

The first cybernetic point is that the huge surge of information into the regulatory system operated as a negentropy pump: instant communication loops sprang into being, and instant decisions were available. This contrasted with the turgid operation of the bureaucratic system, the entropy of which was close to unity — as is so common. Secondly, the inefficiency of the existing distribution system had lead to high physical redundancy — again, as is normal in unplanned economies (think of idle motor transport pools, railway marshalling yards, demurrage); the ability of the cybernetic regulator to survive the hostile action, derived from the effective use of the few physical facilities remaining under the government's control. Thirdly, such a network as this exhibits that very *redundancy of potential command* described in

Chapter 15. This not only helps to absorb proliferating variety: it is decentralizing, and it is robust. Finally, it had at last been made dramatically clear that properly organized information deployed in real time is a major national resource.

As to innovatory praxis, the lessons learned were very clear indeed. Let us first of all note that the cybernetic projects on which we were engaged had the full knowledge and support of the relevant ministers and managers from the President down. We had intellectual assent to the proposition that information constitutes regulation, and we had political commitment to the reorganization that would embody this principle. There were no complaints on either side. But it was not until the top officials and the socially responsible ministers were plunged into the traumatic experience of the *gremio* battle, lived with the problems non-stop, used the tools provided however makeshift, and mastered the revolt, that they fully and deeply understood. We really had been talking about a managerial revolution, and not about the introduction of some rather slick administrative tricks.

It seems little short of a tragedy that this kind of experience cannot be had vicariously, although it can be 'pointed at'. For those involved, perceptions of the management process radically changed. The crisis had come on the night of October 17th, and had been survived. One senior minister said flatly that the government would have collapsed that night if it had not had the cybernetic tools. Meanwhile, the President had preserved his usual posture of calm reassurance. He was reported in a headline in *El Mercurio* thus, *Allende: 'Chile no Está al Borde de Guerra Civil'*. *The Times* in London under the dateline of Santiago, October 18th, translated this: 'Dr Allende said yesterday that the country was near civil war'. Not only was it impossible to translate profound experience; the media reporting in Britain and North America systematically misunderstood the most elementary facts, and the most elementary Spanish.

The Problem of Cybernetic Training in Industry

During the first half of October, while the *gremio* battle raged, I was preparing plans for 'The Extension of Cybernetic Management Systems to the Enterprises', as the paper issued on 14th was called. We had been engaged in training from the beginning (see the first PERT chart); but the subtitle of this paper was: 'A Reconsideration in the political context'. It was explicitly a response to the experience at Los Andes, and proposed a new approach.

As has been explained, the project's OR teams had been charged with the need to explain, to gain help, and to seek approval at all levels of recursion — *in order to create the basic system*. This was accomplished. The training problem now under discussion concerned the replication of the total system **within** each autonomous unit, for all recursions. To this end, all managers and workers' committees required a complete understanding of the theories advanced in this book, so that they could recreate their own managerial systems. Much effort had already gone into this; but after Los Andes it seemed that the two methods we were using might not be appropriate to the openly radical stand it was intended to take. The variety amplifiers that had been developed were based on respectable practice in industrial training for circumstances in which there is plenty of time, and in which the major concern is to upgrade performance in an evolutionary fashion. Chile had very little time, as current events in that October were all too clearly demonstrating; and it had revolutionary intentions about the whole regulatory system. Many 'advanced' countries have less time than they now think to accomplish revolutionary practices in relation to everything from energy policy to arms control, from national 'growth' to individual liberty; and they have not realized that the regulatory system needs changing at all. Thus it is worth recording the options for training as they appeared in the forced climate of the Chilean experience. The paper mentioned identified the two methods already in use in roughly the following terms:

The Method of Prudence:

Choose an enterprise; move in a team of people, with the management's agreement, to set up an internal regulatory system; use this as a 'demonstration model' to convey confidence; use it as a training ground for teams-under-instruction from other enterprises; 'grow' the work to a national scale.

This approach was used in two major companies, with the primary purpose of discovering how to undertake the exercise, how to meet the aspirations of the workers, and how to help them to perform a more useful synergistic role while at the same time preserving autonomy for their own company. A series of intense workshops was held under the direction of Schwember. The workers quickly grasped the problems of production and organization, and linked them both to practical decisions and the political environment. They visited the Operations Room, which they found exciting — if somewhat overwhelming. It was impressive to see Dr Allende move his formal location as president of the republic to an out-of-town factory floor in order to participate. He showed his faith in winning the forthcoming election (as he subsequently did), and also his ability to discuss questions of supplies, foreign exchange, and organization on the shop floor.

These experiences were very positive, and pointed the way towards the genuine partnership between government and industry that has notoriously eluded us in Britain. But as to using the method as a training device, as a variety explosive that would 'seed' the whole social economy, the idea was hardly realistic. It would surely take ten years, even on the basis of exponential expansion (the epidemiological model in which everyone catches new methods like the measles); and that was not on our time scale.

The Method of Selling:

Disseminate information, instruction and enthusiasm outwards from an epicentre of Good News; make convincing presentations to sector committees, then — with their blessing — to the enterprises; 'promote' the product; provide visiting 'circuses'.

Essentially, this was the strategy in use. It was based on an excellent appreciation of the scope and scale of the problem, on a detailed plan of campaign, and a well orchestrated set of approaches to management groups at each level of recursion. How often have all innovating professionals been told: 'you will have to *sell* the idea'. But was this really the whole of the story for us? We were trying to transmit desperately needed tools and scarce computer power to workers' committees who were expecting help. Although there should be no coercion, although factory groups should be left with a genuine choice about their own internal organization (as distinct from their participation in the national Cybersyn as providers of minimal data), we had a duty to offer something positive. What need of cajolery? We could be more forthright. Perhaps, then, when the current programme of presentations was concluded, all of that could be treated as a 'general briefing' phase, in favour of a different and novel approach — based, not on standard practice, but on strong leadership. Hence

The Method of Decision:

Declare a campaign of national action to improve the quality of management, to advance simultaneously across the whole front (therefore not 'prudential'), as a matter of government policy (therefore not 'selling'); take advantage of the Cybersyn management systems **package, flexible, recursive,** in the context of current economic pressures.

Everyone knew that industrial management had been left in a very weak state by departing owners, and the government could be criticized for not giving a strong lead. The idea was to set up a Training Centre in one of the hotels owned by Corfo, and to mount intensive short courses of such panache and effectiveness that there would soon be a clamorous waiting list of management/worker teams asking to come. The objective would be to effect a quantum leap in the managerial prowess of Chile within a year.

To achieve this, the training programme, lasting ten days, would be largely automated. That is, a set of films would be made, to be watched by sixty people at a time, and there would be carefully prepared supportive literature.

Each course was to comprise twelve teams of five people, with four fully qualified tutors — one to three teams. Having understood the basic cybernetics and the tools made available, each team would work out for itself how it intended to proceed when it returned home. If it wished to run its own in-house programme (say, especially, that a sector committee might decide to run local courses for its component enterprises, thus becoming an amplifier), then the films and other course material would be made available to it. Here was the powerful reason for automating the basic teaching: so that in the amplification of variety, information would not be degraded by inadequate transduction.

This was the thinking behind the detailed plan, in which the course was time-tabled and the coverage of ten films was elaborated. They would teach the cybernetic language and principles of this book (but not the neurophysiology), and the written material would provide Chilean examples. The completed plan claimed 'to capture the sense that we are engaged in an economic war. Current approaches look too leisurely, and make too many concessions to 'the way things are done'. If the workers can expropriate ownership, then science must be seen to come to their immediate assistance. If industry is in deep trouble, then the government must be seen to take dramatic action'.

As earlier remarked, these concrete plans resulted from 'reconsideration' following Los Andes. I had already explored the various media for training in Britain and North America, and one British specialist in particular was anxious to make a deal — in return for facilities to make a documentary film about the Chilean process itself. But now the film question arose in a much more potent context than before. It was no longer a matter of having some films available to support the selling method of training: the new plan construed film as the primary transducer of a political as well as a scientific intent. Luciano Rodrigo was the head of Chilean Films, and he entered into the work with enthusiasm, extending the concept of course training by film to the more general context. Especially, he suggested, there should be a preliminary, pre-course film showing enterprises the purpose of the training proposed; there should be a condensed film for refresher courses in-house; and there should be a version of the story that would interest and inform the general public. The only technical problems in sight for Rodrigo were the shortage of 16mm film, and the absence of opportunity to process film quickly: the absurd kinds of constraint with which we were all too familiar. He was silent on the political problems that I knew that he would also face.

I have gone into these plans in some detail here for a special reason. Training (as distinct from education) is conceived as a method of transferring established knowledge. For instance, there is a way of understanding how an internal combustion engine works, and a way of teaching people how to maintain that engine in good order. Training is based on the very solid experience of the trainer, whose credibility as an expert is never in doubt —

any more than the existence of i/c engines themselves is in doubt. Training courses are therefore fundamentally conservative; they conserve established knowledge, and reinforce its cultural grip by admitting new members (when they have passed the training course) to the club of experts in the relevant topic. In the field of management training, this conservative phenomenon is very noticeable — so noticeable, in fact, that training course organizers are usually at pains to insert one or two innovatory or speculative sessions into the programme, to avoid the charge of being dull or out-of-date. Since such sessions are, however, basically inimical to the conservative ethos of the training course, they are likely to be treated as cabaret acts intended to enliven an otherwise boring if necessary occasion (and are consequently often put on after dinner). Not only, then, is very recent knowledge not transferred: it is culturally branded as frivolous, or impracticable, or even meretricious.

Then how can major reform be effected by 'training'? It cannot, according to this model. In the early nineteen-sixties, I had a reasonable hearing on the need radically to transform the British civil service; and I produced a plan for doing this — based on a training school having a number of unorthodox characteristics. In the event, none of the features intended to break the conservative mould could be realized, and eventually the traditional Staff College was created rather on the military model (hence the name). But the 'staff college solution' to a strategic problem is the one that fails to work in the next war, since it is based on the best practice to emerge from the last war. Meanwhile, everything has changed. The Chilean training plan made a conscious attempt to avoid this trap by placing total reliance on the new cybernetic system and the solutions it promoted, and by not discussing anything else at all. Then the issue of credibility would be a central problem: and it is clear that only leadership, rather than pious calls for attention to better methods, could produce the necessary effect. We had understanding now from the ministers and politicians of the party in power, who were ready to give leadership; but we did not yet have unqualified support from senior government officials — many of whom were not, after all, supporters of Popular Unity in the first place.

The October Perspective

The core group struggled with these matters as the *gremio* battle recrudesced, with the prognosis that stocks would finally run out on Tuesday 24th. On 20th, the President was reported in vigorous words: 'Solo me sacaran de La Moneda dentro de un pijama de madera' (They'll only drag me out of the presidential palace in wooden pyjamas'). He meant it. And this time his will prevailed. On the same day I was setting up the research, already mentioned, into the social uses of algedonic meters at CEREN, and wondering how the use of any such tool might affect minority aggression within a democracy. On the same day

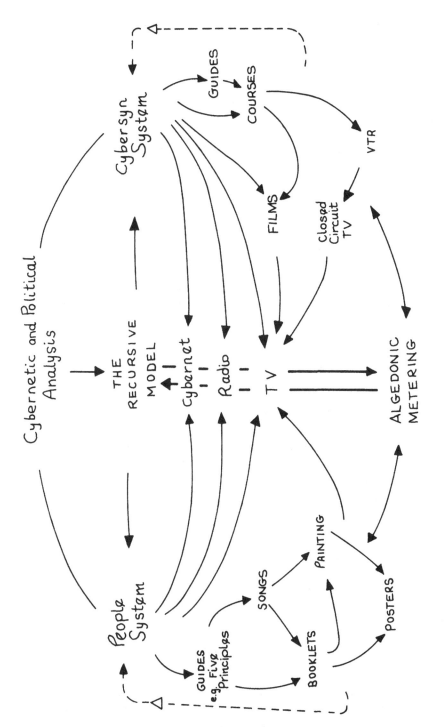

Figure 46

also, I gave the first draft of the diagram at Figure 46 to the Undersecretary. It attempted to give perspective to all that we were doing, and to mark the October turning point in our preoccupations. The picture presented by the diagram does not need a commentary, but it should not be passed over too lightly: it took us a long time to discuss all its implications. Although Project Cybersyn was to continue as planned until the government's overthrow, it was hardly surprising that, from this time, I should devote only a fraction of my time to it. The same was true for other core group members, to the mystified chagrin of many scientists working on Cybersyn, who could not appreciate why we were infrequently seen.

'October' was nearly over. A very long and crucial meeting between Flores, Espejo, Schwember, Farné and myself reviewed the whole experience. We should proceed with all our plans; but they were now secondary to national survival. The training programme should be furthered with all speed, but facilities and funding for the films would be most difficult to arrange — wherever they were made. This problem passed back to me. The new network that had given embodiment to the Third of the *Five Principles* during the crisis must be maintained, built upon, and turned into a permanent feature in support of the new cooperative structures that were rapidly emerging in the countryside. There was much more ....

As the political dust settled, the cabinet resigned en bloc, as was inevitable, so that the President could make fresh dispositions. On 2nd November the new cabinet was formed, and Fernando Flores was now Minister of Economics. The problem area of his direct responsibility had enlarged again. Moreover, the attempts in the reshuffle to accommodate the aspirations of all members of the coalition were to lead to such a degree of sectarian rivalry within the cabinet and the top echelons of administrative power that the viability of the government itself became a more urgent question than the viability of the economy. (The role of the military was an ever-present and shifting complication.)

Back in England during November, I was pursuing many plans already mooted in these chapters, and trying to guide progress with the operations room in Santiago by conversational Telex from London. There were meetings with film makers and financiers about the proposed films, the basic postulate being that ten training films could be made in support of this very book, and sold internationally to management schools at a modest profit, so that Chile would get the set free. Obviously, however, they would need to be more general in their relevance than we should wish in the the context of Cybersyn. Once again, it was frustrating to have important developments at the national level held up by such small considerations. While all these efforts continued in London, quieter moments were devoted to the realities of life eight thousand miles away. They were filled with concern about instability — of the country, of the government, and of the economy at large. Systemic instability is a cybernetic concept, and it has cybernetic solutions; but these have to be formulated within the bounds of political practicability .... The sectarian struggle was destabilizing in itself, while the activities of foreign agencies reflected (as has since been officially documented) deliberate strategy of destabilization. Although it was still possible to discuss these large issues with the minister qua cabinet member, it seemed clear that any action proposal would have to be pitched within the context of his own ministry. Here, his promotion meant that we were addressing *a new level of recursion,* in which the projects so far being developed were attributable as Systems One.

Messages arrived from Chile that confirmed this orientation. There were large questions surrounding the public stance that a relatively unknown minister should adopt: in short, here was a System Five function to fulfil that belonged to a recursion midway between that of the organization for regulating the social economy as a viable system, and that of the collegiate cabinet organization for preserving the state as a viable system. Secondly, and very naturally following the October experience, the organization of the supply of essential goods for the population needed special attention. The population itself, alert to its vulnerability in this respect, was rapidly engaging in measures to confirm and improve the techniques of distribution that had sprung into being during the stoppage. Autonomous, self-organizing units were developing to cover neighbourhoods, then villages, and even working-places, whereby the producer (the worker himself) could be connected to the consumer himself directly. Such development threatened to eliminate 'commerce' as such — and with it, of course, the *gremios.* These developments deserved encouragement; and it seemed that the only administrative intervention that would be needed would be to provide some version of a System Two capable of regulating metabolism in the total system. There would, however, remain policy determinants on the central axis: accute shortages of basic foods must invoke mandatory rationing in some form, and the government still had its social policy for fairer shares than those traditionally awarded according to the extreme socio-economic stratification of the populace.

The architectonics of the new recursion were formulating in my mind, but I wanted to discuss the issues in depth before attempting a written statement. By the end of November I was back in Santiago, arriving just before the President left for Cuba on route to the United Nations. There he was to make a famous address about the Chilean plight under the monstrous burdens of economic blockade and covert political intervention. This provoked world-wide sympathy, and no helpful action whatsoever. But, while I was yet in England, my compatriot and friend Ross Ashby, discoverer of the Law of Requisite Variety, who had retired to his home in the West Country a few years earlier, died at the age of 69. Cybernetics thereby lost the further teachings of a great man, whose genius is still far from being properly recognized. The event left me personally depleted.

A New Recursion

It is easily stated, and perhaps readily understood from this vantage point, that we were now dealing with a new level of recursion — if only because the sponsor of the cybernetic approach had emerged as Minister. It was not obvious at the time, although it was clear that something was different. Some perhaps saw this simply as a gain in prestige and authority for the work; because the man was the same man, and his contribution to the inner councils of the president had always been effective whatever his official job. Again, the ostensible cybernetic effort was perceived as being concentrated at Corfo, where Project Cybersyn had been started and where it was still housed. Its growing professional staff was increasingly remote from the centre of cybernetic activity — the core group, which was in turn expanding. This itself had no institutional focus, and was thereby rendered invisible — even perhaps to its own members, who were wholly preoccupied in urgent political tasks and economic assignments such as directing industrial sectors.

Although Cybersyn itself had still to be scientifically directed, there was much else for me to do, and I did not even meet most of the latterly recruited staff. It was December 1972: after October, the priorities were changed — as I have already said. None knew this better than the Minister himself; and his response was to draw sharply back from Cybersyn — to the consternation of many, the gratification of a few, and the obfuscation of the recursion issue. The consternation was felt by those who regarded Cybersyn as a political instrument, and who thought they saw political support incipiently witheld. The gratification was experienced by the technocratically minded, who wanted effective management regardless of the political framework. The emergence of a new recursion was obscured because all the circumstances recounted in these two paragraphs seemed adequate to explain why 'things were different', and they did not point to any structural problem in the recursive mapping of the economy.

There was one, however. If we think back to the original modelling of November 1971, we find the economy defined in terms of its assets — the land, minerals, industry — and the ownership of those assets, which in turn defined the public and the private sectors. All the emphasis was on the shift from private to public ownership, which was creating what was called 'the Social economy'; it was therefore natural to everyone to structure their approach to organization in terms of the assets owned. The land had its own agricultural ministry. Ownership of that land had been a major political issue for many years, and important changes had already been introduced before this government arrived, although they had been much accelerated. As far as the Ministry of Economics was concerned, ownership related to industry, and economic regulation related in the first place to the effective management of the assets that constituted that industry. Thus it was political reality which originated the hierarchy of enterprises, sectors, ramas, and the administrative apparatus to go with it; and it was cybernetic necessity which mapped that reality onto a recursive nest. So far, so good; but the preoccupation with ownership makes sense only insofar as it betokens ruling power. Increasingly we find that other factors supervene. Hence privately owned industry in the West complains that the trade unions exercise too much power, and dissident minorities in all advanced societies are often accused of holding the majority to ransom. In all contemporary societies where such movement is not forcibly repressed, there seems to be a resurgence in the self-organizing capability of communities to promote themselves as viable systems — independently of, or even set against, a moribund authority that derives from archaic and legalistic courts of appeal. Thus it was in Chile, by the end of 1972; the model we were using until then could not adequately represent changes that had come about during Allende's term, and which had crystallized around the events of October, because these were changes in economic management that had nothing to do with ownership in the legal sense.

To be precise, the 'ownership' model nominated only owned assets (whether public or private) as viable systems, which between them constituted and exhausted System One. The community (considered only in its economic role, of course) was part of the environment with respect to System One, and was connected to System One operations by a homeostatic loop labelled 'demand' in the one direction and 'supply' in the other. The distribution function was depicted as metabolizing that homeostat. Certainly, and continuing the use of the ownership filter on our spectacles, the distribution function was largely owned by the *gremios*, and therefore this homeostat was vulnerable to disruption; but this fact does not necessarily turn commerce into a System One. All subsystems of the viable system, as elucidated by the model, are regarded as essential components of viability in any case — so survival depends on them all. Then so long as the management of assets determined the composition of System One, this mapping of the model obeyed all the cybernetic conventions as well as reflecting political reality, and I still consider it to have been adequate to the task originally imposed upon it. What was happening, however, as described at the end of the last section, powerfully suggested that two levels of recursion were mixed together in that preliminary model. It took a great deal of analysis to understand why this was, how it happened — and therefore what could be done about it. In the end, I think that most of the difficulty experienced at this point was due to an ideological hyperbole. What we had modelled was the public sector of industry in n recursions, and it had the label 'the social economy'. The social economy however, turned out to be more than this; and in order to model the ministerial totality we needed an extra level of recursion.

The evidence that this was so presented itself uniquely in my experience, and this made it difficult to recognize and later to explain. The economic community (something different from the demographic community) was itself a viable system, because it had grown a management that was quite independent of the whole business of ownership. The distributive function (something different from transportation) was also a viable system, because it too had grown a management that was quite independent of *gremio* ownership. These two managements were the Systems Five-Four-Three of two viable systems that were part of the social economy, but *not* part of the set of industrial recursions. Then the social economy and public industry were not after all co-exstensive: *the latter was a System One of the former*. This conclusion identified the missing recursion. It needed to offer an at least tripartite account of the internal economy, in which owned industry was only a component System One — along with various others. The distribution function, or 'commerce' (in quotation marks because it is conceived as independent of ownership), and 'community' (in quotation marks because it is conceived as an economic instrument), had identified themselves, because of their emerging managements — which were, it needs repeating, independent of the norms of the industrial model. Then of course there could be others, as yet not identified . . . .

For the purposes of explaining the new recursion, at any rate, and out of all the activity going on in the countryside, the emergent non-ownership managements to which I drew attention were the neighbourhood councils known as JAPs (Junta de Aprovisionamiento Popular) and the Comandos de Abastecimiento, who were local volunteer bodies supervising provisioning. Both forms of organization had been fundamentally self-generating, but each had an accepted status within administrative policy by this time. Indeed, the development of the Comandos in particular had been considerably influenced by the conceptual use of this viable system model: those closely involved had for example explained how they had rapidly understood the requirement for System Two activity within this initially makeshift distribution system. Then the cybernetic argument for the fresh architectonic took shape. The new recursion should be recognized, with (initally) three Systems One. First would come the nest of industrial recursions with its regulatory procedures embodied in Project Cybersyn, and presided over by the workers' committees at each recursive level. Next would come the nest of economic communities, in which all those regulatory activities already summed under the heading of the People Project would find their embodiement, presided over by the JAPs. These would be linked by the third viable system, replacing existing commerce with the new 'commerce', over which the commandos already presided. The regulatory procedures needed here could be very rapidly provided, because they already existed in the standard tool-kit of operational research; thus an 'Allocation Project' became a possibility, which would seek to satisfy demand in an effective fashion using mathematics as well as organizational techniques.

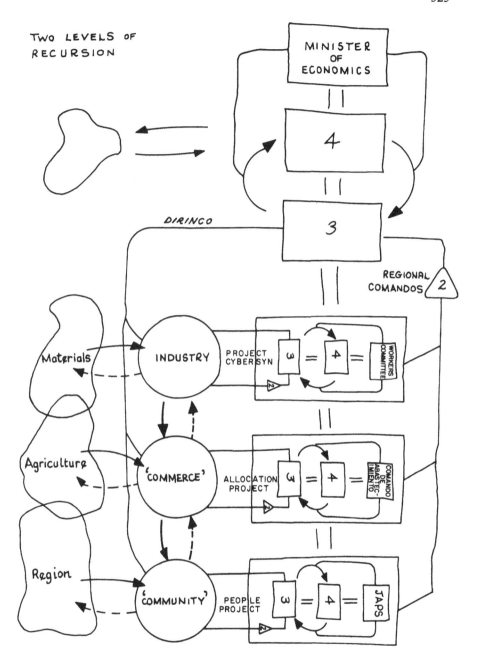

Figure 47. The proposed new level of recursion in the Ministry of Economics, which collects into System One existing projects that may be inspected on a ninety-degree rotation.

The layout of the new level of recursion is shown in Figure 47, with its three Systems One. By turning the page through ninety degrees, the second level of recursion may be inspected. Details of the model for industry would be unchanged from those given in the last chapter. The models for community and commerce would seek to map the nests of recursions already organizing themselves on the ground. For instance, the so called 'industrial belts' were now emerging. These were self-organizing entities (in the cybernetic sense), that arose in response to the bureaucracy of the Sector Committees of CORFO itself. Again, cybernetic workshops were held, and proved to be positive experiences for all concerned. DIRINCO is shown as operating on the parasympathetic loop: this was a government agency concerned with fair trading and price control. It had all the marks of this high-variety regulator, as had been explicitly recognized a year earlier. If we had not been active in its regard, it was because we had compressed two levels of recursion into one. By the same token, we ought to have been able to have predicted the System Two comandos, had the two levels of recursion within the model of the Ministry been teased apart in advance. Now, however, everything was falling into place.

The whole system as depicted in Figure 47 looked robust, but it really needed a new set of communications to vitalize the major loops at the ministerial level of recursion. It was now obvious that the original Cybernet, belonging to the second level of recursion (industry) for which it had been designed, was not adequate at the higher ministerial level of recursion — although it had been successfully dragooned into that role during the October emergency. Again intuitions were sparking ahead of the formal analysis. For the core group had already generated the thought that a new version of the Post Office could provide the network of algedonodes that the Ministry needed for internal regulation at the metasystemic level. Certainly that idea fitted perfectly with this architectonic, and with my own belief that although Cyber*net* could not properly handle the topographical requirements of the ministerial recursion, Cyber*stride* could indeed handle its filtration needs. For I could think of no regulatory indicator appropriate to the two new components of System One at the higher level of recursion that could not readily be expressed as a triple index.

To take an example, and it is no more than that: a community comando knows how much meat it has *got* (Actual) and how much it would *like* (Potential), while a rationing rubric applied to regionally available supplies could quickly compute how much meat it *can* have (Capability). Then a triple-index could be monitored to alert the 'commerce' system to impending shortage at each next-lower echelon, through a supply (equals productivity) quotient; and the appropriate System Four could be alerted to shifts in the investment (or in this case probably import) level required to match not merely need, but desire, through a demand (equals latency) quotient. And so on, throughout the model.

In the outcome, it was Cybernet rather than Cyberstride that was expanded beyond industrial boundaries. It seems that the power of instant communication provides huge advances in regulatory finesse that can quickly be assimilated, and that the filtration system can be relatively crude. Ministries, the Central Bank, and many government agencies were incorporated into Cybernet at this point. The lesson has not yet been understood by other countries.

At that moment (the end of November, 1972, and a year into the work) then, it seemed possible that by understanding the formal cybernetics of the radically changed situation we might start to resolve what I certainly regarded as an alarming degree of political confusion. There was disagreement within the core group on almost every topic. Sets of economic advisors were coming and going, and contradicting each other from within different sections of the ministry. The Minister's priorities, the division of his attention between his ministry and the collegiate responsibility of the cabinet, and his own public posture, were all matters of advice that divided his personal advisors. Probably none of this is very unusual when a government is under intense pressure. But the intellectual hubbub it creates does deafen one to conclusions that might otherwise be heard perfectly clearly. To reach the structural conclusion recorded in Figure 47, to think through the variety engineering implicit in that model (which was eventually to lead to certain theoretical cybernetic advances), and to elaborate the necessary supportive detail as to praxis, was completely exhausting. Therefore it would certainly tax my colleagues, who were already very tired and busy in their own right. These are the realities of the implementation of management science when the situation is very stressful. It is important that the degree of stress be understood: events are moving so quickly in such circumstances that it is almost impossible not to make a mistake. I go into some detail here, because my records of the two relevant weeks are sufficiently thorough as to explain what I think *was* eventually a mistake.

On 30th November 1972 I took Enrique Farné into my confidence as to these proposed new plans. As head of the nationalized automobile agency for the whole country, he was probably under more pressure than any other colleague, but he was the one best placed to collaborate in the implementation of any such ideas. We discussed them for eight hours, and agreed to meet Fernando Flores together as soon as we could. The meeting of the three of us took place next day, Friday at 10.45 in the evening. I left the Flores house at 3.00 a.m. The Minister's departing words are quoted in the log: 'The arguments are so cogent that I have no alternative'. During the next twelve days, I wrote the plan down, in a document entitled: *One Year of (Relative) Solitude*. This title will convey a special meaning to readers of the writer Gabriel Garciá Márquez; but the sub-title was straightforwardly, *The Second Level of Recursion*. These twelve days were exceptionally busy: maybe their influence significantly changed the emphasis of the recommendations as originally advanced. At any rate, this was the gist of the written statement.

Firstly, I was fairly confident about progress with Project Cybersyn considered as a piece of management development. All the project managers were enthusiastic about progress; results were emanating from Checo; the Cyberstride PERT was on course, and meetings with those running inputs from the big nationalized industries were satisfactory; the operations room was under construction, and I was visiting it once or twice every day — often with impatient would-be users. Workers' representatives were becoming very interested, and were full of suggestions. Given the evolution of Figure 47, the advocacy was to stand yet further back from the *management* of its Systems One — which, after all, ought to be autonomous. For instance, there should be a Director of Total Industry as Chairman of System Five in Recursion Two (Industry), who would be a worker, and the tools already developed would be formally handed over. Evaluating the consequences, there ought to ensue a collapse of bureaucracy, a restructuring of the sector committees (if not their total abolition), and a replacement of technocratically oriented OR groups by workers' groups. Then this would change the problem of training as so far conceived. One could look forward to the day when, instead of being enticed into attending government courses, industrial workers' committees would be demanding service on the parasympathetic loop .... Indeed this was to happen, when the dockers required to know why they were not yet involved (which was because transportation as a whole remained such a politically intractable question). And yet there was something manifestly starry-eyed about this set of 'expectations', and a sense of political realism had to insert those quotation marks. More fundamental cybernetic analysis was continuing in an attempt to identify the deeper system whereby such changes are universally resisted, and the topic will reappear in Chapter 19.

Secondly, I could see no problems in developing the two new nests of the new recursion, which would clear the path correctly to design the new metasystem for the ministry. In particular, the advocacy was to found the public posture of the new Minister on the people's use of 'the people's science'. Angel Parra, whom I met twice during those twelve days, and other artists were by now ready to join in such a campaign. (Indeed, Parra sang the 'Litany' in public twice during that period.) Separate meetings with all the members of the core group, and several more with the Minister, led me to hope that all these plans were feasible. Pressing a little too hard, perhaps, the advocacy proposed a series of ministerial broadcasts on television, and the public inauguration of the operations room by the President. Such moves were plausible, and had been discussed before. If they now came over with a touch of overstatement, the error can perhaps be traced to another incident that occurred during the twelve days, when time was at such a high premium. At their own request, I saw a most distinguished pair of British television producers, who had come to make a documentary film about Chile and its 'experiment'. They already knew (after one day) what this documentary should say, and the travesty was eventually broadcast exactly as planned. Presumably my role was intended to be to endorse the product. The impotent rage to which this interview reduced me was surely connected with the advocacy to use the medium properly, and soon.

These days of talks may have changed the emphasis in the written report, as distinguished from the *oral* report. Certainly there was no shift in the perception of social objectives, nor in the managerial cybernetics implicit in the organizational design. What was shifting, even from one day to the next, was the emphasis of sectarian politics. Fernando Flores had emerged from the events of October with an enhanced reputation and a cabinet post; by December he was under constant and vitriolic attack in the press. Thus the question as to what public actions were feasible for him was over-riding. As far as I was concerned, I took little notice of the fact that various people were loudly suggesting that I had completed my contract — a circumstance that I should have taken more seriously.

The report was not finished until breakfast-time on the day of departure, and my close colleagues did not like it. I thought that perhaps there had not been time to take the ideas beyond the 'evangelical' phase and into 'solid theology', and that the meaning of the report would sink in during my brief absence over Christmas. Perhaps it did, insofar as the dual recursion idea was effectively assimilated, and the conceptual model offered (Figure 47) was adopted as a mode of thinking and talking. But there was no outcome in terms of organizational change or ministerial stance, as I had advocated.

Almost any explanation of this could be defended. The probability is that the freedom to manoeuvre in so powerfully constrained a situation is itself curtailed — almost to zero. It is also likely that evangelism does not have requisite variety to complete any theological job. During my first late night walk in Santiago in the fateful year of 1973, which was to see the fall of the government and the death of many friends, I was dispirited. The city was peaceful enough; quiet even. But for the first time in the whole enterprise I felt made alien. The words of Nietzsche were in my head: 'Our steps ring too lonely through their streets'.

CHAPTER NINETEEN

The end of the beginning

January is high summer in Santiago: the one month when people who can afford it decamp to the coast or to the mountains to leave a capital that is like an English summer for the rest of the year. And people say: 'Don't worry, it is too hot for revolutions'.

On the 10th January 1973 I spent all day sweltering in the Operations Room, supervising changes to the Checo screen aparatus — which was not animating properly. Nonetheless, there it all was: the room *existed*. Of course it was not 'running the Chilean economy'. But it was the last of the four Cybersyn tools to be ready. It was a viable transducer. Only the linkages remained to be made. In the next few days, I prepared an inaugural speech for the President; and also a very long explanation of the arrangement of the room and its purposes, which was intended to be recorded for all the visitors that were waiting to come — from every level of recursion. It was this fact that gave rise to considerable disagreement between several of us about the Spanish language version. Were we really talking to ministers, parliamentarians, senior officials, bureaucrats, workers' committees, or the people themselves — and if to them all, as was strictly intended, in what order?

Meanwhile, and simultaneously, there was yet another major change of emphasis on the political front. For complex constitutional reasons, the Ministers of Economics and Finance had changed places. Cybersyn especially was clearly related to Corfo, a branch of Economics; we had already said that 'its tools were ready to be handed over', and all the personnel 'belonged' to Corfo as paymaster. But Fernando Flores was now Minister of Finance; and he continued to be the political director of all our cybernetics. So far as I knew, I was still the scientific director. Thus there began a new series of demands on the core group which had almost no relevance to the prior history. The strain was telling on everyone: two key people were confined to bed for the whole of January and most of February too. The President, as I spoke to him once (though unofficially) in January, seemed more relaxed than anyone, despite the imminence of the March elections.

The point about these was crucial. If the vote for Allende fell from 36% to less than a third, he would be constitutionally compelled to resign — and certainly he would have acquiesced in that. Given all the difficulties since October, such a result seemed a plausible outcome. But Mario Grandi made a detailed political analysis which suggested that the Unidad Popular vote would actually *increase* to at least 40%. In the event, it was 43%; and it is surely a terrifying conjecture for democracy that an increase of 7% in popular support might sign the death warrant of any administration . . . .

The Cybernetics of Public Accountability

It is against this background that we come to consider the whole question of announcements, of which the inauguration of the operations room was intended to be the first. It is first of all necessary to distinguish between the various publics to which such schemes as these are accountable.

The foremost of these is the public who will be actively involved in the scheme. As explained in earlier chapters, we had aimed for participative management of both Project Cybersyn (via workers' committees and individual advisors) and the People Project (via the political parties and the arts connexions). Be it noted, however, that the customarily fine balance between the leadership of a participating group and the dragooning of consenting assistants, which causes difficulty in every 'presidential office' type of organization, is further sharpened by the use of innovative technology. Because the would-be participants do not know what the opportunities are until these novelties have been explained; and it is difficult, if only because of enthusiasm and the need to overcome psychological and intellectual inertia, not to exert pressure in the process.

Even so, the members of the whole participative group involved in setting objectives and taking decisions have direct access to each other. Cybernetically: the network connecting them is anastomotic and not hierarchic: it is in principle capable of generating requisite variety; and it should exhibit the redundancy of potential command (see Chapter 15). It is easy, from within such a network, to perceive when these multinodal characteristics are being lost: the symptom is for the network to tend to centralize, so that actions increasingly become referred to one dominant person, and secondly for one person (not necessarily the same person, but one responding directly to him) to act as gatekeeper between the group and the outside world. Not at all surprisingly, these tendencies ebb and flow in strong correlation with the degree of stress. In normal managerial circumstances, some one person is known to be ultimately accountable for the group's activity; but in placid conditions he is 'the boss' (and the quotations marks are audible in spoken parlance), while as matters become stressful he becomes The

Boss (and the capital letters are audible too). The cybernetics of the multinode show this to be perfectly acceptable, insofar as the greater the stress, the more likely it is that the boss rather than anyone else has the information needed to relieve it, because he has the better contacts among his own organizational peers — so the potential command is momentarily realized in him. The caveat is of course that when placid conditions return, The Boss must again become 'the boss', which is something he may forget to do — having got into the bossy habit. Other members of the group then have certain duties to the boss and to the group which are difficult to discharge: I have experienced the difficulty in both the roles concerned more than once.

The last paragraph, as its final sentence is intended to show, is a generalization based on fitting experience into the cybernetic framework of a viable System Five. It was well borne out in the Chilean work, but it was handled successfully by the group. A test for this success can be proposed. Consider the mismatch existing at any given time between the bossiness of the boss in a participative group, and the degree of external stress that generates the bossiness through the realization of potential command. If the mismatch grows over a period, the danger signals in the network's homeostats will be steadily amplified by positive feedback, until (maybe) homeostatis breaks down. It sounds something like this: 'Look what he's done', '*Now* look what he's done', 'I could see this coming all the time', 'he's *mad* I tell you', 'I resign/you are fired' as the case may be. Whole management groups have been seen to explode into fragments by this process, which obviously ought to be constrained. Because of the stress, such a process often started in the Chilean cybernetic network. But in two years, the names of only three actual casualties occur to me: one who resigned, one who was fired, and one who was as-it-were extruded by mutual consent. The test is more qualitative than quantitative: the group did not explode; its attrition was natural.

Next we come to consider the public that is not directly affected (those who are represented therefore by participation) but who are affected indirectly, and in this case the entire Chilean nation — insofar as these plans intended to change managerial modes of government. Again, then, in this case, there is no method whereby requisite variety can be obtained, except through external amplifiers that are outside the control of the sponsors of the work. This comment refers outstandingly to the political opposition. Remembering that Unidad Popular was a minority govenment, and remembering the case already submitted in these chapters that the cybernetic group was working as a management service to that government, it would make no sense whatever to invite *participation* from the political opposition. As already remarked, there were political opponents working inside the projects, as a matter of professional freedom; but they were not there to *represent* their parties' causes. Had they been no consensus would ever have been reached about anything. (I refer again to the opening arguments of Chapter 16, but do not repeat them here.) It follows that the Law of Requisite Variety can be met only through amplifiers capable of reaching the whole nation, and not only the minority of the nation as represented in participative project management. Such amplifiers are usually referred to as the mass media; and in Chile these were dominated, heavily dominated, by outspoken opposition interests.

This analysis pinpoints a dilemma. It would have been cybernetically wrong (even if it had not been unethical) to try to keep the work a secret, because of the counterproductive consequences of attempting to thwart Ashby's Law. The Law always reasserts itself — and if the mode of amplification (in this case from 40 to 100 per cent, equals times two-and-a-half) were not properly designed, then the government initiatives were likely to be overwhelmed. A two-and-a half-times discrepancy in variety matching hardly lies within experimental error. But the amplifiers could not be designed, since they were under the opposition's control. This being so, we had neither sought secrecy for the work, nor attempted to advertize it, and this was surely the best policy. Up to this point, early in 1973, we went about our business — just circumspectly. Even to do this presented problems. Large numbers of people were involved in our activities, including political opponents (although not in the core group, as I called it before). My own presence in a government office quickly drew attention, and therefore I left it: for the whole of 1972 I worked out of the biggest hotel in Santiago, unnoticed among the celebrities, Chilean and foreign, who were continuously in occupation. But the work was based in Corfo, which was entirely appropriate so long as Flores was in Economics; and we were dealing directly with the industrial economy, rather than with agencies spotlighted as planning or policy-making — which moreover, were regarded as the sectarian 'property' of individual parties within Popular Unity. In this way the force of the Ashbean dilemma was deflected for more than a year. But it is always dangerous to tamper with natural laws, and we were alert to the need to take the initiative in redressing the variety balance at the propitious time. We defined this as the official launching of Cybersyn via the inauguration of the Operations Room. Alternatively, we knew that we needed to act quickly if these matters came to public attention. Meanwhile, silence rather than secrecy was enough — because the media were very slow indeed to catch on to the importance of the work. But as it turned out, they were inconveniently too fast by just one month — as shall be seen.

Returning once again to January 10th and the Operations Room, it was clear that the 'propitious time' for announcements to the larger public was drawing nigh. These announcements stood to be radically perverted by the opposition-dominated media. The Flores solution to this had for a long time been that I should make an announcement about Cybersyn in England at the same time as the Chilean government spoke in Santiago. The idea could be viewed, in public relations terms, as an attempted escalation in credibility — London supporting Santiago, and vice versa. Cybernetically, it was of course an attempt to regulate the amplification process that was not under control in Chile: the hope was that by enlarging the Chilean public to the world-government public, a more objective media-treatment on an international scale would insist that the Chilean media held substantially to the truth.

The machinery was this. I had been asked to deliver the Richard Goodman Memorial Lecture for 1973 at the Brighton Polytechnic in England. Goodman had been a brilliant cybernetician, and a dear friend; but I had felt preoccupied by the Chilean work, and originally contemplated making excuses — at least for that year. Suddenly, the invitation became exactly the right medium through which to make the Cybersyn announcement in England. It was the occasion *par excellence*. Richard Goodman had been dedicated to the under-privileged; he had fought in the Spanish Civil War; thereafter he had devoted his work to ordinary teaching in a college well-known for its Third World student intake, spurning high academic honours. Had he still lived, he would surely have taken sabbatical leave to join me in Chile. Everything fitted together: what a celebration! It was still January 10th. The Richard Goodman Memorial Lecture had by now been fixed for February 14th.

On Sunday, January 7th, the science correspondent of the British *Observer* newspaper, Nigel Hawkes, published an article entitled 'Chile run by computer'. The article gave its own source: 'the underground science newsletter *Eddies*, published in London'. The *Observer* article correctly reported me as 'somewhat taken aback at the disclosure', and said that I should be giving more details in Brighton mid-February. Meanwhile, however, it is noteworthy that the *Observer* pre-empted the whole story, without a detailed interview (I was taken aback only by telephone). This is called a scoop. It thereby set the whole tone of subsequent reportage, not so much by the article itself, as by its title (woe to sub-editors). By Monday 15th, less than a month before the Brighton assignment, the *Observer* article had been widely noticed and a cabinet meeting in Santiago considered the original leak, plus its Latin American copies and speculative elaborations in Colombia, Argentina, and Chile itself (in Valparaiso!). The story had been printed in *Eddies* in the first place, as a result of what I had told a political group in London in the attempt to gain help for the activities earlier called *Externalities*. There had been a 'misunderstanding' about confidentiality, on one man's part.

Nothing, not even the most expensive public relations programme, can generate the requisite variety needed to regulate the media worldwide. All such attempts have fortunately always failed, and will continue to do so as long as free speech is anywhere allowed. Our plans had gone wrong. I gave very strong advice that the government should immediately make a full-scale and high-level press presentation of Cybersyn, with a televised tour of the Operations Room, in order to amplify the government side of the variety equation to the full. The counter-argument was that the place would then need twenty armed guards to resist sabotage by the opposition, not to mention the vulnerability of the hundreds of input stations spread over three thousand miles of country. Various decisions were reached, and then rescinded, at least once a day through the week. Many other things were happening, notably a copper strike. At any rate, the initiative in the battle of Ashby's Law for Project Cybersyn was lost that week. The story had already been filed, as far as the British media were concerned. There was no support nor extra information coming out of Santiago, as had been planned. I left for Europe after an extremely friendly and particularly useful meeting with the Minister, during which this issue was virtually disregarded. Nothing was going to be done about it, obviously; and there was so much else to be done about the other limbs of our work, especially in the circumstances that realists now knew for certain that the administration would not be allowed to run its full term. He gave me a new brief in this regard.

But one thing relevant to Cybersyn still had to happen — namely the delivery of the Goodman Memorial Lecture itself on 14th February 1973. That did happen. The address itself, called 'Fanfare for Effective Freedom', is printed *in extenso* in *Platform for Change* (John Wiley, 1975). Present on this occasion was the Chilean Ambassador to London; absent on this occasion was any one of the twenty scooped journalists invited by the Goodman Trustees. The questions afterwards were mostly elementary, save for those of one well-informed academic, who wanted full details of the relationship of Project Cybersyn to all the planning agencies in Santiago. Naturally (the reasons have already been given in these chapters), I could not go beyond saying that the work came under the aegis of Corfo.

During March I was engaged in *Externalities* matters around Europe, and was not in Chile again until April. By this time, Cybersyn had been praised to the skies and damned to hell by a variety of critics. The details are of no concern to the cybernetics of public accountability, consisting as they do of the usual mixture of carefully considered reviews and *ad hominem* assaults (the latter coming exclusively from two British journals which take a special pride in scientific and social responsibility, but which — perhaps for that very reason — reduced themselves on this occasion to hysteria). This section is concerned only to point out how the attempt to regulate (**not** the media, but) the design of the government's own amplification system failed; and especially how — once such a transducer has become denatured — then, as with a neuron that cannot respond during its refractory period, nothing happens at all. For this was the cybernetic truth: the battle of Ashby's Law for the reputation of Project Cybersyn had (as was said earlier) been lost *in advance*. The algedonic signal constituted by the immediate effects of the first major leak (January 7th) had been ignored. That was the cardinal error. What happened in April in Santiago was not an error, it was the natural reaction of a denatured transducer. Not only was there all the published evidence to consider; not only was there a question of the efficacy of the project to consider; not only was so much else happening at the same time .... the academic member of the Richard Goodman audience whom I had perforce turned aside, chose this moment to make a vitriolic personal denunciation — through a private channel open to her which led straight to the cabinet. This attack nearly finished me in Chile. That it did not was due to the support of the man who had fetched me to Chile in the first place — aided, I suppose, by the general knowledge at cabinet level that at least some of the accusations that had been made in *odium academica* were manifestly false.

All of this argues that public accountability can be discharged *locally*, because the local system can be designed to exercise requisite variety. This means that the negentropy pump called information can successfully offset the entropic drift towards disorganization by invoking the basic cybernetic principles of the multinode, as already discussed. Secondly it argues that on some larger scale the capacity to deploy requisite variety is lost, because control of the design of the amplifiers of regulatory vareity is lost; in the Chilean case this happened, for political reasons, at the national level. Thirdly it argues that by engaging in a yet higher level of recursion (and in this case the international level of governmental systems), negentropy can in principal be pumped back into the intermediate (i.e. national) level of recursion, but that this is a very difficult manoeuvre to handle. In principle, one does not have requisite variety to handle it, and the only recourse is to be exceptionally alert to algedonic warnings of disaster. These, to conclude, were missed in the presentation of the Chilean cybernetics applications ... possibly because my colleagues thought, if so erroneously, that the danger signals were hurt pride in masquerade; much more plausibly because there were too many other things to do; and certainly because there was no *organizational* apparatus for handling algedonic signals outside those built into the social economy regulation itself. We had not got that far.

Healthy and Pathological Autopoiesis

At the end of Chapter 18 the concern was expressed that there had been no organizational consequence of proposals which had allegedly been assimilated into the corporate mind of the group. In the preceeding section of this chapter is recounted the failure of an algedonic signal, which again implicated incapacity in organizational adaptation. The paper issued in April was an attempt to penetrate the basic problem to which these outcomes pointed. It is reviewed here in detail, because it is inevitable that a major confrontation would have occurred between the established bureaucracy (including the party Establishment of the political left itself) and the cybernetic innovators concerning that problem, had the government survived into 1974.

Elsewhere in this book, the concept of homeostasis has been invoked *passim*. It was defined as 'the capability of a system to hold its critical variables within physiological limits in the face of unexpected disturbance or perturbation'. Now we may define autopoiesis as characterizing a special kind of homeostat: one in which the critical variable held steady is *the system's own organization*. This is a very powerful concept indeed, as it needs to be — since autopoiesis was first advanced by Humberto Maturana and his associates as the basic characteristic of a living organism. Hitherto people had placed emphasis on the ability of living things to reproduce themselves. The new approach emphasized that living things produce themselves: 'to make oneself' is the exact meaning of the Greek term used (see Reference 5).

Maturana, distinguished biologist and cybernetician, was the first Chilean whom I had ever met — many years before this current story. I had not met his major collaborator Francisco Varela before. It was a delight to be with either or both of them occasionally during these days, and especially to debate the cybernetics of autopoiesis. For these two were not agreed about the societary implications of their theory; and my own view differed from each of theirs. This must be on record, both in deference to them, and also to free them from any 'guilt by association' with my views.

Naturally I had very closely compared the conditions for life as expounded by the theory of autopoiesis, with the conditions for a viable system as expounded in this very book. To me, they were complementary and mutually enriching. To me, both applied to societary systems. Such a system is (in my view, by applying the discoverers' own thesis) necessarily autopoietic. In order to survive as a viable system, it must produce itself. Then let us proceed to examine the possible autopoiesis of the five sub-systems of the viable system. *Evidently*, System One must be autopoietic, because of the recursion theorem which declares its components to be themselves viable systems. *Evidently,* Systems, Two, Three, Four and Five are not individually autopoietic, because they have no status in their own right. They are subservient systems of the total viable system. (So, too, is System One subservient — but it uniquely has the capacity to survive independently.) Then we may argue:

(i)   a viable system is autopoietic;
(ii) the autopoietic faculty for this viable system is embodied in the totality and in its Systems One, and nowhere else;
(iii) therefore any viable system developing autopoiesis in any of its Systems Two, Three, Four, or Five is *pathologically autopoietic*; and that entails a threat to its viability.

By these definitions and by this argument, all the governments that I have studied have been pathologically autopoietic in *all four* subsystems that are not themselves supposed to be viable systems. There is, moreover, good reason for the general recognition of a network within this quadripartite pathology that is known as the Establishment. This could well be defined as the pathologically autopoietic principle which pervades them. Then the point behind the analysis of the April 1973 paper (called 'On Decybernation') was the recognition that, although we had already effected major change of a sort, we were not impinging on the Establishment's own organization — which therefore retained the ability to nullify our efforts. It was in fact beginning to do so, by the well-worn expedient of lauding and gladly incorporating some individual components of the total cybernetic plan (such as Cyberstride and the Operations Room) within the existing managerial paradigm, rejecting other components (such as Checo) as too exaggerated to belong to that paradigm, and ignoring the whole class of components (such as algedonic metering) as irrelevant which were not even stateable in paradigmatic language. This expedient obviously discards much important work; but the real issue is that it denatures the viability of the plan that was cybernetically designed as a totality. It is to take the cybernetics out of the cybernetic plan; it is to take any actual change out of the set of proposed alterations. In fact, it dismantles the invention altogether.

In arguing this case, the paper made strong use of four statements made by Maturana. They draw a distinction which is so valuable that they are repeated here in his own words:

'The term *structure* emphasizes the relations between the parts as well as the identity of the parts which constitute a whole.'

'The word *organization* emphasizes the relations which define a system as a unity (and thus determine its properties) with no reference to the nature of the components which can be any as long as they satisfy these relations.'

'If the organization of a system changes the identity of the system changes, and it becomes a new one, a different unity with different properties.

Conversely, if the organization of a system stays invariant while its structure changes, the system remains the same and its identity stays unchanged.'

'Although we make these connotational distinctions in the use of the terms structure and organization, we are usually unaware of them, and thus do not realize that the organization of a system is by necessity an invariant. We talk about change of organization without realizing that such a change implies a change of system.'

So: the argument was that the Chilean governmental Establishment was accepting, and would continue to accept *structural* change — but not *organizational* change (and in this they were and are not alone). However, this was the explanation advanced for the two examples of failure that the paper set out to examine. It went on to discuss the extent to which we could regard the whole work as successful — a matter which has since been debated in the forum of management science internationally, mostly from a solid plinth of ignorance as to what actually happened. The following was the view of current success taken by my paper; it is still April 1973.

> 'If what we wanted to do was *to meet the objectives listed* for Cyberstride and Project Cybersyn, then we have succeeded. Those were **technical** objectives, and meeting them may count as success to some people.
>
> If what we wanted to do was *to display that technical achievement* in management action, then we may yet succeed. This is the **technocratic** objective, and meeting it may count as success to some people.
>
> If we wanted to *'help the people'*, this was a **social** objective, and the outcome is ambiguous. For if the invention is dismantled, and the tools used are not the tools we made, they could become instruments of oppression. This would count as failure.
>
> If we wanted *a new system of government*, certainly a **political** objective, then it seems that we are not going to get it. This too must count as failure.
>
> Any one person who has worked on this team may have a complex motivation, in which the above technical, technocratic, social and political objectives are mixed in unique proportions to constitute his own 'objective functional'.
>
> This would explain some current confusion, and the disagreement about success.'

It still does, I think. We had made huge strides in developing non-bureaucratic management by simply ignoring the established bureaucracy — by setting up a separate framework. Please note that this is the ultimate form of *organizational* change, because the *structural* entity is altogether replaced (Maturana's terminology). Then innovations cannot be merely structurally assimilated: they redefine the system.

Having remarked that my own recent proposals for effecting change on this scale had indeed been 'assimilated' rather than 'implemented', the paper complained that other members of the core group were not making any proposals at all to this end. It called for them; and it offered certain criteria that any such proposals ought to satisfy. These are repeated here, not because they have generality (for they do not) but because they do illustrate how a topic sounding as vague and remote as 'the cybernetics of change' can be sharpened to precise ends in an actual situation.

Criteria for Proposals for Organizational Change in Chile (dated 27th April 1973)

1. A proposal must aim to change the organization of the established order, and not be a proposal for simply implementing a system of management.

2. A proposal must involve activity by the workers. The system was designed for them, and they are the variety amplifiers. (I think that doing rather than teaching is the key to this required proposal. That is why I am now so hesitant about making films.)

3. A proposal must identify structural change, which is easily accomplished, in non-bureaucratic terms — these we already know, because of Cybersyn.

4. A proposal must envisage our invention as an instrument of revolution. I mean that 'The Way of Production' is still a necessary feature of the Chilean revolution, but that 'The Way of Regulation' is an extra requirement of a complex world not experienced by Marx or Lenin.

5. A proposal must treat our invention at the right level of recursion.

   The invention needs to be seen in perspective. Some of us see nothing but the invention, and stand to be abandoned by those who see the political setting in which the invention is embedded. Some see nothing but the immediate political crisis (and who shall blame them?) and therefore have forgotten the purposes of the original inventing.

All our endeavours could fall between these two stools.

Obviously this list is based upon the political philosophy of the national management at that time, as these chapters have consistently argued that it should be. It is not the intention of this book to discuss politics *per se*. The list does demonstrate how cybernetic generalizations may be 'sharpened to precise ends in an actual situation'. It was followed by a long commentary on the political implications of any putative proposal. Then it returned to the managerial cybernetics which are our current concern. It claimed that we, the agents of change, were missing our opportunitites, because the facts of the situation could not be understood without reference to some model of that situation which enshrined political beliefs raised upon ideological foundations. The argument was that we were ignoring — therefore 'eliminating' — those facts that did not map onto this model. How common, indeed, this is: it is endemic to the human condition. Such models are paradigms; if there is to be a mapping of the facts onto a paradigmatic model, it will be homomorphic — many-one. The variety reduction involved fails to transmit the information that 'the facts' supposedly constitute.

Three examples of this phenomenon were discussed in the April paper. First was the issue of organizational change, and second our treatment of bureaucracy. The third talked about corruption, which is a problem in so many countries, and is always difficult even to discuss because no paradigmatic model of good government can possibly include corruption as a variable. It can include illegal acts, because these are straightforwardly negations of the law, and their perpetrators are liable to punishment. Corrupt acts are, however, in some sense accepted in a society where they are the norm. These considerations led the April paper to define corrupt acts as 'those acts which explain away actions that are contrary to law'. In discussion of the paper, Maturana proposed this alternative: 'corruption: all those acts which do not validate the system we want to validate'. In any case, it seems clear that the evident epistemological problems faced in trying to deal with such issues are founded in logical mappings that do not exhibit requisite variety. Then this is one of the mechanisms whereby viable systems may the more readily become pathologically autopoietic: a System Two, for example, that is intent on its own survival rather than its dedicated anti-oscillary function, can actually fund this false activity from corrupt acts. Those who concern themselves about this particular System Two, then, are likely to address themselves to the disgrace of the evident corruption, and to fail to understand the pathological autopoiesis; this in turn will make them less capable of rooting out the corruption . . . .

Discussing these matters once in India, a cabinet minister was astonished that anyone should challenge his conviction that the Indian character is distinctively flawed. Of course it is not. If we ask the cybernetic question: 'For which autopoietic system is this flow of corrupt money the salary?' we shall be led straight to the pathological structure that requires diagnosis and treatment.

The End of 'The Peaceful Road'

The situation was still deteriorating. As the months went on, the mounting pressures were tangible in the atmosphere of the Santiago streets. The core group was also completely alert to the foreign activity that meant that the government could not survive for much longer, and certainly not into 1974. Let it be clear that this was understood by all of us, as I am sure that it was by Allende himself. But it was April, still; and the paper I had just written would provoke a response. The immediate facts of the cybernetic activity were these.

The 'troika' that is to say the threesome team, was already inoperative as such. Raúl Espejo was running Project Cybersyn, which was still precisely on course. Enrique Farné was much preoccupied with his automotive sector. Hermann Schwember had moved from Copper to be general secretary of the Agro-industrial sector. Fernando Flores himself was preparing for a crucial meeting of the Latin-American Finance Ministers in Jamaica. I was spending a lot of time, but separately, with each of them. There was really nothing that I could do personally to further the cause of either Project Cybersyn or of the People Project. Cybersyn had by now a professional and politically uncommitted staff of some seventy people; and it was very much part of the changed Corfo that Flores had completely left behind. Twice, the official there who was playing a central role in further planning avoided meeting me. Also, by now, the People Project had entirely embraced and was totally absorbed by political realities of such potency that it was no longer even decorous to speak of cybernetic formalism in its regard (even in my solitude). But *Externalities* certainly remained. And in May I returned to Europe in pursuit of those economic potentialities in which I still believed. *Might* there yet be sufficient time? Many issues were ostensibly poised for action over there . . . .

They awaited the delivery of letters of authorization from the various government agencies concerned with minerals, with wine, and with fish. It was on the eve of my flight that I discovered that I should have to go without the letters; also I discovered the ironic cybernetic reason for that.

Mention was made in the last section of the role of corruption in these Chilean (and internationally comparable) circumstances. The *variety* of corruption had proliferated in many agencies. Obviously the variety of corrupt acts is far greater than the variety of incorrupt acts, since corruption recognizes no boundary. Then suppose that you are an incorruptible president, facing such a variety proliferation of corruption. You do not have Requisite Variety to hold that situation, and you must therefore attenuate it. Allende's solution had been to declare that general abuses had amounted to a public scandal, and that in future all international trading decisions were to be in the hands of one man. This man's reputation was invoilate. He was the head of the International Trading Office. He was upright; he was scrupulous; and he was known to be so by all.

Then that is fine, so far as it goes. But if everything has to pass through a one-man filter, we may be short of time. Secondly, and naturally enough, most of what time there had been was absorbed, because 'the filter' was undertaking his own negotiations abroad. Thirdly, those negotiations had created a protocol, which was highly desirable; but it was a protocol that left its negotiator disinclined to countenance international agreements that were not passed through the international Establishment. My propositions were not of this kind. The Minister of Finance could intervene in that situation, and he did. But still the letters of authorization did not arrive in time; and it is easy to understand why they did not. Corrupt variety proliferation had been designedly attenuated to near-zero via an incorrupt low-variety filter. Then high-variety incorrupt amplifiers were needed after that phase, to restore requisite variety. The people who were needed were there, and I was dealing with them. They had the will and the imagination to act; they did not yet have the constitutional means. And this was probably because they did not have the sectarian 'clout' — even with ministerial support.

The requisite variety equation was never to balance, and the European trip in May 1973 was inevitably a failure in its absence — although I tried. Should I have gone in May, and should I have returned in June? Opponents of Unidad Popular, and even technocrats within our own part of the governmental machine, wanted me to go, and *not* to return: I was a real nuisance, and they made this evident. Because they made this evident, and because of mounting public attention, there were also personal friends who wanted me to go, and not to return — because they thought that I had run into too much personal danger. The core group around the Minister, whom I knew also to be personal friends, resolved the problem by suggesting that I both go and return — but return surreptitiously, to a cottage on the Pacific coast, away from Santiago. This idea I immediately accepted. The arrangements went ahead. Fernando Flores himself found the idea tiresome. Because of a number of international developments, he strongly urged me to stay close to him in Santiago. Certainly there would be no desertion; but it was necessary to interpret what 'close' ought to mean. It was important not to embarrass him in the public eye. In the event, I was anonymously in a cottage by the shore at Las Cruces during (what was to prove) the final visit to Chile, during June and July 1973. It was a good solution. Few people realised that I was in the country at all. But all necessary meetings were held; the movements took place between several cities, whether by me or by others, by night.

On the way to Chile for this last assignment, I was in transit on the last airliner to land at Beunos Aires before the airport was closed to await the ultimate return of President Juan Perón to Argentina. There were two million people around the airport. Because of serious threats, his plane was diverted to a military base: even so, a gun battle broke out. The southern tip of Latin America was clearly in a tempestuous condition. And yet none of our scenarios for Chile, all of which foresaw the end of the government, most of which foresaw the loss of political freedom which a period of military rule entails, and most of which were extremely accurate in evaluating the intentions and involvement of the United States (as Congress subsequently established these in public hearings), none of them foresaw the massive bloodshed and absolute oppression that was to come. The Chilean military gave the appearance of upholding the constitution against all comers, of whatever political complexion. Since, in addition, the Commander-in-Chief, General Prats, was a staunch ally and personal friend of Allende, it was all too easy to be misled.

But he himself faced the gravest difficulties. On 28th June his car was cornered in the public street. No armed attack was made; but the circumstances seemed to have been arranged to mimic the assassination of his predecessor, General Schneider. Perhaps the incident was meant to intimidate him prior to the mutiny of a tank regiment which began the next day, and appeared to herald civil war. Santiago was cleared, and my log says 'went into use as a firing range'. Sixteen offices in the presidential palace were shot up, and holes were blown in the Ministry of Defence building. But no-one else joined the mutiny, and the tank commander concerned was personally disarmed by General Prats. This produced euphoria among government supporters. But it was the beginning of the end: Prats shortly resigned; after the coup, he went into exile in Argentina, where he was later murdered.

Throughout these months, the cybernetic core group were trying to assimilate and to understand the events through which we were living, and to incorporate the lessons in an adaptation of the political theory that had inspired the Chilean experiment which Allende had led. What else could we have done with the insights and tools of cybernetics than what we had done, and what plans could be made, while there was yet the time to plan, for the range of possible futures? It seemed to me that much that was internally amiss could be accounted for in terms of the pathological autopoiesis of the viable system, and could therefore be put right by proper diagnosis and prescription; therefore I began the construction of a whole new theory of social cybernetics based on this proposition (it is still under development). As far as attack from outside is concerned, however, there is no way in which poor countries can protect themselves against rich ones if the latter have a mind to suppress them: this has always been the case, and will remain so unless the problem can be tackled successfully at the next level of recursion. It would mean the cybernetic design of a so-called United Nations that is already so far gone in pathological autopoieses that such a proposal cannot even be mooted.

At the end of July, there were strong political currents felt around Corfo and Project Cybersyn. Several strange messages reached me at the coast; they were coming from the political opposition. It seemed that this was the best project undertaken under Allende's aegis, and that his (self-assumed) successor would continue it in his own way. This way would not, of course, involve any 'nonsense' about worker participation .... I found these overtures obnoxious; but our strategies were well prepared. However, these stirrings came to the ears of the President. He sent a car to the coast to fetch me to Santiago.

While waiting in his outer office, I discussed the military situation at length with the ADC on duty, Arturo Araya, a Captain in the Chilean Navy. He was assassinated that very night: loyalty to the constitution was becoming less possibly daily for even the best of servicemen. The Campañero Presidente was tired and harrassed. He interrogated me closely about the new currents surrounding Cybersyn, and I told him all that I could. Certainly there were many people involved who did not subscribe to industrial democracy as we had planned it. He asked me whether I had anything to ask of him. I said yes; in view of the confusion being generated around the project, would he tell me quite directly the extent to which he expected worker control of the social economy. He replied: 'El maximo'.

During August, a second attempt to bring down the government by *gremio* action was made. Having successfully endured the experience of October 1972, my associates knew what they must do. Two special purpose operations rooms were constructed, and connected to the network of communications through the country which Cybernet embodied. Filtration systems were set up for the spate of messages, and Cabinet Ministers and senior industrial managers dealt with them in *real time*. Raúl Espejo has recorded that during this period between 10 and 30 per cent of the normal lorry fleet was in operation. But thanks to the 24-hour-a-day management of distribution, the levels of fuel and essential food that were normal in the country before the strike were maintained. State enterprises playing a strategic role in the economy received their normal supplies of raw materials. If all this sounds an impossibility, it must be recalled that transportation systems are highly redundant: think of parked lorries, of railway wagons in sidings and under demurrage, and of the notorious delays that happen at docks. This redundancy was mobilized into instantly responsive action in Chile, taking up much of the slack in a system that is normally (and in any free country) allocated to both preparedness to compete and also pure inefficiency. Moreover, the levels of supply to which folk had become accustomed were already depressed by earlier disruption that could now be corrected. Even so, the achievement was still dramatic; and there is little doubt that, as in the previous October, this stoppage would have been successfully handled, despite the influx of foreign money to support it, had events run their course.

The potency of cybernetic thinking was again being vindicated within the country of Chile; but how could this small, poor country withstand the pressures from outside? I have often been asked why we were not able to stipulate a behaviour which would accommodate that threat. It is like complaining that man, who is supposed to be an adaptive biological system, cannot adapt to a bullet through the heart.

On 8th September, the President sent an order to the Cybersyn project team: it was the last that they were to receive. The operations room built on the Avenida Santa Maria was to be moved to the inside of the Palace, La Moneda. He well understood that none of the existing rooms was large enough to accommodate this apparatus, and allocated one of the most traditional and important rooms to be transformed for the purpose. During the next three days, the drawings were completed.

On 11th September 1973, I was fulfilling a last engagement in England prior to returning to Chile. It was in the City of London, and I was expounding these matters, and especially the *Externalities*, to an inner group of the Liberal Party, as represented in 'the City'. The Party Leader sat in the front row. Following the official proceedings, there was considerable informal talk, and the gathering broke up slowly.

Eventually, I left the building alone. It was to confront a newspaper placard in the street outside: ALLENDE ASSASSINATED.

CHAPTER TWENTY

Prospectus

Having undergone the experience recounted in the preceeding four chapters, and drawing a veil over subsequent events — involving as they did much agony for so many, I want to turn if that is possible to positive conclusions. It is only by consolidating what has been learned within some framework that a prospectus for future work can be formulated.

The problem for a long time was to know what the framework is to which so many impressions and facts, lacunae, inferences, and convictions are supposed to relate. Each of us who were colleagues in this affair seems to place the emphasis on what we learned differently, and this is probably because we are all using different reference frames — and even those change at different times. This was a Third World issue. This was a new kind of Marxism. This was a cheap-technology undertaking of high-science. This was a managerial revolution. Yes, and it was many other things too: the cybernetics of the viable system relates to them all, and none seems to be central to such an undertaking as we made — and which could be made again, somewhere else ....

Where else? I went to various countries by invitation to discuss the use of managerial cybernetics in government at a high level. Their circumstances were all different; so were the circumstances of the firms who called me in different. It gradually came home to me that what they all had in common was a recognition that things were not working well, thall all familiar remedies had been tried and had failed, and that a radically fresh approach had to be attempted. Now things are not working well anywhere, or in any institution; but that fact is not always recognized; and if it is, many managers and ministers truly believe that more stringent applications of ineffectual remedies will somehow work in the end. Then in terms of management science, what was dividing the world in two was *the perception of impending crisis*. This was the common condition of my involvement, and it was also enough to set radical reappraisals in motion everywhere.

What counts as a crisis is the expectation of *loss of control:* in other words cybernetic breakdown in the institution. This does not refer to an inability to impose decisions; it means that the institution is out of control itself. We may certainly recall how Operational Research, conceived as the use of transdisciplinary science in tackling ill-formed problems with no known solution, grew and flourished in Britain during the Second World War. This was an extremely radical attack on issues which generals, poring over their between-wars sand tables, had imagined that they could control — an expectation that was rapidly falsified by land, sea and air once hostilities began. At that point crisis was recognized, radical reappraisals could be made, and — much more importantly — the suggested new solutions would actually be tried (and they usually worked). In today's Britain, crisis has been institutionalized — and so has Operational Research. Reappraisals are made by tired people who can be relied upon not to propose new ideas ... in short, matters are very serious indeed.

Returning then to the theme of perceived crisis as the expectation of cybernetic breakdown, it is obvious to me that the first and foremost lesson of the Chilean work was: ACT FAST. We did that, after all, and were able to do so because the threats were imminent and seen to be so. Having understood this lesson, I made speed the essence of my proposals in four other countries — but in each case the impending crisis exploded before work could begin. So far as it goes, this seems to validate both the hypothesis about crisis and the strategy of swift action. (The countries are not named, because I do not want to be side-tracked into case histories, and because progress may yet be made.)

The speed with which this advocacy suggests that managerial cybernetics should be undertaken is abhorrent to the scientist and the bureaucrat alike. No-one is likely to be awarded a Ph.D. for cutting corners and taking decisions on inadequate evidence. But, as I have argued with passion before, and shall again, if a major part of the manager's problem is to reach a decision by Thursday, that is a parameter of his situation with which the management scientists must deal — otherwise, he is no good. It will probably cost him his respectability, because of the way that the scientific Establishment works; but in fact he is doing nothing more opprobrious than to say: 'the probability that my advice is correct is lower than I would like, but as high as can be generated by the evidence that could be collected and analysed in so short a time'. But it is this very limitation that makes it essential for the scientist to have as large an armoury of weapons as he can amass in advance. This is why fundamental research is published, and why experience counts — in every field of application: the speed with which a surgeon acts in crisis comes to mind. As to the bureaucrat, he is greatly threatened by any reappraisal at all, by radical reappraisal especially, and by swift action most of all. Bureaucratic systems, by their very nature, cannot promote swift action (this is the major strength of their autopoiesis, their self-production, because delaying tactics dissipate the energy of reform). By the same token, however, they cannot move fast enough to arrest swift action, if it is sufficiently determined.

Fast action works, in the crisis mode, and nothing else will; but fast action is very hard to effect. Insofar as I can now understand the mistakes made in the Chilean work, they seem to be related to the framework of crisis itself. We all knew the major features of the crisis that Chile confronted, and tried to take them into account. But these features were presented *ad hoc*: this was happening, that was a risk, the other was ... peculiar to the place and time, for sure.

For all these reasons, I have tried to create a framework for the application of radical managerial cybernetics that would be based on fathoming the underlying mechanisms of crisis. This framework will now be presented. And if the following sub-heading, and the many pages devoted to its elucidation, appear to be a lugubrious start to a Prospectus, then it is time to take a realistic look at the world we now inhabit.

The Cybernetics of Crisis

If cybernetics is the science of effective organization, then this science ought to be used in designing the organizational modes that are appropriate to a rapidly changing society and its rapidly changing institutions — of which the firm was initially taken as the example for this book. In the last four chapters, the model of the viable system has been applied at many levels of organizational scope — even to the state itself. Those contending, and some do so contend, that it must be illegitimate to deploy the same structural model and the same informational criteria in such diverse ways have not accepted (or possibly have not understood) that this whole cybernetic theory of the viable system is based on the recursion theorem that demonstrates a particular set of structural invariances in all such systems. Even at the cytological level, for example, it is perfectly convenient to discuss what is going on in the single cell in terms of the language and logic developed here. (The metasystem is contained in the nucleus, which houses the (Five) policy-stuff called DNA, including the (Four) systems of reduplication and adaptation, and the (Three) plan for working the cell. Continuous direction (Three) seems to be shared with the mitochondria in their respiratory activity, which also has a major anti-oscillary (Two) regulatory role in arranging for the use of oxygen. The cilia are the 'limbs' (One) of the cell, which also detect sense-data about their environment.)

There is, however, a different critical contention. It says that, regardless of the correctness or otherwise of the cybernetic theory that has been advanced to account for viability, it is ridiculous to suppose that it can be used to bring about societary change. The reason given for this contention is that the attempt would be — and allegedly in Chile was — politically 'naive'. This word, which labels an approach as 'simple or artless', has pleasing overtones when it is applied to child-like things. There is no doubt, however, that use of the word in the political context is so pejorative as to be intentionally damning; that is because 'artless' means not lacking in artificial contrivance, but lacking in fundamental insight, necessary skill, and relevant experience. If this is the proper denotation of the term, then I shall go on to argue that *all* political acts are naive, and that therefore the attribution of political naivety tells us nothing (except that the commentator manages only to be dismissive in just that context where he most needs intellectual acuity).

Because the character of this Part of the book is founded in personal narrative, I approach the abstract cybernetic argument which will follow with just a few recollections of events which impinged on my own life by their 'political naivety' as just defined. It is done in the hope that the reader will be encouraged to pause and review his or her own experience. If it is parallel, then the cybernetic statements will be more readily understood.

The first instance occurred when I was a boy in 1936. Midway between proclamation and coronation, King Edward VIII abdicated. This was a very startling event for almost the whole of Great Britain, and especially so for a boy being borne along on the general air of jollity. Essentially through the connivance of press barons, the government managed to keep secret a constitutional crisis of the first magnitude until it was almost concluded — and possibly not in a way (there is no means of knowing) that would have been decided by any remotely democratic process. If I was amazed by the event, I was even more amazed by the strong disagreements which the outcome disclosed, even within my own family, among my schoolmasters and schoolmates, and in the press. It was not to be for many more years that the facts known today fully emerged; and it has to be realized that, as with any historical event, there are broadly relevant facts which are lost for ever. But twenty-five to fifty years on, people — and especially those who were not alive at the time — are content to believe that they now have the matter 'in perspective'.

Let us take a leap of ten years. In 1946 I was a young officer in India at the time when the ultimately crucial decisions were being taken about the future of that whole sub-continent. I was naive enough, if that is the word we are discussing, to be amazed at the picture of the situation that was being purveyed in Britain. First of all, it was quite difficult to discover what this was. 'Letters from home', Army instructions, and the responsible Indian press (informed by capitals other than London) told very different stories. This could not have been due simply to connivance by press barons on this occasion. But it was due to *something*: that much was clear. I did not then know that the atomic holocaust, which had curtailed my own preparation for an assault upon Japan, had been approved by Prime Minister Attlee without (as he subsequently declared) his having the faintest idea that what was being perpetrated was anything more than a much bigger bang. Next year, in March

1947, I must have been one of the very last Britons in India ever to propose the mess toast 'to the King Emperor'. And so we left the partitioned India to its massacres, and a legacy of subsequent further divisions, slaughtering, and even formal wars. But of course all that, too, is 'in perspective' now . . . .

The passage of another decade takes us to 1956, a date indelibly stamped on the face of Europe by the events in Hungary. For myself, however, I was working in the British steel industry, and had already made the original applications of cybernetic theory that eventuated in *Brain of the Firm*. But I had not yet been notified of any release from the first line military reserve. At this point came the crisis over the Suez Canal, which had been nationalized by President Nassar of Egypt. Once again, it was completely impossible to determine the truth of what was happenng. Stories leaked out to the effect that Britain, France, and Israel were acting in collusion; but there were strenuous government denials at the time of this now-acknowledged fact. As before, the nation was seriously split on non-party lines, and the entire world appeared to be condemning the incipient British action against Egypt. While the forces were gathering, there were several announcements that the military reserve might well be called upon; and therefore I had to consider in advance what stand should be taken if my name were selected for this task. Now that some quarter of a century later this incident also is seen in perspective, maybe I should be forgiven for a conscientious objection, had it come to that. But for the absolution to be real at the time, one would have to be seen to have been right: this is never on the cards until much later. It was the absence of fact rather than the absence of ethic that was dividing the country — although the facts seem to have been known to everyone else in the world as they happened.

I mentioned at the outset that I would give utterance to these three incidents in the hope of creating resonant recollections in the reader. No further examples are offered, partly because they have proliferated dramatically as the world has 'grown smaller', thanks to its deployment of technology, and partly because as more recent dates are approached there is less likely to be consensus about what really happened. In any case, it is not the current purpose to make an historical analysis of these three moments of history: whole books have already been written about each of them. The purpose is instead to show how our cybernetic vocabulary may be applied to the examination of political systems in the epoch of their developing crisis, and to demonstrate how conclusions may be drawn from thinking in these terms which it would be virtually impossible to gainsay on scientific grounds. That is to say, the case is argued from first principles, those of variety engineering, and the examples are used only to show what is really meant in practical terms by the cybernetic nomenclature.

There are many parties to a crisis, wherever it appears in today's world; and national boundaries are not absolute barriers to many kinds of intervention. In

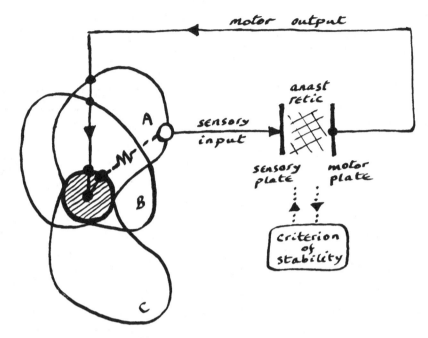

Figure 48. (Compare Figures 6 and 7)

Figure 48, three major interest groups (A,B, and C) are depicted as intersecting (the hatched circle) in an imbroglio of developing crisis. We consider first the behaviour of one of the three, in cybernetic terms.

Party A, whose span of interest is depicted in the diagram by an amoeboid phase space, has first of all to transduce the variety implicit in the crisis into the realm of its own capacity to act on the situation. That is to say, with reference to Figure 6 in Chapter 2, that the sensory input (information about the crisis) to be admitted to the sensorium (in the decision-making 'brain' of Party A) ought to balance and to preserve the variety capable of being generated by the crisis. The same is true of the motor input (the implementation of decision), and its projected impact on the crisis zone, true also then of the anastomotic reticulum connecting the sensory and motor plates (see Figure 7 and the discussion thereon). In a well-regulated system there are four major cybernetic requirements of such stability, which will be discussed in turn.

(i) The System is Obedient to Asby's Law of Requisite Variety

Any situation on which managerial attention is suddenly focused will inevitably prove to exhibit characteristics of explosive variety. All human affairs have such high variety that they are constantly in danger of losing stability. But those attracting special attention, in any phase space at any epoch, are usually proliferating variety at their maximal rate — in an attempt to discover polystable solutions to the imbalances that are occurring in their subsystems. Then it is also typical that any one system (in this case, A) will be committed, for internal reasons, to subsystemic variety generation-absorption on such a scale that it is likely to exacerbate the problems of intersecting systems (in this case, B and C) in terms of its own increasing disequilibrium.

When we consider this comment insofar as the firm itself is concerned, the threat to internal peace is not too alarming. This is because the linkages governing System One in its participation as an operational component of a viable system are strong in terms of shared purpose (as an observer may see it). A powerful constraint on horizontal variety is therefore a likely product of homeostatic interaction on the central vertical axis itself. In larger and less teleologically focused systems, such as whole countries, the prospect of constraining variety at operational intersects is much diminished: just because there is less teleologically shared ground. It is very well worth noting, however, that some countries — and certainly international movements — have more purposive focus than others. Think of the way in which a magnifying glass can focus general sunlight, so as to set fire to grass . . . .

When global situations are our topic, then, prospects are gloomy indeed. Astronauts who have viewed Earth from vast distance have reported that (to such an observer) the planet is clearly an organic entity; therefore its systems A, B, and C — such as the three great power blocs of our time — might be regarded as sharing the purpose of human survival. But such a perception depends on the creation of a *model,* and in that case a model devised by A Man On The Moon. Whether God's model talks in such terms is known only to that Observer; whether the consensus model of Earthlings can rise to lunar heights prescribes the future of our species, at the very least. There is perhaps some comfort in recognizing that all these models of the cosmically viable system are recursions of each other . . . .

These paragraphs are tightly written; and there is a danger that they might develop into the 'wrong' book. The emphasis here is to point out the role of the *model* formulated (Figure 48) within the compass of the anastomotic reticulum, under the criterion of internal stability to which System A subscribes. It is all too obvious that — to someone in Britain at the relevant times — the 1936 model of the Abdication, the 1946 model of Indian Freedom, and the 1956 model of Suez, all lacked requisite variety to the point of the actual loss of democratic control. These were the personal examples that I offered to compare with yours. And if we sat together today, then surely neither of us has the least doubt that pages more could be filled to show how our international, national, and local regulatory systems are so constructed as to try and flout Ashby's Law — and how they conspicuously fail in that attempt. The first reason for this is that the variety exhibited by the crisis situation is necessarily attenuated on the way to model construction within the sensory-motor reticulum.

Although there is empirical evidence (as cited, for example) for this, the contention is more safely advanced by analysis of the instrumentality that is necessarily involved. We have first of all to take account of the inadequacy of the model builder himself. He is not omniscient in his understanding, and he perforce sets up filters within his information-gathering network. This happens even to the individual human being as he peers into and otherwise senses the world that surrounds him: he can see only within the narrow spectrum of visible light, hear within a spectrum of audible sound frequencies, and so forth. When it comes to understanding political situations, those responsible for constructing cognitive models seem to be extremely selective in what is allowed to count as pertinent information. Why should this be? Because a model as it were condenses onto a group of people who have a similar outlook, or a similar vested interest in the situation, or who have selected sources which become the arbiters of what is pertinent. Secondly, although this group may debate its emerging model with zeal, both the group and its individual members have other situations to consider — whereas the participants in *this* situation are devoting themselves to its unfolding on a full-time basis. Thirdly, comes the question of the with-holding of information (as in the case of the Abdication), the grave distortion of information — whether through misapprehension or bias (as in the interpretation of the Indian dilemma), and finally the use of the information channel (as happened in the case of Suez) to tell deliberate lies.

Thus, looking at Figure 48 once more, we see that a sensory input is being made to a model-creating reticulum, which derives immediately from a responsible managerial centre (marked by a circle) within the domain of Party A; this centre is fed by information (shown by a dashed line) which contains an attenuating filter. It is contended that this is the instrumentality whereby Ashby's Law will inexorably rebuke the designers of the system, by ensuring that the model at the reticulum is deficient in variety — repeat *variety,* which is something other than information. This is a point, often misunderstood, which may conveniently be emphasized here, with the example of the Chilean story in mind.

The responsible managerial centre in A might well be the Foreign Office of a country A that is involved in a developing crisis — still represented by the hatched intersect of A, B, and C — in another country, X. Then the transducer (marked in Figure 48 by a solid dot) of information about the developing crisis, will be the A-embassy there. The link between the Foreign Office in A and the A-embassy cannot conceivably be short of *information.* If the home country demands facts from its A-embassy in X, it will certainly get them. If the Ambassador in X has facts relevant to Foreign Office policy, he will certainly send them. Now here is a definition that I have proposed before: information is the set of facts that changes us. The selection of facts demanded and sent about the developing crisis will be those that are *competent to effect change*. This sounds reasonable. In a crisis, who wants to know the albeit undoubted fact that the primroses are in bloom? The ambassadorial arrangements under discussion are designed to convey the facts that have the status to become information, and therefore to procure new decisions or policies. But all of this takes for granted the existence of a diplomatic corps conceptual model in A that has requisite variety to absorb the variety generated by the burgeoning crisis. When requisite variety in that model is lacking, states of the system that are distinct become indistinguishable; therefore valid data are transformed by the operations within the model into false 'information' — which, when it procures change, as it remains competent to do, will generate mistakes in the handling of the crisis from A's direction.

In wondering what, if anything, can possibly be done to avoid implicit variety attenuation in this fashion, we encounter an operational difficulty that is widely recognizable. It was pointed out that the model shared by the A-diplomats 'condenses' onto a group whose members typically have much in common. The group probably does not explicitly agree that it is using a model at all. It sees itself as making wise interpretations of facts; it ignores the points that intepretations are processed through conceptual models of the world rather than through the world itself, and that facts are selectively recognized because they make useful inputs to conceptual models, rather than being recognized free-of-context as if they were independent gems of value found glinting in the sun. But if the condensation of an inexplicit model onto a group were to be forestalled by the deliberate creation of subgroups known to be in disagreement with each other, so that attention were drawn to the models in use and they in consequence attained requisite variety, other disagreeable consequences would surely follow. To invent an extreme example: if the British embassy in Chile had been staffed from top to bottom by declared and convinced Marxists disinclined, as was Allende himself, to the Soviet model of Marxism, British policy could not have taken the course that it did from 1970 onwards to this day — because there would have been no A-group at home and in station of sufficient commonality as to condense a model onto itself. That sounds satisfactory so far as it goes: it is likely to maintain requisite variety. The trouble is that in such conditions, the Foreign Office in London would have found itself unable to believe most of what it heard from its embassy, and unable to process what it did believe through a conceptual model mismatching the model in Santiago. Then it would probably have taken its sensory input from the United States' embassy instead, and matters would have ensued just as they did.

It is surely part of the issue about political naivety that this section undertakes to discuss that any example is likely to trigger strong emotional response, because of its content. The foregoing paragraphs set out to show by one example how difficult it must in general be to maintain requisite variety in the conceptual models tacitly in use, once a crisis burgeons. In 'normal' conditions, if such ever actually obtain these days, requisite variety is provided by low-variety models — because 'normal' is itself a low-variety signal. Hence even when a crisis is expected, and models are made explicit so that variety can be expanded to whatever is requisite, the design task remains extraordinarily difficult. For example, I set up three different systems of communication with three different groups in Chile, ready for use if the expected coup befell (as it did), and I was safely out of the country at the time (as I was). These needed to employ coded information, expressed in casual form, so as not to alert expected censorship. So here were three different models, quite explicit and fully developed, which were supposed to be capable of generating requisite variety to balance that generated by the developing crisis. In the event, none was adequate. One failed completely, but that was probably due to psychological traumata suffered during the coup. A second was successful in adaptation over the fairly short period needed, but would not have continued to generate *variety* for much longer — even though it had large *information*-handling capacity. The third was fully adaptive, and therefore did its job successfully for a long time. But it required strong efforts of both imagination and inference, at both terminals, and eventually became so complicated that it also failed.

Perceive then, please, in the light of Ashby's Law, the enormous difficulties involved in designing systems capable of generating requisite variety in conditions of burgeoning crisis. By definition, a crisis has emotive content; by belief, its successful handling depends upon accurate and timely information. It is hard indeed for anyone involved to withhold emotional response at the time (and with hindsight, I can be as coolly critical of my own design of codes as I remain about the British government's actions). And the importance of information is indeed so great that to feel confidence in the system that provides it is paramount at the time (with hindsight, I can criticize its deficiencies, especially in the linkages *between* the five main levels of the socio-industrial recursion). But whatever degree of emphasis is placed on these two dominating themes within a political crisis, or rather because of it, this underlying requirement must be maintained because it is absolute: that all subsystems standing in homeostatic relationship be capable of generating requisite variety to absorb each other's variety — in very principle, which is to say in terms of the conceptual models which govern both the dynamics of emotion, and the selection of information.

(ii) Information Channels Maintain Variety Entrusted to Them

In the foregoing section, the distinction between variety and information was clearly drawn. Confusions between the two are especially common when the channels carrying information come under review. People are familiar with the notion that a particular channel can transmit only a finite amount of information in unit time, and that this can be measured. Thanks to the seminal work of Shannon (see References D), who established the mathematical rules under which units of information are transmitted down lines of various characteristics, a communication system can be properly designed in the engineering sense. The Tenth Theorem, to which I draw special attention, points out that the channel capacity must *exceed* its notionally adequate bit-handling ability, in order to resolve ambiguities that may arise in passing the message because of 'noise' in the system. But people are also aware that the mathematical theory of communication, concerned as it is with the transmission of bits, does not concern itself with *semantic* information — which is to say, what the bits mean to the recipient. Then often they fail to see the very basic relevance of the Tenth Theorem to management systems. Some people, having perceived the relevance, begin to contend that the Tenth Theorem and the Law of Requisite Variety say the same thing: thus debates have been heard as to whether Ashby or Shannon has proprietorial priority. The political context of the present discussion provides an opportunity to elucidate this problem, which is by no means academic; and the difficulty arises primarily because we seek to distinguish three notions instead of the convenient two (since any dichotomy slices its relevant universe in half). The three notions are: the flow of bits and the flow of variety, both of which are information-theoretic notions, and the flow of semantic meaning, which is not.

This very point begins the elucidation: one bit of information does not have enough variety (the power to discriminate between possible states) to distinguish more than two notions. Well, communication theory can deal with that, by creating capacity for transmitting two bits. This arrangement has the discriminatory power to deal with four possibilities: therefore it can certainly handle three — and with considerable resolving power left over to cope with any ambiguity derived from noise. This will work, in Shannon-terms, so long as there is enough *time* to transmit two bits. It would work, in Ashby-terms, in half the Shannon-time, so long as the 'bit' were replaced by a 'quartit' — the (just-invented) 'quarternary digit'. This illustrates the exact sense in which the two approaches say the same thing about the information channel. It has to be noted, however, that the identity is of interest only insofar as there is freedom to design *either* system. If we must use the Morse Code, we have only long and short buzzes to play with, and cannot add fairly-long and fairly-short buzzes to reach the variety of the quartit; therefore a given message takes longer to transmit. And so on: the practical alternatives proliferate, because the *rate* of transmission can be speeded up — provided that the 'lines' can stand the pace, and that the receiving transducers can decode at equivalent speed. The length of silences can be altered too, as they are between buzzes in Morse to create a single letter, or to distinguish letter-groups: which means that under sufficiently careful definition, Morse transmits quartits after all .... To sum up so far (which means in terms of a binary distinction between the Tenth Theorem and Requisite Variety) Ashby's Law is the more general principle when applied to communication channels, since the trade-off between transmission-time and signal-complexity is not implicitly pre-empted by the choice of a particular base such as the binary digit. But to say so as a criticism of Shannon would be as absurd as it would be laughable, since the very source-book quoted begins with Shannon's examining various numerical bases for achieving intelligible communication. Obviously *any* numerical base could be used, such as a decimal base, or the base *e*, or 26 (considered as the number of alphabetic characters). The base 2 has many advantages (see my *Cybernetics and Management,* Reference B5). But none of this, although it fosters broader thinking in the domain of technical transmission, has yet faced the problem of semantic communication at all.

The burgeoning crisis in the A-B-C intersect will proliferate variety in country X, and Party A knows it. It therefore formulates a plan, the name of which is O (pronounced 'zero'), which it intends to put into action in country X if certain conditions — which it lumps together under the heading of 'the criterion of stability' — are negated. Plan O, we must observe has no hope of success unless it can proliferate variety at the same rate as the crisis: this statement is true, independently of channel capacities, as was seen in (i). Suppose, now, that the crisis deepens. Remotely — in country A — a finger hovers over a button which controls a transmission line sounding a continuous buzz. If the button is pressed, that buzz will change to silence: Plan O goes into operation. The communication system is logically binary, and handles only one bit of information. In practical terms, it had better incorporate redundancy: for example, the button might have to be pressed ten times at regular intervals. This would convey 10 bits of information, instead of the necessary one bit, which is enough channel capacity to discriminate a variety of 1024, rather than 2. Then a mistake due to noise in the system ('what was that again? Did you say Zero?') has a thousandfold protection. But this kind of discussion still concerns variety inside the wiring of the channel, and not the semantic variety of the message.

The *semantic* variety transmitted by the one bit (or, for protection by the Tenth Theorem, ten bits) is the entire variety of Plan O. This could specify a million states; it could specify a billion. How much variety it releases in Country A to deal with a crisis is determined entirely by the ability of the designers of Plan O to foresee the complexity of the crisis in advance. It has nothing whatever to do with the channel capacity of the link, whether Shannon-protected or not, in the sense of the mathematical theory of communication, so long as that one bit, the transition from 1 (the buzz) to

(Plan) O *can be conveyed.* This example, simplification though it be, draws the further distinction that we needed. It also reminds us to realize through those last italics, that the channel's very existence is under threat in any crisis: wires may be cut, emissaries captured, radio signals jammed. The Compleat Cybernetician, therefore, will not hesitate to draw on the genius of Ashby as well as of Shannon, and will certainly be found designing redundancy into the anastomotic reticulum between-channels as well as into the transmission lines within-channels. A review of the Chilean code system to which reference was made just now makes clear all these distinctions:

(a) Each code enabled the use of a variety attenuated channel, since a (say) five-state element in the code could specify a (say) fifty-state element in the crisis (this is what 'encoding' means);

(b) the channel capacity (Shannon-sense) of any one transmission line handled the variety (Ashby-sense) of the code, as a product of a time-epoch and an alphabet of symbols (such as 'one bit each half-second equals one quartit each second') — or in this case, one discrete and discreet letter selected a message from an adaptive range of possible alternatives;

(c) the channel capacity (Shannon-sense) of the entire reticulum could not be calculated, because it was (a) anastomic by structure, and (b) semantic by the inferences it entailed. Thus if this channel capacity were treated as calculable, then in crisis it would not necessarily work — because the self-organizing demands of the reticulum may in principle exceed *any* finite limit;

(d) the adequacy of the entire reticulum as generating a regulatory model (Ashby-sense) could be calculated in terms of the variety it could encode (onto the sensory plate) balanced against the variety that could be decoded from it (via the motor plate) solely in terms of homeostatic equilibrium within the burgeoning crisis — when the loop was closed;

(e) since any one channel leading to or from the reticulum is invariably under threat, both as to its physical existence and as to the integrity of its code, other channels and other codes need to be used, and in this case there were three of each;

(f) the redundancy built into the system presupposed that the three channels intersected at crucial nodes of decision.

As far as the exemplification of these arguments through the Chilean codes is concerned, the dangers and difficulties seem to have been equally spread between the three channels. The first failure, put down earlier to psychological traumata, occurred in the (a), (b) domains above. The second channel worked, but would shortly have failed in the (d) domain. The third success derived, I think by accident, from an *open-ended* coding system which operated very well in the crucial (c) domain — even though it eventually collapsed under its own proliferated complexity. The over-riding failure (mine) was in the (e),(f) domains: this aspect is well worth cybernetic rumination.

The criterion at (f) was taken — all too uncritically — as fulfilled. The people concerned were very close friends; and this seemed (in advance) to mean that their variety would be multiplicative. If each agreed with the other two, that is to say, that the semantic meaning and variety explosion of each of three messages in different codes was the same, then the protection of the motor action's informational integrity and operational validity would be huge. It would be especially large, if each of the three channels had each of the three codes. That would be good cybernetics but bad tactics: obviously, it is very dangerous to the individual (and to any operational plans of the group) to have more detailed knowledge than she/he needs to fulfil a single role, in a crisis that involves armed insurrection. Therefore I made each code specific to one channel, and did not even divulge to any one of the three that there were two others. This led to (f)-type failure, and was therefore a mistake of metasystemic proportions. It is a mistake that I would repeat for the reason given — but seeking meanwhile alternative means of circumventing the difficulty to which it gave rise in (f).

This anecdote about the Chilean codes is recorded not merely for the sake of completeness, nor to embroider a tragic event with trivial flourishes. If people could only see, when locked in conflict, that the distinctions drawn here apply to them and to their situation, *detente* would mean more than airport embraces. As to societary conflict in the post-industrial age: there are always at least three parties (management, workers, government) to a dispute, which makes the customary binary logic inappropriate; and there is a whole range of models and codes in continuous use — which it is not within anyone's interest (or perhaps competence) to acknowledge. Can it be, then, that political naivety is a characteristic of politics itself, rather than of commentators or those who intervene, much as economic naivety is characteristic of economics itself? We cannot of course advert to military naivety in the same terms, because this brand of childishness leaves all the protagonists dead.

In developing Figure 48 into Figure 49, further problems of apparent naivety arise: and that is why these preliminary explanations have been given and commentary made on them. In order to penetrate further into the mechanisms that underly Figure 48, which derived from Figures 6 and 7, we need to see the relevance of control theory in engineering, and to draw on Figure 8 and its accompanying discussion. Here now is the specification for the bridge of understanding that has to be constructed in the mind: the realities of political crisis proliferate enormous variety, which defeats any attempt to depict the anastomotic reticulum that houses the invariants that underlie this complicated behaviour. The bridge crosses from the apparently too chaotic, a tangled skein that beggars description, to the apparently laconic, a few lines and symbols without manifest richness, and back again. The cybernetician spends a professional lifetime walking this bridge; without it she/he may be trapped in a state that is either irrelevant because too spare at one end of the bridge, or otiose because engulfed at the other. Let us try the walk.

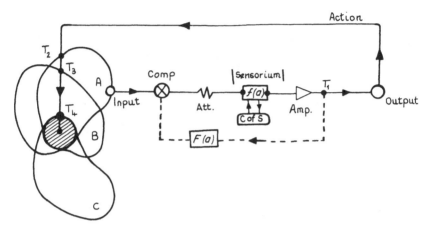

Figure 49. (Compare Figures 6, 7, 8, and 48)

Figure 49 redraws its predecessor, and omits the attenuating connexion that stands for a loss of variety in learning about the nature of the crisis initially, since this has already been discussed at length. The single transmission line that runs from 'input' to 'output' conveys the information that produces action; and we know that this is *not* a single line in reality, but a mass of tangled cabling. Each strand of it is under threat — as to its physical existence, its probity, its susceptibility to be 'noisy', and its internal lack of redundancy. Each strand, then, in the Shannon-sense is a poor risk as a transmitter of valid data; and the tangled cable itself, despite its mostly accidental redundancy, will not offer much improvement — because it has not been properly designed as a redundant net to protect its power to inform. Even so, we are not now primarily concerned with these defects, but with those that attenuate variety. Is it in the nature of the channel that constitutes any strand in the cable to preserve variety, in the Ashby-sense that it can discriminate between all the states of the system that the crisis proliferates? The answer to this is no. And this is the reason why variety is shown as attenuating on the way from its input-in-A to the sensorium, where the conceptual model is now represented as the feed-forward function of the system. Justification for the negative answer could be offered at this stage of the description, but it will be much easier to understand when the description is complete.

The feed-forward function *f(a)* is necessarily a function so complicated that it can never be accurately specified in terms of the unknown equations connecting the myriad unknown variables that the anastomotic reticulum includes and manipulates. This does not mean to say that it cannot be accurately specified at all. Certainly it can; for the sensorium is a black box which operates on an input to produce an output, and (consult the definitions of Chapter 2) the feedforward function is simply the ratio of these two. But, it might well be asked: in this very-high-variety crisis, and amid all the chaos, how can this ratio possibly be labelled 'simple'? How can it even be conceived of as a consistent function at all, when this black box could be merely a random number generator — a box that absorbs inputs, ignores them, and capriciously issues arbitrary outputs? The answer to this question is: well said. The debate enshrines a truth worthy of its few paragraphs.

The sensorium houses a conceptual model, the pattern of operation of which as a decision-taker *constitutes* the feedforward function. We saw in (i) that this model does not have requisite variety. This is precisely why it is able to behave with consistency. In the diagram there appears a solid black dot at the point where 'input' is **transduced** into the sensorium. The transduction involves a homomorphic many-one mapping of the variety. That is to say: input variety (already attenuated though it will be) will again be attenuated insofar as the conceptual regulatory model cannot contain it.

Suppose for example, that we were expected to take action of some kind in response to a scene full of elaborately changing colour patterns, when a certain feature became a particular shade of yellow. If we were forced to survey this scene through a screen of glass filters that reduced the scene to primary colours, then the transmission line would not have requisite variety to distinguish the particular shade of yellow concerned. We should make many errors; but at least all our outputs would be yellow — rather than (say) red. Next suppose that a witch appeared and transformed us into dogs. These dogs have no retinal cone cells, and their conceptual model of the scene is without colour altogether: it is composed in chiaroscuro. Then the mapping of our particular shade of yellow would coincide in our model with shades of other colours as well, at some equivalent level of greyness. This illustration is meant to show that, independently of variety attenuation in the transmission, variety is lost in transduction into the sensorium — because the transducer may recognize only that variety which the conceptual model itself can discriminate.

It follows therefore for Party A that the variety of its own model *decides* the variety of the crisis. Then the reason why its feedforward function is a relatively simple and consistent input/output ratio is because input variety has been attenuated in initial perception, *and* in transmission, *and* finally in recognition within the conceptual model. No wonder that 'better dead than red'; no wonder that this-or-that ethnic group is wicked, while that-and-this ethnic group (namely 'us') is impeccable. And, in the limit: if even these dichotomizing tricks should fail, so that the cumulative effect of the three variety-attenuators just mentioned should result in no-pattern-at-all, however crude, then the sensorium is reduced to a variety of ONE. Something, rather than nothing, has occurred. There is a crisis — but it has no pattern, it is incomprehensible. No wonder, then, that there should sometimes be a random response, as earlier predicted. Yet even this is subject to bias, when we are dealing with viable systems. For the 'random' response has a value in a metasystemic calculus: that of survival itself. Thus we may expect the response that was foreseen to be random to verge toward the catatonic. There is more survival-value in lying low, when you have no idea as to what may be going on, than in leaping on a horse 'and riding off in all directions'.

The next step in the process is strange indeed. It is, as the diagram shows, a variety amplifier — and an amplifier of very high gain. Consider: there is a basic requirement, as argued in (i) — which spoke of a need 'in very principle' — to balance the variety equation across the sensory-motor anastomotic reticulum, because of the pertinence of Ashby's Law within the crisis — given that the regulatory loop is closed. Everything so far discussed about the loop that provides the channels to this end (from a continuous registration of crisis within the hatched area, through the input-at-A, to the model represented by the feedforward function $f(a)$, diminished as it in turn is by subjection to an Established criterion of stability) has led in product to a huge attenuation of variety in the conceptual model. The self-organizing viable system, because it is also self-conscious, recognizes this attenuation. Probably it has no real insight into how that attenuation arose; and that is why we often speak in such circumstances, not of 'a reaction' but of 'over-reaction'. The high-gain variety amplifier over-reacts, because it is 'frightened by Ashby', in the same sense that someone leaning over the rail of the observation platform on top of a skyscraper may be 'frightened by Newton' — and leap backwards, instead of merely withdrawing.

The argument is that the simplifications embedded in the regulatory model deprive it of requisite variety, in recognition of which that variety is ostensibly but not actually restored — essentially by *shouting*. This is not to confuse sound amplification with variety amplification. By declaring a monumental platitude or a crude oversimplification with conviction and an air of authority, the politician seeks to convey the impression that since obviously nothing could be *that* naive, it isn't. There are hidden depths in the underlying conceptual model, comes the implication, which you would not understand, or which it is not in the national interest to divulge. At any rate, says the tacit message, our model can match the variety proliferated by the crisis. It cannot; and the fact that the claim is spurious is often signalled by the hectoring attitude of the speaker, bolstered as it sometimes is by phrases such as: *for heaven's sake; everyone knows* ...; and that favourite North American version, *aw c'm'on now*. They tell us that the regulatory model in *f(a)* does not enjoy requisite variety.

Now if the action taken in the crisis were to be based on the output of this forward transmission line as described, serious mistakes would certainly be made. Then we shall invoke the capabilities of an error-controlled negative-feedback servomechanism (as described in Figure 8, its accompanying text, and the mathematical note at the end of that same Chapter Two). Output is compared with input, as indicated in Figure 49 by the circle with cross inscribed, to generate a signal measuring error that is added in to the forward transmission, according to a set of rules embodied in a feedback function *F(a)*. We saw in Chapter Two the circumstances in which the feedback loop comes to dominate the whole circuit, and the claim was advanced that thanks to its operation 'the output signals will be of greater 'purity' than we had any right to expect' when the input is noisy (as in this case it was demonstrated to be). In the context of crisis analysis, however, this protective device seems not to work properly — maybe because it does not exist. If it does exist, then its operation seems to be counterproductive — in that crises so often tend towards increasing instability and eventual explosion, rather than to damping and eventual equilibrium.

It will perhaps be remembered that the conceptual model informing the forward function *f(a)* is chosen, not because it offers the best available representation of the world, but because it is competent to effect the change within the mores that are acceptable to those in charge. The discovery of a great truth might not be amenable to registration in this conceptual model, simply because *discoveries* are *new;* then the 'great truth' would have no capacity to engage in changing anything. By the same token: the only *F(a)* feedback function that can be heard by the action-taking process on the forward line, must be using a model of *lower variety* than that in use by the conceptual model in *f(a)*. Unfortunately from a cybernetic standpoint that seeks stability, if fortunately for the freedom of speech, such a feedback function does exist — and is indeed counterproductive towards stability. It is, quite clearly, provided by the mass media. They amplify variety in the spurious sense defined above, thereby making the total dynamic system depicted in Figure 49 as dangerously explosive as we know it to be, and as unequipped with requisite variety to handle crisis as we feared. For the variety generated by the crisis is likely to proliferate with time, whereas the 'matching' variety of the regulative mechanism here described must resolutely fall.

(iii) Transducers neither Attenuate nor Amplify Variety

The transduction role has already been mentioned several times in examining the crisis would-be regulator. It is worth a reminder that transducers come into action whenever information has to be encoded or decoded in the course of crossing a boundary in the system, and that a properly designed transducer will have no effect on the richness of variety transduced. In fact, each of the transducers (solid black dots) so far considered has failed this test of good design, and the group of them next to be discussed — which is not designed at all in a free society — seems to be responsible for the problems enunciated at the end of the last section. The members of the group are marked on Figure 49 as T_1, T_2, T_3, and T_4. Trouble begins when information is transduced into the feedback circuit at T_1. Now this transducer, which controls the conceptual model housed in the feedback function $F(a)$, was in the past — even fifty years ago — designed as part of the diplomatic regulator. It probably did preserve the variety carried in the forward transmission; and perhaps it even protected the total crisis-regulator against noise in the input as it is supposed, control-theoretically, to do. But now, as has been said, it appears to have been superseded by a T_1 supplied by the mass media. Or perhaps it would be more accurate to say that the reaction-time of the media is so short that the putatively designed diplomatic element does not have time to take the initiative. Such an hypothesis would account for a role-reversal whose general acceptance seems even stranger than its general appearance — in the West, as will shortly be examined.

At any rate, it seems in practice impossible to separate, within the compass of the crisis regulator whose structure we are attempting to understand, diplomatic transduction from that of the mass media, because each seeks to outwit and to pre-empt the other — or so it appears to the public, and therefore to the astute politician (whether she/he is personally confused by the entanglement or not). For example, statements made by foreign governments or by foreign embassies involved in crisis, are habitually anticipated by the media in advance — whereupon they exert part of their effect, before they are emphatically not-made — because they cannot be un-made — by a denial. Nor is this to do with the speed of response alone, but also with its format — that is to say with the unsurprising dominance of the media by television. It is worth recalling that the processes of the waking brain devote unparalleled activity to visual input as evidenced by the vast variety-capacity at and behind the retina, along the optic nerve, and within the occipital lobe of the cortex. Socially, too, the amazing proportion of time devoted to viewing broadcasts by the average citizen must assuredly lead to an acceptance of the *variety structure* of editorial viewpoint. Views themselves are commonly contested, that is true; and this is taken to be a sign of a free society. But both the richness and connectivity of variety transduced by T_1 will necessarily inform the conceptual model housed in the feedback function $F(a)$, thereby not only making it impossible to register the 'great new truth', but forcing the practical politician to work within a variety-impoverished model imposed on him or her. And woe betide that politician who tries to amplify variety at this point: answers drawn from a richer variety-source must sound (and look) evasive, or blinding-with-science, or daft — but in any case they will be incomprehensible. This seems the sufficiently clear reason why politicians are led away from honest enquiry in public utterance, and towards the naive appeal to 'good sense' and so forth. They must work within the available variety structure; and rely on charisma to generate bogus variety of the kind earlier discussed.

It is from this perversion of the feedback loop — its transduction at T_1, its conceptual modelling and consequential transformation at $F(a)$, and its ultimate dominance of the forward process that leads to action by a decreasingly adequate variety structure — that the disasters derive. First comes the role-reversal in governance. Predictably and observably: politicians are compelled to offer instant response to burgeoning crisis, in terms of a variety-impoverished model, for propagation through a regulatory system that does not exhibit requisite variety. They seek to create extra variety by hectoring; but the variety is bogus, and unless they are extremely astute they are made to look silly. For at this point the 'investigative journalists' (unelected, unaccountable), who have foisted the impoverished variety structure of the feedback function onto the public in the first place, assume the watchdog role of keeper of the public conscience — a role in which the (elected, accountable) politician was originally cast.

Well, however penetrating or otherwise this commentary may be, it seems to be a cybernetic fact that the central feedback system of Figure 49 is not going to function as a damping device: it will accelerate explosion, if we are not extremely careful. Then if role-reversal in governance is the first effect, which is (despite its general acceptability) cybernetically bizarre, the final effect is probably ... war. This is as true of these processes within the family as it is of the human condition at large, as true within the firm as it is within the nation. Folk are fearful that this will be the outcome, because of the violence and belligerence that they see all around them — especially on television. Their explanations for it are mediated through the low-variety structures that are to hand; and because those structures are cybernetically incompetent, the explanations feed the fear and thereby exacerbate the risk.

All this is said of the transducer T_1: perhaps, then equivalently lengthy analyses will be needed to account for the performance of transducers T_2, T_3, and T_4 in Figure 49. There are two answers to this expectation. These three transducers govern the decoding of 'action' information into the phase spaces of the three parties to the crisis — respectively, A, B, and C. Since we have not attempted to say precisely what unites these parties in their common intersect (the hatched area, where the crisis has germinated), or what divides them (each and severally, according to the diagram), they have the same cybernetic status. Each owns a dedicated phase space transducer; and its coding facility depends firstly on the distinctive qualities of the Party serviced. However: they are all alike in sharing the 'action' input to the crisis determined by the output of the regulatory system so far discussed. It is in this respect that they are of such major interest. The detailed *information* encoded and decoded by each of these transducers will heavily depend on the subtlety of the languages available to parties A, B, and C. But the *variety* transduced (which may be attenuated or spuriously amplified by any T) is that variety — and only that variety — preserved at the 'output' stage of the servomechanism recently described. Nuance can be projected into a sufficiently subtle language, but **only** if the variety is built into the transducer that will service the whole range of nuances from which this nuance is selected.

It is this fact that makes it unnecessary to distinguish between the transducers T_2, T_3, and T_4. But doubtless the second expectation was that this little set is markedly different from the feedback transducer T_1, to which so much attention has been devoted; because it sits in the field of affairs, close to the crisis domain, whereas T_1 is part of a regulatory feedback loop that 'belongs' to Party A. This is an incorrect reading — *because the whole system is closed.* T_2-T_3-T_4 and T_1 belong to the same circuit, which is closed through the crisis (as at Figure 48). Hence, over a period of time, and whatever *information* may be flowing round this circuit, and transducing into whatever languages at whichever points, the *variety* of T_1 and T_2 and T_3 and T_4 will tend to equate. This is due to systemic entropy. The negentropy that would be needed to offset this tendency is unrelated to the data-flow within the servomechanism and its transduction into crisis-related information; it is related to the information that distinguishes requisite variety in the conceptual models. Once this is clearly perceived, it will be apparent that the remaining transducers on the circuit (already discussed) belong to the group as well. Thus we have cohesion — a pleasing solidarity, if you will, on behalf of all components to constitute a unitary system. As constituted, however, it has a fatal flaw.

Variety, like any other constructive variable in our universe tends to leak away, unless it is specifically boosted, like a charge on a capacitor. This leakage should be expected to destroy complexity and effective organization, inducing impotence for survival, on a negatively exponential curve. Quite soon, therefore, there may be only one bit of uncertainty left in any crisis. We have met exactly this situation before, in a more sanguine context. It was in Chapter Fourteen, where the multinode was in charge of such a process, deliberately contrived and intended as an aid to controlled decision. In the current analysis, responsibility has been abdicated to an accelerating feedback loop, and the power to decide has been lost to caprice. When the last bit of uncertainty vanishes in any crisis, whether by change of by the intervention of god or devil, the die is cast. The outcome is success or failure, life or death, peace or war, survival or annihilation — depending on the system concerned. It is pity indeed that humankind might lose its prerogative to intervene, simply through a failure to understand the cybernetics of the system; pity too to entertain so strange a fate because of its own prowess in the speed and the slickness of global communication. The picture, even so, becomes yet more complicated, yet more disturbing, in its final phase.

(iv) The time cycle is synchronous for all subsystems

We have so far considered the regulatory system of a crisis from the standpoint of one party (a) of three, and as if just one regulatory model would 'condense'. But as many models will condense as there are interest groups to pay attention to the world situation under consideration. The diagrams at Figures 48 and 49 indicate the existence of three parties actually implicated in the burgeoning crisis, and in the final diagram all three will be considered as subsystems of the larger system that has that 'crisis' name. But it ought to be noticed that each of the three subsystems acknowledges subsystems; and that there is consequently a whole raft of difficulties to be resolved under the recursion theorem of the viable system. These difficulties have to be resolved, that is to say, in any specific application of managerial cybernetics. They cannot be resolved in general principle; even so there are general principles that bear on them. Consider firstly the role of the sub-systems . . . .

The government is not homogeneous — it has its 'wings', and so has the political party. By the same token, still less is parliament homogeneous; less still again, the public itself. And typically, every aspect of organized society — from financial people in the City to business exporters, from trade union enclaves to soccer clubs, from one learned profession to another — will each be forming its own model of any crisis that impinges on them all. It is just because there is a plurality of models, and known to be so, that each model loses intrinsic variety in the attempt to *condense* it to the point where it is recognizable to its adherents, and distinguishable from the rest. That is to say that although the process of consensus for each group of model builders aims at revealing the highest common factor between them, it is likely to produce the lowest common multiple. Maybe this was one of the tragedies of Allende's Unidad Popular in Chile: vital synergy was thereby lost. Once again we must note that this 'process' is not a sustained and rigorous procedure to which all subscribers to the model are dedicated; yet more possible states of the system become blurred one with another . . . . Variety is as usual, because of entropy, running into the sand.

Three models only are depicted in all these diagrams, although (as argued above) there are in principle many more. Needless to say, the models interact with each other, as opposing points of view are debated and given public airing. These are depicted in the new diagram, Figure 50, the basis of which is the triplication of Figure 49.

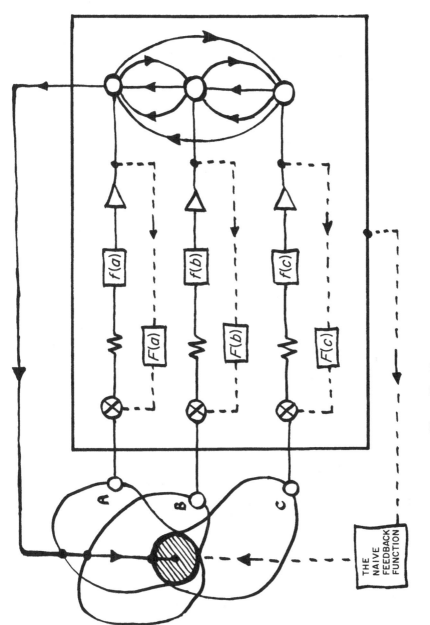

Figure 50. (Compare Figure 49)

Now if we consider any one of the three stages of the total interaction, we may follow its output along the action route to its effect on the crisis, noting its transduction into the phase spaces of its own and the other two Parties on the way. The action route appears to be shared between all three outputs, and this is not only a matter of diagrammatic convenience. The total picture deals with a *continuous* crisis; all loops shown in the diagram tend to be in synchrony, because a time cycle is imposed upon everyone by the rhythm of the working day as it moves around the globe with the sunlight. Thus the three regulators are indeed compelled to share the available public channels simultaneously, unless any one of them refuses to make public utterance as a matter of policy. The technique is interesting: in constructing this model, I have often noted this strategy's disruptive effect on the escalation of crisis. It ought indeed to produce detente; but it runs the risks that silence will look sinister, or appear as a sign that 'we have got them on the run'. Again the low structural variety of the media model is threatening.

In any case, however, it will remain difficult to be sure which of the three regulators has produced a specific effect in such circumstances, and the diagram shows two-way interactions between each output and the other two. These loops are modifiers of potential action rather than conversational channels, and it seems only rarely that any protagonist will break such a loop. It has to be an act of courage or bravado to do so ('regardless of your options for action, *I* do *this*'), and the insight that can recognize which is which is a valuable asset. The policies of Unidad Popular in Chile can be studied in this light; and the judgment seems to depend upon the judge's recognition of the historical perspectives within which those policies were formulated. It is all too easy to make judgments based on one's own sense of appropriate time scales, not to mention the value subjectively put on self-preservation; but these will tell you only that had *you* made a particular stand it would have been an act of courage or bravado. The same issue (*mutatis mutandis*) is observable in all major crises: for example, a government declares to its people that there will be (say) three dreadful years of recession while inflationary spirals are checked, after which comes the new economic dawn. Whether this announcement, which ignores the loops denoting continuous modification of potential action, is courageous or stupid depends less on the wisdom of the policy itself than on the likelihood that a government espousing that policy will last three years.

The model of crisis is completed by the addition, in Figure 50, of the large rectangular box which encapsulates all the regulatory mechanisms that have so far been discussed. This indicates the existence of a *second-order* model, or metamodel, which takes account of everything that is going on, and gives rise to the over-riding naive political feedback that was noted at the start of this section. This ultimate regulator of the system is, like its contained sub-regulators, a device compounded of diplomatic and political and media-generated elements, in inseparable admixture. The people concerned are the first indication that such a metasystem exists. The diplomats and politicians that belong on this loop are not emissaries and foreign secretaries acting in that capacity: they are *world statesmen*. The media-people who belong on this loop are not the reporters-on-the-spot and the newsreaders at home: they are *masterminds of global compass*. These two small groups interview each other on television in searching programmes of high prestige, capturing large audiences of influential people, which often last for as long an an hour. The second indication that this metasystem exists is yet more compelling: the models housed in the naive feedback have much *larger* scope, and far *less* structural variety than those of the ABC sub-regulators.

The history of the nineteen-seventies will indelibly record the activities of world-statesman Dr Henry Kissinger on this loop, acting as a regulator operating a model enshrining structural variety of either three or five — as he has been at pains to point out. As Chairman of the forty Committee that allocated the funds for 'destabilizing' Chile (see Reference 6), he knew how Latin America looked through such attenuating filters; and he knew how the Middle East looked too, in his role as door-to-door mediator there. On the media side of this classical symbiosis, Mr David Frost will not be forgotten, because his image will constantly reappear on archival videotapes of the period. The structural variety of the models he projects is also very low, limited as it has to be by an hour's-length of channel capacity and an international size A4 clipboard. These invocations of two personalities are briefly made to illustrate the theme, rather than to scorn those mentioned. People in the hot seats of international counsel all have the problem of grappling with inordinate variety, and of reducing that to a level at which 'the people' can ostensibly decide: whether by electing this or that president, paying for a budget without civil disobedience, and so forth — which, in the limit, may mean going to war. But, in fairness to them, those in other vocations do the same thing, perhaps in all cases because there seems to be no choice: the individual, as audience, supplicant, slave, or citizen has limited variety with which to absorb variety bombardment from all sources. Hence to the would-be saviours of the world: *variety is rationed*. It is so much more plausible for a government minister to manage to act on a monetarist theory of the economy, rather than to enjoin the cybernetic penetration of its effective organization; because the monetarist model has such low structural variety. It is so much more attractive for people to manage and act out a daily twenty-minute period of transcendental meditation, rather than to change every aspect of their world-views and behaviour; because 'instant nirvana' has such low structural variety. Thus Dr Friedman and the Maharishi will also figure in the archives of the 'seventies'.

Whether low-variety participation by every humble human being in the world's destiny, in global communication, in economic control, in spiritual sanctity, or in anything else, is what she/he ought to be engaged in, should be a matter for the individual. If there is any teaching to be done, it is perhaps in guidance to that end. Because the human resource in this incarnation, namely in terms of time and neurons, space and energy, is finite, it can easily be spread too thin. The worst, because utterly meretricious, form of such bare existence is determined for us by the Naive Filter. Perhaps there is no withstanding its employment and effect, though each of us may try to withstand by withholding consent, and by concentrating personal variety on the issues she/he selects rather than those selected by the filters. But for the majority to withdraw from those crises that beset the behaviour of our species would open a rapid route to universal oppression by the remainder. It seems to follow that the investigation of the cybernetics of crisis is worthwhile, and might eventually lead to the design of more effective mechanisms than we have now for containing it. In the meantime, a model such as that presented here should offer a basis for interpreting tendencies in the escalation of crisis in systemic terms.

Here for example is a series of five comments that derive from a perception of the total model, working in its synchronous cyclic mode. It gains cohesion and develops meaning when viewed against the background of the cybernetic structure now completed.

- The metamodel that generates the naive feedback function necessarily reduces the sum of the structural variety which is generated by all the models that have so far condensed within it. This is simply because the space and time available to the media to communicate the composite metamodel cannot be adequate to report in equivalent detail all the alphabets of internationally-fraught trouble spots at any one time; there must on average be a variety attenuation at this point. In particular instances the mass media will make a special effort to preserve the variety inherent in the collection of sub-models, if only to combat the contention that they dangerously oversimplify the issues. But they face a dilemma of their own: the more the variety of one world situation is deployed to the various publics, the less time and space is available for others. Thus in the effort to avert the charge of oversimplification of some issues, the expectation has to be that they will not only have to oversimplify but actually to *polarize* others. And this expectation is certainly fulfilled on many occasions — when, for instance, the public finds that its only choice is to decide whether a particular and newly emerged national leader with a revolutionary government in some distant country is 'good' or 'bad', and of course that its choice has been made for it by the slant of a two-minute presentation.

● When the naive feedback function impinges on the crisis itself, it changes all the *information* flowing through the system, but more especially its *variety*. This will change the character of all the transducers, attenuators and amplifiers, which must perform their functions in terms of an ever-diminishing power of discrimination. The system will soon be galloping round its own loops at an ever increasing pace — driven on and gaining momentum by infuriated responses to its very naivety. Here then are the dynamics of the polarizing tendency referred to in the previous point. As to the synchronicity of all sub-regulators, it seems to impart a 'beat resonance' to the development of events; and that can in theory (and for instance in practice when flying a helicopter) shake the system to pieces.

● The cybernetic regulatory system as described runs primarily on the analysis of options as recognized within and elucidated by regulatory models that do not display requisite variety. Insofar as this process is fed by inspired leakages from the supposed seats of power, this apparently journalistic activity could be regarded as a form of decision or action on the part of a government itself. It is noteworthy that what would strictly *be* a political decision ('they shall not pass') or a political action ('send a gunboat') is frequently avoided by its simulation through the low-variety models of these regulatory loops. In itself, this has cathartic effect. But the situation that is depicted in these quasi-imaginary terms stands to break down — because the regulator does not contain an adequate model of that which it seeks to regulate. This circumstance would appear to increase the likelihood of both covert action (which, so long as it remains covert, is not susceptible to this system of naive filtration), and of surprise action (namely that action which the system did not envisage and cannot therefore handle). Covert action by the United States throughout the Chilean story, which has been freely admitted by now and documented, is an example of the former; the Entebbe raid by Israel on Uganda is an outstanding example of the latter.

● When because of the entropic drift that steadily erodes variety in this crisis regulator, polarization is eventually induced (because no more than two states of the system can now be discriminated), it may be recognized by agonizing displays of insincerity. These arise because the induced dichotomy is spurious. The rights of neither pole can be discussed rationally, and therefore become the subject of 'moral' stance, and outpourings of sanctimonious 'ethical' dicta. This is not to argue that there can be no such thing as a genuine ethical position: there can. But if ethical stands which appear to be based on value judgments are in fact generated merely by differences in the premises of the models that have been inadequately constructed and meretriciously purveyed, then this would explain their apparent insincerity — in that politicians palpably adopt inconsistent ethical standards from one world crisis to the next. This has recently become a scandal of such proportions that (I suggest) no morality will sustain its credibility for much longer. What then will become of the motivation to warfare? It would be naive indeed to answer: peace.

● Finally, there is one very simple consequence (aside from war itself) of the systematic loss of systemic variety as the process depicted in Figure 50 unfolds. The crisis generates possibilities within the world situation of such complexity that they cannot even be *expressed* within the model structures made available. Thus all possible solutions to the problem are rendered unacceptable to at least one faction. This is, I think, outstandingly true of the apparently endless war of attrition in Northern Ireland. And it has to be conceded that the same point could be made about Allende's problem in unifying his own coalition.

These comments complete the present account of the cybernetics of crisis. The whole exposition of this model has been put forward under four headings, which were introduced many pages ago as 'four major cybernetic requirements' of homeostatic stability. To recapitulate:

(i)   The system is obedient to Ashby's Law of Requisite Variety;
(ii) Information channels maintain variety entrusted to them;
(iii) Transducers neither attenuate nor amplify variety;
(iv) The time cycle is synchronous for all subsystems.

The extent to which a self-organizing system recognizes these requirements, seeks to obey them, flouts them (by accident or design), and finally achieves its come-uppance at their instigation, will indeed determine that system's viability. The outlook, by these tokens, for crisis regulation must be adjudged bleak.

These four requirements were drawn respectively from the four Principles of Organization enunciated in this book's companion volume, *The Heart of Enterprise*. They are exemplifications of those general principles.

The model offered here, however, is merely a start in elaborating the cybernetics of crisis. In working on it, a haunting question has been in the forefront of my vision. It is an important quesion, and one attending all utterances that could be labelled 'managerial cybernetics'.

If it is naive to reduce the variety of real-life crises by employing attenuators of the kind described (which, for example, include the use of pungent variety-destroyers such as sarcasm and dramatic irony); then is it not also naive and indeed equivalently dangerous, to propose relatively simple models of crisis regulation (using, on recent occasion, somewhat similar expository tricks)?

I wish precisely to restate two fundamental tenets of any science, of which cybernetics is an example: that all natural processes exhibit formal invariances; and that the corpus of scientific knowledge is composed of statements which not only state but suitably constrain such invariant relations within the compass of their applicability. In this book (then in seeking to disclose a model of any viable system) and in this section of the book (then in seeking to disclose a model of societary crisis) vast amounts of variety have been discarded. This has sometimes been done explicitly, as for example by dismissing it in sarcasm or dramatic irony; but usually it has been done implicitly, by privately selecting what should be included in, and what excluded from, the developing models. If mistakes have been made, the models can be tested — to destruction. They seem to me to be useful; but they are cheerfully submitted to Popperian criteria of disproof. This is not true of the variety reduction engaged in by crisis manipulators themselves. *They are not seeking invariances.* If I went on to say what they are seeking, it could be called an expository trick; but they themselves neither doubt nor deny the pragmatic values to which they answer, and on behalf of which variety is justifiably axed to the bone.

Perhaps this statement will dismiss Banquo's ghost, the spectre of less-than-requisite variety, from the cybernetic feast: I hope so. But I shall end this section on the cybernetics of crisis with a reference to another spectre, and another feast.

Soon after the beginning of the work in Chile in 1971, and I think that the date was in January 1972, the Chilean government formally applied to the British government for financial aid — under an existing scheme — in support of all that we were intending to do. This was not my application; and I even refused to endorse it. I had travelled eight thousand miles to work independently of my familiar friends in England, the 'can't-be-doners' of those days. This I explained in Santiago; but I did not try actually to veto this alarming proposal: considerable hard-currency sums were due to be spent in England, after all, in projects, salaries, and equipment.

The Chilean request must have been duly processed, because I eventually found myself having lunch in London with an officer of the Department of Overseas Aid. He wanted to know how things were going, and I told him how they had gone. The work had been on course. Unfortunately, exactly ten days earlier there had been an armed insurrection. President Allende, thousands of his friends, and some of mine had been killed. Every life and every freedom was at risk. The long-cherished tradition of democracy and constitutional government in Chile had been brought to an abrupt halt. The project, after two dramatic years, was over. The gentleman actually asked why.

We have been discussing naivety. We could map this incident onto the model. Who was naive? Was it the Chilean government, who asked for support — two years too soon? Was it the British government, who could not understand what the support was for — until ten days too late? Was it the government of the United States, who funded the *coup d'état*? Or was it I, who paid for the lunch?

The Cybernetics of Progress

In Chapter 15, before the 'old book' concluded, lessons learned from the operation of the ascending reticular formation of the brain stem were applied to the notion of *behavioural modes*. There is a small number of basic modes, it was argued, and an organization that is a viable system will lock onto one of them at a time. The first three that were distinguished belong to what has usually been considered as 'normal' behaviour. Of these, the first was 'normal' normality: sustained activity. On either side of this, steady growth or steady retrenchment from the norm could also be regarded as 'normal', the three modes forming a coherent scale. The other three modes considered could not be regarded as exhibiting normal behaviour at all. They were the crisis, the moribund, and the self-destructive modes. In this chapter, the focus has become the crisis mode — for reasons already advanced. And if crisis is indeed our central preoccupation today; if the crisis mode is in a real sense 'normal' now wherever we may turn; then it could be regarded as the potential progenitor of any of the other modes, or unfortunately of a fresh version of itself. That is: systems experiencing crisis, and seeking any escape, may very easily *learn* to subsist in a permanently trapped state. The only recognizable way out is the way back in.

The cybernetic model of crisis completed in the last section was sponsored by the observation that 'normal' behaviour — with its modes of steady, growing or retrenching activity — is today a fiction in which we should like to believe, and not a reality at all. Perhaps the reason why that tripartite model of normalcy is somehow incorporated into our expectations of institutional behaviour, is that a retrospective rationalization of the so-called industrial revolution implanted it in socio-economic theories: theories that our new model would have to call naive. This in turn would be because they all took it for granted that the industrial revolution had at any rate defined Progress. Thus half-way through the couple of hundred years from (say) 1750 under review, the iron-master and the cotton king who believed that Progress would inevitably flow from the deployment and compounding redeployment of invested capital, were in basic agreement with the man who denounced the capitalist system itself as containing the seeds of its own destruction — because both envisaged the road ahead as the Way of Production. Today, when the total work-force is far less a proportion of the total population than it then was (thanks to the better nourishment, general conditions and health care that keep the rest alive), and when less than half of *that* is engaged in production as such (thanks to the rise of the professions and service industries), such a definition of Progress is today decreasingly adequate for the Rich World.

In all fairness, this is currently being recognized by many who seek to redress the oppression and exploitation of peoples, and to abandon the rape of finite planetary resources. But here is a large and challenging BUT: nothing is done to help the Poor World to define Progress in any other terms than those already proven to drive an advance society *moribund,* thence into *crisis,* and thence, quite possibly, into *self-destruction* — rather than back to the erstwhile if only occasional 'normalcy'. Of course there are twin reasons why nothing is done. In the first place, the leaders of modern civilization could not bear to admit, even if they knew, that the values of ancient cultures have greater insight into the human condition than those of latter-day institutional Christianity and the industrial revolution — with their low-variety models of fulfilment. Secondly, if these leaders suddenly declared as much, the Poor World would rise up and kill them.

This is a predictable outcome of all the conditioning that has been applied to both Second and Third World countries over the last hundred-and-more years (which in the Third World means 'for ever' in relation to Rich World dominance). I referred to a challenge: it could prove to be the most fearsome double-bind in the history of humankind, and the explicit detonator of biological extinction. It is a double-bind because Progress has been written into the socio-economic culture in such a way that *not to progress is to regress,* whereas the implanted presumptions about the nature of Progress make Progress *itself regressive.* We follow our technological noses wherever they may be pointing: upwards to the moon, downwards to microbiotic and neurological warfare. We fulfil our energy needs with lethal equipments that threaten our albeit wiser progeny for a million years, and draw the warlike bows whose every quiverful of arrows could single-handedly volatilize the planetary biosphere.

International agencies and firms bring Progress from the Rich World to the Poor. The net effect has always been to widen the economic gap between them. The replacement of venerably and humanly satisfying cultures by the philosophic garbage of the West is reflected in material terms: gadgetry takes over from craft; soap opera and titillation from legend and dance; and bodily nurture through the means of lovingly prepared repasts and feasts gives place to sustenance by junk foods and soda pop. However: infant mortality decreases, life-expectancy rises, 'fair play' is exalted, and — in whatever form it takes — 'the trains run on time'. Besides, and in any case, everyone knows that you can't *stop* Progress — whatever it is.

Progress at the individual level in our culture seems to be the analogue of this. The belief, held in the teeth of all sage counsel since philosophy began, that to amass personal wealth is a proper goal, means that Progress is measured in the possession of goods and the control of services. To be at the appropriate point on that road for one's age and style is the measure of Progress. Yet no-one doubts that there is more to life than this; and therefore there is leisure, which must be properly used. Hence there is Progress also in the proper use of leisure; and it turns out that this too is measured by the possession of goods and the control of services. The time is almost here when the stress of maintaining the ownership of adult toys such as ski-outfits and snomobiles, boats and aqualungs, film-making and videorecording apparatus, and so forth, not to mention the stress of deploying them, travelling with them, and then actually undertaking to play with them, will account for more illness, madness and death than did the stressful acquisitive activity which leisure was devised to alleviate in the first place. But 'devised' is the operative word: exhausted executives who are allowed to lie in the sun and chew a blade of grass will not underwrite a multi-million-dollar industry for leisure ....

Should someone, however, resting a chin on a hand, and laying a forefinger down the side of the face, presume to say: 'yes, but what do we *really mean* by Progress?', the Great Audience would switch off in a hurry. The question sounds boring; the question is threatening; and in general we do not seem to be equipped to discuss it in practical terms. The meaning of this is to say that whatever we might manage to work out abstractly, the fact would remain that we are caught up in a process the name of which is Progress (hence the capital P) which it is difficult indeed even to question.

Surely we may question the meaning of this process in our individual lives; and it is possible, though difficult and arduous, to change the process — thereby changing the *meaning* of its name, Progress, for ourselves.

If we do the same in the context of society, whether locally, nationally or globally, we shall perforce engage in politics. That is because the same effect is unavoidable: simply to affect the process is to define the Progress. But this cannot be done unilaterally where society is concerned; other people will demand a role in the hot debate as to what Progress 'really' is. Then this debate is necessarily political, because the interests of all taking part (and those whom they represent) are being 'progressed' — or not — in wholly subjective terms.

We often hear the slogans that sport should keep out of politics, that art should keep out of politics, that (this is the really big joke) religion should keep out of politics. But all these activities impinge on both personal and societary processes to massive effect. Just how they impinge will determine what Progress those caught up in the process consider themselves to be making — and the political utterance is *ipso facto* made.

If, because of these arguments, it can be agreed that the notion of Progress is politically relative, an important start will have been made in trying to express what is to count as the criterion of action in any managerial situation — whether we are managing ourselves, or a firm or society. The achievement of the intentions that we are able to articulate can be measured by Progress, but only in a political context. At the societary level, this form of words is sufficiently clear. But so, by extension, should it be clear for the individual level. All of one's associates — and notably oneself — will adopt differing opinions as to one's personal Progress. That is because Progress is 'politically' defined even for the individual — defined that is in relation to some common cause. But beyond these intentions lie meta-intentions: that is to say, there is something to be achieved which is *politically invariant*.

There is no ordinary English word that expresses the criterion of action to which this discussion points. But as usual, 'the Greeks had a word for it'. Many years ago, seeking a word for social ease — easi*ness* — that did not connote euphoria (as perhaps the word 'happiness' might), I followed the initiative of Charles Goodeve and sought renewed currency for Aristotle's word eudemony (roughly, 'well-being'). The term caught on quite well, so that I now feel emboldened to invoke Aristotle once again. The meta-intention that provides the politically-invariant criterion for managerial action expresses *the realization or complete expression of some function*; it manifests *a condition in which a potentiality has become an actuality*. The italicized words lend the authority of the Oxford English Dictionary to this definition of Aristotle's word **entelechy.** (His usage is distinguished from Leibnitz's later use of the word to characterize his monads.)

Those who find Aristotle and the *OED* somewhat abstruse may prefer to recall the song of the folk group called *The Eagles*: 'Take it to the limit one more time'. This potent song certainly captures for me the *practicalities* of the pursuit of entelechy. If the word is to regain its currency after two-and-a-half millenia, which could be helpful, let us be quite clear why it is needed, and why it is politically invariant. Consider this sentence: 'Chile is making rapid Progress towards a full and untrammelled democracy'. Salvador Allende might have said that in 1972; Augusto Pinochet might have said it in 1974. No politically sensitive observer could possibly have agreed with both of them. It is not conceivable that 'Progress' for the Chilean people could have veered through a hundred and eighty degrees during the morning of September 11th, 1973. But it *is* possible to say that each man's actions recognized the entelechy to which his policy was inevitably directed, and that this entelechy provided each his own criterion of managerial action.

Managers and their management scientists are driven by a meta-intention embodied as an entelechy. Their *plans* are embodiments of straightforward intentions, and *progress* towards the fulfilment of those plans is measurable in the political currency appropriate to the *platform* publically mounted by the managers. The search for entelechy is something separate from all of this: therefore the methods to be adopted can be prescribed in advance only in terms of ethical imperatives. For example, neither a manager nor a scientist should be engaged in developments for which she/he will not personally accept moral responsibility; and therefore it will always be a necessity to define what would constitute an indefensibly oppressive version of otherwise acceptable plans. For example, it may properly be decided to make efforts to restrain an exploding birth rate; but most of us would refuse to adopt the method of killing all young babies on sight. Then obviously there are other methods in between this approach and mere exhortation, and each has to be considered separately.

There is in fact no serious problem in pointing out and debating moral issues in this way, because an ethical metasystem is well-recognized — even by the amoral. So, vital as the moral issues are, the notion of entelechy was not introduced to aid an analysis that has its own meta-language already. The analysis I want to make concerns the *methodology* of management science. Let us first of all note that this term usually refers (on university courses, for instance) to a collection of techniques. People *talk* about problem-solving, but few can understand it. Instead, they classify the problem through the taxonomy of established techniques, and their litanies emphasize some rather than others — depending, not on the problem, but on the local expertise that is available to serve the technique. Thus we have apostles of queueing theory, high priests of mathematical programming, and so on. But we cannot say in advance whether any particular technique will be relevant; especially we cannot say it if the situation is likely — as has been argued — to be characterized by crisis. This is precisely because available descriptions of plans and measures of progress *do not yet bear on the entelechy* — and perhaps they never will.

Before this allegation is discarded as preposterous, each should reflect on the applications of management science to dangerously unstable situations that s/he has studied. There are startlingly few exceptions to the rule which shows *x,* who is a master of x-ish technique, solving x-type problems. That is quite unobjectionable *insofar as* there really is an x-type problem: who better than x to solve it, and why not send for him? But in contexts such as those discussed in this chapter, it is very worrying indeed to observe the intervention of x, and to hear him declare that x-ish technique is the thing to use. It is a monumental coincidence that it should be appropriate, after all; but consult the subsequent report — in which we may see why. Coincidences, it seems are multiplicative. Though the situation was an unstructured muddle, in a terrible mess, subsisting in crisis mode, and surrounded by an environment of fast-changing chaos, it was *fundamentally* an x-type problem after all. How fortunate. Whole institutes operate on the basis of such serendipity.

The methodology that it would be gratifying to be able to pinpoint, but which these arguments tend to show cannot be specified in advance, must be focused on problem rather than technique. The difficulty is that the problem is not apparent until the crisis from which it emerges has to some degree matured. For example, nothing remotely sensible could have been said about solving Chile's 1971 problems at a time only a year or so earlier, when no-one — not even Unidad Popular itself — seriously contemplated that the minority coalition of Allende would become the government, no-one could predict (what was to be) an extremely complicated international reaction to that democratic result, and no-one had any means of testing the good faith of potential allies either inside or outside the country. The famous technique of 'scenario building' is flawed in a *quantitative* sense in such circumstances: it simply cannot generate requisite variety. Nor can the Delphi technique hope to do so either. Because in this approach, as I have experienced it, variety is even further squeezed in the corset of the peer group's mutual suspicion and fear of being outrageously instead of simply wrong.

The strange and alarming thing is that techniques such as these begin to work only at the point where the variety of the real world has been repeatedly decimated by the cyclic operation of the crisis mode — as indicated by the model of the last section. When superpowers artificially delimit structural variety to values of three or five, so that only these states will be physically permitted, then it *is* possible to construct this number of scenarios, and it *is* possible for the peer group of Delphi to converge on the likely outcome. But the scientific techniques are then accessories before the fact, rather than problem solvers; and the whole strategic edifice crumbles immediately when an ingenious opponent, or nature itself, expands the variety that the analysts and activists have jointly conspired to contain. The extra variety that may be reassembled at this moment is *the variety of the entelechy*, less its so far realized 'three or five'.

Now an attempt was made at the beginning of this chapter to say something that would hold in general about the nature of crisis. Whether we can conclude the chapter by saying anything definite about solving an as yet unidentified problem, depends on our ability to conjure a methodology of the entelechy itself. The following story is intended to illuminate the issue.

The early work of Taylor and Gilbreth in the creation of time and motion study appeared towards the end of the nineteenth century. A little later, Frank Gilbreth, who was an industrial engineer, and his wife Lilian, who was a psychologist, pioneered the movement in production management which eventually came to be known as Work Study. Much of this was extremely effective: productivity improvements ranging from some thirty to some three hundred per cent were generally recorded. The analysis of repetitive movements into small elements termed 'therbligs' (which of course is the word 'Gilbreth' spelt — roughly — backwards) became a teachable skill. Later, the story of these two remarkable people, and their extremely large family, was to reach a very much wider public than that of the industrial shop floor through both a book and a film about the family: it was called *Cheaper by the Dozen*. Frank Gilbreth died before I was born. His wife Lilian, however, lived on to a splendid old age.

In the mid 1950s, I was directing management sciences for the largest steel company in Britain, United Steel. (This was before the final nationalization of the industry.) The name of the organization was The Department of Operational Research and Cybernetics; but it included the responsibility for other branches of management science, notably the development of computer applications — and for Work Study. This latter arrangement was extremely unusual, because an absurd 'civil war' had broken out in Britain between the leading specialists in Work Study (who tended to regard Operational Research scientists as mathematical narcissists) and OR scientists (who tended to regard Work Study engineers as the Tony Lumpkins of industry). Problems were certainly generated by the fact that the Work Study Manager of United Steel was a member of my own management team at Cybor House. At any rate, it was at about this time (though perhaps during its preparatory stage) — that to my total astonishment and intense delight — I found myself entertaining Lilian Gilbreth to dinner in Sheffield. Dr Gilbreth was consumed with curiosity about the internecine warfare in management advisory circles to which I have just referred. She knew that the problem existed in Britain, which it did not in her native United States, and she required explanations of me as to how anything so ridiculous could have occurred. I thought that I understood the essentially 'political' reasons quite well, and spent a long time in explaining what had happened. At the end of it all, I asked her this very direct question: 'Were your husband alive today, where would he stand in this argument?' She unhesitatingly replied: 'He would be President of the Operational Research Society'.

How can this story be interpreted? In *Decision and Control* I contended that Archimedes was the first OR scientist, because of the uses he made of science in advising King Hieron II about his strategy in defending the city of Syracuse against the Roman seige. What was Gilbreth doing in the early years of this century? He did not attempt to burn down a fleet of ships by focusing a large magnifying glass on their sails, that much is certain. And had he been President of the OR Society in the 1950s, it seems very unlikely to me that he would still have been analysing the motions of industrial workers on a production line which had probably been automated by that time .... In short, the contention is that at all times in the history of the world, there have been perspicuous minds seeking to improve managerial competence and societary eudemony in every conceivable way, and by the use of the very latest knowledge available to them — both of technique and also of problem diagnosis. It is these activities that might well be grouped together as a methodology towards entelechy.

It is interesting that the initially obtrusive features of such a methodology are negative, in that they run counter to so much common practice. Not only does the methodology not depend on a taxonomy of technique — because this is simply something dictated by time and place; it is antipathetic to any other fixation of that kind. Readers may have noticed the Latin motto devised for the dedication of this book: it was very seriously intended. When we discover that a particular technique works, we train a cadre of people in its use. This is a sensible thing to do, in its way; but the grotesque consequences have by now been so often repeated that we should take note of them. The people who have been trained in a set of techniques that have been found to work in occasional contexts proceed to institutionalize their activities: they constitute themselves a profession, they provide themselves with protective sanctions, they cease to be innovative, and they do what they can to block the fresh initiatives of others. This is why Lilian Gilbreth said instantly that her late husband would not by that date have been content with the Work Study label. It seems that every generation of innovators has to crystallize a point of view — which cannot go far beyond the limitations of its own time and place. If it attempts to do so, it cannot be properly understood, and even the well-disposed will defensively declare it to be 'twenty years ahead of its time'. What is observed to happen next is that the institutionalization of such technique-oriented approaches to the managerial task eventually becomes counter-productive. This is partly because the time and place change, partly because innovation remains by definition something that has *not* been tried before, and partly because the motivation for supporting new managerial thrusts and for supporting a feather-bedded career are wildly different. The manager himself is compelled to live with that dilemma; so must the management scientist with whom she/he is in double harness.

Having spoken first of what is not, in order to clear presupposition and prejudice to one side, let us now attempt a positive statement about

A Tentative and Final Methodology towards Entelechy

- The methodology is directed primarily to the recognition of people's legitimate meta-intentions insofar as they will affect other people.

  Its skills are therefore based in human rather than technological or theoretical factors.

- It must however command the transdisciplinary insight and skills to support such recognition, and subsequent diagnoses.

  Collection and screening mechanisms are therefore needed to ensure that no knowledge, model, technique, hardware nor software that may have relevance is either left out of account, or dragged irrelevantly into the arena.

- Since entelechy represents the actualization of a potentiality, its methodology must be able to measure performance — quantitatively defined in Chapter 11 as the ratio of the two estimates.

  The triple-index described will measure the *residual* potentiality from today's actuality, as the component indices of productivity and latency both approach unity.

- The methodology becomes thereby (Chapter 11, Figures 28 and 29) the tool of normative planning that brings the entelechy into focus.

  Importance is not attached to an accuracy in making these measurements that would be spurious in any case. The concern is with two other functions of measurement that are only incidentally concerned with any degree of precision:

    to compare orders of magnitude,
    as a means of allocating effort;

to monitor secular trends, the
detection of which depends more
on consistency than on precision.

● The methodology must be able to detect, recognize, measure and adapt to **shifts** in the structural variety of unrealized potential.

For example: we detect hundreds of possible states in a given potentiality. Suddenly the government declares only three to be admissible, and of these one is evidently the best. Work on this problem should automatically cease (but it does not). The example may be reversed, concluding that work on that problem should automatically begin (again, it does not).

● It must be functionally organized, in obeying these precepts, so as to **move fast.**

If it is unable to move fast enough, the methodology will certainly fail (this outcome's counting as part of the entailment of 'enough'). Then the methodology itself must be equipped to determine what is 'enough'.

Then, by cybernetic theorem, the methodology must generate a model of its own activity.

Compiling and many times rewriting this 'charter' for a methodology towards entelechy has taken so long that reading it so quickly may have left you breathless. It is highly compressed. Let us therefore return to the encapsulating metalanguage in which this section was introduced.

Archimedes, whom people probably called a geometer, was a mathematician who would very likely have submitted some version of this statement to King Hieron as an account of his role as a management scientist — whether at Syracuse or as directing *Project Heureka* from his bathtub on the same monarch's behalf. The industrial mathematician of today would not subscribe to such a charter — why should he? He is otherwise engaged in (for example) modelling crystal structures by algebraic topology. The government statistician of today would not subscribe to it. And why should he? He is advancing the demography of the census by computerized topography. (Maybe those two should get together, but there the matter ends.)

Frank Gilbreth, industrial engineer *par excellence,* and surely also Lilian Gilbreth, psychologist *par excellence,* could (on her own showing) surely have improved on this draft — had they been available. Today, most industrial engineers and also psychologists undertake great works, rightly and productively, without talking about entelechies. Why should they?

And so the procession goes on. Some of the OR men from the 1940s, some of the founders of General Systems Theory, some of those who talked and from their talk put forth the name of Cybernetics, might also have written some version of this methodological statement. But many distinguished OR men, GST men, and cyberneticians today are — as a matter of fact — doing something else under those respective banners. In this lies no complaint.

The point is just this: something methodological connects the approach to societary and managerial change of those who, in their time and place, and whatever the banner they seized or were given to hold, might have written or subscribed to a statement of this kind. I have not invented the methodological notions that I have selected to focus on the concept of entelechy — and I did not invent that either. What this 'something methodological' may be is suggested (by circular definition) in the statement itself, by allusion and illustration in the stories told to embellish it, and by noting the *unexpectedness* of the approach used in the domain of the problem itself when it matures — which happens because, under this methodology, the problem is not defined by the problem-solving technique.

If these complicated methodological considerations make it quite difficult to recognize who would have been, might now be, or might henceforth become, a 'signatory' of the 'charter', an infallible and very practical guide can be inferred from the principles put forward themselves. No-one who thought that the principles were right would sign any charter that sought to embody them; no-one who understood them would try to found a learned society, a professional institution, or a journal that sought to uphold them; and no-one who acted upon them would take any interest in giving a name to the methodology itself. The methodology, as the sub-heading under which this is written tried by oxymoron to say, is intrinsically tentative, absolute in practice, and in general an expository device.

On Technological Method

The employment of a methodology subsumes the deployment of a technology that serves those methodological ends. It is too glib to assume that the technology that should be used is fully explicated by the 'state of the art'. For one thing there may be financial restraints on the slice of available hardware that can be purchased, and there may be humanpower constraints on the software servicing that can realistically be undertaken. For another thing, in a novel situation where a new methodology is embraced, the state of the art itself stands to be extended. As earlier chapters showed, all these considerations applied in the Chilean experience.

There is yet more to it than that, of course. The technology that we hold in our hands — literally, as the extension of our brain-directed limbs — determines the very nature of the problem-solving homeostat. In part, it creates the technology that makes it possible. In part, through its informational techniques and global communications system, technology nourishes the problem, as was seen through the model of crisis. Certainly, and in so many ways, technology is also part of the solution to the problem. The point is that the technology deployed can never be judged *aside* from the problem-solution homeostasis in which it inheres, and to which it helps import form. Many people seem to think that it can; they are prepared to take a stand, as it were in a vacuum, as to whether technology is a 'good' or 'bad' thing.

This position is untenable, because life cannot be sustained without tools. When they are appropriate, they may appropriately be cherished: the master craftsman handles his tools with love; and it is a fact that computer programmers (the better ones) relate becomingly to their machines, much as good car-drivers do. Then it sounds as though the 'good' and 'bad' appellations relate more to the user than to the technology used. Speaking personally, I have learned to minimize technological intervention between myself and nature; but this is a reasonable strategy only within the limits of viability of the system concerned. Taking the personal case as an example, there is a vocation as well as a physiology to keep viable. In the aid of the latter, I use the minimum technology required to make minimal garments and furniture, comestibles and heat. In the aid of the former, I use the pen and the light without which these words could not now be written; I will use trains and aeroplanes to reach the scene of action when required, but not otherwise. Telephone, television, computer terminals and the like have been eliminated; and since it is possible to do arithmetic mentally and to carry water, there is no need for calculators or water-pipes. In short: the adoption of technology can and should be carefully gauged, not simply taken for granted — as it usually is.

At the level of the firm, the social service, or the nation, this homely example illustrates a form of analysis that is rarely formally made. The difficulty is to counsel caution to any group that has been already *imprinted* with the epitome of 'Progress'. Imprinting destroys variety: the Progress imprint seduces the mass to behave as if one criterion alone should really matter — and off they go, like a swarm of bees, or perhaps a colony of lemmings. Obviously, this imprinting is not accidental, and there is a vast advertising industry to prove it — which, it may cybernetically be noted, makes major use of positive feedback. But whatever the cause, it was profoundly shocking to me, on first arrival in Chile, to discover how far this social process had already gone —

because I had not expected that. The result was to influence the recommendations on the use of regulatory technology. I had expected (given that Chile is three thousand miles long) that the motor car would be an issue. But to find eudemony measured on the *linea blanca,* that is by the provision of 'white line' goods such as washing machines and refrigerators, was too much. Even with hindsight, however, and realizing the possibly malign influence of these shocks on the recommendations, it is hard to envisage offering an abacus rather than a computer to a *linea blanca interventor.*

Then let us be very cautious with the complicated problem, and not dismiss it with naivety. In India there is a research laboratory (at Hyderabad) dedicated to the deployment of high science in aid of the ordinary villager — not indeed to supply refrigerators, and so to determine what she/he eats, nor indeed to mass-produce television sets, and so to determine what she/he thinks. It exists to improve the design of potter's wheels, cooking ovens, irrigation systems, small enterprise .... No computer, no wind tunnel, no international recourse is barred to these projects, which exploit every known scientific aid: the standard is excellence, without cultural perversion. Does that approach solve the problem, or is it condescendingly paternalistic? And why was the harijan ('untouchable') community that I entered alone on this visit (1974) still remote from its parent village — just as it would have been when I was first shocked by that phenomenon (1945) — after a quarter of a century of Independence? Part of the answer is that there are severely practical impediments to change which the outsider does not understand. For example: it is easy to talk about the 'modernization' of transportation in India, and to say that it is religious prejudice that maintains the bullock cart. In fact, most of the capital in India is tied up in these transports: it cannot simply be written-off, discarded. In any case, as we survey the world energy scene, India may have the best answer already — even at the expense of Progress (with the capital P).

Reviewing the two preceeding paragraphs, and apart from noting their author's uncharacteristic propensity to be shocked, nothing is clear beyond the absolute necessity to think in terms of entelechy rather than prediction, of realizing potential rather than concocting technique-oriented plans. Significantly, both Chile and India had ambitious National Plans which failed. The Chilean case has already been reviewed; India had one of the earliest Plans to fail in the free world — and this happened despite its having been directed by a man of brilliance, Mahalanobis, who might well have been also a saint. We must not minimize, therefore, the problem of choice in developmental technology; and the sense in which that problem is bound into the homeostasis of unfolding crisis has surely been established above. Then now, perhaps, is the moment to restore the balance (as the personal story of my own *modus vivendi* tried to do in adumbration), by considering the sense in which any **particular** technology — in this examination called 'automation' — may also be irrelevant to the problems of humankind.

'This sketch (of an automated factory) does not dwell lovingly on the colossal achievements of engineering, on the lines of transfer machines, on the huge electronic information-handling systems. Perhaps we have congratulated ourselves enough on these advances already. The sketch is drawn at a deeper level. It js a picture of an industrial society undergoing a second industrial revolution, a society which has focused its attention on a particular and narrow manifestation of its own inventive ability in the belief that this manifestation, automation, constitutes the revolution. This is a society with a sense of unease, sometimes amounting to guilt, about its own future. Because it is creating for itself problems which it cannot honestly say it knows how to handle, problems which have a significance deeper than engineering or economics can bestow.'

further on:

'I am not attacking automation. I am attacking the apotheosis of automation.'

We constantly hear about the automative significance of the silicon chip, of microprocessors. The above quotations reflect doubts about the relevance of automative technology to the underlying nature of the problem. Yet it has just been argued that technology *inheres in,* and *helps to impart form to* that problem. The quotation ends:

'Cybernetics is about all manner of control, all kinds of structure, all sorts of system. Automation belongs here. But to the science of cybernetics as a thinking-tool for solving the control problem that besets industry, automation is irrelevant.'

The speaker, then, was not talking about the system in which technology inheres — he was indicating an entelechy. He was not, moreover, talking about microprocessors, but about the newly-emerged transistors. For the date was September 1958, and the occasion was the Second International Congress on Cybernetics. The title of the plenary address was indeed: *The Irrelevance of Automation.* What was true then of automative transistors is true now of automative microprocessors — they radically restructure the problem-solution homeostat. What was true then and remains true now about 'cybernetics as a thinking tool' is that the principles and laws of the science always obtain, whatever the technology through which they are disported. Until **this** is clearly perceived, then there is only — and nonsensically — 'good' or 'bad' technology; afterwards there is *technological choice* — at the behest of 'good' or 'bad' people. May they choose well.

[It must be bad manners to quote approvingly one's own words that have gathered the dust of more than twenty years. But it is necessary to demonstrate consistency, and also to renounce an undeserved reputation for belief in technocracy. This recent comment is typical: 'They appear to think that you are saying that if the world would just give you a computer, you'd solve its problems'. Marx said: 'Thank God I'm not a Marxist'. Well, it seems that I am not a Beerian.]

The enquiry *On Technological Method,* in short, is long. To précis the approach presented here: we should look first to the entelechy, then consider the problem-solution homeostat and the range of possible technologies that relate it to that entelechy. The objective is to offer **choice.** And that is to say exactly the same thing as this: let the number of possible states of the system proliferate that will at the least make available Requisite Variety.

There is only one more matter of substance to review, namely the dynamics of these relationships. The question of speed has several times been raised; and that may have appeared to advocate the quick flash of the *coup.* Not so: the problem-solution homeostat is central to the issue of speed, because it has its own dynamic — although this is subject to modification by the mass media, as we saw earlier. Please consider this series of points.

- The speed of events as perceived determines the rate at which the continuously cycling problem-solution homestat must work, if it is to be an effective regulator.

- Most existing administrative systems in all kinds of institution have not been designed to operate at this pace, and cannot adapt to it. Then the alternatives are to redesign those systems, or to by-pass them. The first alternative has nowhere (to my knowledge) been tried in government, at least: redesign there certainly has been, but without regard to cybernetic canon.

- All viable systems are autopoietic, which is to say that part of their activity is necessarily devoted to the homeostasis of their own internal organization: they *produce themselves* (see Chapter 19). If more than necessary effort goes into this task, however, the autopoietic system may be called pathological (see *The Heart of Enterprise* for the arguments). When this condition obtains, and it appears to be pandemic, the energy that drives the problem-solution homeostat will be absorbed to some degree by the cancerous autopoiesis; the homeostat will then slow down and may become ineffectual;

● Communications between managers/ministers and their administrators depend absolutely on adequate variety reduction, and this is technologically undernourished at the best of times. The memoirs of senior ministers in successive British governments, moreover, continually assert (my terminology, of course) that this transduction is actively thwarted by a civil service propensity to invent filters designed to reduce the variety that the minister can recognize in problem-solution homeostasis. On the face of it, this should speed things up; in practice it is more likely to produce deadlock, albeit rapidly — because of the loss of regulatory requisite variety.

● 'The Principle of Minimum Dissipation states that among the set of movements that have passed through the filter of other selection principles, that particular movement is realized which produces a minimal increase in entropy. Nature is thus organized in such a way that two mutually complementary processes continually take place — namely a continuous growth in disorganization, which is measured by entropy, and a counterbalancing striving to maintain organization, which is expressed in the Laws of Conservation and in the Principle of Minimum Dissipation.' (This is NN Moiseev speaking, of the USSR Academy of Science, as translated by PI Meadow of York University, Ontario.) According to this principle, when it operates through the filtration system mentioned in the preceding point, we must expect a reinforcement of the tendency towards pathological autopoiesis.

The series of five points has been presented in this pithy form, whereas whole chapters could have been written about each, because their net impact is sufficiently clear. These are some of the inter-related cybernetic mechanisms that bear upon our capacity to do anything at all that will effect change — and the outlook is bleak, particularly in crisis mode. Ponderous theory is moreover borne out by instant experience whenever a new leadership or novel policy is installed. It seems to be generally accepted in the public mythology that there is a 'honeymoon' period, during which all is sweetness ('give them a chance') and journalists present statements about 'The First Hundred Days'. After that, the criticism begins to mount. This is surely not because the public, still less their hard-bitten media folk, have genuinely been seduced by the initial propaganda; nor is it because the new approach was honestly tried and honestly failed. It is simply because the system opposing change (see the five points) is instantly *denatured* by the sheer novelty of fresh inputs: it does not know how to react, because it needs time to translate and reclassify. As soon as it understands the new language, syntax and grammar, it can succeed once more in preventing the problem-solution homeostat from effective regulation.

If this is what happens, it is certainly a signal to the innovators to act fast. The argument might well have been elaborated, then, under the first sectional heading: *The Cybernetics of Crisis*. It has been reserved to conclude the second section called *The Cybernetics of Progress* instead — and, you may think remarkably, to complete a sub-section *On Technological Method*. This is by no means an oversight: please consider in just this context a strong and contentious issue as it was manifested in Chile.

If we denounce technocracy; if we put human values first; if we look preferentially to cybernetic principle rather than to technological convenience: then maybe it was a mistake to bother with electronics, and computers, and futuristic-looking operations rooms. Perhaps these were merely frills. After all, the basic success was due more to **organizing structural variety** than to anything else. In that case, a final chapter called *Prospectus* should discount the technological element, and concentrate on people first and people-structures second.

New paragraph: the previous paragraph has weight, and should stand there on its own, for due consideration. It has a very good case to make; and my own psyche leans towards it. Nevertheless, on balance I disbelieve its humanistic promise. The reason why finally explains the placing of this argument in this section. The **requirement for speed** in the operation of the problem-solution homeostat makes this outstandingly a technological issue: if we are to redesign all our administrative systems, then we must choose — and choose with care — the technology on which that redesign will be based. It may certainly be hoped that this contention does not, in the limit, conflict with the humanitarian position just expressed. Tools of some kind are essential, ran the argument previous to that; and the nature of the tools chosen will condition every solution. Let us then preserve the possibility of choice, but not neglect to make it. And let us not fail to make use of advanced technology simply because its very mention is anathema to those whom it affrights.

The Cybernetics of Prospectus

Cybernetics, remember, is the science of effective organization. The question arose, when this chapter was planned: what is the effective organization of a *prospectus?*

The provisional answer was to say: list all the questions to which the Chilean experience gives rise, and try to answer them on the basis: **this** we learned how to do better next time.

It turns out that not a single question can even be clearly formulated (much less answered) without specifying an attendant set of circumstances in great detail. Unless this were a merely theoretical exercise, then, or perhaps a novel, it would be necessary to predict a future that is known only to God.

Managers, their staffs and their scientific aides ought to be problem-solvers, not fortune-tellers. In this chapter, therefore, we have studied the effective organization of a **progress** that cannot be determined *in vacuo,* and also the effective organization of the **crisis** in which that progress is likely to be embedded. In any real-life situation, then, we should expect to interpret the cybernetics of the viable system (as understood through either the neurocybernetic model of this book, or the a-prioristic model of *The Heart of Enterprise*) in terms of the potentiality dormant in its actuality.

This is the Prospectus of the Entelechy. The futurological prospectus does not have requisite variety.

References explicit to these five chapters

1. HARRISON, P.J., and STEVENS, C.R. — 'A Bayesian Approach to Short-term Forecasting, *Operational Research Quarterly,* Vol. 22, No. 4, December 1971
2. BEER, STAFFORD
    'A Technique for Standardizing Massed Batteries of Control Charts', *Applied Statistics,* Vol. 2, No. 3, 1953
    'The Productivity Index in Active Service', *Applied Statistics,* Vol. 4, No. 1, 1955
    Cybernetics and Management, English Universities Press, 1959 (Chapter XVI)
    Decision and Control, John Wiley, 1966 (Chapters 13 and 15)
    The Heart of Enterprise, John Wiley, 1979 (Part Four, Note Four)
3. BONSIEPE, G.U.
    Teoría y Practica del Diseño Industrial, Editorial Gustavo Gili, Barcelona, 1975
    Teoria e Practica del Disegno Industriale, Fertrinelli, 1975 (translation of above).
4. POWERS, WILLIAM T.
    Behavior: The Control of Perception, Aldine, Chicago, 1973
5. MATURANA, HUMBERTO R. and VARELA, FRANCISCO J.
    Autopoiesis and Cognition, D. Reidel, Dordrecht, Holland, 1980
6. US GOVERNMENT
    United States and Chile during the Allende Years, 1970-1973 (Hearings before the Subcommittee on Inter-American Affairs of the Committee on Foreign Affairs, House of Representatives), Washington 1975

Notes

(i) The following book contains many important papers relevant to the Chilean debacle, prepared by IDOC (International Documentation on Chile):

BIRNS, LAURENCE — *The End of Chilean Democracy,* The Seabury Press, New York, 1973

(ii) The following further publications, written by leaders of the project herein described, bear on the Chilean experience:

BARRIENTOS, JORGE and ESPEJO, RAUL — 'A Cybernetic Model for the Management of the Industrial Sector', *National Research Institute of Chile, Review Number 4* (in Spanish), June 1973.

BEER, STAFFORD — 'Cybernetics of National Development', the inaugural lecture for the *Zaheer Science Foundation,* New Delhi, December 1974.

SCHWEMBER, HERMANN — 'Project Cybersyn: An Experience with New Tools for Management in Chile', *Computer Assisted Policy Analysis* (Ed: Bossel), Birkhauser Verlag, Basel, 1977.

ESPEJO, RAUL — 'Cybernetic Praxis in Government: The Management of Industry in Chile 1970-1973', *Journal of Cybernetics,* Vol 10, No 3.

PART FIVE

APPENDIX

Glossary of cybernetic terms used in this book

There is no standard authority for cybernetic definitions, and these are my own. Some of the words come from other sciences, and may be used by cyberneticians in a rather special or restricted way.

The words 'algedonode' and 'multinode' are my inventions; 'algedonic' is not in general cybernetic use (I thought for twenty years that I invented this too, and only now discover that it dates from 1894).

There is no glossary of neurophysiological terms, because those I have used are mainly names for bits and pieces inside the body rather than for definable concepts.

ALGEDONIC (ἄλγος, pain, ἧδος, pleasure); pertaining to regulation in a non-analytic mode.
For example, we may train others to perform a task by explaining analytically the 'why' and the 'how', or algedonically by a system of rewards and punishments which offer no such explanation.

ALGEDONIC LOOP a circuit for algedonic regulation, which may be used to over-ride an analytic control circuit.
For example, acute discomfort may stop us from performing a task we perfectly understand and wish to complete; fail-safe devices may be used to switch-off a whole plant when some critical variable is exceeded, without knowing why it has happened.

ALGEDONODE (algedonic + node); an algedonically modulated probabilistic switch.
That is: algedonic information is used at this node to alter the probability that something (which could otherwise be decided either analytically or by chance) will happen.

ALGORITHM a comprehensive set of instructions for reaching a known goal (cf. HEURISTIC).

ANASTOMOTIC branching and reconnecting, like streams in a river delta.
Note: no pathway from A to B is unique.

ENTELECHY the realization of a potentiality in actuality.

ENTROPY the measure of a system's inexorable tendency to move from a less
to a more probable state
(cf. NEGENTROPY).
Note 1. This entails an evening-out of the energy available to the system,
which reaches a standstill at unit entropy (= maximal probability).
Note 2. For a viable system unit entropy = death.

FEEDBACK the return of part of a system's output to its input, which is
thereby changed.
Positive feedback takes an increase in output back to increase the input;
negative feedback takes back an output increase to *de*crease the input — and
is therefore stabilizing in principle.
Note: this term is often *incorrectly* used to mean simply 'a response to a
stimulus'.

HEURISTIC (contraction of 'heuristic method'); a set of instructions for
searching out an unknown goal by exploration, which continuously or
repeatedly evaluates progress according to some known criterion (cf.
ALGORITHM).

HOMEOSTASIS the capability of a system to hold its critical variables within
physiological limits in the face of unexpected disturbance or perturbation.

METALANGUAGE, METALOGIC the language and the logic of a metasystem (q.v.).

METASYSTEM a system over and beyond a system of lower logical order,
and therefore capable of deciding propositions, discussing criteria, or
exercising regulation for systems that are themselves logically incapable of
such decisions and discussions or of self-regulation (because the metalogic is
inaccessible to the system's logic, or the metalanguage is capable of
statements inexpressible in the system's language).
Note: a metasystem is of a higher *logical* order than a system, and not
necessarily of higher 'seniority' in the sense of command. For example: the
school timetable is metasystemic to the timetable of a single class.

MULTINODE a machine, brain, system or management-group made up of
individual decision-making elements and capable of reaching a corporate
decision.

NEGENTROPY the measure of negative entropy, equalling the active information content of a system (cf. ENTROPY).
Note: systems gaining in entropy are equivalently losing information, and vice versa.

PARADIGM an exemplar or pattern; a basic way of doing something recognizable beneath many superficial variations.

RETICULUM (Latin: a net); a network of connections in which unique pathways may or may not be specifiable (cf. ANASTOMOTIC).

TRANSDUCER a machine, device, protocol or rule by which information is changed to an appropriate form and introduced into a system.

TRANSFER FUNCTION an expression relating input to output; the operation performed on an input to provide an output.

ULTRASTABILITY the capacity of a system to return to an equilibrial state after perturbation by unknown or unanalysed forces (against the intervention of which the system was therefore not explicitly designed).

VARIETY the total number of possible states of a system, or of an element of a system.

Select bibliography

The preparation of bibliographic references for this book has proved a problem of the utmost difficulty. Because of its interdisciplinary character, a full-scale cybernetic bibliography would fill a large book. Besides, I am neither an historian nor an archivist: my own knowledge of the literature is bound to be eclectic. The simplest course would have been to enter here the entire contents of my personal library, but — at whatever risk of being unfair — I have had to make some kind of selection. The following pages are arranged according to a plan that I will now explain.

A. Source Books in Neurophysiology

This is a careful selection of books meant to provide an adequate neurophysiological background for the model proposed in *Brain of the Firm*. All have been my close companions over the years. I have of course used a good many others too, as well as countless papers. None of the entries here has anything directly to do with cybernetics, and the authors (who may never have heard of the subject) cannot be blamed for the use I have made of their work.

B. Selections in Neurocybernetics

We next turn to the marriage of neurophysiology with cybernetics, which has provided a vast literature usually referred to under the heading of 'neurocybernetics'. *Brain of the Firm* must acknowledge a debt to this literature, though not often in a specific context. Accordingly, I have given some key historical references, and a sample of works from the origins until now, arranged in chronological order. There may well be embarrassing omissions.

C. General Introductions to Cybernetics Itself

As to cybernetics itself, the difficulty becomes overwhelming. I have taken a different approach here, listing only five introductory works which set out (in their different ways) to be comprehensive, and explaining why each is included. There are many, many more books of importance — the list has been kept so short by grimly enforcing that criterion of comprehensiveness. In particular, this has eliminated some wonderful books on the subject of General Systems Theory, which I take to be co-extensive with the subject of cybernetics.

D. Explicit References

This short list of works to which the text makes direct allusion is not at all representative. If I wanted to refer to someone's work while I was writing, I did so — and that accounts for the disproportionate number of references to my own work too.

A. Source Books in Neurophysiology

1. The Nervous System in General

A brilliantly illustrated (perspective, colour) general-though-technical account:
NETTER, FRANK H., *The Nervous System,* C.I.B.A. Publications, New Jersey, 1953. Vol. 1 of the C.I.B.A. Collection of Medical Illustrations.

A good, straightforward, general introduction:
WYBURN, G.M., *The Nervous System,* Academic Press, London, 1960.

2. The Brain in General

The classic:
ECCLES, SIR JOHN, *The Neurophysiological Basis of Mind,* Oxford, 1953.

A splendid presentation, using a three-dimensional technique of overlays in colour:
KRIEG, WENDELL J.S., *Brain Mechanisms in Diachrome,* Brain Books, Evanston, Illinois, 1957.

A short perceptive account of the brain in its alert aspect:
MAGOUN, H.W., *The Waking Brain,* Thomas, Springfield, Illinois, 1958.

A Russian account of the brain in quantified terms:
BLINKOV, SAMUEL M. and GLEZER, IL'YA I., *The Human Brain in Figures and Tables*, Plenum Press, New York, 1968.

3. Chemical Aspects of Neurophysiology

A valued source book:
GOODMAN, LOUIS S., and GILMAN, ALFRED, *The Pharmacological Basis of Therapeutics*, Macmillan, New York, 1965.

4. Specific Neurological Systems

On the information flow itself:
HODGKIN, A.L., *The Conduction of the Nervous Impulse*, Liverpool University Press, 1965.

On Autonomics (Systems One-Two-Three):
MITCHELL, G.A.G., *Anatomy of the Autonomic Nervous System*, Livingstone, Edinburgh, 1953.
ECCLES, SIR JOHN, ITO, MASAO and SZENTAGOTHAI, JANOS, *The Cerebellum as a Neuronal Machine*, Springer-Verlag, Berlin, 1967.

On 'arousal' mechanisms (System Four):
BRODAL, ALF, *The Reticular Formation of the Brain Stem*, Oliver and Boyd, 1957.
KILMER, W.L., BLUM, J. and McCULLOCH, W.S., *The Reticular Formation*, Air Force Office of Scientific Research, Arlington, Virginia, 1969.

On the Cortex (System Five):
BURNS, B. DELISLE, *The Mammalian Cerebral Cortex*, Edward Arnold, 1958.
SHOLL, D.A., *The Organization of the Cerebral Cortex*, Methuen 1956.

On the question of pain (Algedonics):
KEEL, K.D., *Anatomies of Pain*, Blackwell, 1957.
NOORDENBOS, W., *Pain*, Elsevier, Amsterdam, 1959.

On the issue of specific command:
FULTON, JOHN F., *Functional Localization in the Frontal Lobes and Cerebellum*, Oxford, 1949.

B. Selections in Neurocybernetics

1. Early (and Seminal) Works 1940-1960

Three from the United States:
McCULLOCK, WARREN S., *Embodiments of Mind*, M.I.T. Press,

Cambridge, Mass., 1965. Contains his major papers from 1943.
JEFFRESS, LLOYD A., *Cerebral Mechanisms in Behaviour,* John Wiley, 1951. The Hixon Symposium, 1948.
SHANNON, C.E. and McCARTHY, J., *Automata Studies,* Princeton University Press, 1956.

Three from Britain:
ASHBY, W. ROSS, *Design for a Brain,* Chapman & Hall, 1952.
WALTER, W. GREY, *The Living Brain,* Duckworth, 1953; Penguin, 1968.
NATIONAL PHYSICAL LABORATORY, *Mechanization of Thought Processes,* H.M.S.O., 1959. Symposium, 1958.

2. Selections (Datal Order) — The Sixties

GEORGE, FRANK H., *The Brain as a Computer,* Pergamon, 1961.
MUSES, C.A. (Editor), *Aspects of the Theory of Artificial Intelligence,* Plenum Press, New York, 1962.
WIENER, NORBERT and SCHADÉ, J.P., *Nerve, Brain and Memory Models* Elsevier, Amsterdam, 1963.
GOODWIN, B.C., *Temporal Organization in Cells,* Academic Press, London, 1963.
YOUNG, J.Z., *A Model of the Brain,* Oxford, 1964.
CARNE, E.B., *Artificial Intelligence Techniques,* Spartan Books, Washington, 1965.
KIMBER, DANIEL P. (Editor), *The Anatomy of Memory,* Science & Behavior Books, Palo Alto, 1965.
FOGEL, LAURENCE J., OWENS, ALVIN J. and WALSH, MICHAEL J., *Artificial Intelligence Through Simulated Evolution,* Wiley, New York, 1966.
DEUTSCH, SID, *Models of the Nervous System,* Wiley, New York, 1967.
STARK, LAURENCE, *Neurological Control Systems,* Plenum Press, New York, 1968.
PROCTOR, LORNE D. (Editor), *Biocybernetics of the Central Nervous System,* Little, Brown & Co., Boston, 1969.

3. The Emergent Science

The following massive volume is the first attempt to lay out a study programme of a wholly interdisciplinary kind:
QUARTON, G.C., MELNECHUK, T. and SCHMITT, FRANCIS O., *The Neurosciences,* Rockefeller University Press, New York, 1967.

C. General Introductions to Cybernetics Itself

1. The original major book (American)

WIENER, NORBERT, *Cybernetics: or Control and Communication in the*

Animal and the Machine, Wiley, New York, 1948.
Difficult, quixotic, immensely stimulating (then and now), *Cybernetics* split
the scientific world (for those who read it) down the middle. Think of it like
this: the great man (he really was) holds forth to his friends after dinner,
ruins the tablecloth by scribbling mathematics all over it, sings a little song
in German, and changes your life. It is tough going: you have to stay the
night.

2. The original usable book (English)

ASHBY, W. ROSS, *An Introduction to Cybernetics,* Chapman & Hall,
1956.
Not difficult at all, if you grit your teeth and work at it, this was the first
major attempt to teach the subject in its own right — to people with plenty
of intelligence and no special knowledge. It is an education in itself,
complete with exercises, which means that the author has done most of the
hard work himself. It demonstrates (see above) that great men do not *have*
to hold dinner parties, and that you can change your life quietly as well as
dramatically.

3. The Russian Viewpoint

GLUSHKOV, VIKTOR M., *An Introduction to Cybernetics,* Academic
Press, New York, 1966. Published in Russian, 1964.
An *Introduction* this may be, but for sophisticated scientists only, by the
leading Soviet cybernetician. Given that the book has the same title as the
previous reference, anyone could be forgiven for not seeing much
connection — which perhaps demonstrates the scope of cybernetic science.
By Western usage, in short, the book is badly titled; I would have suggested
Advanced Cybernetics. In any case, it is another great book — a text of real
importance.

4. Next, a book first written (1965) in Czech:

KLIR, JIRI and VALACH, MIROSLAV, *Cybernetic Modelling,* Iliffe
Books London, 1967.
This book is a 'must' for serious students of cybernetics — it is possibly the
best book for them to read first. It is derivative where Ashby was original
(but this was ten years later), but it makes a genuine textbook. Unlike
Glushkov, it is not highly mathematical. Readers having success with this
book should look for the subsequent publications in America of George J.
Klir — who is the first author.

5. Finally

BEER, STAFFORD, *Cybernetics and Management,* English Universities
Press, 1959.

This was the first attempt to tell the story of cybernetics, and to expound its fully interdisciplinary nature, from a managerial standpoint.

D. Explicit References

Here are the full references to works actually referred to in the text, often simply by use of the author's name:

ASHBY, W. ROSS, *Design for a Brain,* Chapman & Hall, 1952.

BAYLISS, L.E., *Living Control Systems,* English Universities Press, 1966.

BEER, STAFFORD, *Cybernetics and Management,* English Universities Press, 1959.

BEER, STAFFORD, 'Towards the Cybernetic Factory', *Principles of Self-Organization,* Pergamon, 1962. Symposium, 1960.

BEER, STAFFORD, *Decision and Control,* Wiley, London, 1966.

BEER, STAFFORD & CASTI, JOHN, 'Investment Against Disaster', *Working Paper,* International Institute for Applied Systems Analysis, 1975.

BEER, STAFFORD, *The Heart of Enterprise,* Wiley, London, 1979.

BREMERMANN, H.J., 'Optimization Through Evolution and Recombination', *Self-Organizing Systems 1962,* Spartan Books, Washington D.C., 1962.

DAVENPORT, H., *The Higher Arithmetic,* Hutchinson University Library, 1952.

FORRESTER, JAY W., *Industrial Dynamics,* M.I.T. Press, Cambridge, Mass., 1961.

INNES, JOCASTA, *The Pauper's Cookbook,* Penguin, 1971.

McCULLOCH, WARREN S., 'Living Models for Lively Artefacts', *Science in the Sixties,* University of New Mexico, 1965.

McCULLOCH, WARREN S., *Embodiments of Mind,* M.I.T. Press, Cambridge, Mass., 1965.

PRIBAN, I.P. and FINCHAM, W.F., 'Self-adaptive Control and the Respiratory System', *Nature,* Vol. 208, No. 5008, London, 1965.

SHANNON, CLAUDE and WEAVER, WARREN, *The Mathematical Theory of Communication,* University of Illinois Press, 1949.

THOM, RENE, *Stabilité Structurelle et Morphogénèse,* W.A. Benjamin, 1972.

WADDINGTON, C.H., *The Strategy of the Genes,* George Allen and Unwin, 1957.

NOTE

References explicit to Part IV will be found on page 397.

Index